Portraits of the L2 User

SECOND LANGUAGE ACQUISITION
Series Editor: Dr David Singleton, *Trinity College, Dublin, Ireland*

This new series will bring together titles dealing with a variety of aspects of language acquisition and processing in situations where a language or languages other than the native language is involved. Second language will thus be interpreted in its broadest possible sense. The volumes included in the series will all in their different ways offer, on the one hand, exposition and discussion of empirical findings and, on the other, some degree of theoretical reflection. In this latter connection, no particular theoretical stance will be privileged in the series; nor will any relevant perspective – sociolinguistic, psycholinguistic, neurolinguistic, etc. – be deemed out of place. The intended readership of the series will be final-year undergraduates working on second language acquisition projects, postgraduate students involved in second language acquisition research, and researchers and teachers in general whose interests include a second language acquisition component.

Other Books of Interest
Cross-linguistic Influence in Third Language Acquisition
 J. Cenoz, B. Hufeisen and U. Jessner (eds)
English in Europe: The Acquisition of a Third Language
 Jasone Cenoz and Ulrike Jessner (eds)
Foreign Language and Culture Learning from a Dialogic Perspective
 Carol Morgan and Albane Cain
The Good Language Learner
 N. Naiman, M. Fröhlich, H.H. Stern and A. Todesco
An Introductory Reader to the Writings of Jim Cummins
 Colin Baker and Nancy Hornberger (eds)
Language and Society in a Changing Italy
 Arturo Tosi
Languages in America: A Pluralist View
 Susan J. Dicker
Language Learners as Ethnographers
 Celia Roberts, Michael Byram, Ana Barro, Shirley Jordan and Brian Street
Language Revitalization Processes and Prospects
 Kendall A. King
Language Use in Interlingual Families: A Japanese-English Sociolinguistic Study
 Masayo Yamamoto
The Languages of Israel: Policy, Ideology and Practice
 Bernard Spolsky and Elana Shohamy
Multilingualism in Spain
 M. Teresa Turell (ed.)
The Other Languages of Europe
 Guus Extra and Durk Gorter (eds)
Reflections on Multiliterate Lives
 Diane Belcher and Ulla Connor (eds)
The Sociopolitics of English Language Teaching
 Joan Kelly Hall and William G. Eggington (eds)
World English: A Study of Its Development
 Janina Brutt-Griffler

Please contact us for the latest book information:
Multilingual Matters, Frankfurt Lodge, Clevedon Hall,
Victoria Road, Clevedon, BS21 7HH, England
http://www.multilingual-matters.com

SECOND LANGUAGE ACQUISITION 1
Series Editor: David Singleton, *Trinity College, Dublin, Ireland*

Portraits of the L2 User

Edited by
Vivian Cook

MULTILINGUAL MATTERS LTD
Clevedon • Buffalo • Toronto • Sydney

Library of Congress Cataloging in Publication Data
Portraits of the L2 User/Edited by Vivian Cook
Second Language Acquisition: 1
Includes bibliographical references and index
1. Second language acquisition. I. Title: Portraits of the second language user.
II. Cook, V.J. (Vivian James). III. Second language acquisition (Buffalo, N.Y.): 1
P118.2 .P67 2002
418'.0071–dc21   2001055822

British Library Cataloguing in Publication Data
A catalogue entry for this book is available from the British Library.

ISBN 1-85359-584-5 (hbk)
ISBN 1-85359-583-7 (pbk)

Multilingual Matters Ltd
UK: Frankfurt Lodge, Clevedon Hall, Victoria Road, Clevedon BS21 7HH.
USA: UTP, 2250 Military Road, Tonawanda, NY 14150, USA.
Canada: UTP, 5201 Dufferin Street, North York, Ontario M3H 5T8, Canada.
Australia: Footprint Books, PO Box 418, Church Point, NSW 2103, Australia.

Typeset by Wordworks Ltd.
Printed and bound in Great Britain by the Cromwell Press Ltd.

Contents

Acknowledgements

Above all I am grateful for the inspiring work of all the contributors; it has been a great privilege working with them and I hope they are reasonably satisfied with the result. Without the music of Brad Mehldau, Sonny Rollins and Thelonious Monk, the book would never have been completed; indeed like many Europeans I owe an immense debt to Willis Conover, who opened this door to me.

Contributors

Ellen Bialystok: York University, Canada: ellenb@yorku.ca

Vivian Cook: University of Essex, England: vcook@essex.ac.uk

Kees de Bot: University of Nijmegen, The Netherlands: c.debot@let.kun.nl

Annette de Groot: University of Amsterdam, The Netherlands: pn_groot@macmail.psy.uva.nl

Jean-Marc Dewaele: Birkbeck College, England: dewaele@french.bbk.ac.uk

Franco Fabbro: Istituto Scientifico 'E.Medea', Italy: fabbro@bp.lnf.it

Suzanne Flynn: MIT, USA: sflynn@mit.edu

Fred Genesee: McGill University, Canada: genesee@ego.psych.mcgill.ca

Francisco Gomes-da-Matos: Universidade Federal de Pernambuco, Brazil: fcgm@cashnet.com.br

Madeleine Hulsen: University of Nijmegen, The Netherlands: M.Hulsen@its.kun.nl

Barbara Lust: Cornell University, USA: bcl4@cornell.edu

Roy Major: Arizona State University, USA: roy.major@asu.edu

Aneta Pavlenko: Temple University, USA: apavlenk@astro.temple.edu

Clive Perdue: University of Paris VIII, France: clive@univ-paris8.fr

Chapter 1

Background to the L2 User

VIVIAN COOK

Introduction

Portraits of the L2 User treats a wide range of topics from the perspective of the second language (L2) user as an independent speaker of language. They range from vocabulary to phonology, Universal Grammar to language teaching, brain functions to personal identity, treated by writers from a variety of backgrounds. The book thus provides a unique overview of second language acquisition (SLA) theories, results and methods, related to a common theme. It is intended for students and researchers working with second language use and acquisition in psychology, SLA research, bilingualism, linguistics and language teaching. It serves both as an introduction to current SLA research and as an account of the L2 user. Each chapter has a brief introduction relating it to the broader themes and issues of SLA research.

The purpose of the present chapter is to introduce some of the background, themes and consequences of the L2 user perspective. It should not, however, be assumed that all the contributors are necessarily in complete agreement with all of this chapter, or indeed with each other, as will be seen from their own contributions.

L2 Users and L2 Learners

An L2 user is any person who uses another language than his or her first language (L1), that is to say, the one learnt first as a child. He or she may be an English schoolchild staying with a family in Germany on an exchange, Luc Vandevelde the Belgian head of Marks and Spencer in England, the tennis-player Martina Hingis with Czech L1 being interviewed in English, a London newsagent using Bengali and English to his customers, a Canadian trucker with L1 English driving through French-speaking Montreal, a street trader in Singapore switching between English and two Chinese dialects, Kirsten Flagstad the Norwegian opera singer singing Wagner in German in New York, a Greek student using Italian to study in Perugia,

1

Billy Wilder code-switching from English to German to explain how he directed *Some Like it Hot,* a child in Vancouver speaking Chinese at home and English at school, an Arabic businessman switching to English for e-mails.

In other words an L2 user can be almost anyone anywhere. Using a second language is a commonplace activity. There are few places in the world where only one language is used. In London people speak over 300 languages and 32% of the children live in homes where English is not the main language (Baker & Eversley, 2000). In Australia 15.5% of the population speak a language other than English at home, amounting to 200 languages (Australian Government Census, 1996). In the Congo people speak 212 African languages, with French as the official language. In Pakistan they speak 66 languages, chiefly Punjabi, Sindhi, Siraiki, Pashtu and Urdu.

A country with many languages does not necessarily have many inhabitants who use more than one language, as seen in the distinct geographical regions for the various languages in Switzerland, Belgium and Canada. So it is almost impossible to estimate how many L2 users there are in the world. Though only 8% of the inhabitants of Pakistan speak Urdu as a first language, most of them use it as the official language, change to Arabic for religious purposes, and probably know English as well. In Singapore 56% of the population are literate in more than one language; in Europe 53% of people say that they can speak at least one European language in addition to their mother tongue, 23% speak two other languages (European Commission, 2001). One 12-year-old London child uses Lingala, French and English at home, Kiluba and Limongo with relatives and others outside the home; another speaks Aku at home, English, Spanish and Wolof outside (Baker & Eversley, 2000). Supposedly monolingual societies conceal a large number of L2 users; Japan for example, often cited as the most monolingual country, has 900,000 speakers of Okinawan and 670,000 speakers of Korean (Ethnologue, 1996); all Japanese children learn English in the senior secondary school. Arguably the majority of people in the world are multi-competent users of two or more languages rather than mono-competent speakers of one language, and there are as many children brought up with two languages as with one (Tucker, 1998).

L2 users are not necessarily the same as L2 learners. Language *users* are exploiting whatever linguistic resources they have for real-life purposes: they are reporting their symptoms to a doctor, negotiating a contract, reading a poem. Language *learners* are acquiring a system for later use: they are memorising a list of vocabulary, pretending to be customers in a shop, repeating a dialogue on a tape. The difference is that between decoding a message when the code is already known and codebreaking a message in order to find out an unknown code. Sometimes using and learning come to the same thing: an asylum-seeker in a new country learns by using the language for everyday survival, as does a child whose parents speak two languages.

Some L2 learners study the language in the classroom or on their own for diverse reasons set by themselves or by their educational systems. Vast numbers of students are involved; 83% of young people in the European Union have studied a second language (Commission of the European Communities, 1987); the British Council (1999) estimates that over one billion people are studying English. Some of these L2 learners become L2 users as soon as they step outside the classroom: the Indonesian child acquiring Dutch in Amsterdam, for example. Others use the second language to talk to their friends with different first languages inside the classroom: for example a Swedish student talking to a French student in English at a summer school in Dublin.

But many L2 learners are studying a second language as an academic subject alongside other school subjects such as geography or physics; it has no current purpose in their lives as a language for immediate use, and marginal relevance for their futures. Children learning English in China have little reason to use it while at school; few of them will find it useful in their future careers. The goal of using the second language is only one of the reasons for studying it; the UK National Criteria for GCSE in Modern Languages, for instance, stress the insight into other cultures and the promotion of general learning skills, not just the ability to use the language for communication (DES, 1990). Hence there are L2 learners who have no intention of becoming L2 users. Most obviously this is the case for teaching Latin and Classical Greek as 'dead' languages; less obviously it applies to any 'living' language taught for educational reasons other than possible use.

In a sense L2 users have no more in common than L1 users; the whole diversity of mankind is there. Some of them use the second language as skilfully as a monolingual native speaker, like Nabokov writing whole novels in a second language; some of them can barely ask for a coffee in a restaurant. The concept of the L2 user is similar to Haugen's minimal definition of bilingualism as 'the point where a speaker can first produce complete meaningful utterances in the other language' (Haugen, 1953: 7) and to Bloomfield's comment 'To the extent that the learner can communicate, he may be ranked as a foreign speaker of a language' (Bloomfield, 1933: 54). Any use counts, however small or ineffective. People use language, whether their first or second language, for their own purposes. L2 use succeeds or fails in the same ways as L1 use does. Some people write epic poems, some write e-mails; one businessman may win a contract, another may not. Inevitably there is a gap between people's intentions and their achievements. A person who tries to hit a particular language target may miss it for one reason or another: my attempts to write a sonnet never succeeded, even in my first language. In a second language, speakers are perhaps more aware of the gap between plan and execution.

The term *L2 user* can then refer to a person who knows and uses a second language at any level. One motivation for this usage is the feeling that it is demeaning to call someone who has functioned in an L2 environment for years a 'learner' rather than a 'user'. A person who has been using a second language for twenty-five years is no more an L2 learner than a fifty-year-old monolingual native speaker is an L1 learner. The term *L2 learner* implies that the task of acquisition is never finished, and it concentrates attention on how people acquire second languages rather than on their knowledge and use of the second language. Hence SLA research is a far broader discipline than first language acquisition research since it includes, not just the developmental aspects of first language acquisition, but all the aspects of the L2 user's language covered in other areas of linguistics and psychology. The first international organisation for second languages, EUROSLA, carefully made this point by having the 'A' in its name stand for *association*, not *acquisition* – European Second Language Association – to show that it was concerned with all aspects of second languages, not only with acquisition. The term *bilingual* in turn has so many contradictory definitions and associations in popular and academic usage that it seems best to avoid it whenever possible.

Characteristics of L2 users

The main aim of this book is to look at the nature of L2 users. The assumption here is that the L2 user is a different kind of person, not just a monolingual with added extras. What then are the characteristics of L2 users? Here we can summarise some of these; the other chapters explore them at length.

The L2 user has other uses for language than the monolingual

Do L2 users use language differently from monolinguals? The most obvious difference is that, as well as uses of language that can be carried out in either language, L2 users can perform specific activities that L1 users cannot. When they are aware that the other person knows both languages, L2 users often code-switch from one language to another. Take, for example, one Japanese student talking to another in England:

<u>Reading</u> sureba suruhodo, <u>confuse</u> suro yo. Demo, <u>computer lab</u> ni itte, <u>article</u> o <u>print out</u> shinakya.

(The more reading I have, the more I get confused, but I have to go to the computer lab and need to print out some articles.)

L2 users can also take something said in one language and translate it into another. An interpreter at the European Parliament, for instance, may listen to a speech in his or her L2 Danish and translate it into L1 Spanish at the same time.

Some see these uses as essentially extensions to the way monolinguals switch dialects and paraphrase (Paradis, 1997). Nevertheless there seems a qualitative as well as a quantitative jump from L1 paraphrase to the L2 ability to translate; L1 paraphrase for example seldom leads to distinct social roles such as acting as an intermediary between two other people, whether as a professional or an amateur. Nor does L1 dialect switching often occur within the production of single utterances or within the same conversation (except perhaps for purposes of humour), as is typical of code-switching between languages.

Some L2 users use these abilities directly for their jobs whether as professional translators, journalists, bilingual secretaries or other jobs: the skills they employ need specialist training. 'Natural' L2 translators are often children acting as mediators for their elders (Malakoff & Hakuta, 1991), say during a medical consultation for a mother who does not speak the doctor's language. So L2 users are capable not just of uses that overlap those of monolinguals, but also of uses that go beyond them.

The rest of the L2 user's language use is also in a sense invisibly different from that of a monolingual. When speaking their first language, L2 users are still affected by their knowledge of another language – its rules, concepts and cultural patterns. The L2 user stands between two languages, even when apparently using only one, having the resources of both languages on tap whenever needed, as we see below.

The L2 user's knowledge of the second language is typically not identical to that of a native speaker

Is the second language of L2 users different from that of native speakers of the language as a first language? In one sense the answer to this is obviously yes: few L2 users can pass for native speakers; their grammar, their accent, their vocabulary give away that they are non-native speakers, even after many years of learning the language or many decades of living in a country. A German student's spelling of *live* as *life*, of *England* as *Englan* or of *institute* as *institude* shows the carryover of the L1 voicing system to English spelling. There is little dispute that L2 users have different knowledge of the second language. The controversial issues have usually been whether this applies inevitably to all L2 users, and what its causes might be.

Some SLA research has concentrated on 'ultimate attainment' in L2 acquisition: can L2 users *ever* speak like natives? Those who think they cannot cite research that showed that Americans living in France for many years still had a different awareness of grammaticality in French from that of native speakers (Coppetiers, 1987). Those who think that it is possible for L2 users to speak like natives point to a handful of L2 learners who indeed pass for native speakers, whether in pronunciation (Bongaerts *et al.*, 1995) or in syntax (White & Genesee, 1996). Both sides of the debate judge the L2 user against the native speaker; ultimate attainment is a monolingual standard rather than an L2 standard. Differences from native speakers represent failure; 'Very few L2 learners appear to be fully successful in the way that native speakers are' (Towell & Hawkins, 1994: 14).

While the question of what ultimate attainment means in a second language is not yet resolved, there is no intrinsic reason why it should be the same as that of a monolingual native speaker. We should not be paying too much attention to the select handful of specially gifted individuals who can arguably pass for natives, but should take heed of the vast majority of people who are distinctive L2 users; we would not make the mistake of basing the study of human speech on a specially talented group such as opera-singers or mimics.

The L2 user's knowledge of their first language is in some respects not the same as that of a monolingual

Does the first language of L2 users also differ from that of monolinguals who speak the same language natively? This question has so far barely been broached in the SLA research field, except in the context of language loss, to be discussed in De Bot's chapter. Evidence for the effects of the second language on the first includes:

- *Phonology.* The L2 users' pronunciation of their first language moves towards that of the second language in respects such as Voice Onset Time for plosives such as /t/ and /d/ (Nathan, 1987) (discussed in Major's chapter).
- *Vocabulary.* The L2 users' understanding of L1 words is affected by their knowledge of the meanings and forms of the second language; a French person who knows English has the English meaning of the word *coin* (money) activated even when reading *coin* (corner) in French (Beauvillain & Grainger, 1987); loan-words have different L1

meanings for people who know the second language from which they are derived, for example Japanese *bosu* (gang-leader) has a more general meaning for Japanese who know English *boss* (Tokumaru, in progress).

- *Syntax.* Grammaticality judgements of French middle verb construction are affected by the second language (Balcom, 1995); cues for assigning subjects in the sentence are affected in Japanese by knowing English (Cook *et al.*, in preparation); Hungarian children who know English write more complex Hungarian sentences than those who do not (Kecskes & Papp, 2000).
- *Reading.* L2 users in some respects read their first language differently from monolingual natives: Greeks who know English read Greek differently from those who don't (Chitiri *et al.*, 1992).

Though the differences may not be great or even noticeable in everyday situations, the L1 knowledge of the majority of L2 users is not identical to that of monolinguals, as detailed in the volume *Effects of the L2 on the L1* (Cook, in preparation).

L2 users have different minds from monolinguals

Do L2 users think in different ways from monolinguals? Acquiring another language alters the L2 user's mind in ways that go beyond the actual knowledge of language itself, as we see in the chapters by Bialystok and Genesee. For example L2 users:

- *Think more flexibly.* Bilingual English/French children score better than monolingual children on an 'unusual uses' test (Lambert *et al.*, 1973).
- *Have increased language awareness.* Spanish/English bilingual children go through the early stages of grammatical awareness more rapidly than monolingual children (Galambos & Goldin-Meadow, 1990).
- *Learn to read more rapidly in their L1.* English children who learn Italian for an hour a week for five months learn to recognise words better than monolinguals do (Yelland *et al.*, 1993).
- *Have better communication skills in their L1.* For example English-speaking 6–7-year-olds who knew French were better able to communicate the rules of a game to blindfolded children than those who spoke only English (Genesee *et al.*, 1975).

The mind of an L2 user therefore differs from that of a monolingual native speaker in several ways other than the possession of the second language; multi-competence is not just the imperfect cloning of mono-competence, but a different state. The cogent title of Grosjean (1985) is 'The bilingual as a competent but specific speaker–hearer'. While the positive side of difference has been emphasised here, some aspects may of course be negative. Magiste (1986) and Ransdell and Fischler (1987) found L2 users had slight cognitive deficits on certain tasks compared with monolingual native speakers; Makarec and Persinger (1993) found that male L2 users, but not women, had some memory deficiencies compared with monolinguals. Nevertheless earlier research that showed ill-effects of bilingualism has mostly been refuted.

Completeness and Interlanguage

A commonsense approach to first language acquisition is to start from the adult and work backwards: the language of children is a defective version of the language of adults. A child who says *Help jelly* actually intends to say the adult sentence *Could you help me to some jelly?* The aspect of Chomsky's early thinking that can be called the independent grammars assumption (Cook, 1993) recognised that the child's language is a complete system in its own right, rather than an imperfect adult system. A child's sentence such as *Help jelly* relates to the child's grammar which has, say, rules that Verbs (help) are followed by Objects (jelly) and that sentences do not have to have subjects, rather than to the adult English rules of question formation, compulsory subjects and use of prepositions. In other words children are real children, not imitation adults; each stage of their development of language forms a complete system. The grammar of the two-year-old is as much a grammar as the grammar of the twenty-year-old, the language of the two-year-old as genuine as that of the adult. While the final adult state of competence provides a convenient yardstick that is historically related to the interim stages that children go through, it does not invalidate the existence of complete language systems at each stage of development. The independent grammars assumption meant that children's grammars should be evaluated in their own terms, not in terms of adult grammars, thus severing the child's grammar from the adult's. Linguistic competence is whatever it is at the particular moment that it is being studied, not a partial imitation of what it might become one day.

When applied to L2 learning, the independent grammars assumption meant treating L2 learners too as having language systems of their own. It was adapted to SLA (second language acquisition) research by several people at roughly the same period as 'transitional idiosyncratic dialect' (Corder, 1971), 'approximative system' (Nemser, 1971) and 'interlanguage' (Selinker, 1972), leading to the wave of SLA research of the 1960s and 1970s.

The grammars of L2 learners were seen to have their own characteristics rather than being pale reflections of the second language or transfer from the first language.

Take a sentence such as *Is policeman on the road* produced by a Punjabi-speaking user of English. Its characteristic is, not the distortion of either English or Punjabi, but the omission of non-lexical subjects such as *there*, common in early L2 grammars, as seen in other sentences spoken by the same user such as *Eating* and *After it's going from there try to go to back jail.* The L2 grammar is neither a defective version of the monolingual native grammar nor a partial transfer from the second, even if there are elements of both within it, but a creation of its own. In L1 acquisition the independent grammars assumption meant decoupling the child's grammar from the adult's. In L2 acquisition it means decoupling the L2 user's grammar from that of the monolingual native speaker. The L2 learner's grammar is to be judged as an L2 system in its own right, not against that of the native speaker.

This consequence was not in fact fully heeded by SLA research, which continued to assume that L2 users are failures compared with native speakers. This is seen in remarks such as 'Relative to native speaker's linguistic competence, learners' interlanguage is deficient by definition' (Kasper & Kellerman, 1997: 5), a sentiment echoed in almost every book on SLA. Labov (1969) trenchantly argued that members of one group should not be criticised for not meeting the standards of another group to which they can never belong, leading to this approach being outlawed in linguistics, though not in popular discussions. In academic discourse, women are not said to speak worse than men, nor Black English people worse than white, nor New Yorkers worse than Bostonians, however large the differences may be between these groups. While we can learn something by comparing apples with pears, apples inevitably make rather poor pears, however delicious.

As we have seen above and shall see throughout this book, the minds, languages and lives of L2 users are different from those of monolinguals. L2 users are not failures because they are different. To demonstrate a similar point in a different context, Williams (1975) found white American children scored 51% on the BITCH-100 test (Black Intelligence Test of Cultural Homogeneity) compared to their black contemporaries' 87%. Using the logic of deficit, the English of white Americans is extremely deficient. Monolingual native speakers are also incompetent at speaking second languages, tautologous as this may be to point out. Some people continue to insist that L2 users are a special case where the goal of one group is genuinely to be like another group: the ultimate state of L2 learning is indeed to pass as native. This argument of specialness seems a last defence, no more convincing in a second language context than it was in the area of human rights or racial or sexual discrimination. It also ignores the main use of international languages like English for non-native speakers to speak to other non-native speakers rather than to natives. This is not to say that the 'monolingualist' belief in the supremacy of the native speaker is not shared by many L2 users, who apologise for not speaking like native speakers, according to Grosjean (1989), because they 'assume and amplify the mono-lingual view'.

So it is dangerous to imply that either children or L2 users are incomplete versions of some complete final state. L1 children may use the word *more* in an apparently adult-like fashion; it is only when they are tested experimen-tally that it becomes apparent that they do not distinguish 'more apples' from 'less apples' (Clark, 1971). Looked at from the adult perspective, they have a partial meaning for the words; looked at from their own system, they have two synonyms. Intermediate L2 users of English often use the word *interesting* when a native speaker would say *interested*, as in *I am really interesting to help*. In native terms their meaning is incomplete; in L2 terms, it has a meaning of its own. Major discusses the idea of completeness applied to phonology more fully in his chapter.

In the absence of the native speaker, there is no single uniform criterion against which L2 users can be measured. Some use the language for comparatively simple daily exchanges such as commuting to work. Some lead their entire lives through the second language, the most extreme examples being spies. Hence the concept of a complete knowledge of a language is meaningless: competence is whatever it is. We communicate with an L1 child who says *Want more up* despite the differences in concepts and syntax. Our lexical knowledge of a word's meanings and behaviour may be incomplete compared with the entry in the dictionary, but our competence in English is not incomplete because we do not know that, for people in Cumbria, the word *man* means 'a cairn or pile of stones marking a summit or prominent point of a mountain'. What is complete is the system at a given moment for a given user. However, while there are names for the L1 and for the L2 interlanguage in the user's mind, no single term covers the overall system made up of the L1 and the interlanguage. Cook (1991) therefore introduced the term *multi-competence* to refer to 'the knowledge of more than one language in the same mind'.

The Integration Continuum Between L1 and L2

The overall question about L2 users is then how two or more languages relate in the same mind: what does multi-competence consist of? The three logical possibilities are:

- total separation in which the two languages are independent;
- interconnection in which they are connected to a greater or lesser degree;
- total integration in which they form a single system.

These reflect points on an integration continuum between complete separation for the two languages at one end and complete integration at the other (Francis, 1999), shown in Figure 1.1.

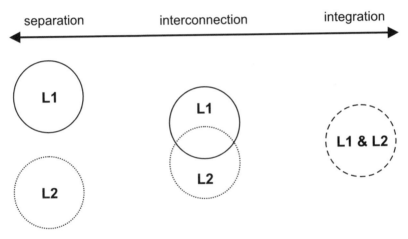

Figure 1.1 The integration continuum of possible relationships in multi-competence

This integration continuum applies across different areas of language. Take phonology. The sounds of the two languages might be quite distinct for the L2 user – separation. Or the two sounds might form a single element in the same hybrid phonological system – integration. Evidence of integration, for instance, comes from a study by Holmes (1996) in which L2 users were slower to react to possible and impossible words in English and German, such as THROG (possible in English, not German) or ZWUCK (possible in German, but not English) and, unlike monolinguals, did not make a clear break between them. The chapter by Major discusses this issue at greater length.

In grammar the same continuum applies. The grammars of the first and second languages could be entirely separate. L2 users of Japanese might know the Japanese word order Subject Object Verb (SOV), as in *Watashi wa hono kaimasu* (I book buy), regardless of whether their L1s have English SVO or Arabic VSO word orders. Or the L2 user might arrive at the Japanese order by connecting it to their L1 order, SOV to SVO for English, SOV to VSO for Arabic. Or L2 users might have a single system in their minds that shifts from L2 SOV to the L1 SVO or VSO when needed. Work by Cook *et al.* (in preparation) shows that the L2 indeed influences the L1 processing of Japanese people who know English, thus indicating some interconnection at least in this area of syntax.

The much-used concept of 'balanced bilingualism' applies only at the separation end of the continuum. At other points it has little meaning in terms of multi-competence, since the languages affect each other in both directions to a greater or lesser extent rather than being two discrete entities in balance. In other words the metaphor of balance applies to two objects, not to two inter-permeating systems.

Clearly neither total separation nor total integration can be completely true. Total separation is belied by the use of the same mouth and ears for both languages; total integration is denied by the L2 user's ability to keep to one language at a time. In particular the relationships could vary in several dimensions:

- *Different relationships could apply to different areas of language.* An L2 user might have an interconnected vocabulary but entirely separate grammars, or use grammatical structures independently but depend on the first language for L2 pragmatic functions. Paradis and Genesee (1996), for example, showed that L2 children developed the syntactic properties of English and French separately.
- *The relationship might change according to the stage of development or of language attrition.* At the early stages of L2 acquisition the languages might be tightly linked by translation and transfer, at later stages unified into one system. For instance Taeschner (1983) found an initial stage at which children had a single lexical system, which separated at the next stage into two lexicons with one syntax. The Asymmetrical Model described in De Groot's chapter is an example of such a developmental model.
- *Closeness of languages may affect the relationship.* For various historical reasons the first language and the second language can be related to each other (like English and Dutch), or totally unrelated to each other (like Japanese and Spanish). L2 users with L1 writing systems similar to that of the second language can, within limits, make use of their L1

system; L2 users with completely different L1s need to acquire a new system. For example, Chinese students with a meaning-based L1 writing system read English at a speed of 88 words per minute, compared to 110 words per minute for Spanish students with a sound-based L1 writing system (Haynes & Carr, 1990).

- *The relationship might vary from one person to another.* Some individuals keep the languages predominantly separate, others integrate them massively. Every mind does not necessarily relate two languages in the same way; there is no single final state of L2 use common to everybody, as we saw above. These variations might be due entirely to the users' minds, or might be the product of the language situations they find themselves in or of the teaching they have been subjected to or of the age at which they learnt the second language.

Relationships between Concepts and Language in the L2 User's Mind

The additional complication that is developed in several contributions to this book is the relationship of language to the concepts in the L2 user's mind; the background to this area can be found in Pavlenko (1999). This already assumes the existence of a conceptual level separate from language itself – that language and thinking are at some level distinct. The relationship between language and thinking raises the classic dilemma of linguistic relativity, alias the Whorf–Sapir hypothesis: does the way people speak condition the way they think, or are thought and language independent? English lacks an everyday word for children of the same parent found in, say, German *Geschwister* or Bahasa Melayu *suadara*; English people may just speak differently from speakers of German or Bahasa; or they may have different concepts of family relationships. The classic test-case is colour perception, currently having a revival as an area of research. For example Berinmo speakers in Papua New Guinea and English speakers have two pairs of colours *nol/wor* and *blue/green* with different boundaries between them (Davidoff *et al.*, 1999). Colour concepts then link to the speaker's language.

So do people who speak two languages have two different ways of thinking? Or is there one human mode of thinking that is expressed in different ways in different languages? The various possibilities for linking the integration continuum to a conceptual level are developed informally in Figures 1.2 to 1.4; a slightly different set based on experimentally tested models will be found in De Groot's chapter below. These figures assume for convenience of exposition that words and concepts are unitary wholes rather than made up of systems, features and networks of meaning, a view challenged in De Groot's chapter. While vocabulary is used for illustration, essentially the same points apply to grammatical concepts such as tense.

Separation

When the two languages in the mind are separate at one pole of the integration continuum, two classical links between language and concepts have been made, shown in Figure 1.2, corresponding to two of the three types of bilingualism detailed in Weinreich (1953).

- *Compound.* A single concept links to different words in both languages. The meanings of the second language are the same as those of the first, but are expressed by different words. So the concept ✈ links both to the English word *plane* and to the French word *avion*. The implication is that human beings have only one way of thinking, which can be expressed equally well in two languages; translation is possible via the mediating concept.
- *Coordinate.* The two languages are in separate compartments. The two concepts are as separate as the two languages. So the L1 concept ✈ links to the English word *plane*, the L2 concept ✈ to the French word *avion*. Speakers of different languages have very different concepts; it was for instance difficult for English speakers to operate with the Berinmo colours *nol* and *wor* (Davidoff *et al.*, 1999). The individual may find it impossible to go from one language to the other by translating *plane* into *avion* since the words have no conceptual level in common.

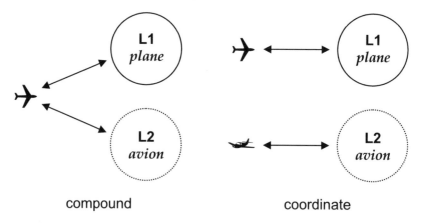

Figure 1.2 Relationships between concepts and separate L1 and L2

Interconnection

If the two languages are interconnected in the mind, that is to say in the middle of the integration continuum, there are overlaps between them. This will vary according to what links to what, how many links there are, how strong they are, whether the links are asymmetrical, and so on. The three main possibilities are seen in Figure 1.3.

- *Subordinate*. This is the third type in Weinreich (1953): the L2 is parasitic on the first language; the L2 vocabulary is accessible only through the first language. So the concept ✈ links to the L1 word *plane* which links to the L2 word *avion*. The L2 is tied in completely to the L1; the second language is a way of recoding the first language, like a complex form of Morse Code. Everything in the second language is essentially reached by translation. The L2 user's concepts do not change, as the second language is simply a spin-off from the L1.
- *Overlapping languages, same concepts*. The two systems are closely related without one being subordinated to the other; the L2 user is employing both L1 and L2 lexicons in conjunction, say to code-switch. The L1 word *plane* and the L2 word *avion* are linked together in the lexicon, particularly true for words that are cognates, say *airport* and *aeroport*. But a single concept ✈ underlies both languages. This is called the Asymmetric Model by De Groot, following Kroll; it allows many differences in terms of the amount and strength of the overlap between the languages and the links to the concepts.

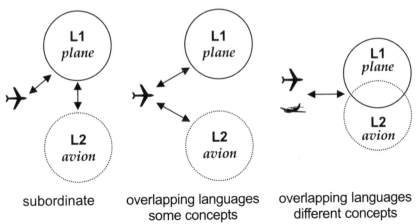

subordinate   overlapping languages some concepts   overlapping languages different concepts

Figure 1.3 Relationships of concepts and language in interconnected L1 and L2

- *Overlapping languages, different concepts.*This allows for the possibility that separation extends to the conceptual level and that people with different languages do have different ways of thinking. Thus there may be two slightly different concepts, ✈ and ✈, which relate to the overall linked systems of the L2. For example Athanasopolos (2001) found Greek speakers who knew English had a different perception of the two Greek words covered by English *blue*, namely γὰλὰζιο (*ghalazio*, 'light blue') and μπλε (*ble*, 'dark blue'), than monolingual Greek speakers.

Integration

The remaining overall relationship at the other pole of the integration continuum is integration: the two languages form one indivisible system, seen in Figure 1.4.

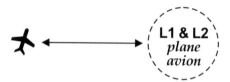

Figure 1.4 Relationships of concepts and language in integrated L1 and L2

There is no more separation between the two languages in the multi-competent mind than there is between different styles and genres in the monolingual; *plane* and *avion* are choices for expressing the same concept, just as say *plane* and *jet* are choices for the monolingual. The L1 concepts are not separate from the L2 concepts but merge into a new identity distinct from either in which 2 + 2 = 5; combining the concept ✈ with the concept ✈ yields a new concept ✈ for which two words *plane* and *avion* are available. Caskey-Sirmons and Hickson (1977), for example, found that monolingual speakers of Korean use the colour term *paran sekj* (blue) to mean something greener and less purple than Koreans who know English. Their colour concepts form a single system in which there is no L1 value, no L2 value, but a combined L1/L2 value.

These relationships with concepts can be incorporated into the integration continuum, as seen in Figure 1.5. This simplification misleads slightly by reducing the variety of possibilities at the interconnection stage to one. As before, the different points along the continuum may reflect different areas of language, stages of development, closeness of the two languages, or individual variation between users.

Other Consequences of the L2 User Perspective

Clearly this schematic approach to the possible relationships between first and second language fails to deal with some other crucial dimensions.

Universal aspects of language

What about the features that languages have in common? Languages do not vary arbitrarily, but only within certain limits, preferring certain clusters of features over others, and totally excluding some logically possible alternatives. The contribution of universal aspects of language to second language acquisition are developed in the chapters by Flynn and Lust on syntax and Major on phonology. For example, a language with Object Verb order, say Japanese *hono kaimasu* (book buy) and adjective before noun *atarashii hono* (new book), is very likely to have the genitive before the noun *chomusukino hono* (Chomsky's book) (Hawkins, 1983: 64). The first and second languages are therefore constrained by the same overall properties of language. L2 users apply these implicational universals to the language they are acquiring, 90% of them for example extrapolating that a language with Object Verb order also has nouns followed by postpositions rather than preceded by prepositions (Cook, 1988). Cutler *et al.* (1992) showed that L2 users of French or English divided speech according to syllables or to stress depending on which language was dominant; that is to say, they had an either/or choice from two possibilities for language, but could not have both at once. The Universal Grammar (UG) theory interprets universals as built-in aspects of the human mind; the two languages L1 and L2 may be

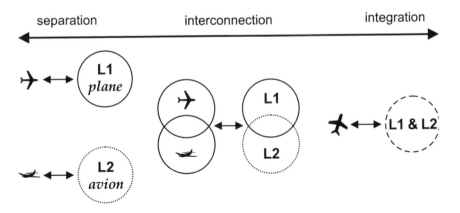

Figure 1.5 Sample points on the integration continuum of possible relationships between L1, L2 and concepts in multi-competence

related by drawing on the same potential in the human mind. Recognising that aspects of language are universal does not, however, necessarily commit one to a particular theory of language.

The notion of transfer

Placing the L2 user on an integration continuum means to some extent reinterpreting the notion of transfer that is popular in SLA research (Cook, 2000). The verb *transfer* implies that someone moves something from one place to another: *John transferred his bank account from the NatWest to the HSBC.* It presupposes a process of movement and three separate objects; the learner (object 1) transfers (process) L1 SOV (object 2) to L2 English SVO (object 3). The relationships described here do not fit this schema, since there are not necessarily discrete objects labelled L1 and L2 and no process of moving something from one place to another. The integrative continuum does not treat the source and destination as separate mental objects with defined edges but as merged or overlapping systems; language acquisition or use is not transferring something from one part of the mind to another, but two systems accommodating to each other. The terms 'transfer' and 'cross-linguistic influence' seem to imply separate languages and movement rather than overlapping systems. For example Gawlitzek-Maiwald and Tracy (1996) prefer to see L1 to L2 transfer as a way in which the child can 'boot-strap' into the second language, in a sense reviving the idea that transfer is motivated by ignorance (Newmark & Reibel, 1968).

'Gating out' languages in the mind

Wallace Lambert posed a crucial question:

> How is it that the bilingual is able to 'gate out' or set aside a whole integrated linguistic system while functioning with a second one, and a moment later, if the situation calls for it, switch the process, activating the previously inactive system and setting aside the previously active one? (Lambert, 1990: 203–204)

L2 users not only have two languages in a complex relationship in the mind but that they can also quickly flip from a bilingual mode in which they are code-switching from one language to another to a monolingual mode in which they use only one language (Grosjean, 1989). The bilingual mode raises questions about when, how and why the L2 user switches from one language to another; this is a natural ability in many L2 users and rarely a sign of confusion or incompetence, even in small children. The monolingual mode raises questions about if, how, when and to what extent the person can use a single language and exclude the other; as we have already seen, much of the research suggests that, even in monolingual mode, the L2 user is still tapping into the other language. As Genesee points out in his chapter, one definite addition to the bilingual child's repertoire is the ability to keep the languages separate.

Physical properties of the L1/L2 relationships in the brain

So far the relationships between languages in the mind have been discussed as abstract properties of two language systems. But the integration continuum may also reflect differences in how the languages are actually stored in the brain. The highly influential early work by Lenneberg (1967) saw storage as distributed between the two hemispheres of the brain, right and left. It would be very neat if the first language were stored in the left hemisphere, the side most concerned with language, and the second in the right, but this turns out to be easier to say than to prove. Or there might be differences of location within the same hemisphere, say within the parts known to be involved with language, namely Broca's and Wernicke's areas. As we see in Fabbro's and Dewaele's chapters, a new generation of research has employed techniques for investigating how the different areas of the brain are activated during L1 and L2 processing, ranging from the electrical stimulation of the brain during surgery to measuring the blood supply and electrical activity. The fascinating possibility is that the relationships of the integration continuum and the variation between L2 users' abilities could be reflected in the physical development and organisation of their brains.

Implications of the L2 User Perspective

If this approach is correct, it has consequences not only for SLA research itself but also for linguistics. Implications for language teaching are considered in the final chapter.

Implications for SLA research

As we see throughout this book, the L2 user concept alters the perspective of SLA research. The same areas, the same results, the same theories, all look different from this angle and lead to different research questions. SLA research is no longer about finding excuses why L2 users are failed native speakers but can explore what makes L2 users what they are.

The overall questions to be asked concern the relationships between the languages in the L2 user's mind and how these develop. The rest of this book poses a broad spectrum of questions, given here in the order in which they appear:

- What are the relationships between the two stores of vocabulary in the mind and how are they used in comprehension and production? (De Groot, Chapter 2)
- How do L2 learners balance universal aspects of language and L1 transfer as they create an L2 phonological system? (Major, Chapter 3)
- How does the knowledge of syntax in the L2 learner's mind relate to properties of Universal Grammar in the Chomskyan sense? (Flynn and Lust, Chapter 4)
- How do L2 users develop functional grammars for communicating meaning? (Perdue, Chapter 5)
- How are children's minds affected by the acquisition of more than one language? (Bialystok, Chapter 6)
- How do young children develop the ability to separate and to mix two languages systematically? (Genesee, Chapter 7)
- How are the two languages physically organised in the brain of the L2 user? (Fabbro, Chapter 8; Dewaele, Chapter 9)
- What accounts for the variation in fluency of L2 users? (Dewaele, Chapter 9)
- How do the user's first or second languages change with time as they are affected by the other language? (De Bot and Hulsen, Chapter 10)
- How does a second language constitute part of the L2 user's multiple social identities? (Pavlenko, Chapter 11)
- What rights can L2 learners lay claim to? (Gomes da Matos, Chapter 12)
- How can we best help people to become L2 users? (Cook, Chapter 13)

Treating the L2 user as an independent person not only yields questions like these but also in principle forces SLA research to reject research methods that treat the L2 user as a defective native speaker, a claim justified at greater length in Cook (1997a). The acceptance of the independent grammars assumption by SLA research in the 1970s did not substantially change the kinds of research methods that were employed. Many saw grammatical development as adding the rules of the language one at a time, building a house brick by brick; interlanguage is 'the sum of all the rules a learner has acquired so far' (Pienemann, 1989: 54); the bricks involved are rules of the native speaker grammar, not of L2 user grammar. The revealingly-titled Error Analysis technique typically combs L2 user speech for deviations from *native* speech; the technique of obligatory occurrences checks L2 users' sentences for omission of elements that *natives* would use; the grammaticality judgements of L2 users are mostly referenced against *native* speakers; the question of age in second language acquisition is 'whether the very best learners actually have native-like competence' (Long, 1990: 281).

Despite the lip-service to interlanguage, the language systems of L2 users have commonly been treated in terms of the native speaker. The only rigorous attempt to build a whole L2 user grammar in its own terms is perhaps the cross-national European Science Foundation project (Perdue, 1993), which established a basic grammar for L2 users independently of the L1 or the L2 concerned, as we see in Perdue's own chapter.

Comparison is indeed a useful research technique: the development of children and chimpanzees can for example be compared in order to reveal the distinctively human factors in development (Tomasello, 1999), without assuming that one should be measured by the standards of the other; chimpanzees are not failed human beings. What is unacceptable from the L2 user perspective is not so much the use of native speaker comparison as a tool but drawing conclusions from it that treat the L2 user as a deficient native speaker, whether this is couched as failure 'to acquire the target language fully' (White, 1989: 41), 'to achieve native-speaker competence' (James, 1998: 2) or 'to become native speakers' (Felix, 1987: 140). The comparison technique misses precisely the ways in which L2 users go outside the bounds of monolinguals; the ultimate achievements of L2 users are constrained to those that duplicate or do not duplicate native performance. Suppose for example that aspects of Universal Grammar are activated only in minds that store more than one language, the typical human condition; these will never be discovered by methods that investigate the presence or absence in L2 grammars of aspects of monolingual grammars.

It should not of course be presumed that there are no circumstances when L2 users should try to speak like native speakers. L2 users do sometimes have to communicate with monolingual native speakers, who may well prefer to hear native-like speech, whatever their motivations may be, for example, British businessmen negotiating in English with their Japanese counterparts. But they form only one of the many types of person that the L2 user may encounter. In the absence of more specific L2 user models, the model that a language teacher puts forward, for instance, might well be the native speaker, partly because of the students' expectations, partly because of the convenience of a lowest common denominator for all students to aim at. This issue is discussed further in the final chapter.

A major problem with the comparison technique is that the changes in the L2 mind may in themselves affect the measuring instrument employed. L2 users do not treat the research tasks in the same way as monolinguals do, for example they translate sentences back into their first language, an impossibility for monolinguals (Goss *et al.*, 1994); their strategies for making judgements vary between their first and second languages (Davies & Kaplan, 1998). Despite the well-known problems with the grammaticality judgements technique (Birdsong, 1989; Cook, 1993), this technique is massively used in SLA research, particularly in UG studies. Sometimes the comparison with native speaker judgements is explicit, sometimes the comparison is implicit in the choice of sentences that are or are not grammatical by the standards of a native speaker. Yet a well-established effect of L2 learning is that the metalinguistic judgement of L2 users is altered, as we see in Bialystok's chapter. The grammaticality judgements technique is bound to reveal differences between monolinguals and L2 users, because the actual measuring instrument is not neutral. A related issue is the use of data based on recorded conversations of L2 users where it is either not specified or not seen as relevant whether the researcher/interviewer knows the L1 of the L2 user. Code-switching is after all natural in bilingual situations, but peculiar where one person does not know both languages, and varies according to the extent of the L2 knowledge the speaker imputes to the listener (Grosjean, 1997).

Implications for linguistics

As several contributors suggest, if this line of reasoning is correct, it raises issues for linguistics itself. The basic stance here is the 'multilingualist' view that it is normal for human beings to know more than one language rather than the 'monolingualist' view that it is normal to know only one (Cook, 1997b). Here we can sketch, as starkly as possible, some of the implications that are likely to be hotly disputed by most linguists.

Even for linguists who see the monolingual as central, a disturbing consequence of multi-competence is that comparatively minor exposure to other languages changes the individual speaker, affecting *inter alia* their knowledge of their first language and their ability to carry out grammaticality judgements. If the native speaker informants that linguists consult are not 'pure' monolinguals unsullied by contact with other languages, the speech they produce and their judgements of language are affected by the other languages they know. This monolingual purity is increasingly hard to find these days. With one billion people learning English, for instance, it is difficult to find informants or subjects for experiments who have not had at least minimal exposure to English; there are few Japanese speakers who have not been taught English at school except among the old or those outside mainstream education.

This consequence also affects linguist-observers, whose linguistic intuitions about their first language may be contaminated by the other languages they know. The transformation in the L2 user means linguistics needs to be careful to use as pure monolinguals as possible; any research that does not specify whether the subjects or the researcher speak more than one language is suspect, in so far as it purports to describe monolingual native speakers. Taken to an extreme, this would then presumably mean distrusting the judgements of virtually every twentieth century linguist because of the other languages they know. For example the judgements about English of Bloomfield, Halliday or Chomsky are not trustworthy, except where they are supported by evidence from 'pure' monolinguals. In practice much linguistics is already in practice L2 users talking about other L2 users. Linguistics should either acknowledge that the normal human being actually uses more than one language, and so accept that much of its descriptions concern L2 users, or it should restrict its scope to the dwindling handful of isolated pockets of 'pure' monolinguals, now hard to find even in the mountains of Papua New Guinea.

More specifically, the notion of linguistic competence usually disregards the L2 user. Like the other aspects of linguistic competence, monolingualism is a simplifying assumption rather than reality: no-one denies that many human beings speak more than one language. The fact that people know more than one language is taken to have no more bearing on the study of competence than the existence of different social or geographical dialects or different styles and registers. Mono-competence is seen as the norm, multi-competence as an exception.

But, if all human beings can potentially acquire more than one language, the ways that their minds are organised must permit this from the beginning. It is accidental that some children only hear one language; linguistics has to take into account what *any* child can do, not just those with comparatively impoverished linguistic environments. An analogy would be the absurdity of considering lung functions in terms of the 'simpler' case of people with a single lung. Given the appropriate environment, two languages are as normal as two lungs. If we take multi-competence seriously, Chomsky's goals for linguistics of observing, describing and explaining the knowledge and use of language (Chomsky, 1986) need to be rephrased by making the word 'language' plural (Cook, 1993):

- What constitutes knowledge of languages?
- How is knowledge of languages acquired?
- How is knowledge of languages put to use?

The goals of linguistics are now to describe and explain knowledge, acquisition and use of languages, the single language being an exception. Indeed one could start to speculate whether counting languages in one mind – L1, L2, L3, etc. – is a valid approach. Chomsky (1982: 5) claimed 'The grammar in a person's mind/brain is real; it is one of the real things in the world. The language (whatever that may be) is not'. The reality is the grammar stored in the mind, not a language or languages. The language system in the mind varies in everyone, bilingualism being simply an extreme case: '"multilingualism" is a vague intuitive notion; every person is multiply multilingual in a more technical sense' (Chomsky, 2000: 44)

Satterfield (1999) argues from learnability theory that existing explanations of language acquisition have not recognised that many children learn two languages simultaneously. The basic UG (Universal Grammar) scenario of acquisition has to widen to allow the child essentially to set parameters in two ways right from the beginning, rather than seeing this as an add-on extra. 'A theory purporting to account for universal language learnability cannot be considered adequate if it excludes the non-monolingual speakers of this world' (Satterfield, 1999: 137). Any theory about the acquisition of languages by ordinary human beings has to account for the fact that many of them acquire two languages simultaneously from the beginning, and that many others acquire one or more other language consecutively at a later time. 'Bilingualism should stand as a rigorous barometer for measuring the feasability of our most developed linguistic theories' (Satterfield, 1999: 137). If any child exposed to two languages can acquire them, the standard account of language acquisition has to accommodate children who, at the same time, know two languages with two sets of parameter-settings. It is misleading to restrict acquisition theories to children who have been brought up in an environment where they only hear one language.

References

Athanasopolos, P. (2001) *L2 Acquisition and Bilingual Conceptual Structure.* MA thesis, University of Essex.

Australian Government Census (1996) *AusStats.* Online document: http://www.abs.gov.au/ausstats

Baker, P. and Eversley, J. (2000) *Multilingual Capital.* London: Battlebridge.

Balcom, P. (1995) Argument structure and multi-competence. *Linguistica Atlantica* 17, 1–17.

Beauvillain, C. and Grainger, J. (1987) Accessing interlexical homographs: Some limitations of a language-selective access. *Journal of Memory and Language* 26, 658–672.

Birdsong, D. (1989) *Metalinguistic Performance and Interlanguage Competence.* New York: Springer.

Bloomfield, L. (1933) *Language.* New York: Holt.

Bongaerts, T., Planken, B. and Schils, E. (1995) Can late starters attain a native accent in a foreign language? A test of the Critical Period Hypothesis. In D. Singleton and Z. Lengyel (eds) *The Age Factor in Second Language Acquisition* (pp. 30–50). Clevedon: Multilingual Matters.

British Council (1999) Frequently asked questions. Online document: http://www.britishcouncil.org/english/engfaqs.htm#hmlearn1.

Caskey-Sirmons, L.A. and Hickerson, N.P. (1977) Semantic shift and bilingualism: variation in the colour terms of five languages. *Anthropological Linguistics* 19 (8), 358–367.

Chitiri, H-F., Sun, Y. and Willows, D. (1992) Word recognition in second language reading. In R. Harris (ed.) *Cognitive Processing in Bilinguals* (pp. 283–297). Amsterdam: Elsevier.

Chomsky, N. (1982) *Some Concepts and Consequences of the Theory of Government and Binding*. Cambridge, MA: MIT Press.

Chomsky, N. (1986) *Knowledge of Language: Its Nature, Origin and Use*. New York: Praeger.

Chomsky, N. (2000) *The Architecture of Language*. New Delhi: Oxford University Press.

Clark, E. (1971) On the acquisition of 'before' and 'after'. *Journal of Verbal Learning and Verbal Behaviour* 10, 266–275.

Commission of the European Communities (1987) *Young Europeans in 1987*. Brussels: EC Commission.

Cook, V.J. (1988) Language learners' extrapolation of word order in phrases of Micro-Artificial Languages. *Language Learning* 38 (4), 497–529.

Cook, V.J. (1991) The poverty-of-the-stimulus argument and multi-competence. *Second Language Research* 7 (2), 103–117.

Cook, V.J. (1993) *Linguistics and Second Language Acquisition*. Basingstoke: Macmillan.

Cook, V.J. (1997a) Monolingual bias in second language acquisition research. *Revista Canaria de Estudios Ingleses* 34, 35–50.

Cook, V.J. (1997b) The consequences of bilingualism for cognitive processing. In A.M.B. de Groot and J.F. Kroll (eds) *Tutorials in Bilingualism: Psycholinguistic Perspectives* (pp. 279–300). Hillsdale, NJ: Lawrence Erlbaum.

Cook, V.J. (2000) Is transfer the right word? Paper presented at the International Pragmatics Association (IPRA) conference, Budapest. Online document: privatewww.essex.ac.uk/~vcook/OBS8.htm.

Cook, V.J. (ed.) (in preparation) *The Effects of the L2 on the L1*. Clevedon: Multilingual Matters.

Cook, V.J., Iarossi, E., Stellakis, N. and Tokumaru, Y. (in preparation) Effects of the second language on processing the first. In V.J. Cook (ed.) (in preparation) *The Effects of the L2 on the L1*. Clevedon: Multilingual Matters.

Coppetiers, R. (1987) Competence differences between native and near-native speakers. *Language* 63, 3, 545–573.

Corder, S.P. (1971) Idiosyncratic errors and error analysis. *International Review of Applied Linguistics* 9 (2), 147–159.

Cutler, A., Mehler, J., Norris, D. and Segui, J. (1992) The monolingual nature of speech segmentation by bilinguals. *Cognitive Psychology* 24, 381–410.

Davidoff, J., Davies, I. and Roberson, D. (1999) Colour categories in a stone-age tribe. *Nature* 398, 18 March, 203–204.

Davies, W.R. and Kaplan, T.I. (1998) Native speakers versus L2 learners: Grammaticality judgments. *Applied Linguistics* 19 (2), 183–203.

DES (1990) *Modern Foreign Languages for Ages 11 to 16*. London: Department of Education and Science and the Welsh Office.

Ethnologue (1996) *Ethnologue: Languages of the World, Fourteenth edition*. Online document: http://www.sil.org/ethnologue/.

European Commission (2001) *Special Eurobarometer Survey 54 'Europeans and Languages'*. Online document: http://europa.eu.int/comm/education/languages.html.

Felix, S. (1987) *Cognition and Language Growth*. Dordrecht: Foris.

Francis, W. (1999) Cognitive integration of language and memory in bilinguals: Semantic representation. *Psychological Bulletin* 125 (2), 193–222.

Galambos, S.J. and Goldin-Meadow, S. (1990) The effects of learning two languages on metalinguistic awareness. *Cognition* 34, 1–56.

Gawlitzek-Maiwald, I. and Tracy, R. (1996) Bilingual bootstrapping. *Linguistics* 34, 901–926.

Genesee, F., Tucker, R. and Lambert, W.E. (1975) Communication skills of bilingual children. *Child Development* 46, 1010–14.

Goss, N., Ying-Hua, Z. and Lantolf, J.P. (1994) Two heads may be better than one: mental activity in second language grammaticality judgments. In E.E. Tarone, S.M. Gass, and A.D. Cohen (eds) *Research Methodology in Second Language Acquisition* (pp. 263–286). New Jersey: Erlbaum.

Grosjean, F. (1985) The bilingual as a competent but specific speaker-hearer. *Journal of Multilingual and Multicultural Development* 6 (6), 467–477.

Grosjean, F. (1989) Neurolinguists, beware! The bilingual is not two monolinguals in one person. *Brain and Language* 36, 3–15.

Grosjean, F. (1997) Processing mixed language: issues, findings, and models. In A.M.B. de Groot and J.F. Kroll (Eds) *Tutorials in Bilingualism: Psycholinguistic Perspectives* (pp. 225–254). Mahwah, NJ: Lawrence Erlbaum Associates.

Haugen, E. (1953) *The Norwegian Language in America*. Philadelphia: University of Pennsylvania Press.

Hawkins, J.A. (1983) *Word Order Universals*. New York: Academic Press.

Haynes, M. and Carr, T.H. (1990) Writing system background and second language reading: A component skills analysis of English reading by native-speaking readers of Chinese. In T.H. Carr and B.A. Levy (eds) *Reading and its Development: Component Skills Approaches* (pp. 375–421). San Diego: Academic Press.

Holmes, F. (1996) Cross-language interference in lexical decision. *Speech Hearing and Language: Work In Progress* Volume 9. University College London, Department of Phonetics and Linguistics. Online document: http://www.phon.ucl.ac.uk/home/shl9/freddieh/holmef.htm.

James, C. (1998) *Errors in Language Learning and Use: Exploring Error Analysis*. Harlow: Longman.

Kasper, G. and Kellerman, E. (eds) (1997) *Communication Strategies: Psycholinguistic and Sociolinguistic Perspectives*. Harlow: Longman.

Kecskes, I. and Papp, T. (2000) *Foreign Language and Mother Tongue*. Hillsdale, NJ: Lawrence Erlbaum.

Labov, W. (1969) The logic of non-standard English. *Georgetown Monographs on Language and Linguistics* 22, 1–31.

Lambert, W.E. (1990) Persistent issues in bilingualism. In B. Harley, P. Allen, J. Cummins and M. Swain (eds) (1990) *The Development of Second Language Proficiency*. Cambridge: Cambridge University Press.

Lambert, W., Tucker, C.R. and d'Anglejan, A. (1973) Cognitive and attitudinal consequences of bilingual schooling. *Journal of Educational Psychology* 85 (2), 141–159.

Lenneberg, E. (1967) *Biological Foundations of Language*. New York: Wiley and Sons.

Long, M. (1990) Maturational constraints on language development. *Studies in Second Language Acquisition* 12, 251–86.

Magiste, E. (1986) Selected issues in second and third language learning. In J. Vaid (ed.) (1986) *Language Processing in Bilinguals: Psycholinguistic and Neurolinguistic Perspectives* (pp. 97–122). Hillsdale, NJ: Lawrence Erlbaum.

Makarec, K. and Persinger, M. (1993) Bilingual men, but not women display verbal memory weakness but not figural memory differences compared to monolinguals. *Personality and Individual Differences* 15 (5), 531–536.

Malakoff, M. and Hakuta, K. (1991) Translation skills and metalinguistic awareness in bilinguals. In E. Bialystok (ed.) *Language Processing in Bilingual Children* (pp. 141–166). Cambridge: Cambridge University Press.

Nathan, G.S. (1987) On second-language acquisition of voiced stops. *Journal of Phonetics* 15, 313–322.

Nemser, W. (1971) Approximative systems of foreign language learners. *International Review of Applied Linguistics* 9, 115–24.

Newmark, L. and Reibel, D. (1968) Necessity and sufficiency in language learning. *International Review of Applied Linguistics* 6, 145–64.

Paradis, J. and Genesee, F. (1996) Syntactic acquisition in bilingual children: Autonomous or interdependent? *Studies in Second Language Acquisition* 18, 1–25.

Paradis, M. (1997) The cognitive neuropsychology of bilingualism. In A.M.B. de Groot and J. Kroll (eds) *Tutorials in Bilingualism. Psycholinguistic Perspectives* (pp. 331–354). Mahwah, NJ: Lawrence Erlbaum.

Pavlenko, A. (1999) New approaches to concepts in bilingual memory. *Bilingualism: Language and Cognition* 2, 209–30.

Perdue, C. (ed.) (1993) *Adult Language Acquisition: Cross-Linguistic Perspectives* (two volumes). Cambridge: Cambridge University Press.

Pienemann, M. (1989) Is language teachable? *Applied Linguistics* 10 (1), 52–79.

Ransdell, S.E. and Fischler, I. (1987) Memory in a monolingual mode: When are bilinguals at a disadvantage. *Journal of Memory and Language* 26, 392–405.

Satterfield, T. (1999) *Bilingual Selection of Syntactic Knowledge: Extending the Principles and Parameters Approach*. Dordrecht: Kluwer.

Selinker, L. (1972) Interlanguage. *International Review of Applied Linguistics* X (3), 209–231.

Taeschner, T. (1983) *The Sun is Feminine*. Berlin: Springer.

Tokumaru, Y. (in progress) A study on cross-linguistic interactions between Japanese Katakana-go and English words in the mind of 'multicompetent' Japanese–English users.

Tomasello, M. (2000) *The Cultural Origins of Human Cognition*. Boston: Harvard University Press.

Towell, R. and Hawkins, R. (1994) *Approaches to Second Language Acquisition*. Clevedon: Multilingual Matters.

Tucker, G.R. (1998) A global perspective on multilingualism and multilingual education. In J. Cenoz and F. Genesee (eds) *Beyond Bilingualism: Multilingualism and Multilingual Education* (pp. 3–15). Clevedon: Multilingual Matters.

Weinreich, U. (1953) *Languages in Contact*. The Hague: Mouton.

White, L. (1989) *Universal Grammar and Second Language Acquisition*. Amsterdam: John Benjamins.

White, L. and Genesee, F. (1996) How native is near-native? The issue of ultimate attainment in adult second language acquisition. *Second Language Research* 17 (1), 233–265.

Williams, R. (1975) The BITCH-100: A culture-specific test. *Journal of Afro-American Issues* 3, 103–16.

Yelland, G.W., Pollard, J. and Mercuri, A. (1993) The metalinguistic benefits of limited contact with a second language. *Applied Psycholinguistics* 14, 423–444.

Introduction to Chapter 2

Lexical Representation and Lexical Processing in the L2 User, Annette de Groot

VIVIAN COOK

The chapter by Annette de Groot takes a psychological approach to one of the fundamental issues about the L2 user: how do the vocabularies of two languages fit together in the same mind? In broad terms the area of L2 vocabulary has been approached in three ways. One, typically practiced by 'applied linguists', applies linguistic description to language teaching: find out the frequencies of words, look at the ways in which linguists organise vocabulary in fields and semantic features, and then organise language teaching accordingly. Some of the papers in Schmitt and McCarthy (1997) represent the good points of this approach. The second, typically produced by 'SLA researchers' or 'language testers', studies L2 acquisition of vocabulary through detailed experiments on the transfer of meaning from one language to another, investigation of learners' strategies, and so on. A good representative might be Nation (2001). The third approach, practised mostly by psychologists investigating bilingualism, studies L2 vocabulary as pairings of words and concepts within strictly controlled experiments.

While these approaches sometimes overlap, they often have difficulty in appreciating each other's points of view. The applied and SLA approaches tend to question the psychologists' dependence on word-forms as the central units, rather than the networks of meanings, collocations and forms found in the linguist's lexical entry. The SLA and psychological approaches are sceptical of the value of an applied approach not firmly based on studies of actual L2 acquisition. The psychological approach tends to regret the lack of research rigour and absence of learning theory of the other two. David Singleton's book (Singleton, 1999) bravely attempts to bring together these diverse fields.

A distinctive element in the psychological approach is the use of models that are tested step by step against experimental evidence, most famously in Levelt's model of speech production (Levelt, 1989). Chapter 1 sketched some informal models of L2 users. Here De Groot starts from the basic three-component two-level model seen in Figure 2.1.

The first question De Groot deals with is how these three components connect to each other across the lexical and conceptual levels. Learning the English word *bicycle* in the L1 means linking it to the concept 🚲; understanding the word *bicycle* means accessing the concept 🚲. A word in a second language needs to be tied in to this concept/word *bicycle*/🚲 pair in one way or another. The concept 🚲 might link to the English word *bicycle*, which leads to the French word *bicyclette*; this relationship is called word association, i.e. word-to-word rather than concept-to-word. (This should not be confused with 'word association' in tasks where participants produce the first word that comes to mind, an area of SLA research in its own right.) Alternatively the L2 word might link directly to the concept, that is to say 🚲 links to both English *bicycle* and French *bicyclette*. This is called concept mediation since the links between the languages are indirectly mediated by the concept rather than direct.

The second question is whether these three components and two levels of representation are adequate. De Groot presents the more complex BIA and BIMOLA models and develops an argument that initial access to the mental lexicon is independent of the language being processed.

Her chapter then describes a number of the lexical avenues explored in contemporary experiment-based research. It shows some of the complexity of the organisation required in the L2 user's mind and the difficulties that this raises for research, compared say to that involved in studying minds with only one language.

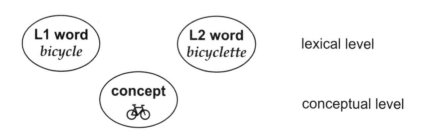

Figure 2.1 The three-components two-levels overall model of L2 lexical representation

References

Levelt, W. (1989) *Speaking: From Intention to Articulation*. Cambridge, MA: Bradford Books.

Nation, P. (2001) *Learning Vocabulary in Another Language*. Cambridge: Cambridge University Press.

Schmitt, N. and McCarthy, M. (eds) *Vocabulary: Description, Acquisition and Pedagogy* (pp. 199–227). Cambridge: Cambridge University Press.

Singleton, D. (1999) *Exploring the Second Language Mental Lexicon*. Cambridge: Cambridge University Press.

Chapter 2

Lexical Representation and Lexical Processing in the L2 User

ANNETTE M. B. DE GROOT

Psycholinguistic research into bilingualism during the past 15 years has been dominated by two related questions concerning representation and processing:

(1) How is the bilingual's vocabulary knowledge of his or her two languages represented in memory?
(2) What exactly happens within the bilingual's mental lexicon from the moment an externally presented word (whether in the L1 or the L2) is input to the language system to the moment it is understood (in comprehension), and from the moment a lexical concept is delivered by some internal conceptualiser to the moment it is verbalised in the appropriate language (in production)?

Research focusing on the representation question (1) tries to decide whether bilingual memory contains two separate language-specific stocks of knowledge, one for each of the bilingual's two languages, or, instead, a single stock that is shared between the two languages. Research addressing the processing question (2) tries to choose between selective access and non-selective access. In the non-selective access view, an external or internal input to the bilingual language system is processed by both of the bilingual's language subsystems that the system as a whole is assumed to consist of; in the selective-access view it is processed by the contextually-appropriate language subsystem only.

In this chapter I will review studies that have dealt with one or the other of these two research questions (or with both at the same time). I will present the common current models of bilingual lexical-memory representation and of how the stock of bilingual lexical knowledge is accessed during word comprehension and word production. I will also provide experimental support for these models, and discuss some of their defects.

Lexical knowledge consists of various different types of knowledge (e.g.

what syntactic class the word belongs to; how it is morphologically structured; how it is spelled; what it means). The ensuing discussion will primarily focus on just two of these, namely, on knowledge of the words' surface forms (how they are spelled and sound) and of their meanings. Further constraints are that many of the studies to be reviewed have primarily tested nouns, and in many cases the tested nouns referred to concrete concepts only (that is, concepts that can be perceived by one or more of the senses). These facts evidently constrain the scope of the models to be presented.

Bilingual Lexical Representation

Three-component representation of translation pairs

The most common view of bilingual lexical memory is that it is 'hierarchical' in the sense that it consists of at least two layers of memory representations (or 'nodes'). One of these layers of nodes stores the meanings of words and the second stores their forms. The crucial support for the existence of such a layered structure comes from monolingual studies that have shown a dissociation between lexical and semantic factors (see Smith, 1997, for a review). For instance, in a study where participants had to judge whether pairs of letter strings contained the same letter (Besner _et al._, 1990), performance was affected both by the lexical status of the letter strings in a pair and by the semantic relation between the two letter strings of a pair when both of these were words: response times were _shorter_ for pairs in which the letter strings were real words (e.g. _table-cigar_) than for pairs consisting of two non-words (e.g. _nable-pigar_). Furthermore, when the letter strings of a pair were words, response times were _longer_ when these words were semantically related to one another (e.g. _lion-tiger_) than when they were unrelated (e.g. _lion-flower_). The combined results of a facilitatory effect of the lexicality of the letter strings and an inhibitory effect of a semantic relation between the words in a pair suggests the existence of a two-layered memory structure, one layer storing the words themselves and a second storing their meanings.

Given such a two-layered structure, a question of interest for the bilingual research community is whether the memory units in each of the two levels are segregated by language or instead integrated across languages. Segregation implies that the stored units are language-specific; that is, there is a separate representation for each of the two words in a translation pair (e.g. one for the word _girl_ and one for its French translation _fille_ in an English/French bilingual). In the case of integrated representations the memory units for the two words in a translation pair are (partly or completely) shared between the two languages such that there is just one representation for the words *girl* and *fille*. A third alternative is that segregation by language holds for one of the two levels, whereas integration holds for the other level. This third view is supported by a set of pertinent studies: the surface forms of the two words that constitute a translation pair appear to be represented in two separate, language-specific representations (maybe with the exception of the surface forms of cognate translations, that is to say, translations that share surface form across a bilingual's two languages, e.g. *flower=fleure* in an English/French bilingual (Sánchez-Casas *et al.*, 1992); in contrast, word meanings appear to be stored in representations that are shared between the two languages. In other words, according to this view the representation of translation pairs (e.g. the English/French pair *apple-pomme*) in memory consists of (at least) three components: two word-form representations, one for each language, L1 and L2, and one meaning representation common to the two languages. Form representations are often referred to as 'lexical' representations, which can cause confusion, as a word's lexical knowledge consists of more than just the form of the word (indeed, its meaning is also part of its lexical knowledge). Similarly, meaning representations are often called 'conceptual' representations, because typically the relevant models do not distinguish between word meanings and concepts (but see Pavlenko, 1999, for an exception). Different versions of this hierarchical, three-component model have been proposed, which will be discussed in detail in the next section.

Crucial evidence for such three-component memory structures comes from studies that have looked at the effects of 'repetition priming' across languages. In monolingual studies, the term 'repetition priming' refers to the finding that the prior presentation of a word (the 'prime') speeds up the processing of this same word when it is presented again later in the experiment (e.g. Forbach *et al.*, 1974), typically with many unrelated words presented in between the two occurrences of the critical word. In this line of research, word recognition is thought to come about when the word's lexical (word-form) representation is activated beyond some critical activation threshold. The facilitatory effect of repetition priming is then attributed to residual activation in a word's lexical representation when it is presented once again; relatively little additional activation needs to be collected for the threshold to be exceeded. In the analogous bilingual studies, instead of presenting the same word twice, an earlier word (e.g. the French word *pomme*) is followed by its translation (the English word *apple*) at some later time. The question of interest is whether a 'cross-language repetition effect' or a 'translation-priming' effect occurs; that is, whether a word (e.g. *apple*) is responded to faster when it follows the presentation of its translation (*pomme*) earlier on in the experiment than when not preceded by its translation but by some other, unrelated, word instead (say the French word *femme*, meaning 'woman'). The occurrence of such an effect would suggest that one and the same representation is contacted by each of the two words in a translation pair (and would then, again, be attributed to residual activation in this representation). In other words, it would suggest language integration. The absence of a translation-priming effect would indicate that different representations are accessed by the two words in the translation pair, thus suggesting language-specific representations.

The results obtained in the relevant experiments depend on what the participants are asked to do with the targets; more precisely, they depend on whether the participants have to perform a 'data-driven' task or a 'conceptually-driven' task instead (see e.g. Durgunoglu & Roediger, 1987). A data-driven task focuses the participant's attention on processing the surface forms of the stimuli. Examples are fragment completion (where the participants are presented with fragments of words and have to fill in the empty letter positions; e.g. *el--h-nt* = elephant) and lexical decision (where participants are presented with letter strings that constitute words and non-words and are asked to decide for each of these whether it is a word or not; so, when presented with the letter string *house*, they should press a 'yes' button and, when presented with the letter string *pouse*, they should press a 'no' button). Given a layered memory structure that consists of a word-form level of representation and a meaning-level of representation, data-driven tasks presumably tap activation in the form representations. In contrast, a conceptually-driven task focuses attention on the conceptual (meaning) information associated with the stimuli. Examples would be free recall of the words in a list presented earlier or some semantic-decision task (such as categorising the referents of the presented words as concrete or abstract, or as animate or inanimate). Conceptually-driven tasks presumably tap activation in the meaning (conceptual)-level of representation.

Data-driven tasks typically show null-effects of translation priming (e.g. no difference in response time between a response to *apple* preceded by *pomme* and a response to *apple* preceded by *femme*), at least when the translation pairs consist of non-cognates (translation pairs with completely different forms in the two languages concerned, such as in the pair *apple-pomme*; Gerard & Scarborough, 1989; Kirsner *et al.*, 1980; Kirsner *et al.*, 1984). These results suggest that different memory representations are contacted by each of the words in a non-cognate translation pair; in other words, they suggest that non-cognate translations are represented language-specifically at the form-level of representation. In contrast, conceptually-driven tasks *do* show a translation-priming effect, on cognate and non-cognate pairs alike, suggesting that one and the same representation is contacted by a word and its translation, and that this holds for both cognates and non-cognates. In other words, performance in conceptually-driven tasks suggests that, at the meaning-level of representation, cognates as well as non-cognates are stored in representations that are shared between the bilingual's two languages.

The conclusion that meaning representations of translation-equivalent words are shared between the two languages receives additional support from the finding that 'semantic-priming' effects occur not only within a language but between languages as well. Semantic priming is an experimental procedure where a target is preceded by a semantically related prime. In monolingual studies the prime and target are words from the same language (e.g. prime: *love*; target: *hatred*), whereas in cross-language studies prime and target are words from the different languages of the bilingual participant (prime: *love*; target: *haine*, in an English/French bilingual). One of the most robust findings in the word-recognition research field is that a word is processed faster when it follows a semantically related word than when it is preceded by an unrelated word. This semantic-priming effect occurs not only when prime and target are words from the same language (see Neely, 1991, for a review), but also when the prime is a word from one of the participant's two languages, and the target is taken from the other (Chen & Ng, 1989; De Groot & Nas, 1991; Jin, 1990; Kirsner *et al.*, 1984; Meyer & Ruddy, 1974; Schwanenflugel & Rey, 1986; Tzelgov & Eben-Ezra, 1992). In some of the critical studies the inter-language effect was in fact as large as the intralanguage effect. This latter finding constitutes particularly compelling evidence that meaning representations are shared between a bilingual's two languages.

In sum, the view that memory representations of translation pairs in bilinguals consist of two form components and a single meaning component receives support from a substantial number of studies. Nevertheless, many deficiencies and limitations of the model can be pointed out. But before doing so, I will present a number of different versions of the three-component model that have been proposed and the evidence on which they were based; the various alternative formulations of the three component, two level model are represented in Figures 2.2–2.5.

Different versions of the hierarchical, three-component model

Word-association versus concept mediation

Potter *et al.* (1984) reintroduced two versions of the hierarchical three-component model that about three decades earlier had already been advanced by Weinreich (1953), but under different names. The two versions differed from one another in terms of the connections between the assumed three components of the above hierarchical bilingual representations. In the version of the model that is called the word-association model (see Figure 2.2), the word-form representations in the first language (L1) and the second language (L2) of the translation pairs are directly connected with one another, and only the L1 word-form representation has a connection with conceptual memory.

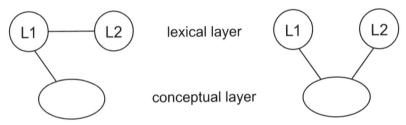

lexical layer

conceptual layer

Figure 2.2 The word-association model

Figure 2.3 The concept-mediation model

In the concept-mediation model (see Figure 2.3) the L1 and L2 word-form representations of a translation pair are not directly connected with one another, but both are connected to the conceptual representation common to the two words. Weinreich (1953) referred to the word-association and concept-mediation models as *subordinative* and *compound* structures, respectively.

Given a word-association structure, understanding and speaking the second language exploits the L1 word-form representations. For instance, a visually presented L2 word first accesses its L2 word-form representation; the corresponding L1 word-form representation is then accessed via the link between the two word-form representations; finally, the L2 word form is assigned a meaning via the connection between the L1 word-form representation and the associated meaning representation. In other words, the L2 word is in fact assigned the L1 word's meaning. Given a concept-mediation structure, L2 is processed in basically the same way as is L1; an L2 word is assigned meaning directly via the connection between the L2 word-form representation and the meaning representation shared between the L1 and L2 words. In these two versions of the model (as in the asymmetry model to be introduced below), the labels L1 and L2 not only indicate the order in which the two languages were acquired, but also the relative strength (dominance) of the two languages. The reason is that the two are typically confounded, with the language acquired first (the native language) typically being the stronger of the two (of course, there are exceptions). In fact, in the relevant studies (e.g. Kroll & Stewart, 1994; Potter *et al.*, 1984) differences in processing the two languages have been attributed to strength differences between them, not to a difference in acquisition order. Even though the reports of these studies were quite explicit about the pivotal role of language strength, the common labelling (L1 and L2) has unfortunately led to confusion and apparent misconceptions (Heredia, 1997). In this article I will follow the common practice of using the label L1 for the native and stronger language, and L2 for the second and weaker language.

Potter *et al.* (1984) considered an intermediate model, also referred to as the developmental model (Kroll & De Groot, 1997), which assumed that with practice the word-association links were replaced by the concept-mediation links between the L2 word forms and conceptual memory. They put the intermediate model to the test by comparing performance of a group of proficient (Chinese/English) bilinguals and a group of non-fluent (English/French) bilinguals on two tasks: picture naming in L2 and word translation from L1 into L2. The authors argued that a word-association memory structure predicts longer response times in the former task than in the latter, whereas a concept-mediation structure predicts equally long response times in the two tasks (see Potter *et al.*, 1984, for details). Both the proficient and the non-fluent groups responded equally quickly in the two tasks, a finding that disqualifies the intermediate (developmental) model and, instead, suggests concept-mediation memory structures at both levels of language proficiency.

Potter *et al.* (1984: 34) explicitly acknowledged the fact that the participants in their two experimental groups differed on more dimensions than L2 proficiency alone (e.g. the specific language combination; the age at which L2 acquisition started). But they deemed it unlikely that any of these were responsible for the fact that L2 proficiency did not critically affect the response pattern. However, they *did* acknowledge the possibility that proficiency effects might have been obtained if L2 users even less fluent than their non-fluent L2 users had been tested: 'It remains to be seen whether there is a stage at the very beginning of second-language learning ... in which direct word associates do play a role in second-language retrieval'

(Potter *et al.*, 1984: 36). The validity of this suggestion is supported in studies by Kroll and Curley (1988) and Chen and Leung (1989). These authors also compared picture naming and translation in L2 in beginning and proficient bilinguals, but with beginners that presumably had a lower command of L2 than Potter *et al.*'s non-fluent bilinguals. The beginners in both of these studies indeed showed the response pattern that is consistent with the word-association model; in contrast, the proficient groups showed the concept-mediation pattern of results. In both studies the combined results for the two participant groups thus supported the developmental model.

The revised hierarchical or asymmetry model.
Kroll and her colleagues (Kroll, 1993; Kroll & Sholl, 1992; Kroll & Stewart, 1994; Sholl *et al.*, 1995) proposed a third version of the hierarchical three-component model (see Figure 2.4). It assumes both a direct link between a translation pair's L1 and L2 form representations (and vice versa) and an indirect connection between them through the conceptual node shared between L1 and L2 (a connection that includes a direct link between the L1/L2 conceptual node and the L2 word-form node). In a way this model combines the word-association and concept-mediation models into one. But the new model is more than a mere fusion of the earlier two. It explicates directional strength differences between the various types of connections and holds these responsible for, e.g. particular effects of translation direction in translation tasks (translating from L1 into L2 or from L2 into L1) and for asymmetrical semantic-priming effects in cross-language semantic-priming studies.

The broken lines in Figure 2.4 represent relatively weak connections; the solid lines represent strong(er) connections. The link between the L1/L2 conceptual node and the L1 form node is stronger than the link between this conceptual node and the L2 form node because of the differential command of the two languages, with L1 being the stronger of the two. The

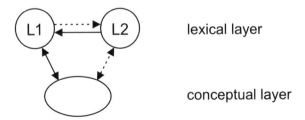

Figure 2.4 The asymmetrical model

likely underlying source of this language imbalance is differential experience with the two languages, with L1 having been used more than L2. Furthermore, instead of just one connection between the two word-form nodes, as in the word-association model, the asymmetry model assumes two: a strong connection from L2 to L1 and a weak one in the opposite direction. The L2 to L1 link is assumed to be relatively strong because, according to the authors, second language learners first acquire L2 words through L2/L1 translation pairs (Kroll & Stewart, 1994: 158). Gradually, with increasing exposure to L2, direct connections between L2 word-form representations and the L1/L2 conceptual representations are established, but while this happens, the direct connections between the L1-form and L2-form representations do not disappear (or, worded more precisely, they do not pass into total disuse). It may be clear from this description that, in addition to specifying directional effects of L1 and L2 processing, the asymmetry model is a developmental model as well: the processing of L2 by non-fluent bilinguals will parasitise L1 word forms more often than will L2 processing by proficient bilinguals.

Kroll and Stewart (1994: Experiment 3) put this model to the test in a translation task where fluent bilinguals translated L1 words into L2, and vice versa. According to the authors, owing to the strength differences between the various connections in the underlying memory structures, translation proceeds qualitatively differently in the two directions of translation. L2 to L1 translation primarily employs the strong direct connections between the L2 and L1 form representations, whereas L1 to L2 translation primarily employs the indirect connections that implicate the L1/L2 conceptual representations. If this is true, response times for L2 to L1 translation may be expected to be shorter than response times for L1 to L2 translation, the reason being that the route to the translation response would be shorter in the former case. Furthermore, since conceptual (meaning) representations are usually implicated when L1 words are translated into L2, but not (or hardly ever), when translation proceeds in the opposite direction, meaning-related variables should clearly affect L1 to L2 translation, but they should not noticeably affect L2 to L1 translation. Both these findings were obtained by Kroll and Stewart (the meaning-related variable in question being whether the words to be translated were clustered in semantic categories during presentation or presented in random order instead), and provide support for the asymmetry model (see Kroll & Sholl, 1992, for other studies that produced the direction effect on response times). Further support for the model was obtained by Sholl *et al.* (1995), who observed a facilitatory effect of earlier picture naming on subsequent translation of the words depicted (and named) in the picture-naming task when translation was from L1 to L2, but not when it was from L2 to L1. Picture naming is known to involve access to conceptual memory. The priming effect of earlier picture naming on L1 to L2 translation thus suggests that concepts are also accessed while performing the latter task; in contrast, the absence of a priming effect of earlier picture naming on L2 to L1 translation suggests that concepts are not implicated when L2 words are translated into L1.

Other studies, however, have produced results that are problematic for the asymmetry model. A number of studies did not show the direction effect on translation speed that the model predicted. Instead, null-effects of translation direction on response times were obtained (De Groot *et al.*, 1994: Experiment 1; the highest-proficiency group in De Groot & Poot, 1997; La Heij *et al.*, 1996: Experiment 4; Van Hell & De Groot, 1998), whereas other studies have even obtained the opposite effect of faster translation from L1 into L2 (the two lowest-proficiency groups in De Groot & Poot, 1997; La Heij *et al.*, 1996: Experiment 3). Furthermore, several studies have shown an influence of semantic variables when words were translated from L2 into L1 (De Groot *et al.*, 1994; De Groot & Poot, 1997; La Heij *et al.*, 1996; Van Hell & De Groot, 1998a), and in some cases the size of the relevant semantic effects was equally large in both directions of translation. The latter studies in particular suggest that conceptual memory is implicated to the same extent in both translation directions. Kroll and De Groot (1997: 184–185) discuss possible reasons for these conflicting results.

A further set of results that is problematic for the asymmetry model (as well as for the developmental model discussed earlier) is that from the very initial stages of L2 vocabulary learning onwards, learning performance is better for concrete words than for abstract words (De Groot & Keijzer, 2000; Ellis & Beaton, 1993; Van Hell & Candia-Mahn, 1997). This finding suggests that new L2 words are immediately associated with meaning (see also Altarriba & Mathis, 1997, who arrived at the same conclusion using a different experimental procedure). The concreteness effects were equally large with productive testing (L1 words are presented and the newly learned L2 words have to be produced; i.e. translation from L1 into L2) as with receptive testing (the newly learned L2 words are presented and the corresponding L1 words have to be produced; i.e. translation from L2 into L1; De Groot & Keijzer, 2000). This finding also appears to challenge the asymmetry model, which would have predicted larger concreteness effects with productive testing.

Determinants of Bilingual Memory Representation

The data patterns obtained in the studies by Chen and Leung (1989) and Kroll and Curley (1988) suggested word-association representations for bilinguals at a very low level of L2 proficiency, and concept-mediation representations for bilinguals relatively fluent in L2. An important conclusion to be drawn from this is that bilingual memory representation is not uniform across all bilingual populations. Apparently, level of L2 proficiency is a variable that determines how translation pairs are represented in bilingual memory. Other support for the same idea comes from bilingual Stroop studies (e.g. Chen & Ho, 1986; Tzelgov *et al.*, 1990).

De Groot and Hoeks (1995) further specified the role of language proficiency in bilingual memory representation. They tested trilinguals who had Dutch as their native language, English as their strongest foreign language, and French as a weaker foreign language (cf. Abunuwara, 1992). When concrete and abstract Dutch words were translated into English, a strong concreteness effect was obtained. This finding suggests concept mediation translation (and the concomitant memory structures) at a high level of foreign-language proficiency. In contrast, when concrete and abstract Dutch words were translated into the weaker language French, no such effect was obtained, a finding that suggests word-association translation (and the corresponding memory structures). It thus appears that foreign-language proficiency affects memory representation not only across subject populations but also within one and the same person. The important conclusion is that within one and the same multilingual mind different types of bilingual memory representations – word-association representations as well as concept-mediation representations – may co-exist.

In De Groot (1995) I discussed a number of other determinants of bilingual memory representation. One of them makes exactly this same point that different types of representations may coexist within multilingual memory, but takes it one step further by showing that, even for one and the same language combination, different structures may exist within one multilingual mind (and that the state of 'mixed-representations' may thus also hold for bilinguals). The determinant I am referring to here is word type. Many bilingual studies have shown that different types of words are processed differently in a number of tasks (e.g. primed lexical decision, word translation). The most robust effects are those of 'cognate status' and of concreteness. Words that have a cognate translation in the participant's other language (e.g. *appel-apple* in a Dutch/English bilingual) show a response pattern different from that of non-cognates (e.g. *pomme-apple* in a French/English bilingual), and words with a concrete referent (e.g. *wheelchair*) show results that are different from those obtained with abstract words (e.g. *mystery*). Typically the data suggest that the bilingual memory structures for cognates and concrete words are more integrated across a bilingual's two languages than the structures for non-cognates and abstract words (for a review, see De Groot, 1993).

In addition to concreteness and cognate status, word frequency appears to determine bilingual memory representation. This can be concluded from the fact that, in translation studies, concreteness effects tend to be larger for high-frequency words than for low-frequency words (De Groot, 1992a), suggesting that the former are relatively often translated via the concept-mediation route and the latter relatively often via the direct connections between a translation pair's L1-form and L2-form representations. Worded in terms of memory structures, not processes, the results suggest that relatively many high-frequency words are stored in concept-mediation representations, whereas relatively many low-frequency words are stored in word-association representations. The important underlying variable is presumably the amount of practice that bilingual language users have had with a word and its translation in L2. By definition, high-frequency words will have been used more often than low-frequency words (this holds not only for L1 words but also for the corresponding L2 words; word frequency is highly correlated between languages). As a consequence, the direct connections between the representations of a word's surface forms in L1 and L2 on the one hand and the (shared) conceptual representation will both be strong, promoting concept mediation. For low-frequency words, the direct connections between the L2-form representation and conceptual memory will be relatively weak (owing to the lack of sufficient practice of particularly low-frequency L2 words), frustrating concept mediation; consequently word-association translation will have to be relied on relatively often.

It is likely that over time (more precisely, with increasing L2 experience) even low-frequency L2 words will ultimately have been practiced often enough to have developed sufficiently strong links between the L2 word-form representations and conceptual representations for these to be exploited efficiently in L2 processing and in cross-language tasks. In terms of the underlying representations, we could say that concept-mediation structures will have replaced the word-association structures that existed earlier for these words. This account of the relation between word frequency and the way it is reflected in bilingual memory is completely compatible with the view on the relation between L2 proficiency and bilingual memory presented earlier. Proficient bilinguals have presumably practised the L2 enough to have developed a preponderance of concept-mediation structures for frequent and infrequent words alike (and show the concept-mediation data pattern in the relevant experiments). Non-fluent users have had little practice in L2 and, as a result, the links between the L2 form representations and conceptual memory will still be weak for *all* words. They will therefore have to rely on word-association processing relatively often; in other words their memory consists primarily of word-association structures. In a way then, the present word-frequency variable mimics within one and the same bilingual mind the (between-individual) effect of language proficiency. The important new insight provided by this analysis is that lexical change is likely to take place at the level of individual words, rather than that, when some critical level of L2 proficiency has been reached, all representations in bilingual memory suddenly change from word-association structures to concept-mediation structures. Earlier I phrased this idea as follows:

> The representational structure for any given pair of translations gradu-ally develops over use or disuse of that particular translation pair. This view is more plausible than the assumption that at one point in time all memory structures, all being of one type, are miraculously replaced by structures of a different type. (De Groot, 1995: 174)

In addition to L2 proficiency and word type, the L2 learning method, or more generally, the L2 learning environment, is yet a further possible deter-minant of bilingual memory organisation. The results of studies by Chen (1990) and Lotto and De Groot (1998) suggest that indeed learning method (e.g. whether the L2 word to be learned is presented with the corre-sponding L1 word during learning or instead with a picture representing the meaning of the L2 word) plays a role, at least during the very initial stages of L2 learning. Picture learning resulted in 'picture-association' representations (that contain links between the representations of the L2 word forms and those of pictures that depict the referents of these words), whereas word learning resulted in word-association representations. (In the same study, Chen ruled out the learner's age as a critical factor in bilin-gual representation.) However, Chen's study also demonstrated that already after a rather small number of learning trials, learning method no longer mattered: irrespective of learning method, concept-mediation patterns were obtained, suggesting concept-mediation representations for both learning conditions. These relatively recent studies on the effect of learning method on bilingual memory representation in fact exemplify the much older idea that the environment in which the L2 is learned affects what type of memory structures emerge (Ervin & Osgood, 1954; Lambert *et al.*, 1958). The results of Chen's (1990) study in particular may account for the fact that in this older work little support has been obtained for the idea that learning environment affects bilingual representation (Kolers, 1963): the memory structures may differ only during the very initial stages of L2 learning. If this is true, studies that test bilinguals beyond this stage will not show any effects of learning environment.

To summarise this section, the memory of a bilingual language user presumably contains structures of different types; the different structures occur in different proportions across bilinguals, and the individual structures change over time (with practice). The change involves the strengthening of initially weak links between the various components of the bilingual memory structures. The consequence of such strengthening of links that were weak before is that they will start to dominate processing, and that, accordingly, the response patterns change, e.g. from a word-association to a concept-mediation pattern. What this description of change highlights is that the different versions of the three-component model should not be viewed as qualitatively different from one another, but merely as functionally different.

Caveats and Qualifications

So far I have presented a general model of bilingual memory that assumes three-component representations of translation pairs that each contain two language-specific word-form representations and one conceptual (meaning) representation that is shared between the languages. I then presented the various versions of this general model that have been suggested and some of the experimental evidence and counter evidence. Finally, I made the point that the different versions can co-occur within one and the same bilingual mind. Together, these views provide an account of bilingual memory that is lacking in several respects. In this section I will detail a number of its shortcomings.

A first obvious fault of the model is that it does not specify the exact nature of particular types of lexical knowledge in detail, and ignores other types altogether. For instance, I consistently talked about word-form representations, as if these were of a unitary type. But many languages come in two forms, one written and one spoken, and literate users of such a language must have stored representations for each of them in memory. These two types of form representations, one orthographic and one phonological, are likely to be stored in separate subsystems of the word-form store (plausibly with a connection between a word's form in each of the two subsystems), and the elements of *both* subsystems map onto the conceptual representations one way or the other. For bilinguals who are literate in both of their languages, this situation holds for both languages. All this has been ignored in the discussion so far, but will ultimately have to be taken into account. In doing so, many new questions will probably present themselves. For example, do direct connections between the L1 and L2 word-form representations exist only for form representations of the same kind (both orthographic or both phonological), or are there bilingual cross-form connections as well (e.g. from the orthographic representation of *pomme* to the phonological representation of *apple*?)

Another caveat is that language users' knowledge about words obviously encompasses much more than what words look or sound like (their form) and what they mean. For instance, users may know what letters a word contains, to what syntactic class it belongs, and what its morphological structure is. Furthermore, bilingual language users will generally know to which one of their two languages a particular word belongs. Therefore, a complete description of monolingual and bilingual lexical representation should contain more layers than just the two distinguished above, and the content of the separate layers may be richer than suggested above. For instance, Levelt's serial model and Dell and O'Seaghdha's interactive model of monolingual speech production (Dell & O'Seaghdha, 1991; Levelt, 1989) specify morphological, phonological, semantic and syntactic lexical information, as do bilingual speech production models that are derived from these (for reviews, see Hermans, 2000; Poulisse, 1997). Moreover, the well-known bilingual representation models that have focused on the process of word recognition (rather than on how word forms and word meanings map onto one another) have distinguished between layers that were not explicit in the three-component model. The bilingual interactive activation (BIA) model for *visual* word recognition (Grainger & Dijkstra, 1992; Dijkstra & Van Heuven, 1998; see Figure 2.5) contains four layers that store the representations for letter features, letters, words, and language, respectively. The bilingual model of lexical access (BIMOLA), an interactive model of *spoken* word recognition (Léwy & Grosjean, 1999; Grosjean, 1997; see Figure 2.5), contains separate representation layers for phoneme features, phonemes and words (see Grosjean, 1997). The word layer in both models is similar to the word-form level in the present three-component model and, although both models include levels not specified in the three-component model, neither of the two models contains a layer that stores word meanings. Recently, however, Van Heuven (2000) extended the BIA model such that it also contains representations of word meanings as well as a phonological lexicon; the extended model is called SOPHIA (Semantic, Orthographic, and PHonological Interactive Activation Model). Which layers of representational units are specified in a particular model depends on the specific question posed by the bilingual researcher (for example: how does visual or spoken word recognition come about? how do words map onto meaning? how are L2 words retrieved and output during L2 production?), and on the set of data the model is meant to account for.

Another distinction that several authors consider to be important, but that is nevertheless not reflected in the three-component model is one between semantic and conceptual representations (e.g. Paradis, 1997; Pavlenko, 1999). Pavlenko defines the semantic component of bilingual memory representations as 'explicitly available information which relates the word to other words, idioms and conventionalised expressions in the language; it is characterised by polysemy'. In contrast, the conceptual component is thought to store 'non-linguistic multi-modal information, which includes imagery, schemas, motor programs, and auditory, tactile

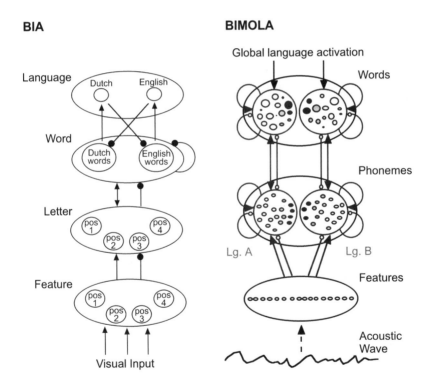

Figure 2.5 The Bilingual Interactive Activation (BIA) model of bilingual visual word recognition (e.g. Grainger & Dijkstra, 1992) and the Bilingual Model Of Lexical Access (BIMOLA), a model of bilingual spoken word recognition (e.g. Léwy & Grosjean, 1999; Grosjean, 1997).

(Published with the permission of the authors.)

and somatosensory representations, based on experiential world knowledge (Pavlenko, 1999: 212). The three-component model conflates these two types of knowledge. This may turn out to be a crucial flaw of the model, although I have argued elsewhere (De Groot, 2000) that conflating them may be the logical consequence of the facts that pinpointing the difference between semantic and conceptual knowledge is a tedious task, and that both types of knowledge plausibly originate from one and the same source.

Finally, the three-component model cannot readily account for the fact that the two words in translation pairs very often (maybe even most often) do not share meaning completely. In early research into bilingual memory this cross-language non-equivalence of meaning was a reason to assume completely separate conceptual memories for a bilingual's two languages (Kolers, 1963; Weinreich, 1953: coordinate bilinguals). However, given a word-association structure, the meaning assigned to an L2 word is simply the meaning of the L1 word. The way the concept-mediation model is usually described suggests the same (the crucial difference between the two models being that L2 words are directly assigned this meaning in the one case, but indirectly – via the L1 word forms – in the other case). Yet, I believe that the completely-shared-meaning assumption is not inextricably bound up with the concept-mediation hypothesis.

In an earlier paper (De Groot, 1992b), I zoomed in on the content of the conceptual representations in, *inter alia*, the concept-mediation structures to stress the point that these representations are likely to contain sets of more primitive-meaning elements. The exercise led to the proposal of a model of bilingual memory (see Masson, 1991, for the monolingual version) in which a word's meaning was presented as 'distributed' across a number of more elementary representation units that each stored some elementary part of the word's meaning (say, one semantic feature). From there on it was a small step to account for the non-equivalence of word meaning across languages, namely by assuming that the two words in a translation pair do not have to share exactly the same set of such elementary meaning elements. This state of affairs is depicted in Figure 2.6 (see Kroll & De Groot, 1997 and Van Hell & De Groot, 1998b, for more recent versions of this 'distributed' model that also assume distributed word-form representations). In addition to accounting for cross-language non-equivalence of meaning, this 'distributed' model can also readily explain the fact that conceptual knowledge is not static. It changes all the time and, furthermore, differs between individuals (Pavlenko, 1999). Elements may be added to the conceptual set or disappear from it, and across individuals differences may occur in the set that represents a particular word's meaning.

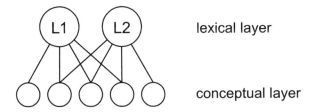

Figure 2.6 Distributed model

The point to be made here (see also De Groot, 2000) is that, had the proponents of the present three-component models explicitly focused on the content of the conceptual representations, they might also have arrived at the conclusion that meaning representations may consist of sets of more primitive elements. The next step, again, might have been to allow for the existence of L1-specific and L2-specific meaning elements in the conceptual representations of the concept-mediation memory structures and the asymmetrical memory structures (but not in those of the word-association structures, because these store only L1 meanings). However, the fact remains that the three-component models do not explicitly split up conceptual representations in component parts and, consequently, provide no *ready* explanation for cross-language non-equivalence, the non-static nature of the content of conceptual representations, and for the fact that different individuals can assign different meanings to one and the same word.

The points raised in this section all lead to the conclusion that the various versions of the hierarchical three-component model are all still rather incomplete accounts of bilingual memory. Because of their focus on representation, and in particular on how word forms map onto meaning within the memory structures, they have ignored the question of how other types of linguistic knowledge than a word's surface form and meaning are stored, and they also have had little to say about the way bilingual memory is accessed. The next section reviews work that primarily dealt with the latter question.

Bilingual Lexical Access

Presumably the currently most central question in research on lexical processing by bilinguals is whether or not they can somehow 'switch off' the contextually inappropriate language during comprehension or production in the targeted language, or, phrased in today's more common terminology, whether bilingual lexical access is language-non-selective or

language-selective instead. The selective-access view of language comprehension holds that the visual or spoken input is processed by the contextually appropriate language system only. Similarly, the selective-access view
of language production holds that during the process of speech production,
lexical elements from the non-target language do not compete to be output
with lexical elements from the targeted language system. In contrast, the
corresponding non-selective-access views hold that in comprehension
both of a bilingual's language systems respond to a language input and that
in production lexical elements of both language systems compete for selection. The occurrence of unintentional use of words from the non-target
language in the speech of bilinguals suggests that bilingual language
production is non-selective. Similarly, the accidental assignment of the
non-target language's meaning to an input letter string that constitutes a
word in both of a bilingual's two languages (e.g. the letter string *coin* in a
French/English bilingual; *coin* means 'corner' in French) would suggest
that access during comprehension is non-selective. These errors do occur,
though in surprisingly small numbers. For instance, Poulisse (1999)
reported an average of just one L1 speech error among 350 L2 words
produced by unbalanced bilinguals whose stronger language is L1. The
opposite, that is, intrusions from the weaker L2 into the stronger L1 is likely
to occur even less often. The low incidence of such errors might well be
taken to indicate that bilingual language comprehension and production
are generally language-selective. Yet, the majority of the pertinent studies
suggest that, instead, non-selectivity is the rule.

Support for language-selective access?

Apparent support for selective access comes from a set of studies that
looked at the effect of language switching (or language mixing) on performance. The typical result is that alternating between the two languages in
input and/or output slows down the response. For instance, MacNamara
& Kushnir (1971; see also Kolers, 1966) showed that silent reading of paragraphs that contained language switches took longer than silent reading of
unilingual paragraphs. Similarly, true–false judgements took longer for
written and spoken sentences containing switches than for monolingual
sentences. Response times increased as the number of language switches
within the sentences increased. For instance, a sentence such as *Un citron est
yellow* (one switch) took shorter to respond to than a sentence such as
Turnips sont vegetables (two switches; examples taken from MacNamara &
Kushnir, 1971). The data suggested that every switch took about 200
milliseconds. The authors interpreted these results as support for the existence of an automatically operating input switch that directs the input to

the appropriate linguistic system. In case of a change of language in the input, the input switch has to be pulled over, as it were, to the other linguistic system in order for the latter to be able to process the input. This operation takes time and, hence, leads to an increase in response time.

Soares and Grosjean (1984) examined the effects of language-switching locally (that is, at the exact position of the switch) instead of globally (by measuring response times for whole sentences), by registering response times to targets in a phoneme-triggered lexical-decision task (see Soares & Grosjean, 1984, for details). Response times were shorter when all the words in the sentence, including the target, were in the same language than when the target involved a change of language. Finally, Grainger and Beauvillain (1987) obtained the analogous pattern of results, but this time for English and French words that were presented not as parts of sentences but in lists of unrelated words and non-words to which the participants performed 'language-neutral' lexical decisions (respond 'yes' if the letter string is a word in either French or English; respond 'no' if it is not a word in either of these languages). The critical words were presented either in pure lists (containing, in addition to non-words, exclusively French or exclusively English words) or in mixed lists (containing words from both languages). Mixing the two languages again slowed down performance. This finding is consistent with the idea that the language-context information provided by the pure lists always directed the incoming information straight to the appropriate language system, which is then searched immediately. In the mixed list the incoming information may initially be directed to the inappropriate language system. Only after a search through this system has failed will the information be directed to the appropriate language system. Longer response times for the mixed condition will consequently be obtained. Another set of studies (MacNamara *et al.*, 1968; Meuter & Allport, 1999) has examined the effect of switching the language of *output* (e.g. in number naming tasks), unconfounded by input switching. The results agree with those of the input-switch studies in that, again, language switching was detrimental for performance.

At first sight, the data from the above comprehension and production studies all appear to support the views that:

(1) A bilingual's mind contains two separate language subsystems (e.g. the two word-form systems assumed by the hierarchical three-component model discussed earlier, and also by the BIA and BIMOLA word-recognition models depicted in Figure 2.5).

(2) During the process of word comprehension and production the two subsystems are not searched (or activated) simultaneously but serially

(and the second of the two only if the first has not come up with a satis-factory output).

The first view is generally not contested, but in most of the more recent work the latter is, because it does not fit the data of a large set of (especially comprehension) studies, to be discussed later, which suggest that the two language subsystems of a bilingual are simultaneously active during language processing.

Grainger and Beauvillain (1987) and Grainger (1993) solve the puzzle by pointing out that a detrimental effect of a language switch in the input does not provide unequivocal support for selective access (and an associated switching device), but is perfectly compatible with the view that at least the initial stages of lexical access are language-non-selective. Similarly, Grosjean (1997: 250) points out that the slowing-down effect of mixing the language input provides 'insubstantial and indirect' support for the existence of some mental language-switch device. He remarks that 'It is not because bilinguals may, at times, process code-switches more slowly than base language words that researchers can conclude there is a language switch/monitor involved in the processing; the delay could be due to numerous other factors' (Grosjean, 1997: 250; see also Grosjean, 1988). Grainger and Beauvillain (1987) present two initially non-selective bilin-gual word-recognition models that could account for their data. One of these two models is the Bilingual Activation Verification (BAV) model; the second is (an earlier version of) the Bilingual Interactive Activation Model introduced earlier (see Figure 2.5). Because this latter model in particular has been advanced in much of the very latest work on bilingual visual word recognition (e.g. Dijkstra & Van Heuven, 1998; Van Heuven *et al.*, 1998), I will briefly explain Grainger and Beauvillain's (1997) language-switch data in terms of this model (see e.g. Grainger, 1993, for an account in terms of the BAV model).

BIA is an extension of McClelland and Rumelhart's (1981) interactive activation model of visual word (and letter) recognition in monolinguals, which consists of three layers of memory nodes, representing letter features, letters and words, respectively. In the BIA model, a fourth layer of language nodes is added, containing one node for each of the bilingual's two languages, and mounted on top of the word-nodes layer. Irrespective of language context, when a word is presented to the language system, it activates (through the relevant feature and letter nodes) word-level nodes in both language subsystems. Subsequently, each of the activated word nodes passes activation on to the corresponding language node through the excitatory connection that connects the two (see Figure 2.5). The activated language node then sends back inhibitory excitation through the inhibitory connections between this language node and the other language's word nodes, or in other words, it suppresses the activation of all words in the other language's lexicon. The effect will be that the subsequent processing of a word from this other language (that is, the word presented on a switch trial) will be slowed down as compared to processing a word on a no-switch trial.

The important conclusion is that Grainger and Beauvillain's (1987) language-mixing effect can be explained in terms of a model that assumes lexical access to be initially language-non-selective. Moreover, there is no a priori reason why the switch data obtained in the mixed-paragraph and mixed-sentence experiments discussed above could not be explained similarly. As already pointed out above, researchers of spoken word recognition also reject the idea of a language-switching device and the selective-access process that it imposes (Grosjean, 1988; 1997).

Support for language-non-selective access

In this section, four sources of support for the view that bilingual lexical access is initially language-non-selective will be presented. Because of space limitations, I will focus entirely on comprehension studies. Therefore, the conclusion to be drawn – that bilingual lexical access is non-selective – should not thoughtlessly be generalised to production studies. Indeed, the relevant production studies (e.g. Costa *et al.*, 1999; Hermans, 2000; Hermans, *et al.*, 1998) do seem to arrive at conflicting conclusions.

Interlexical homograph studies

A set of studies on the processing of 'interlexical' (or 'interlanguage') homographs by bilinguals has provided compelling support for the view that bilingual lexical access in comprehension tasks is (initially) non-selective (Beauvillain & Grainger, 1987: Experiment 1; De Groot *et al.*, 2000; Dijkstra *et al.*, 1998; Dijkstra *et al.*, 1999). Interlexical homographs are words that have one and the same written word form but different meanings in the two languages of a bilingual. An example is the word form *glad*, meaning 'slippery' in Dutch, in a Dutch/English bilingual. The studies just mentioned have all shown that processing times for interlexical homographs differ from those of frequency-matched control words. No obvious difference exists between the homographs and their controls other than the fact that the former mean different things in the bilingual's two languages whereas the latter mean something in only one of her two languages. This *homograph effect* suggests that a homograph activates both of the language subsystems. In other words, it suggests that lexical access is language-non-selective. If the bilingual participants in these experiments had managed to 'switch-off' (deactivate) one of their languages, homographs and controls might have been expected to be processed equally rapidly.

Importantly, the homograph effect does not occur only in *bilingual* tasks, that is, tasks that can be performed only if both language systems are simultaneously activated (e.g. word translation). It also occurs in *monolingual* tasks, that is, tasks that *per se* do not require the simultaneous activation of the two lexicons of the bilingual, and that, in fact, under certain circumstances would be easier to perform when the non-target language is deactivated (see De Groot *et al.*, 2000, for example tasks and more detail). The fact that the effect occurs even when completely deactivating the non-target language would have produced better results constitutes strong evidence that switching off the non-target language is simply no option. In contrast, on the basis of the results of an earlier, similar study, Gerard and Scarborough (1989) concluded that access to bilingual memory *is* language-selective, but other authors have suggested that, in fact, Gerard and Scarborough's findings are largely compatible with the language-non-selective view (e.g. De Groot *et al.*, 2000).

Analogous to the interlexical homograph effect, Dijkstra *et al.* (1999) obtained – with *visual* stimulus presentation – an interlexical *homophone* effect, that is, a difference in processing time for matched controls and words that sound approximately the same in a particular bilingual's two languages but that carry different meanings in these two languages (e.g. the pair *leaf-lief* in a Dutch/English bilingual; *lief* means 'sweet' in Dutch). Interestingly, the direction of the homophone effect (slower than their controls, i.e. homophone inhibition) differed from the direction of the homograph effect in the same study (faster than their controls, i.e. homograph facilitation). However, inhibition for interlexical homographs has been obtained in other studies (De Groot *et al.*, 2000; Dijkstra *et al.*, 1998), and Dijkstra *et al.* (1998) demonstrated that the direction of the homograph effect may vary, depending upon task demands. What is presently more important than the direction of the homograph (and homophone) effect, however, is the fact that an effect is obtained at all. Whatever its direction, the occurrence of the effect *per se* supports the non-selective-access view.

Phonological activation studies

A second source of support for the non-selective-access view comes from a set of studies that, in various ways, all suggest that upon the visual presentation of a word, non-target-language phonology is activated (in addition to target-language phonology). For instance, Nas (1983) had

Dutch/English bilinguals perform English lexical decisions to visually presented letter strings (if the letter string is a word in English, respond 'yes'; if not, respond 'no'). 'No' decisions took longer for non-words that sounded like a Dutch word if pronounced according to English grapheme–phoneme correspondence (GPC) rules (e.g. *deef* and *vay*, when pronounced according to English GPC rules, sound like the Dutch words *dief en vee*, respectively, meaning 'thief' and 'cattle') than for non-word controls (such as *prusk* or *blane*), that, if pronounced according to English GPC rules do not sound like Dutch words). Apparently the phonological forms, encoded according to the English GPC rules, activate the phonological forms of the Dutch words *dief en vee*, inducing a bias towards responding 'yes' (these are words). This bias has to be overcome, thus delaying the correct 'no' response.

Conceptually similar studies by Altenberg and Cairns (1983), Jared and Kroll (2001), Tzelgov *et al.* (1996), and Van Leerdam *et al.* (in preparation), also all showed, in different ways and employing different tasks, phonological activation in the non-target language subsystem. The latter authors employed an interesting new matching task, in which on each trial a *printed* English (L2) word and a 'phonological word body' (that is, the medial vowel(s) and final consonant(s) of a one-syllable word) were simultaneously presented and the participants had to decide whether or not the two match, that is, whether or not the final part of the printed word would, when pronounced, sound like the phonological body. For example, when the printed word *blood* is presented together with the phonological body /aɪd/, as in *bride*, the participant should respond 'no'. The result that is of particular interest here is that relatively many errors were made on mismatch trials where the phonological body concerned the typical L1 pronunciation of the printed L2 word's 'orthographic' body (the letter sequence that corresponds with the phonological body). For instance, the orthographic body *ood* of the English L2 word *blood* is typically pronounced as /əʊd/ (as in the English word *load*) in Dutch. Trials of this type (e.g. the printed English word *blood* presented with the Dutch /əʊd/ pronunciation of the 'ood' letter cluster) resulted in extremely poor performance (47% errors; in other words, 47% incorrect 'yes' responses). This finding strongly suggests that the visual presentation of an English word (e.g. *blood*) not only activates representations in the English language subsystem, but also in the Dutch subsystem (e.g. *brood, nood, dood*). On this specific example trial, the phonological representations of the activated elements in the Dutch subsystem match with the /əʊd/ phonological body presented on that trial, thus leading to an incorrect 'yes' response.

Interlanguage neighbourhood studies

The study by Van Leerdam *et al.* (in preparation) demonstrates that the non-target language's 'phonological neighbourhood' affects target language processing. This finding converges with results of a set of earlier studies that looked at 'orthographic neighbourhood' effects across a bilingual's two languages. A word's neighbourhood is the set of words in the language user's mental lexicon that are to a large extent similar to the target word. In early monolingual work, a word's neighbourhood was specifically defined in terms of orthography, namely, as all the other words in the target language that share all but one letter with the target word (for instance, the English word *hand* has, among others, the words *land, band, hang* and *hind* as English neighbours). Related bilingual work (Grainger & Dijkstra, 1992; Grainger & O'Regan, 1992; Van Heuven *et al.*, 1998) distinguished between a word's intralanguage orthographic neighbourhood and its interlanguage orthographic neighbourhood. The latter consists of the words in the non-target language that share all but one letter with the target word; for example, the Dutch word *hond,* meaning 'dog', is an interlanguage orthographic neighbour of English *hand*). The main question addressed by this bilingual work was whether or not a word's neighbours in the non-target language affect processing the word in the target language. This finding would, again, demonstrate language-non-selectivity of bilingual lexical processing. In different ways the studies just mentioned indeed show this interlanguage effect, e.g. in lexical decision (Grainger & Dijkstra, 1992) and in a so-called 'progressive demasking' task (see Van Heuven *et al.*, 1998). The above study by Van Leerdam *et al.* (in preparation) shows the analogous effect of a word's interlanguage 'phonological' neighbourhood (the set of words in the non-target language that share a large part of their phonological structure with the target word), as does a conceptually similar study by Jared and Kroll (2001) that employed the word-naming task (in which presented words simply have to be read aloud).

Studies on the effect of 'cognate status'

A final source of support for initially language-non-selective bilingual lexical access comes from a number of studies that have looked at the effect of a word's 'cognate status' on task performance. Cognates are words that translate into the bilingual's other language into largely similar (or exactly the same) word forms (e.g. the Dutch words *appel* and *hand*, that translate into the English *apple* and *hand*, respectively). Non-cognates share only meaning, not form, across languages (e.g. the Dutch words *hond* and *fiets*, that translate into *dog* and *bike*, respectively). (Note that, in contrast, the interlexical homographs discussed earlier share form but not meaning across languages.)

At least three lexical-decision studies have shown that lexical decisions in the weaker language of a bilingual are faster for cognates than for non-cognates (Caramazza & Brones, 1979; Dijkstra *et al.*, 1998: Experiment 1; Van Hell, 1998: Chapter 4). Moreover, a recent study by Van Hell and Dijkstra (submitted) showed the analogous result for lexical decision in the stronger language. Again, these studies support the view of language-non-selective bilingual lexical access: the representation of the cognate's similar or identical form in the non-target language appears to be coactivated when a cognate is presented, a coactivation that somehow speeds up the target word's processing. The study by Van Hell and Dijkstra is especially important, because it shows that not only is the processing of the weaker language affected by activation of the stronger language, but also that processing the dominant language is not immune to influences from the non-target language (see also De Groot *et al.*, 2000: Experiment 3). However, these authors also show that, for this interlanguage influence from the weaker to the stronger language to occur, some minimal level of L2 proficiency has to be attained.

Control

In sum, many studies support the conclusion that bilingual lexical access is initially language-non-selective. It is still a topic of debate whether initial non-selectivity is total or only partial. Total non-selectivity would mean that, irrespective of contextual factors (such as the characteristics of the addressee, the conversational topic, the specifics of an experimental setting) a particular external language input (in comprehension) or a conceptual content (in production) always initially activates both of the bilingual's two language subsystems – and always to the same extent. Of course, an external language input will ultimately have to be recognised by the targeted language subsystem (in comprehension) and a concept will ultimately have to be verbalised in the targeted language (in production). An initially non-selective system could reach this goal through a process of inhibitory control that reactively suppresses the activated elements of the non-target language (see Green, 1998, and the peer commentaries to that article).

The alternative view is that to some extent language control can be exerted proactively (a term dubbed by De Groot, 1998), by adapting the relative activation levels of the 'guest' (non-targeted; non-selected) and 'base' (targeted; selected) languages to the specific characteristics and demands of the communicative context (or experimental task). For instance, according to Grosjean (e.g. 1997; 2001) bilinguals respond to the specifics of a conversational setting (such as the topic of the conversation and the L2 proficiency level of the addressee) by moving on a 'language mode continuum' where the various positions on the continuum are reflected in differences in the relative activation levels of the base language and the guest language. The bilingual language user is said to be in a 'bilingual' mode if both the guest language and the base language are highly activated (but the base language more so than the guest language); she is said to be in a 'monolingual' mode if she has deactivated the guest language as best as possible. According to Grosjean, in the monolingual mode the guest language is also activated to some extent. One could therefore say that language non-selectivity also holds for this mode, but only partially.

That bilinguals can adapt to the specific demands of the conversational context is uncontested and is, indeed, convincingly demonstrated experimentally by Grosjean (1997). For example, he showed that the number of switches to the L2 guest language increases as the L2 fluency level of an imaginary addressee increases. It remains to be seen, however, whether such adaptation indeed involves variability in pre-set activation levels (proactive control), which is the view defended by Grosjean. A qualitatively different but equally plausible view is that adaptation to the task and setting involves variability in the degree in which the output of the bilingual lexical system (that may be totally non-selective initially) is monitored and censored (before it is actually articulated). For instance, a situation where a switch to the L2 guest language is likely to cause a communicative breakdown (because of the low L2 proficiency of the addressee) might invite more stringent monitoring and censoring than a situation where a language switch would not harm communicative fluency.

In sum, the exact locus of control and the nature of the mechanism(s) exerting control have yet to be determined. A full understanding of these issues of control will not only complement the current models of language processing in normally functioning bilinguals but is also likely to impact on theories of bilingual aphasia (for details see Green, 1986; Paradis, 1997).

To conclude this section, most of the pertinent studies suggest that bilingual lexical access in comprehension is initially language-non-selective, that is, that both of a bilingual's language sub-systems initially respond to a language input. Whether or not non-selectivity also holds for bilingual language production is a question that was only briefly touched upon, and remains unanswered, in the present review of the literature.

References

Abunuwara, E. (1992) The structure of the trilingual lexicon. *European Journal of Cognitive Psychology* 4, 311–322.

Altarriba, J. and Mathis, K.M. (1997) Conceptual and lexical development in second language acquisition. *Journal of Memory and Language* 36, 550–568.

Altenberg, E.P. and Cairns, H.S. (1983) The effects of phonotactic constraints on lexical processing in bilingual and monolingual subjects. *Journal of Verbal Learning and Verbal Behavior* 22, 174–188.

Beauvillain, C. and Grainger, J. (1987) Accessing interlexical homographs: Some limitations of a language-selective access. *Journal of Memory and Language* 26, 658–672.

Besner, D., Smith, M.C. and MacLeod, C.M. (1990) Visual word recognition: A dissociation of lexical and semantic processing. *Journal of Experimental Psychology: Learning, Memory, and Cognition* 16, 862–869.

Caramazza, A. and Brones, I. (1979) Lexical access in bilinguals. *Bulletin of the Psychonomic Society* 13, 212–214.

Chen, H-C. (1990) Lexical processing in a non-native language: Effects of language proficiency and learning strategy. *Memory and Cognition* 18, 279–288.

Chen, H-C. and Ho, C. (1986) Development of Stroop interference in Chinese-English bilinguals. *Journal of Experimental Psychology: Learning, Memory, and Cognition* 12, 397–401.

Chen, H-C. and Leung, Y-S. (1989) Patterns of lexical processing in a non-native language. *Journal of Experimental Psychology: Learning, Memory, and Cognition* 15, 316–325.

Chen, H-C. and Ng, M-L. (1989) Semantic facilitation and translation priming effects in Chinese-English bilinguals. *Memory and Cognition* 17, 454–462.

Costa, A., Miozzo, M. and Caramazza, A. (1999) Lexical selection in bilinguals: Do words in the bilingual's two lexicons compete for selection? *Journal of Memory and Language* 41, 365–397.

De Groot, A.M.B. (1992a) Determinants of word translation. *Journal of Experimental Psychology: Learning, Memory, and Cognition* 18, 1001–1018.

De Groot, A.M.B. (1992b) Bilingual lexical representation: A closer look at conceptual representations. In R. Frost and L. Katz (eds) *Orthography, Phonology, Morphology, and Meaning* (pp. 389–412). Amsterdam: Elsevier Science Publishers.

De Groot, A.M.B. (1993) Word-type effects in bilingual processing tasks: Support for a mixed-representational system. In R. Schreuder and B. Weltens (eds) *The Bilingual Lexicon* (pp. 27–51). Amsterdam: John Benjamins.

De Groot, A.M.B. (1995) Determinants of bilingual lexicosemantic organisation. *Computer Assisted Language Learning* 8, 151–180.

De Groot, A.M.B. (1998) Retroactive or proactive control of the bilingual system. *Bilingualism: Language and Cognition* 2, 86–87.

De Groot, A.M.B. (2000) On the source and nature of semantic and conceptual knowledge. *Bilingualism: Language and Cognition* 3, 7–9.

De Groot, A.M.B., Dannenburg, L. and Van Hell, J. G. (1994) Forward and backward word translation by bilinguals. *Journal of Memory and Language* 33, 600–629.

De Groot, A.M.B., Delmaar, P. and Lupker, S.J. (2000) The processing of interlexical homographs in translation recognition and lexical decision: Support for non-selective access to bilingual memory. *Quarterly Journal of Experimental Psychology* 53, 397–428.

De Groot, A.M.B. and Hoeks, J.C.J. (1995) The development of bilingual memory: Evidence from word translation by trilinguals. *Language Learning* 45, 683–724.

De Groot, A.M.B. and Keijzer, R. (2000) What is hard to learn is easy to forget: The roles of word concreteness, cognate status, and word frequency in foreign-language vocabulary learning and forgetting. *Language Learning* 50, 1–56.

De Groot, A.M.B. and Nas, G.L.J. (1991) Lexical representation of cognates and non-cognates in compound bilinguals. *Journal of Memory and Language* 30, 90–123.

De Groot, A.M.B. and Poot, R. (1997) Word translation at three levels of proficiency in a second language: The ubiquitous involvement of conceptual memory. *Language Learning* 47, 215–264.

Dell, G.S. and O'Seaghdha, P.G. (1991) Mediated and convergent lexical priming in language production: A comment on Levelt *et al.* (1991). *Psychological Review* 98, 604–614.

Dijkstra, A., Grainger, J. and Van Heuven, W.J.B. (1999) Recognition of cognates and interlingual homographs: The neglected role of phonology. *Journal of Memory and Language* 41, 496–518.

Dijkstra, A. and Van Heuven, W.J.B. (1998) The BIA model and bilingual word recognition. In J. Grainger and A.M. Jacobs (eds) *Localist Connectionist Approaches to Human Cognition* (pp. 189–225). Mahwah, NJ: Lawrence Erlbaum Associates.

Dijkstra, A., Van Jaarsveld, H. and Ten Brinke, S. (1998) Interlingual homograph recognition: Effects of task demands and language intermixing. *Bilingualism: Language and Cognition* 1, 51–66.

Durgunoglu, A.Y. and Roediger, H.L. (1987) Test differences in accessing bilingual memory. *Journal of Memory and Language* 26, 377–391.

Ellis, N.C. and Beaton, A. (1993) Psycholinguistic determinants of foreign language vocabulary learning. *Language Learning* 43, 559–617.

Ervin, S M. and Osgood, C.E. (1954) Second language learning and bilingualism. *Journal of Abnormal Social Psychology,* Supplement, 52, 139–146.

Forbach, G.B., Stanners, R.F. and Hochhaus, L. (1974) Repetition and practice effects in a lexical decision task. *Memory and Cognition* 2, 337–339.

Gerard, L.D. and Scarborough, D.L. (1989) Language-specific lexical access of homographs by bilinguals. *Journal of Experimental Psychology: Learning, Memory, and Cognition* 15, 305–315.

Grainger, J. (1993) Visual word recognition in bilinguals. In R. Schreuder and B. Weltens (eds) *The Bilingual Lexicon* (pp. 11–25). Amsterdam: John Benjamins.

Grainger, J. and Beauvillain, C. (1987) Language blocking and lexical access in bilinguals. *Quarterly Journal of Experimental Psychology* 39a, 295–319.

Grainger, J. and Dijkstra, T. (1992) On the representation and use of language information in bilinguals. In R.J. Harris (ed.) *Cognitive Processing in Bilinguals* (pp. 207–222). Amsterdam: North Holland.

Grainger, J. and O'Regan, J.K. (1992) A psychophysical investigation of language priming effects in two English-French bilinguals. *European Journal of Cognitive Psychology* 4, 323–339.

Green, D.W. (1986) Control, activation, and resource: A framework and a model for the control of speech in bilinguals. *Brain and Language* 27, 210–223.

Green, D.W. (1998) Mental control of the bilingual lexico-semantic system. *Bilingualism: Language and Cognition* 1, 67–81.

Grosjean, F. (1988) Exploring the recognition of guest words in bilingual speech. *Language and Cognitive Processes* 3, 233–274.

Grosjean, F. (1997) Processing mixed language: Issues, findings, and models. In A.M.B. de Groot and J.F. Kroll (eds) *Tutorials in Bilingualism: Psycholinguistic Perspectives* (pp. 225–254). Mahwah, NJ: Lawrence Erlbaum Associates.

Grosjean, F. (2001) The bilingual's language modes. In J.L. Nicol (ed.) *One Mind, Two Languages: Bilingual Language Processing*. Oxford: Blackwell.

Heredia, R.R. (1997) Bilingual memory and hierarchical models: A case for language dominance. *Current Directions in Psychological Science* April (6) 34–39.

Hermans, D. (2000) Word production in a foreign language. PhD thesis, University of Nijmegen, Nijmegen.

Hermans, D., Bongaerts, T., De Bot, K. and Schreuder, R. (1998) Producing words in a foreign language: Can speakers prevent interference from their first language? *Bilingualism, Language, and Cognition* 1, 213–229.

Jared, D. and Kroll, J.F. (2001) Do bilinguals activate phonological representations in one or both of their languages when naming words? *Journal of Memory and Language* 44, 2–31.

Jin, Y-S. (1990) Effects of concreteness on cross-language priming in lexical decisions. *Perceptual and Motor Skills* 70, 1139–1154.

Kirsner, K., Brown, H.L., Abrol, S., Chadha, N.K. and Sharma, N.K. (1980) Bilingualism and lexical representation. *Quarterly Journal of Experimental Psychology* 32, 585–594.

Kirsner, K., Smith, M.C., Lockhart, R.S., King, M.L. and Jain, M. (1984) The bilingual lexicon: Language-specific units in an integrated network. *Journal of Verbal Learning and Verbal Behavior* 23, 519–539.

Kolers, P.A. (1963) Interlingual word association. *Journal of Verbal Learning and Verbal Behavior* 2, 291–300.

Kolers, P.A. (1966) Reading and talking bilingually. *American Journal of Psychology* 79, 357–376.

Kroll, J.F. (1993) Accessing conceptual representations for words in a second language. In R. Schreuder and B. Weltens (eds) *The Bilingual Lexicon* (53–81). Amsterdam: John Benjamins.

Kroll, J.F. and Curley, J. (1988) Lexical memory in novice bilinguals: The role of concepts in retrieving second language words. In M.M. Gruneberg, P.E. Morris. and R.N. Sykes (eds) *Practical Aspects of Memory: Current Research and Issues. Vol. 2: Clinical and Educational Implications*. Chichester: John Wiley and Sons.

Kroll, J.F. and De Groot, A.M.B. (1997) Lexical and conceptual memory in the bilingual: Mapping form to meaning in two languages. In A.M.B. de Groot and J.F. Kroll (eds) *Tutorials in Bilingualism: Psycholinguistic Perspectives* (pp. 169–199). Mahwah, NJ: Lawrence Erlbaum Associates.

Kroll, J.F. and Sholl, A. (1992) Lexical and conceptual memory in fluent and non-fluent bilinguals. In R.J. Harris (ed.) *Cognitive Processing in Bilinguals* (pp. 191–204). Amsterdam: Elsevier Science Publishers.

Kroll, J.F. and Stewart, E. (1994) Category interference in translation and picture naming: Evidence for asymmetric connections between bilingual memory representations. *Journal of Memory and Language* 33, 149–174.

La Heij, W., Hooglander, A., Kerling, R. and Van der Velden, E. (1996) Non-verbal context effects in forward and backward word translation: Evidence for concept mediation. *Journal of Memory and Language* 35, 648-665.

Lambert, W.E., Havelka, J. and Crosby, C. (1958) The influence of language-acquisition contexts on bilingualism. *Journal of Abnormal and Social Psychology* 56, 239–244.

Levelt, W.J.M. (1989) *Speaking: From Intention to Articulation.* Cambridge, MA: Bradford Books/MIT Press.

Léwy, N. and Grosjean, F. (1999). BIMOLA: A computational model of bilingual spoken word recognition. Paper presented at the 2nd International Symposium on Bilingualism, University of Newcastle-upon-Tyne.

Lotto, L. and De Groot, A.M.B. (1998) Effects of learning method and word type on acquiring vocabulary in an unfamiliar language. *Language Learning* 48, 31–69.

MacNamara, J., Krauthammer, M. and Bolgar, M. (1968) Language switching in bilinguals as a function of stimulus and response uncertainty. *Journal of Experimental Psychology* 78, 208–215.

MacNamara, J. and Kushnir, S.L. (1971) Linguistic independence of bilinguals: The input switch. *Journal of Verbal Learning and Verbal Behavior* 10, 480–487.

Masson, M.E.J. (1991) A distributed memory model of context effects in word identification. In D. Besner and G.W. Humphreys (eds) *Basic Processes in Reading: Visual Word Recognition* (pp. 233–263). Hillsdale NJ: Lawrence Erlbaum Associates.

McClelland, J.L. and Rumelhart, D.E. (1981) An interactive activation model of context effects in letter perception, Part 1: An account of basic findings. *Psychological Review* 88, 375–405.

Meuter, R.F.I. and Allport, A. (1999) Bilingual language switching in naming: Asymmetrical costs of language selection. *Journal of Memory and Language* 40, 25–40.

Meyer, D.E. and Ruddy, M.G. (1974, April) Bilingual word recognition: Organisation and retrieval of alternative lexical codes. Paper presented at the Eastern Psychological Association Meeting, Philadelphia, Pennsylvania.

Nas, G. (1983) Visual word recognition in bilinguals: Evidence for a co-operation between visual and sound based codes during access to a common lexical store. *Journal of Verbal Learning and Verbal Behavior* 22, 526–534.

Neely, J.H. (1991) Semantic priming effects in visual word recognition: A selective review of current findings and theories. In D. Besner and G.W. Humphreys (eds) *Basic Processes in Reading: Visual Word Recognition* (pp. 264–336). Hillsdale, NJ: Lawrence Erlbaum Associates.

Paradis, M. (1997) The cognitive neuropsychology of bilingualism. In A.M.B. de Groot and J.F. Kroll (eds) *Tutorials in Bilingualism: Psycholinguistic Perspectives* (pp. 331–354). Mahwah, NJ: Lawrence Erlbaum Associates.

Pavlenko, A. (1999) New approaches to concepts in bilingual memory. *Bilingualism: Language and Cognition* 2, 209–230.

Potter, M.C., So, K.F., Von Eckardt, B. and Feldman, L.B. (1984) Lexical and conceptual representation in beginning and proficient bilinguals. *Journal of Verbal Learning and Verbal Behavior* 23, 23–38.

Poulisse, N. (1997) Language production in bilinguals. In A.M.B. de Groot and J.F. Kroll (eds) *Tutorials in Bilingualism: Psycholinguistic Perspectives* (pp. 201–224). Mahwah, NJ: Lawrence Erlbaum Associates.

Poulisse, N. (1999) *Slips of the Tongue: Speech Errors in First and Second Language Production.* Amsterdam: John Benjamins.

Sánchez-Casas, R., Davis, C.W. and García-Albea, J.E. (1992) Bilingual lexical processing: Exploring the cognate/non-cognate distinction. *European Journal of Cognitive Psychology* 4, 293–310.

Schwanenflugel, P.J. and Rey, M. (1986) Interlingual semantic facilitation: Evidence for a common representational system in the bilingual lexicon. *Journal of Memory and Language* 25, 605–618.

Sholl, A., Sankaranarayanan, A. and Kroll, J.F. (1995) Transfer between picture naming and translation: A test of asymmetries in bilingual memory. *Psychological Science* 6, 45–49.

Smith, M.C. (1997) How do bilinguals access lexical information? In A.M.B. de Groot and J.F. Kroll (eds) *Tutorials in Bilingualism: Psycholinguistic Perspectives* (pp. 145–168). Mahwah, NJ: Lawrence Erlbaum Associates.

Soares, C. and Grosjean, F. (1984) Bilinguals in a monolingual and a bilingual speech mode: The effect on lexical access. *Memory and Cognition* 12, 380–386.

Tzelgov, J. and Eben-Ezra, S. (1992) Components of the between-language semantic priming effect. *European Journal of Cognitive Psychology* 4, 253–272.

Tzelgov, J., Henik, A. and Leiser, D. (1990) Controlling Stroop interference: Evidence from a bilingual task. *Journal of Experimental Psychology: Learning, Memory, and Cognition* 16, 760–771.

Tzelgov, J., Henik, A., Sneg, R. and Baruch, O. (1996) Unintentional word reading via the phonological route: The Stroop effect with cross-script homophones. *Journal of Experimental Psychology: Learning, Memory, and Cognition* 22, 336–349.

Van Hell, J.G. (1998) Cross-language processing and bilingual memory organisation. PhD thesis, University of Amsterdam.

Van Hell, J.G. and Candia Mahn, A. (1997) Keyword mnemonics versus rote rehearsal: Learning concrete and abstract foreign words by experienced and inexperienced learners. *Language Learning* 47, 507–546.

Van Hell, J.G. and De Groot, A.M.B. (1998a) Disentangling context availability and concreteness in lexical decision and word translation. *Quarterly Journal of Experimental Psychology* 51, 41–63.

Van Hell, J.G. and De Groot, A.M.B. (1998b) Conceptual representation in bilingual memory: Effects of concreteness and cognate status in word association. *Bilingualism: Language and Cognition* 1, 193–211.

Van Hell, J.G. and Dijkstra, T. (submitted) Foreign language knowledge can influence native language performance: Evidence from trilinguals.

Van Heuven, W.J.B. (2000). Visual word recognition in monolingual and bilingual readers: experiments and computational modelling. PhD thesis, University of Nijmegen.

Van Heuven, W.J.B. Dijkstra, A. and Grainger, J. (1998) Orthographic neighbourhood effects in bilingual word recognition. *Journal of Memory and Language* 39, 458–483.

Van Leerdam, M., Bosman, A.M.T. and De Groot, A.M.B. (in preparation) Bilingual word perception: Within-language and between-language spelling-to-sound consistency effects.

Weinreich, U. (1953) *Languages in Contact: Findings and Problems.* New York: Linguistic Circle of New York. (Reprinted in 1974 by Mouton, The Hague.)

Introduction to Chapter 3
The Phonology of the L2 User, Roy Major

VIVIAN COOK

Phonology has been one of the areas of research most sympathetic to the idea of the L2 user. Pioneers such as James Flege and Roy Major have not only looked at the effects of the L2 on the L1, but have also actively considered whether in fact L2 users have a single integrated system for both languages.

One fruitful topic has been voice onset time (VOT). Languages signal the differences between pairs of plosive consonants such as /p/-/b/ and /k/-/g/ by varying the brief moment of silence between the air being obstructed and released, known as the VOT. Voicing for the vowel after the plosive *either* starts more or less at the same moment as the release of the obstruction by the tongue or the lips, giving rise to a voiced /b/, /g/ etc., *or* starts a few milliseconds later than the release, yielding voiceless /p/ /k/ etc. The difference between voiced and voiceless plosives is not a matter of *whether* voicing occurs, but *when* it occurs. Hence the difference between voiced and voiceless plosives becomes a matter of convention rather than absolute; the VOT difference between voiced and voiceless varies from one language to another. More discussion of VOT in an SLA context can be found in Cook (2001)

The L2 user has a long way to go to achieve this delicate timing, starting from the VOTs in the first language and ending up with VOTs unlike monolinguals in either language. Spanish/English bilinguals, for example, use more or less the same VOT in both English and Spanish, despite the differences between these two languages (Williams, 1977). French learners of English pronounce the /t/ sound in *French* with a longer VOT than monolinguals (Flege, 1987). Watson (1991: 44) sums up the sizeable research as follows: 'In both production and perception, therefore, studies of older children (and adults) suggest that bilinguals behave in ways that are at once distinct from monolinguals and very similar to them.' VOT reveals an area where the L2 user indeed is a unique user of language. Major goes on from evidence such as this to describe the L2 user phonological system as a balance between the first language, the second language, and the universal properties of the human mind that apply to any phonological system.

SLA research does not take place in isolation from other aspects of language. Languages develop over centuries; individuals change during their lives; languages come into contact with other languages, dialects with other dialects. It would be surprising if these did not reflect some of the same properties of human minds and lives as SLA research. Major's chapter expands the issues beyond SLA research by seeing the use of second languages as part of the continual adaptation to alternative forms of language influenced by the universal properties of the mind, here seen in phonological terms. He provides an insight not only into the type of phonological model necessary to account for L2 acquisition and use, but also into the links between these and the rest of language.

References

Cook, V.J. (2001) *Second Language Learning and Language Teaching* (3rd edn). London: Edward Arnold.

Flege, J.E. (1987) The production of 'new' and 'similar' phones in a foreign language: Evidence for the effect of equivalence classification. *Journal of Phonetics* 15, 47–65.

Watson, I. (1991) Phonological processing in two languages. In E. Bialystok (ed.) *Language Processes in Bilingual Children*. Cambridge: Cambridge University Press.

Williams, L. (1977) The perception of consonant voicing by Spanish English bilinguals. *Perception and Psychophysics* 21 (4), 289–297.

Chapter 3
The Phonology of the L2 User

ROY C. MAJOR

Introduction

The L2 user often differs significantly from monolingual speakers, meaning that the L2 user's L1 and L2 systems differ from those of a mono-lingual native speaker (NS) of both languages. The L2 user's L2 system, or interlanguage (IL), in turn affects the L1 system as well. From one perspective, one might be tempted to say that L2 users are NSs of neither L1 nor L2, because their systems are different from monolingual NSs of both languages. However, from another perspective, these speakers have competence in two languages, albeit a different type of competence from monolingual speakers of these two languages.

Taking the view that L2 users can have completely developed systems in two languages, I present an original model describing the principles involved in the formation of L2 phonological systems, and the change in L1 phonological systems that results from exposure to an L2; portions of this chapter are based on Major (2001). This model also applies to situations not traditionally considered second language acquisition (SLA), including various forms of languages in contact, such as bilingualism and multi-lingualism, pidgins and creoles, dialects in contact, and international vari-eties. For example, bilingual Spanish/English speakers in the American Southwest have Spanish systems that are unlike monolingual Spanish speakers, and English systems that are unlike monolingual English speakers. Yet both the Spanish and English of these speakers are completely developed systems, not deficient realisations of monolingual systems. Creoles and world Englishes have evolved in the same way. Thus, Haitian creole and Singapore English are not viewed as deficient or incomplete varieties of standard varieties, but rather as legitimate varieties themselves. So too 'standard French' in Haiti is different from standard French in other countries, just as Mandarin Chinese in Singapore is different from Chinese varieties in China.

An IL is the L2 user's system. SLA research has demonstrated that there are three principal factors involved in its formation – the L1, the L2 and universal principles. For example, it is commonly observed by French teachers that an English speaker of French may pronounce the final French [l] with a velarised English [ɫ], demonstrating the influence of L1 or transfer; however, this learner may correctly produce French [R] as opposed to using English [r], indicating the L2 component. Still further, the same learner may produce a centralised rounded vowel [ʉ], instead of the French [ü]. Since [ʉ] is neither native French nor native English, this sound must be the result of universals.

Universal Grammar (UG) is also part of the set of linguistic universals. Although the nature of UG is continually under debate (see Flynn and Lust, this volume), UG usually means the *principles*, or the core grammar of all languages, and the *parameters*, or the specific settings that each language has. However, the set of linguistic universals (U) embraces more than UG, and includes learnability principles, markedness, underlying representations, rules, processes, constraints and stylistic universals. For example, there are sonority universals, whereby sonority tends to decrease at the edges of syllables; in L1 acquisition, children acquire consonant-vowel (CV) syllables before consonant-vowel-consonant (CVC) syllables.

Viewing IL as a combination and product of L1, L2 and U has far-reaching implications for areas not traditionally subsumed under SLA. From a broad perspective, everyone speaks an IL. The L1 component is by definition one's NL. However, an L2 can include outside linguistic influences on one's L1, which everyone experiences, including exposure to different dialects and languages. This L1 and L2 interaction in turn is affected by universal principles governing language acquisition and change (U). Thus, everyone can be said to speak an IL, since one's L1 system is continually undergoing change because of outside influences (the L2 component). The change may be large, e.g. an immigrant whose L1 competence decreases dramatically over the course of his or her lifetime and also becomes very competent in the L2. The change may be small, e.g. a US Easterner or Midwesterner who loses the /ɔ/-/a/ distinction in casual speech (but not in formal speech), owing to the influence of a Western dialect.

The Ontogeny Phylogeny Model of Language Acquisition and Change

The Ontogeny Phylogeny Model (OPM) is a modification of the ontogeny model (OM; Major, 1987). The OM states that transfer processes decrease over time, while developmental processes increase and then decrease. Although I believe these claims are sound, there are some problematic areas for the OM. The OM refers to L1 transfer and developmental processes, yet says nothing about how the L2 component develops in relation to the other components. In addition, although the OM model claims there are more *transfer* processes for similar phenomena but more *developmental* processes for phenomena that are 'further apart' (Major, 1987: 109), it does not imply anything about the chronological stages of development. Finally the OM makes no claims regarding markedness. The OPM accepts the basic premises of the OM, but addresses these problematic areas. In addition, the OPM adds phylogeny to the model. In biology, ontogeny deals with the life cycle of a single organism (e.g. caterpillars metamorphosing into butterflies), and phylogeny deals with the evolution of groups of organisms (e.g. giraffes evolving long necks). In terms of language, ontogeny is an individual's language development and change, and phylogeny is evolution and change of whole languages including historical change, dialect variation, language loss and language contact phenomena. The OPM includes both these dimensions.

I consider IL to have the components L1, L2 and U, such that IL = parts of L1 + parts of L2 + parts of U that are not already part of L1 and L2. At the outset of acquisition the ideal learner has only L1; there is no L2, and U is dormant. By being dormant, I mean there is no observable U component that is not already part of the L1 grammar. For example, the U process of final obstruent devoicing is not apparent in Japanese learners of English, for those who always epenthesise vowels for word final obstruents (e.g. *bosu* for *boss*); therefore, IL = L1. During acquisition an L2 system develops, and, in the idealised learner, eventually the L2 is completely mastered, i.e. IL = L2. However, since few people attain native-like competence in the L2, throughout their L2-using lifetime most L2 users have a system composed of L1, L2 and U.

The Ontogeny Phylogeny Model (OPM) claims an interrelationship between L1, L2 and U: L2 increases, L1 decreases, and U increases and then decreases. This model assumes access to U, since IL frequently has phenomena that are neither L1 nor L2. Specific corollaries of the OPM pertain to chronology, style, markedness and similarity.

The Ontogeny Component of the OPM

Chronology

Chronological Corollary of the OPM
   IL develops chronologically in the following manner: (1) L2 increases, (2) L1 decreases, and (3) U increases and then decreases. This corollary applies

to normal phenomena, that is phenomena that are neither marked nor similar (explained in later sections).

The model is demonstrated graphically in stages 1–5 in Figure 3.1. The circles in these figures represent the IL, with each sector representing proportions of the three subsystems, L1, L2 and U.

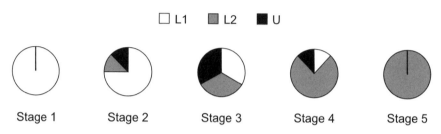

Stage 1   Stage 2   Stage 3   Stage 4   Stage 5

Figure 3.1 The Ontogeny Phylogeny Model (OPM) for 'normal development': The chronological corollary (each circle represents the learner's mind at one stage)

The proportions of the various components in the figures are hypothetical, varying from learner to learner, and from phenomenon to phenomenon. At the beginning stages, the OPM claims that the L1 component is so strong that it prevents U from surfacing. Later, L2 components start to develop, but simultaneously many of the learner's attempts result in non-native-like speech (neither L1 nor L2), indicating that U is exerting its influence. Then in later stages, the influence of U decreases as the L2 becomes more developed.

Some frequently observed examples of individual phenomena illustrate the OPM principles of the model (these are hypothetical examples, though frequently observed by teachers of these languages):

(1) *L1 English/L2 Spanish /r/ (the trilled [r])*. The L2 user first substitutes English [ɹ] exclusively; thus, L1 = 100%, L2 = 0%, and U = 0%. Later the speaker has moderate success with [r] but also produces a uvular trilled [R], in addition to [ɹ]. As acquisition proceeds, the proportions change; [r] continues to increase until it reaches 100%, while [ɹ] and [R] decrease until they reach zero.

(2) *L1 Japanese/L2 English final voiced obstruents*. Since Japanese has no final obstruents (either voiced or voiceless), the L2 user first epenthesises a vowel, e.g. [nido] for 'need' (an L1 process). Later the learner no longer epenthesises but instead devoices the [d]: [nit] (a U process). Finally, the person successfully produces final [d].

Logically the OPM should be true from our concept of what IL is and from well-documented cases of how it develops. The learner begins with 100% L1 and 0% L2. At the final stage, an idealised learner has 0% L1 and 100% L2. This means that over time L2 increases and L1 decreases. Because L1 is 100% at the beginning stage and at the final stage L2 is 100%, U must be 0% at both these stages. However, in the intermediate stages as U appears it must rise and fall. Consider hypothetically a point where L1, L2 and U are equal (e.g. stage 3 in Figure 3.1). After this point, as L1 continues to decrease and L2 continues to increase, U has to decrease, since mathematically L1 + L2 + U = 100%.

During the early stages, L1 transfer is much more important than U, rather than vice versa. This logically follows from long-known principles of learning theory dealing with transfer (Ausubel, 1963, 1967; Ausubel *et al.*, 1978; Ausubel & Robinson, 1969; Bruce, 1933; Bugelski, 1942; Cheng, 1929; Gagné, 1977; McGeogh, 1942; Schultz, 1960; Travers, 1977). Research has continually demonstrated that one relies on existing cognitive structures when learning new structures, i.e. transfer occurs: 'It is impossible to conceive of any instance of such learning that is not affected in some way by existing cognitive structure. This learning experience, in turn, results in new transfer by modifying cognitive structure' (Ausubel *et al.*, 1978: 165). In terms of SLA, this means that L1 transfer will dominate early stages because the learner has little knowledge of the L2. However, during acquisition the 'existing cognitive structure' (i.e. the IL) becomes modified by L2 exposure. Because these modified structures are new, they cannot be L1, rather they must be either U or L2. Thus, continued exposure to L2 modifies these new structures; therefore, the influence of pure L1 transfer will decrease, while L2 will increase, and U will also increase (because attempts at the L2 prove to be non-native-like). As the learner becomes increasingly proficient, more and more nativelike forms will replace U. This is precisely what the OPM claims: L1 will decrease over time, L2 will increase, and U will first increase and then decrease. This general pattern also applies to L1 loss, where immigrants' L1s become increasingly different from monolingual speakers in their countries of origin (see the 'First language loss' section below).

A great deal of SLA research supports the claims of the Chronological Corollary of the OPM. That transfer is the most important factor at early stages of acquisition is widely accepted. Even without empirical research to support this, the very notion of what it means to have a heavy foreign accent substantiates this claim. A heavy foreign accent is synonymous with an early stage, and those familiar with a speaker's L1 can easily identify the person's L1 when that person speaks the L2, indicating that L1 transfer predominates.

The OPM's claim that U increases and then decreases is more difficult to support directly because of the dearth of longitudinal studies documenting the frequency of L1 and U. However, one important early longitudinal study supports the OPM. In his study of the acquisition of English by his four German-speaking children, Wode (1981) observed the following stages in all four of his children acquiring English /r/: [R] (occurring in native German) > [w] > [ɹ] > [r] (In Wode's symbols, [ɹ] = 'central frictionless continuant' and [r] = 'target-like retroflex'.) These stages would be predicted by the OPM. The early substitutions are due to transfer ([R]), later substitutions are due to U ([w] and [ɹ]), and finally L2 is mastered. That these latter two substitutions are due to universals is confirmed by the fact that that they are very common substitutions of monolingual L1 learners of English.

Studies demonstrating that U occurs in learners other than true beginners provides indirect support for the OPM. Accordingly, if acquisition continues to completion (if L2 is mastered), this necessarily means that U decreases during the later stages. A number of studies indicate the role of U in non-beginners. These include Nemser (1971), who found that Hungarian learners produced [sθ] for English [θ], and Johansson (1973), who documented that American English and German speakers produced sounds occurring neither in L2 Swedish nor in their L1 (e.g. [ʉ] for [ɯ]). Obstruent devoicing studies are also numerous (Altenberg & Vago, 1983; Edge, 1991; Flege & Davidian, 1984; Hodne, 1985; Riney, 1989; Yavaş, 1997). In L2 users whose L1s do not have final obstruents, devoicing must be attributed to U. Musau (1993) also found U in the L2 acquisition of Swahili by native speakers of Bukusu, Kamba, Kikuyu, Massai, Nandi, Somali and Luo.

Recent research by Hancin-Bhatt and Bhatt (1997) provides theoretical support to for the OPM. Using an OT (Optimality Theory) framework they conclude:

> In so doing, we can begin to give a linguistic-theoretic interpretation to Major's (1986, 1987, 1994) ontogeny model ... that L2 learners have mostly transfer-related errors in early stages of learning, but that, over time, developmental errors become more prominent, whereas both taper off in advanced L2 speakers. (Hancin-Bhatt & Bhatt, 1997: 386)

Speech style

The OPM claims that stylistically the patterns of L1, L2 and U vary as they do chronologically:

Stylistic corollary of the OPM

IL varies stylistically in the following manner: as style becomes more

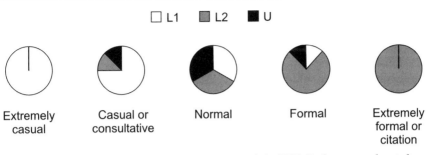

Figure 3.2 The Ontogeny Phylogeny Model (OPM) for speech styles: Stylistic corollary (each circle represents the learner's mind for one style)

formal, (1) L2 increases, (2) L1 decreases, and (3) U increases and then decreases (Figure 3.2).

It is widely observed that the influence of transfer is less as the task becomes more formal. Nearly every teacher has observed that L2 users are usually more accurate when pronouncing isolated words (e.g. minimal pairs) than in conversation, where L1 transfer is more prevalent. One reason for this pattern is that, with increasing formality, the speaker pays more attention to form. This means more monitoring, and in general, the more monitoring the greater the accuracy.

A number of studies support the OPM's claim that transfer decreases with formality (Dickerson & Dickerson, 1977; Gatbonton, 1975, 1978; Nemser, 1971; Petrenko, 1989; Sato, 1985; Schmidt, 1977; Tarone, 1979, 1982, 1983, 1988; Wenk, 1979, 1982; Wilson & Møllergard, 1981). The observation that transfer decreases and L2 increases as style becomes more formal does not directly predict the U pattern. However, it is implicit. Given that a very formal style is pure L2 and a very casual style is pure L1, then, when shifting from a formal to casual style, U has to appear and then disappear, i.e. increase and then decrease.

Wode's study of his daughter Birgit's L1 German/L2 English supports the stylistic claims of the OPM (Wode, 1981: 228). In spontaneous speech she produced more L1 transfer (German [R]) than in 'imitation-like check ups', where she would 'produce or attempt [w] or something [w]-like'. Thus, the two main factors were L1 and U, L1 being more prominent in casual speech, but U more prominent in formal speech. An example from dialects in contact further supports the OPM. Labov's 'Bill Peters effect' (Labov, 1994: 363) indicates that someone acquiring a second dialect performs better in more formal speech than in informal speech. Bill Peters (aged 80) made an /ɔ/ and /ɑ/ distinction in spontaneous speech but merged them in minimal pairs, typical of younger speakers (the L2 dialect).

His greater competence in formal speech (minimal pairs) than in his spontaneous speech is in perfect accordance with the claims of the OPM. A number of similar cases are documented by Labov (1994).

Similarity

For more than three decades it has been observed that phenomena very similar to the L1 are more difficult to learn than phenomena that are less similar or dissimilar. However, there have been no explicit claims regarding the relative roles of L1 and U. Although Flege's Speech Learning Model (Flege, 1995) claims that in similar phenomena L1 persists and that dissimilar phenomena ('new sounds') are acquired more easily, the model does not deal with the role of U. Although the OM claims '... there will be more interference processes for similar phenomena and more developmental processes for phenomena that are further apart' (Major, 1987: 109), it says nothing about whether L1 will decrease more rapidly or less rapidly in comparison to other phenomena. Furthermore, it does not say how U patterns chronologically compared to other phenomena. The Similarity Corollary of the OPM is explicit about these relationships:

Similarity corollary of the OPM
In similar phenomena, IL develops chronologically in the following manner: (1) L2 increases slowly, (2) L1 decreases slowly, and (3) U increases slowly and then decreases slowly. Thus, the role of L1 is much greater than U, compared to less similar phenomena. By implication, the less similar the phenomena (i.e. the more dissimilar), the more important the role of U is compared to L1.

These claims are represented in stages 1–7 in Figure 3.3. *Slowly* means more slowly than in normal overall development (i.e. the chronological

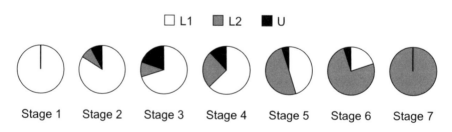

Figure 3.3 The Ontogeny Phylogeny Model (OPM) for similar phenomena: The similarity corollary (each circle represents the learner's mind at one stage)

corollary of the OPM, Figure 3.1). These differences can be observed by comparing Figure 3.1 with Figure 3.3. For example, in stage 3, compared with Figure 3.1, Figure 3.3 shows a smaller L2, a larger L1, and a smaller U; the greater L1/U proportion continues through stages 4–6 until stage 7 (Figure 3.3).

These claims rest on mathematical logic and well-known facts about similarity. Because L2 increases slowly and L1 influence is strong and persistent, logically U must increase slowly and decrease slowly. Therefore, U must be relatively less important than L1 because L1, L2 and U have to add up to 100%. One reason for these relative proportions in similar phenomena is that learners assume that L1 and L2 phenomena are the same. The result is that they rely on L1, and thus the role of U is smaller. One psycholinguistic reason why L1 transfer has a more important role than U is perceptual salience: minimal differences are less likely to be salient, which results in non-learning or L1 transfer. Thus, an English speaker uses English alveolar-aspirated /t/ when speaking Italian because the unaspirated dental /t̪/ occurring in native Italian is very similar. However, the same speaker may notice that the Italian trilled /r/ is very different from English /ɹ/, and thus may substitute non-English, non-Italian, sounds, i.e. it is due to U. True transfer can operate only when there are relevant phenomena to transfer. Ausubel *et al.* (1978) note that past experience has 'impact on relevant properties of cognitive structure' (Ausubel, *et al.*, 1978: 165). However, properties that are not 'relevant properties' cannot transfer (cf. Andersen, 1983). Thus, transferring English /k/ to Arabic /q/ is more likely than transferring English /k/ (or any other English sound) to Bantu clicks, where learners often produce non-English sounds, demonstrating that U plays an important role.

This pattern may seem paradoxical because, if L1 and L2 phenomena are maximally similar, transfer should be the greatest and result in non-learning. However, as L1 and L2 approach identity, 'negative' transfer will actually be 'positive' transfer because the two phenomena are virtually indistinguishable. For example, the VOTs (voice onset times or amount of aspiration) of a Spanish learner of Portuguese may be slightly different from a native speaker of Portuguese, but the differences are so slight that native Portuguese listeners may hear them in a native-like way. Although learning seemingly has taken place, it is merely a free ride of positive transfer. This 'similarity paradox' was discussed more than 50 years ago by Charles Osgood (1949).

A long line of research on similarity suggests the OPM pattern. Virtually all research has demonstrated that in similar sounds L2 acquisition is slow, and L1 transfer predominates; thus, U necessarily has a relatively minor role. Wode (1978, 1983a, 1983b) claimed that transfer occurs only when 'crucial similarity measures' are met (Wode, 1983a: 180) under 'specifiable similarity requirements' (Wode, 1983a: 185). If these conditions are not met, he claims that developmental stages characterising L1 acquisition occur (i.e. U). Thus, negative transfer occurs for similar phenomena, but for less similar phenomena transfer is less likely to operate, resulting in U substitutions.

The prolific work of Flege, including his Speech Learning Model (Flege, 1995) and much of his earlier work (Flege, 1987a, 1987b, 1990, 1993), support the claim that in similar phenomena L2 acquisition is slow, while L1 transfer predominates and persists. By implication, this means that U plays a minimal role. However, dissimilar phenomena often can be acquired with native-like accuracy. For example, Flege (1987a) found that advanced L1 English/L2 French speakers accurately produced French /ü/ but not French /u/. Major and Kim's (1996) Similarity Differential Rate Hypothesis claims that similar phenomena are acquired more slowly than dissimilar phenomena, but makes no claims about the role of U. Thus, both the Speech Learning Model and Similarity Differential Rate Hypothesis imply part of the similarity corollary of the OPM: L2 increases slowly, while L1 is prominent and persists. However, neither the Speech Learning Model nor Similarity Differential Rate Hypothesis nor other research explore the relative role of L1 compared with U, nor the reasons. The similarity corollary of the OPM thus addresses these shortcomings.

Markedness

The role of markedness in L1 and L2 acquisition has been known for sometime (Jakobson, 1941/1968; numerous works of Eckman, e.g. 1977, 1981, 1991, and Carlisle, 1991a, 1997, 1998). Markedness has been defined in many ways. As it applies to the OPM, I use markedness in the following ways: marked phenomena are relatively rare compared to less marked phenomena; if x and y are in a markedness relationship, x is more marked than y if the presence of x implies the presence of y. In L1 and L2 acquisition, marked phenomena are acquired later than less marked phenomena. In both L1 and L2 acquisition, more marked phenomena are acquired later and more slowly than less marked phenomena. However, the OM and other models and theories do not address the relative roles of L1, L2 and U in marked phenomena. The markedness corollary of the OPM does address this.

Markedness corollary of the OPM

In marked phenomena, IL develops chronologically in the following manner: (1) L2 increases slowly, (2) L1 decreases and then decreases slowly and (3) U increases rapidly and then decreases slowly. Thus, except for the earliest stages, the role of U is much greater than L1, compared to less marked phenomena.

These patterns are depicted in stages 1–7 in Figure 3.4. The terms *slowly* and *rapidly* mean more slowly and more rapidly than for normal phenomena (chronological corollary of the OPM, Figure 3.1). Thus, L2 increases more slowly throughout its development than in normal phenomena. In addition, the patterns for L1 and U differ. In the initial stages, L1 decreases at a rate comparable to normal phenomena, but then it decreases more slowly. At the same time U increases rapidly, but then decreases slowly. In the earlier stages L1 is the most prominent component for all phenomena (normal, similar, marked), but in marked phenomena the model claims that, after transfer has decreased substantially, then the relative proportion of U to L1 will become greater than for less marked phenomena. (In contrast, for similar phenomena the proportion of L1 to U is greater, as noted in the previous section.) Figure 3.1 and Figure 3.4 illustrate these differences. Thus, at stage 2, Figure 3.4 has the same L1 proportion, a slightly larger U, but a smaller L2 and U compared with Figure 3.1; at stage 3, Figure 3.4 has the same L1 but a much larger U compared with Figure 3.1. Later, at stage 4, Figure 3.4 depicts an even larger U compared with Figure 3.1. Thus, in marked phenomena, the U/L1 proportion continues to be large until acquisition is complete at stage 7.

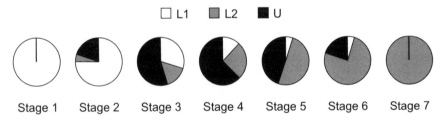

Figure 3.4 The Ontogeny Phylogeny Model (OPM) for 'marked' phenomena: The markedness corollary (each circle represents the learner's mind at one stage)

There are a number of reasons for these patterns. Since marked phenomena are acquired more slowly than unmarked phenomena, this means a smaller component of L2 throughout (Figure 3.4). But why does L1 at first decrease normally and then decrease more slowly, and why does U increase rapidly and then persist? One reason is mathematical logic. If x is more marked than y, but x and y do not differ in degree of similarity (say to L1 phenomenon z), then transfer should be equally important for x and y.

However, since x is more marked than y, the L2 component for x (i.e. native-like x) will increase more slowly than for y. But, since the L1 component is the same for both phenomena, this means that U will increase more quickly in x than in y, since L1 + L2 + U = 100%. In later stages U for x will decrease, but it will do so more slowly than for y because L2 for x increases slowly. This also means that L1 continues to decrease, although more slowly than during the early stages. If L1 continued to decrease at a normal rate, this would mean it would reach zero before acquisition were complete. This is unlikely, because L1 transfer tends to continue throughout acquisition.

The markedness claims of the OPM make sense, given what we know about SLA in general. At early stages L1 is the most likely substitution. However, realising that the L1 will not always suffice spurs the learner to try something other than the L1. If the attempt is neither L1 nor native-like L2 speech, it must be the result of U. Because marked phenomena are intrinsically difficult, the learner tries but fails more frequently than with normal phenomena, meaning there are more U substitutions than in normal phenomena. A continual overcoming of L1 influence while not achieving L2 accuracy means that the U rises rapidly but, because L2 is acquired slowly, this in turn means that U persists or decreases slowly.

The portion of the markedness corollary that claims that L2 increases slowly in marked phenomena is supported by much research, such as voicing contrasts (Altenberg & Vago, 1983; Eckman, 1977; Edge, 1991; Major & Faudree, 1996; Yavaş, 1994) and consonant clusters (Anderson, 1987; Broselow, 1983; Carlisle, 1991a, 1991b, 1997, 1998; Major, 1994; Osburne, 1996). The claim that U is greater than L1 is more difficult to support directly from the research because there are very few longitudinal studies, and far fewer that trace the frequency of both L1 and U. Two empirical studies of my own support this claim, although to the best of my knowledge there is no other empirical support or refutation. In a study of the Spanish trilled /r/ and flap /ɾ/ (Major, 1986), U substitutions (e.g. [ʀ] or [ʁ]) were more prevalent for the /r/ than for /ɾ/ (where either the American English [ɹ] or [ɾ] were frequent). Because /r/ is more marked than /ɾ/, the predominance of U for /r/ supports the U pattern claimed by the OPM. In another study (Major, 1996), investigating consonants in 9 environments, I found that the more marked the environment, the greater the probability of U. Thus, in syllable codas, the probability of U was 0.854 for double stops, 0.590 for fricative plus stop, but 0.083 for a singleton stop.

Comparison of normal, similar, and marked phenomena

Table 3.1 and Figures 3.5–3.7 compare the chronological development of normal, similar, and marked phenomena.

Table 3.1 Comparison of normal, similar and marked phenomena

Normal Phenomena	*Similar Phenomena*	*Marked Phenomena*
L2 acquired	L2 acquired slowly	L2 acquired slowly
Earlier stages: L1 dominates	*Earlier stages:* L1 dominates	*Earlier stages:* L1 dominates
Earlier stages: L1 decreases	*Earlier stages:* L1 decreases slowly	*Earlier stages:* L1 decreases
Later stages: L1 decreases	*Later stages:* L1 decreases slowly	*Later stages:* L1 decreases slowly
Earlier stages: U minimal	*Earlier stages:* U minimal	*Earlier stages:* U minimal
Earlier stages: U increases	*Earlier stages:* U increases slowly	*Earlier stages:* U increases rapidly
Later stages: U decreases	*Later stages:* U decreases slowly	*Later stages:* U decreases slowly

The unifying feature for both similarity and markedness is that acquisition progresses more slowly than for other phenomena ('normal' phenomena). In the initial stages, the component of L1 is large and U is small for all phenomena (stages 1 and 2, Figures 3.5–3.7). Later, the patterns diverge. In similar phenomena (Figure 3.6) L1 persists but the proportion of U to L1 becomes relatively smaller throughout (compared to normal and marked phenomena). However, in marked phenomena (Figure 3.7) the proportion

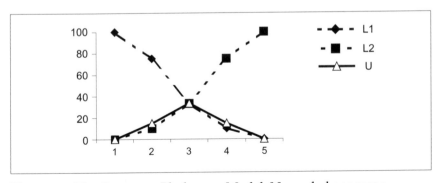

Figure 3.5 The Ontogeny Phylogeny Model: Normal phenomena

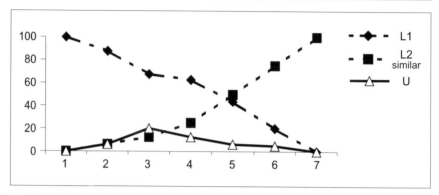

Figure 3.6 The Ontogeny Phylogeny Model: Similar phenomena

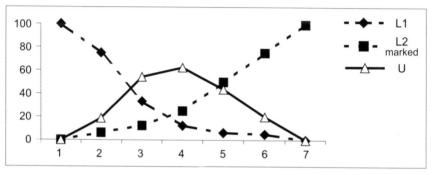

Figure 3.7 The Ontogeny Phylogeny Model: Marked phenomena

of U becomes larger and persists; thus, U/L1 becomes relatively large. Both similarity and markedness slow acquisition, but at the later stages they differ significantly in the relative importance of L1 and U components. That is, the importance of L1 and U becomes reversed for marked and similar phenomena. Thus, stages 4, 5 and 6 for similar and marked phenomena can be mirror images of each other (Figures 3.3 and 3.4).

First language loss

First language loss, or attrition, is frequent in speakers who have continuous L2 exposure and also in those who use their L1 less and less frequently. A typical situation is that L1 influences L2 and vice versa, as in societal bilingualism. For example, the VOTs of Canadian French/English bilinguals are intermediate between monolingual speakers of each language (Caramazza *et al.*, 1973). Although in one sense these bilinguals have 'lost' their native competence in both languages, a more reasonable point of view is simply that these speakers have competence in two languages, albeit different from that of monolingual speakers.

The OPM is a claim about all second-language phenomena, including the effects that L2 has on L1. Given this, the stages of L1 loss should mirror L2 acquisition. Many (e.g. Jakobson, 1941) have observed that L1 loss in aphasic and senile adults mirrors L1 acquisition. For example, many elderly native English-speaking adults lose [s]–[š] distinctions, mirroring L1 acquisition (since [s]–[š] distinctions are acquired late). These patterns of L1 loss through age should be the same as L1 loss due to L2 acquisition, that is, L1 loss should mirror L2 acquisition. The *last acquired first lost* principle should apply to L1 and U phenomena as predicted by the OPM. Accordingly, L2 will transfer to L1, just as L2 transfers to L3. Likewise U phenomena play a role in L1 loss. For example, in L1 attrition an L1 English/L2 Spanish speaker may merge the English vowels /ʌ/ and /æ/. Since Spanish has neither vowel, this merger must be due to U, since there is no Spanish transfer process predicting this. Thus, the OPM claims that L1 loss mirrors L2 acquisition, meaning that the patterns in Figure 3.1 also represent patterns of L1 loss.

The Phylogeny Component of the OPM

The previous sections have dealt with ontogeny, i.e. the development and change in an individual over a period that can range from merely a few moments up to a lifetime. This section deals with phylogeny, i.e. the development and change in groups over part of a generation or over many generations, in addition to historical changes in languages and language families. Although the OPM does not claim to account for all types of language change, it does address change due to languages in contact, including bilingualism and multilingualism, pidgins and creoles, and dialects in contact. In the following sections, I argue that an individual learning one or more second or foreign languages is analogous to groups of people who speak different languages coming into contact with the subsequent changes occurring in succeeding generations.

Bilingualism and multilingualism

One outcome of languages in contact is bilingualism and multilingualism, which are intermediate between complete language maintenance (isolation) and language shift (assimilation). In societal bilingualism the likelihood of speakers having two completely separate systems is extremely rare or non-existent, since it is hard to imagine a situation where the two languages in contact do not influence each another. The degree of influence depends on a number of factors, such as the extent to which one language dominates and how interchangeable the two languages are in the same social situations.

The mutual influence of the two languages occurs even at the fine-grained phonetic level. In bilinguals, phoneme boundaries are often intermediate between monolingual speakers of both languages (Elman *et al.*, 1977; Williams, 1977), for instance VOTs (Caramazza *et al.*, 1973). In the US Southwest, a number of monolingual speakers of Spanish and English report that both Spanish-accented English and English-accented Spanish occur in many Spanish/English bilinguals. For example, some bilinguals merge /č/ and /š/ in English, but surprisingly make /b/–/v/ distinctions in Spanish, even though native Latin American Spanish does not.

Given that there is mutual influence of both languages in bilingual societies, societal bilingualism can be viewed as an intermediate stage in bilingual acquisition. As a result (not necessarily an ongoing process, but a state), bilinguals have two language systems having components of both languages, showing mutual transfer, remnants of U, and a mutually shared core system. Speakers who have a fairly balanced proficiency in both languages A and B have two separate but equal systems of A and B (these are idealised speakers, and few if any exist). However, part of each system has components of the other, in addition to U and a mutually shared system.

Such a system is shown in Figure 3.8. Part of each system is identical to that of monolingual speakers, but part is *not* because of the mutual influence of the two systems. In most bilinguals one language is dominant over the other. If A is dominant, then the influence of B on A is minimal; in addition, the influence of the two other non-A components on A is also minimal (i.e. U and the mutually shared A and B). In contrast, A highly influences B. This situation is graphically represented in Figure 3.9. Such a situation is typical in the US in many Spanish/English bilinguals where Spanish is dominant. Their English is often syllable-timed with a great deal of Spanish segmental phonology.

Language A   Language B

Figure 3.8 The Ontogeny Phylogeny Model (OPM) for non-dominant bilingualism (each circle represents language A or B in one learner's mind)

Language A   Language B

Figure 3.9 The Ontogeny Phylogeny Model (OPM) for dominant bilingualism (each circle represents language A or B in one learner's mind)

Pidgins and creoles

When individuals sharing no common language come into contact, a *pidgin* can form; if it becomes nativised, it is called a *creole* (see Baker & Corne, 1982; Bickerton, 1981; Romaine, 1988; and Singler, 1987). Schumann (1978) likened L2 acquisition to pidginisation, and Bickerton's (1981, 1984, 1988) bioprogram hypothesis stressed the importance of U in the formation of a pidgin, as have many researchers in traditional SLA research. In traditional pidginisation, often speakers do not have continual contact with the dominant language, yet classroom students often do. However, even in and outside the class, students talk amongst themselves in the absence of a NS or near-NS of the language they are learning. Thus, there are close similarities between traditional SLA and pidginisation.

Consider a case of pidginisation with four languages in contact, A, B, C and D (more or fewer languages make no difference to my claims), with language A the dominant language. At the beginning, a pidgin is purely a mixture of these languages, and this stage is similar to a novice L2 learner having only his or her L1. This first stage pidginisation is represented in Figure 3.10 stage 1 (compare this with Figure 3.1, stage 1). However, a pidgin forms, not by speakers becoming proficient in the others' languages, but rather by speakers forming a shared system. U operates with increasing influence, but the influence of the various component languages decreases,

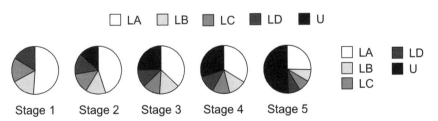

Stage 1   Stage 2   Stage 3   Stage 4   Stage 5

Figure 3.10 The Ontogeny Phylogeny Model (OPM) for pidginisation (each circle represents languages A, B, C, D in contact)

although A still remains more important than B, C and D. As U continues to increase, the component languages must decrease, since all components must add up to 100%. These stages are depicted in Figure 3.10. One reason for the strong U component is that speakers share little knowledge of each other's languages. In order to communicate, they resort to whatever means they can because being 'correct' has little meaning, the pidgin in formation having no set standards. This results in speakers resorting to universal principles, i.e. U.

After a pidgin forms, it can evolve into a more elaborate form and become nativised, i.e. a become a creole. It can continue to change and undergo decreolisation or hypercreolisation. Continual contact with the dominant language favors decreolisation, while cessation of this contact favours hypercreolisation. This highly oversimplified scenario has many exceptions because of factors such as identity and solidarity. Thus, Hawaiian Creole English speakers have continual contact with standard English, but apparently the creole is not becoming decreolised. In decreolisation the dominant language continues its influence, thus the other components become less influential. In contrast, in hypercreolisation U becomes more important, but the component languages become less important because contact is cut off. Decreolisation and hypercreolisation are shown in Figure 3.11.

Decreolisation   Hypercreolisation

Figure 3.11 The Ontogeny Phylogeny Model (OPM) for creolisation (each circle represents languages A, B, C, D in contact)

The process of creolisation and hypercreolisation can be likened to an individual language learner. Decreolisation is analogous to an L2 user with continual access to NSs or near NSs of the L2 and because of this the user's L2 becomes more and more nativelike. Hypercreolisation is analogous to an L2 user being cut off from contact with NSs or near NSs of the L2, yet the person continues to use the L2 with other NNSs from different language backgrounds. Because of this, the L2 will continue to develop independently without the influence of NSs of the L2. Such a process, which is analogous to hypercreolisation, is continually taking place in international Englishes (see Trudgill & Hannah, 1994, for a reference guide).

Dialects in contact

Dialects in contact are similar to bilingualism, multilingualism, and pidgins and creoles, since the difference between language and dialect is not often based solely on linguistic criteria but rather on political, ethnic and social criteria. Indeed Einar Haugen reportedly said that a language is a dialect that has an army and a navy. The claims I have made concerning bilingualism and pidgins and creoles also obtain to dialects in contact, since the language/dialect distinction is not clear-cut.

It is well-documented that the more frequent and intense the contact, the more frequent the mergers. Just as phonological distinctions are often lost in bilingual communities and in pidgins and creoles, so too are they frequent in dialects in contact. In general, in the US there are more distinctions in the East, fewer in the Midwest, and even fewer in the West. This pattern follows from immigration and migration patterns, the West experiencing the greatest change. For example, large western cities, such as Los Angeles, Las Vegas, and Phoenix, have fewer native-born residents than many Midwestern and Eastern cities. The principle *more contact more mergers* is seen in the following examples: the /æ/ and /ɛ/ distinction before /r/ (e.g. *marry/merry*) occurring in the East, does not occur in the Midwest or West; the /ɑ/–/ɔ/ distinction in the East is lost in parts of the Midwest and in the entire West; in the West speakers often merge *heel/hill*, *mole/mull*, *pole/pull*.

The parallels between pidgins and creoles and dialects in contact may at first not be apparent. In general, in dialect-contact situations the differences between the mother dialects and resulting dialect are less dramatic than in pidginisation, where the pidgins and creoles are usually very distinct from the mother languages. One explanation is that in dialects in contact the dialects usually share a large core of phenomena, but in pidginisation they do not. For example, standard US Western dialects have /θ/ and /ð/, coda consonant clusters and coda voiced obstruents simply because the majority dialects involved in the formation of these dialects also have these phenomena. In contrast, many English creoles do not have /θ/ and /ð/, final consonant clusters or voiced obstruents, e.g. Tok Pisin (see Verhaar, 1995). This may be due to simplification and to the fact that most of the mother languages do not share these phenomena. Regardless of the degree of overlap in the mother languages, in both pidginisation and dialects in contact the result is a mixed variety, or hybrid that is not purely any of the mother varieties. If the L1 learner hears this mixed variety as the L1 (by being exposed to either a pidgin or a mixed dialect), the learner will necessarily hear different variations of a particular phenomenon because it is a mixed variety. During acquisition the child will form a compromise or intermediate system, the result being a creole or new dialect, now with NSs.

Dialect contact phenomena can be explicated from the basic claims of the OPM, i.e. transfer decreases over time, L2 increases, and U increases and then decreases (as explained earlier). The situation where one dialect is dominant is analogous to the speakers of the non-dominant dialects learning an 'L2' – the dominant dialect. Initially, the speakers simply use their native dialects, i.e. transfer predominates. As the dominant dialect (the L2) is being acquired, the other dialects (the L1s) decrease and U increases and decreases. Rather than numbered stages for dialects in contact, in Figure 3.12 I have chosen two stages to represent the early and late stages; the late stage is analogous to a typical case of bilingualism, where the minority language is assimilated, and to decreolisation (Figure 3.11). In dialects in contact where one dialect dominates, a compromise or a combination of the component dialects results. Furthermore, when contact with the mother dialects cease, the emergent dialect can evolve in a fashion similar to hypercreolisation (Figure 3.11), where the role of U becomes increasingly important.

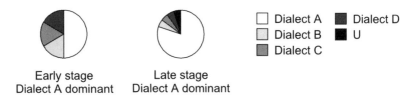

Early stage   Late stage
Dialect A dominant   Dialect A dominant

Figure 3.12 The Ontogeny Phylogeny Model (OPM) for dialect contact (each circle represents dialects A, B, C, D in contact)

The similarity and markedness corollaries of OPM are also relevant to contact phenomena, as seen earlier. The OPM claims that in similar phenomena L1 has a stronger influence than U, whereas in marked phenomena U has a stronger influence than L1. If these claims are true, they explain why in pidgins and creoles U predominates, but in dialects in contact U is much less important. Pidginisation often produces a language very distinct from the mother languages, indicating the large influence of U. In contrast, in dialects in contact, the resulting dialect is often very similar to one or more of the mother dialects, indicating the major influence of transfer. Because dialects in contact are often similar to each other, U plays a lesser role and transfer plays a greater role. On the other hand, since the mother languages are very dissimilar to one another in pidginisation, this predicts the increased role of U over transfer.

According to the OPM, in marked phenomena the role of U is greater than in similar phenomena. This claim as it applies to dialects in contact is represented in Figure 3.13. These figures represent an idealisation, since clearly there is no dialect marked in all respects, nor two dialects similar in all respects. Figure 3.13 (similar dialects) is analogous to initial pidgin-isation stages, where all languages take part (Figure 3.10, stage 2). Note that in Figure 3.13 (similar dialects) there is no dominant dialect. However, an important difference is that for similar dialects the component languages persist (Figure 3.13) because of the OPM principle that transfer persists in similar phenomena. However, for pidgins, component languages diminish more rapidly since they are not similar (Figure 3.10). Figure 3.13 (marked dialects) is analogous to hypercreolisation, U having an important role (as seen in Figure 3.11). In hypercreolisation, U is important because the creole is cut off from the dominant language; in marked dialects in contact, U is important because in marked phenomena it plays a major role.

Similar dialects   Marked dialects

□ Dialect A   ■ Dialect D
□ Dialect B   ■ U
■ Dialect C

Figure 3.13 The Ontogeny Phylogeny Model (OPM) for similar dialect contact (each circle represents dialects A, B, C, D in contact)

It is important to point out that, in pidgins and creoles, marked forms are frequently lost but they often survive in dialects in contact. For example, US Western dialects have /θ/ and /ð/, /æ -/ʌ/-/a/ distinctions, and final consonant clusters, simply because the mother dialects also have these forms, i.e. positive transfer occurred. However, these phenomena are rare in English-based pidgins and creoles, and because of U mergers result.

Conclusion

The Ontogeny Phylogeny Model (OPM) makes explicit claims concerning the interrelationship of L1, L2 and U, in addition to the effects of similarity and markedness. The OPM claims that IL behaves in the following manner: over time and as style becomes more formal, L2 increases, L1 decreases, and U increases and then decreases. In addition, the proportions of L1, L2 and U are different, depending on whether phenomena are normal, similar or marked. L2 increases slowly in similar and marked phenomena, compared with normal phenomena. In similar phenomena L1 is relatively more important than U, but in marked phenomena the situation is reversed. I claim that the OPM holds true both for individuals and for groups of speakers over generations, such as languages and dialects in contact.

The OPM is purposely stated without the machinery of any particular linguistic framework, such as generative phonology, feature geometry or Optimality Theory. If the OPM were stated and confined to a particular linguistic framework then, as the framework changed, became outdated or was disproven, so too would the OPM be discredited. My claims can probably be framed and translated into future frameworks as they appear. Furthermore, it should be possible to design research that can support or refute the OPM, using various linguistic theories. If 40 years ago the OPM had appeared and had been stated within a Contrastive Analysis framework, the U component would naturally be missing since all errors were attributed to transfer. The OPM would then be discredited today.

The OPM makes very general claims without details concerning specific phenomena, e.g. the fine-grained phonetic and phonological details in the acquisition of voiced coda clusters. The OPM's lack of specifics again is purposeful, since an encompassing theory would have to include an inordinate number of details. The OPM is stated at a macrocosmic level. Microcosmic levels of investigation of particular phenomena are a necessary and important ongoing endeavour in SLA. Because the OPM provides a general framework for testing individual phenomena, research may support or falsify the OPM. If research supports the OPM, this suggests that the OPM is an accurate description of how the human linguistic mind operates.

Clearly I view L2 in a very broad sense: an L2 is simply a variety that is not one's native variety, including a different language or dialect. The OPM describes the components of an L2 user's competence. The circles in the various figures throughout this chapter represent complete systems, with the different components varying from situation to situation and from speaker to speaker. None of these 'stages' is a more 'complete' system than another, since they may be final states for many speakers and indeed for whole societies. Accordingly, it would be ludicrous to claim that a Tok Pisin speaker's native language is an incomplete system of standard English, that Indian English is incomplete British English, or that Singapore English is underdeveloped British or American English.

Acknowledgement

I thank Thomas Scovel for bringing the Osgood article to my attention.

References

Altenberg, E. and Vago, R. (1983) Theoretical implications of an error analysis of second language phonology production. *Language Learning* 33, 427–447.

Andersen, R. (1983) Transfer to somewhere. In S.M. Gass and L. Selinker (eds) *Language Transfer in Language Learning* (pp. 177–201). Rowley, MA: Newbury House.

Anderson, J. (1987) The Markedness Differential Hypothesis and syllable structure difficulty. In G. Ioup and S.H. Weinberger (eds) *Interlanguage Phonology: The Acquisition of a Second Language Sound System* (pp. 279–291). New York: Newbury House/Harper & Row.

Ausubel, D. (1963) *The Psychology of Meaningful Verbal Learning*. New York: Grune and Stratten.

Ausubel, D. (1967) *Learning Theory and Classroom Practice*. Toronto: The Ontario Institute for Studies in Education (OISE).

Ausubel, D.P., Novak, J.D. and Hanesian, H. (1978) *Educational Psychology: A Cognitive View* (2nd edn). New York: Holt, Rinehart & Winston.

Ausubel, D. and Robinson, F.G. (1969) *School Learning: An Introduction to Educational Psychology*. New York: Holt, Rinehart & Winston.

Baker, P. and Corne, C. (1982) *Isle de France Creole: Affinities and Origins*. Ann Arbor, MI: Karoma.

Bickerton, D. (1981) *Roots of Language*. Ann Arbor, MI: Karoma.

Bickerton, D. (1984) The language bioprogram hypothesis. *Behavioral and Brain Sciences* 7, 173–221.

Bickerton, D. (1988) Creole languages and the bioprogram. In F.J. Newmeyer (ed.) *Linguistics: The Cambridge Survey* (pp. 267–264). Cambridge: Cambridge University Press.

Broselow, E. (1983) Non-obvious transfer: On predicting epenthesis errors. In S.M. Gass and L. Selinker (eds) *Language Transfer in Language Learning* (pp. 269–280). Rowley, MA: Newbury House.

Bruce, R.W. (1933) Conditions of transfer of training. *Journal of Experimental Psychology* 16, 343–361.

Bugelski, B.R. (1942) Interferences with recall of original responses after learning new responses to old stimuli. *Journal of Experimental Psychology* 30, 368–379.

Caramazza, A., Yeni-Komshian, G.H., Zurif, E.B. and Carbone, E. (1973) The acquisition of a new phonological contrast: The case of stop consonants in French–English bilinguals. *Journal of the Acoustical Society of America* 54, 421–28.

Carlisle, R.S. (1991a) The influence of environment on vowel epenthesis in Spanish/English interphonology. *Applied Linguistics* 12, 76–95.

Carlisle, R.S. (1991b) The influence of syllable structure universals on the variability of interlanguage phonology. In A.D. Volpe (ed.) *The Seventeenth LACUS Forum 1990* (pp. 135–145). Lake Bluff, IL: Linguistic Association of Canada and the United States.

Carlisle, R.S. (1997) The modification of onsets in a markedness relationship: Testing the interlanguage structural conformity hypothesis. *Language Learning* 47, 327–361.

Carlisle, R.S. (1998) The acquisition of onsets in a markedness relationship: A longitudinal study. *Studies in Second Language Acquisition* 20, 245–260.

Cheng, N.Y. (1929) Retroactive effect and degree of similarity. *Journal of Experimental Psychology* 12, 444–449.

Dickerson, L.B. and Dickerson, W.B. (1977) Interlanguage phonology: Current research and future directions. In S. Corder and E. Roulet (eds) *Actes du 5éme Colloque de Linguistique Appliquée* (pp. 18–29). Neuchâtel: Faculté de Lettres.

Eckman, F.R. (1977) Markedness and the contrastive analysis hypothesis. *Language Learning* 27, 315–330.

Eckman, F.R. (1981) On predicting phonological difficulty in second language acquisition. *Studies in Second Language Acquisition* 4, 18–30.

Eckman, F. R. (1991) The Structural Conformity Hypothesis and the acquisition of consonant clusters in the interlanguage of ESL learners. *Studies in Second Language Acquisition* 13, 23–41.

Edge, B.A. (1991) The production of word-final voiced obstruents in English by L1 speakers of Japanese and Cantonese. *Studies in Second Language Acquisition* 13, 377–393.

Elman, J., Diehl, R. and Buchwald, S. (1977) Perceptual switching in bilinguals. *Journal of the Acoustical Society of America* 62, 971–974.

Flege, J.E. (1987a) The production of 'new' and 'similar' phones in a foreign language: Evidence for the effect of equivalence classification. *Journal of Phonetics* 15, 47–65.

Flege, J.E. (1987b) Effects of equivalence classification on the production of foreign language speech sounds. In A. James and J. Leather (eds) *Sound Patterns in Second Language Acquisition* (pp. 9–39). Dordrecht: Foris.

Flege, J.E. (1990) English vowel production by Dutch talkers: More evidence for the 'similar' vs. 'new' distinction. In J. Leather and A. James (eds) *New Sounds 90: Proceedings of the Amsterdam Symposium on the Acquisition of Second-Language Speech* (pp. 255–293). Amsterdam: University of Amsterdam.

Flege, J.E. (1993) Production and perception of a novel, second language phonetic contrast. *Journal of the Acoustical Society of America* 93, 1589–1608.

Flege, J.E. (1995) Second language speech learning: Theory, findings, and problems. In W. Strange (ed.) *Speech Perception and Linguistic Experience: Issues in Cross-linguistic Research* (pp 233–277). Timonium, MD: York Press, Inc.

Flege, J.E. and Davidian, R. (1984) Transfer and developmental processes in adult foreign language speech production. *Applied Psycholinguistics* 5, 323–347.

Gagné, R.M. (1977) *The Conditions of Learning* (3rd edn). New York: Holt, Rinehart & Winston.

Gatbonton, E. (1975) Systematic variations in second language speech: A sociolinguistic study. PhD thesis, McGill University.

Gatbonton, E. (1978) Patterned phonetic variability in second-language speech: A gradual diffusion model. *Canadian Modern Language Review* 34, 335–347.

Hancin-Bhatt, B. and Bhatt, R.M. (1997) Optimal L2 syllables: Interactions of transfer and developmental effects. *Studies in Second Language Acquisition* 19, 331–378.

Hodne, B. (1985) Yet another look at interlanguage phonology: The modification of English syllable structure by native speakers of Polish. *Language Learning* 35, 405–422.

Jakobson, R. (1941) *Kindersprache, Aphasie, und Allgemeine Lautgestze*. Translated in 1968 as *Child Language, Aphasia, and Phonological Universals* (A.R. Keiler, trans.). The Hague: Mouton.

Johansson, F.A. (1973) *Immigrant Swedish Phonology.* Lund, Sweden: Gleerup.

Labov, W. (1994) *Principles of Linguistic Change* (Vol. 1). Oxford: Blackwell.

Major, R.C. (1986) The Ontogeny Model: Evidence from L2 acquisition of Spanish *r*. *Language Learning* 36, 453–504.

Major, R.C. (1987) A model for interlanguage phonology. In G. Ioup and S.H. Weinberger (eds) *Interlanguage Phonology: The Acquisition of a Second Language Sound System* (pp. 101–125). New York: Newbury House/Harper & Row.

Major, R.C. (1994) Chronological and stylistic aspects of second language acquisition of consonant clusters. *Language Learning* 44, 655–680.

Major, R.C. (1996) Markedness in second language acquisition of consonant clusters. In D.R. Preston and R. Bayley (eds) *Variation Linguistics and Second Language Acquisition* (pp. 75–96). Amsterdam: Benjamins.

Major, R.C. (2001) *Foreign Accent: The Ontogeny and Phylogeny of Second Language Phonology.* Mahwah, NJ: Lawrence Erlbaum Associates.

Major, R.C. and Faudree, M.C. (1996) Markedness universals and the acquisition of voicing contrasts in Korean speakers of English. *Studies in Second Language Acquisition* 18, 69–90.

Major, R.C. and Kim, E. (1996) The similarity differential rate hypothesis. *Language Learning* 46, 465–496.

McGeogh, J.A. (1942) *The Psychology of Human Learning.* New York: Longmans, Green, and Co.

Musau, P.M. (1993) *Aspects of Interphonology: The Study of Kenyan Learners of Swahili.* Bayreuth, Germany: Bayreuth University.

Nemser, W. (1971) *An Experimental Study of Phonological Interference in the English of Hungarians.* Bloomington: Indiana University Press.

Osburne, A.G. (1996) Final consonant cluster reduction in English L2 speech: A case study of a Vietnamese speaker. *Applied Linguistics* 17, 164–181.

Osgood, C.A. (1949) The similarity paradox in human learning: A resolution. *Psychological Review* 56, 132–143.

Petrenko, A.D. (1989) Stylistic variants of pronunciation in second language instruction (*Stilistische Varianten der Aussprache im Fremdsprachenunterricht*). *Deutsch als Fremdsprache* 26, 267–272.

Riney, T. (1989) Syllable structure and interlanguage phonology. *Kansas Working Papers in Linguistics* 14. Lawrence: University of Kansas.

Romaine, S. (1988) *Pidgin and Creole Languages.* London: Longman.

Sato, C.J. (1985) Task variation in interlanguage phonology. In S.M. Gass and C.G. Madden (eds) *Input in Second Language Acquisition* (pp. 181–196). Rowley, MA: Newbury House.

Schmidt, R.W. (1977) Sociolinguistic variation and language transfer in phonology. *Working Papers in Bilingualism* 12, 79–95.

Schultz, R.W. (1960) Problem solving behaviour and transfer. *Harvard Educational Review* 30, 61–77.

Schumann, J.H. (1978) *The Pidginisation Process: A Model for Second Language Acquisition.* Rowley, MA: Newbury House.

Singler, J. (1987) Remarks in response to Derek Bickerton's 'Creoles and universal grammar: The unmarked case? *Journal of Pidgin and Creole Languages* 1, 141–145.

Tarone, E. (1979) Interlanguage as chameleon. *Language Learning* 29, 181–191.

Tarone, E. (1982) Systematicity and attention in interlanguage. *Language Learning* 32.

Tarone, E. (1983) On the variability of interlanguage systems. *Applied Linguistics* 4, 142–164.

Tarone, E. (1988) *Variation in Interlanguage*. London: Edward Arnold.

Travers, R.M.W. (1977) *Essentials of Learning* (4th edn). New York: Macmillan.

Trudgill, P. and Hannah, J. (1994) *International English: A Guide to Varieties of Standard English* (3rd edn). London: Edward Arnold.

Verhaar, J.W.M. (1995) *Toward a Reference Grammar of Tok Pisin: An Experiment in Corpus Linguistics*. Honolulu: University of Hawaii Press.

Wenk, B.J. (1979) Articulatory setting and de-fossilisation. *Interlanguage Studies Bulletin* 4, 202–220.

Wenk, B.J. (1982) Articulatory setting and the acquisition of second language phonology. *Revue de Phonetique Appliquée* 65, 51–65.

Williams, L. (1977) The perception of stop consonant voicing by Spanish–English bilinguals. *Perception and Psychophysics* 21, 289–297.

Wilson, D. and Møllergard, E. (1981) Errors in the production of vowel no. 10 /ʌ/ by Norwegian learners of English. *International Review of Applied Linguistics* 19, 69–76.

Wode, H. (1978) The beginning of non-school room L2 phonological acquisition. *International Review of Applied Linguistics in Language Learning* 16, 109–125.

Wode, H. (1981) *Learning a Second Language*. Tübingen: Narr.

Wode, H. (1983a) Phonology in L2 acquisition. In H. Wode (ed.) *Papers on Language Acquisition, Language Learning and Language Teaching* (pp. 175–187). Heidelberg, Germany: Groos.

Wode, H. (1983b) Contrastive analysis and language learning. In H. Wode (ed.) *Papers on Language Acquisition, Language Learning and Language Teaching* (pp. 202–212). Heidelberg, Germany: Groos.

Yavaş, M. (1994) Final stop devoicing in interlanguage. In M. Yavaş (ed.) *First and Second Language Phonology* (pp. 267–282). San Diego, CA: Singular.

Yavaş, M. (1997) The effects of vowel height and place of articulation in interlanguage final stop devoicing. *International Review of Applied Linguistics* 35, 115–125.

A Minimalist Approach to L2 Solves a Dilemma of UG, Suzanne Flynn and Barbara Lust

VIVIAN COOK

How does the fact that most people know more than one language affect the Chomskyan theory of innate Universal Grammar? One approach is to ignore the issue by saying that the language of a mixed community 'would not be "pure" in the relevant sense, because it would not represent a single set of choices among the options permitted by UG but rather would include "contradictory" choices for certain of these options' (Chomsky, 1986: 17), i.e. treat second language use as one of the impurities to be filtered out of the study of linguistic competence. Another approach is to assert that Universal Grammar is beside the point in adult L2 acquisition; L2 learning has no relationship with Universal Grammar, but instead uses general cognitive processes and learning abilities of the human mind. The third approach, exemplified by Satterfield (1999) and this chapter, recognises that L2 acquisition and use has to be accommodated within the mainstream theory of language.

Two metaphors of language acquisition have been used virtually simultaneously in Chomskyan theory (Cook, 1994):

- *The boxes model.* This treats acquisition as a process of input going into a 'black box' – at different periods labelled the Language Acquisition Device (LAD) or UG – and output coming out in the shape of knowledge of language (linguistic competence, generative grammar, etc.). UG is the processor that takes input and transforms it into output. It is therefore separate from the grammar that is acquired.
- *The states model.* The language faculty (alias UG) starts in a zero state, S_0, and is changed by experience of a particular language to a steady state S_S, i.e. adult competence, as seen in Flynn and Lust's Figure 4.1. 'The language faculty has an initial state, genetically determined; in the normal course of development it passes through a series of states

in early childhood, reaching a relatively stable steady state that undergoes little subsequent change, apart from the lexicon' (Chomsky & Lasnik, 1993). UG then becomes the grammar that is acquired.

Much L2 research has accepted the boxes view of UG as an unchanging processor in the mind, seeing its aim as showing whether or not L2 learners' grammars exhibit the constant principles of language that learners could not have acquired from their first language, or parameter-settings that reflect those of their first language. This view essentially limits the grammar of the L2 user to that of the L1 monolingual; success is whether the L2 user gains native settings, not whether the combination of L1 and L2 yields unique new settings not available to the monolingual. Each new language a person learns is a distinct new object with its own instantiation of the principles and parameters from UG (or not), to be measured against the L1. The learner's mind is not a whole in which the first and the second language exist in a single 'state' of the mind, but in different compartments.

Suzanne Flynn and Barbara Lust explore the implications of these two metaphors for L2 acquisition, arriving at a new definition of the initial state as initial with relationship to a particular task rather than being simply the *first* state prior to all experience. Hence the L2 learner may be in an initial state for learning the L2, despite his or her previous language experience. Indeed recent work with first language acquisition suggests that, prior to the initial point of syntax learning as parameter-setting, etc., the L1 child already has some experience with structure (Marcus *et al.*, 1999) and with constructing shared points of view (Tomasello, 2000).

References

Chomsky, N. (1986) *Knowledge of Language: Its Nature, Origin and Use*. New York: Praeger.

Chomsky, N. and Lasnik, H. (1993) Principles and parameters theory. In J. Jacobs, A. von Stechow, W. Sternefeld and T. Vennemann (eds) *Syntax: An International Handbook of Contemporary Research* (pp. 506–569). Berlin: de Gruyter.

Cook, V.J. (1994) The metaphor of access to Universal Grammar. In N. Ellis (ed.) *Implicit Learning and Language* (pp. 477–502). New York/London: Academic Press.

Marcus, G.F., Vijayan, S., Bandi Rao, S. and Vishton, P.M (1999) Rule learning by seven-month-old infants. *Science* 283, 77–80.

Satterfield, T. (1999) *Bilingual Selection of Syntactic Knowledge: Extending the Principles and Parameters Approach*. Dordrecht: Kluwer.

Tomasello, M. (2000) *The Cultural Origins of Human Cognition*. Boston: Harvard University Press.

Chapter 4

A Minimalist Approach to L2 Solves a Dilemma of UG

SUZANNE FLYNN AND BARBARA LUST

Introduction

A fundamental dilemma persists regarding the relation of second language (L2) acquisition to linguistic theory. Chomsky has suggested that, if Universal Grammar (UG) principles are 'wired-in' and 'distinguished from the acquired elements of language, which bear a greater cost' (Chomsky, 1995: 140), then this entails that at the end-state or steady-state the UG principles remain distinct from language-particular properties. He goes on to state that 'Suggestive work by Flynn (1987) on second language acquisition supports this conclusion' (Chomsky, 1995: 164); 'Her work suggests that at least some principles of UG remain active in adult acquisition, while parameter-changing raises difficulties ...' (Chomsky, 1991: 24). A dilemma emerges, however: as Chomsky also notes (we) '... want to distinguish between the transition from the initial state of the language faculty ... to various subsequent states, including ... a steady state that undergoes only limited and marginal change' (Chomsky, 1991: 14). The dilemma raised is the following: if UG is continuous between the initial state and the end state, then how can the distinction between initial and end states be maintained and in what does it consist? Moreover, on empirical grounds, how can the wide array of L2 acquisition facts be related to this theory? These issues concerning L2 acquisition overlap with issues current in the study of L1 acquisition regarding whether or not UG is continuous in L1 acquisition or subject to maturation of some form (e.g. Lust, 1999). Together, these issues concern the foundations of the nature of language development in real time and the power of the theory of UG to account for this.

The focus of the chapter

In this paper, a theoretical resolution to this paradox is proposed and supported with evidence from empirical studies of both L1 and L2 acquisition. In doing so, it outlines the foundation for a new theory of language acquisition that accounts for the developmental relation between the initial state and the end state. At the same time, the proposed theory maintains the Strong Continuity Hypothesis of UG and applies it to both L1 and L2 acquisition. Critically this paper maintains the position that it is difficult on the basis of L1 acquisition alone to determine if UG is continuous or not, as, in the child, some form of maturation necessarily to some degree confounds the language acquisition process. The fundamental question that both this paper and a theory of language acquisition are concerned with is whether or not this maturation involves UG. The adult is presumably post-maturation. For this reason, converging the study of adult L2 acquisition with the study of L1 acquisition can assist in resolving the issues raised above, as well as in shedding important new light on the fundamental nature of UG or the language faculty. The work presented here builds upon previous attempts to relate L1 and L2 (e.g. Cook, 1973) and in addition develops more precisely matched experiments for both the L1 and L2 populations investigated.

Since the adult is presumably beyond the point of any general maturation that might be involved in L1 acquisition, certain critical predictions can be made in this paradigm. If the nature of L2 acquisition can be shown to resemble L1 acquisition in fundamental ways, and that similarity can be linked to a theory of UG (for example if it can be shown that there is evidence of certain UG principles or parameters in L2 as well as in L1), and it can be shown that this knowledge is *not* derived (for example, by transfer from the L1), then this would provide critical confirmation for the central claims of this paper. Although it is possible that L1 and L2 learners would develop similarly or perform similarly or make comparable types of errors for completely different reasons, it can be assumed that the null hypothesis must be that they are occurring for the same reason. (The more similarity can be identified, the more difficult it would be to provide an alternative explanation for these phenomena, without being clearly ad hoc.)

Three sets of empirical data are adduced in support of the claims in this paper. First, by comparing L1 and L2 acquisition, we verify that UG principles and parameters do continuously and effectively constrain the L2 acquisition process, as they do the L1 process. Second, we argue that more precise analyses of empirical L2 acquisition data also provide evidence for UG in L2 acquisition (See also discussion in Epstein *et al.*, 1996). Third, converging evidence from more refined analyses of the linguistic theory of UG are presented, thus providing for more refined analyses of the empirical facts. Together these data suggest a resolution to the dilemma raised both theoretically and empirically by a theory of UG. Taken together, the results of this paper lead to the basis for a new, more comprehensive theory of language acquisition, one that unifies both L1 and L2 acquisition. The development of such a proposal provides the basis for a resolution of a fundamental theoretical and empirical dilemma with regard to language acquisition in the field of linguistics today. Current revisions in the linguistic theory of UG lead to sharper formulation of this more comprehensive theory.

Definition of a theory of UG

For the purposes of this paper, UG is defined as a theory of the language faculty and a theory of the initial state. It is a set of specifically linguistic principles and parameters that has cardinality and is discrete and finite. Following from this definition, at least two possible models of language acquisition are possible: the Maturation model in Figure 4.1 and the Strong Continuity model in Figure 4.2. These models suggest that a fundamental indeterminacy persists in the interpretation of a theory of UG and its role in L2 acquisition as well as in L1 acquisition. The question is, which model provides a more reasonable representation of UG for language acquisition, the Maturation model in Figure 4.1 or the Strong Continuity model in Figure 4.2? Both would appear to be compatible with a theory of UG.

Possible Models of Universal Grammar in Second Language Acquisition

The Maturation model

In the Maturation model in Figure 4.1, UG over time, in some sense, actually becomes the language-specific grammar (English, Spanish, and so on) that is being acquired. Stated somewhat differently, UG and the L1 become indissociable from each other. Under this scenario, UG itself must change in the language acquisition process. (UG must change or, viewed another way, *access to UG may change* (Chomsky, personal communication). This distinction does not significantly challenge the points we make in this chapter. Under either view, UG is not fully available until L1 is fully acquired.)

$$S_1 \rightarrow S_2 \rightarrow S_3 \rightarrow S_{(n)} \rightarrow CORE \rightarrow L_2 \rightarrow L_n$$
$$GRAMMAR$$

$$L1 \rightarrow UG$$

Figure 4.1 The Maturation model (S=state of grammar development)

This interpretation is equivalent to what has been termed a 'maturation' theory of UG (e.g. Chomsky, 1988: 70; Chomsky, 1965) in the field of L1 acquisition1:

> ... it might very well be true that a series of successively more detailed and highly structured schemata (corresponding to *maturational* stages, but perhaps in part themselves determined in form by earlier steps of language acquisition) are applied to the data at successive stages of language acquisition. (Chomsky, 1965: 202, fn 19)

Maturation theory asserts that the function that 'maps' acoustic input to knowledge undergoes change. That is, the mapping function is defined as UG itself. As such, UG will be different at different developmental stages in language acquisition. Such a model would suggest that for a language learner (L1 or L2), hearing sentences containing examples of a particular syntactic structure does not necessarily trigger knowledge of the structure. For example, hearing the sequence of language sounds associated with the utterance 'John was arrested' does *not* give the learner the ability to understand that 'John' is the object of the verb 'arrested'. At some later developmental stage, howeverthe function defined as UG changes in such a way that such data-exposure *does* lead to a change in the learner's grammar.

The Strong Continuity Model

On the other hand, in the Strong Continuity model in Figure 4.2, UG remains distinct from the language specific grammar that is being acquired, and it remains constant over time. UG is continuously available to assist in the construction of various language-specific grammars. This

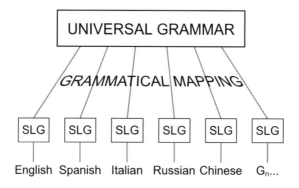

Figure 4.2 The Strong Continuity model (SLG = specific language grammar)

interpretation involves the 'Strong Continuity Hypothesis' in the study of L1 acquisition (see Lust, 1999; Boser *et al.*, 1995). In contrast to the Maturation model in Figure 4.1, the function=UG does not change over time in the Strong Continuity model illustrated in Figure 4.2. UG remains constant and distinct from specific language grammars during the lifetime of an individual and hence is available to guide the learner in the construction of new grammars throughout the individual's lifetime. If the learner's use of input changes over time, this is not due to changes in UG.

A dilemma

If, as theorists assume, UG is a finite and discrete set of principles and parameters, *how can* there be maturation of UG as suggested in Figure 4.1, unless subsets of this finite set of principles are recognised? But these subsets by definition are not equivalent to UG; only the full finite explicit set of principles is. Thus, UG cannot be a model of the *initial state* under this maturational interpretation. Alternatively, if UG is a model of the *initial state*, then under maturation theory, there must be at least two theories of UG: *pre*-matured and *post*-matured. Alternatively stated, there must exist an *initial state*-UG and an *end state*-UG, where these UGs differ; in fact, if language acquisition is viewed as 'stages', more than two UGs may exist. Given multiple UGs, in what meaningful sense can it be said that 'UG is a model of the *initial state*'?

Fundamental questions

Empirical questions regarding L2 language acquisition correlate with this theoretical paradox. (For extended discussion, see Epstein *et al.*, 1998.) For example:

(1) Do the UG principles remain distinct from the language-specific properties in the end state as they do in the initial state?
(2) As a corollary, can an adult who approaches a new language in adulthood access UG or the language faculty in the same way as the child does for L1 acquisition at the so-called 'initial state'?

Given the Maturation model described above, the answers to questions (1) and (2) would presumably be *no*. UG in this model is *not* distinct from the language-specific grammar in the end state, and consequently the adult *cannot* access UG again, after the 'initial state', defined as S_0. New language knowledge must of necessity be accessed through some other means, perhaps through L1 in some transfer-based way. The Maturation model would be predicted to hold, for example, if maturation under some form of genetic programming underlay much of the essential course of L1 acquisition. Presumably there would be actual 'brain change' (as yet undefined) under this model, which correlates with the course of acquisition of an L1. The brain would never be in the same state again in this model, after the language state S_1 (or perhaps more accurately, state zero $[S_0]$), with respect to the language faculty.

Given the Strong Continuity model of UG illustrated in Figure 4.2 above, however, the opposite set of answers to questions (1) and (2) would be predicted. That is, we would predict that UG *does* remain distinct from the language-specific grammar, and the adult can return to the so-called *initial state* (representing the language faculty) at the time of acquisition of a new target language. The acquisition of new language knowledge benefits from the language faculty, as does L1 acquisition. In this model, UG would be presumed to be biologically programmed to remain genetically fixed and constant throughout the course of L1 acquisition and thus available throughout one's life for new language acquisition. Adult language acquisition may differ in some ways from child language acquisition, but these differences do not result from a change in the language faculty, UG.

More specific claims of the Strong Continuity model of UG

In the following sections of this paper, empirical evidence will be presented in support of the following claims:

(a) The Strong Continuity model of UG (as illustrated in Figure 4.2) is a valid approximation of the language acquisition process.
(b) The answers to the fundamental questions in (1) and (2) above are: *yes*. In the end-state, UG remains distinct from specific language grammars.
(c) UG remains available in its entirety to the adult L2 learner. UG is continuously available for the adult during the course of acquisition of a target language.
(d) With regard to UG, new language knowledge in adulthood is not acquired in a fundamentally different manner from the L1, contrary to what the Maturation model (illustrated in Figure 4.1) suggests.

Importantly, this chapter does not propose that there are no differences between L1 and L2 acquisition. However, it is argued that such differences are not due to changes in UG (e.g. Epstein *et al.*, 1998). Critically, L1 acquisition is also not explained through changes in UG itself (Lust, 1999). This chapter will review and analyse examples of evidence of this sort. New analyses of the developmental course in L2 acquisition will be presented, based on existing data relevant to parameter setting. Under careful analysis of L2 acquisition, evidence will be given concerning the effects of specific components of UG, which resemble those found in L1 acquisition. This chapter will not focus on the factors that explain differences between L1 and L2 acquisition. Rather it will concentrate on arguing that these differences do not indicate that UG is either *not* available to the adult L2 learner or that the adult L2 learner accesses UG fundamentally differently from the L1 learner, e.g. by some form of transfer from L1. It will be suggested that the L2 acquisition delays/errors often noted to differentiate L1 and L2 acquisition reflect a number of different factors, all of which are compatible with the Strong Continuity model of UG. Thus, by disconfirming a false hypothesis, the chapter will clarify the research paradigm for future exploration of differences between L1 and L2. It will suggest that these differences reflect processes involved in the 'grammatical mapping' from UG to the language-specific grammar, as they do in child L1 acquisition, thus proposing a new approach to this research paradigm. In addition, the work presented here will in turn lead us to a clarification of the definition of the term 'initial state,' and thus to an avoidance of the dilemma associated with the Maturation Model illustrated in Figure 4.1 above.

Language Acquisition Results

A selection of data from a series of experimental research studies that involve Japanese adults acquiring English as a Second Language (ESL) is used to support the claims made here. These L2 results will be compared to both Japanese and English children learning their L1s, as well as to Spanish adults learning ESL. This domain of investigation involves a parametric difference between the directionality of Japanese and English (or Spanish) phrase structure.

If there were effects of parameter setting on early L2 acquisition as there are in early L1 acquisition, this would provide evidence for the Strong Continuity model of UG in Figure 4.2 above rather than the Maturation model of UG in Figure 4.1. This is because a maturational model would appear to predict that once a parametric value is established, the alternative value would cease to be available to the L2 learner if needed for the construction of a new target grammar. Only if the L2 can be directly modeled on L1 constructions can new language acquisition occur. Only a parameter value instantiated in the L1 would be directly available under the Maturation model.

L1 acquisition

In early work on L1 acquisition, it has been argued that a parameter of phrase structure directionality is set very early, and critically affects and constrains the course of L1 acquisition (e.g. Lust, in preparation; Lust & Chien, 1984; Lust & Mazuka, 1989; Mazuka, 1996). Without going into detail, this parameter differentiates Japanese or Chinese from English and at the same time it takes in English and Spanish. Japanese has functional and lexical heads on the right of the phrase and also leftward subordinate clauses. English and Spanish, on the other hand, instantiate the reverse, with left lexical and functional heads and adverbial subordinate clause adjunction to the right. Glossing over detail, the abstract differences between the left- and right-branching languages are suggested in Figure 4.3. [2]

Abstract configurations of phrase structure directionality

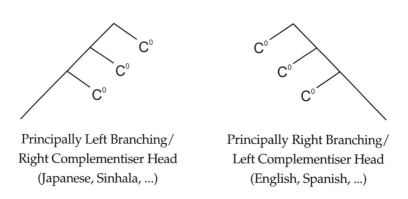

Principally Left Branching/   Principally Right Branching/
Right Complementiser Head   Left Complementiser Head
(Japanese, Sinhala, ...)   (English, Spanish, ...)

Figure 4.3 Principal branching direction configurations

Japanese is head-final	English is head-first
Prepositional phrase	
nihon-*ni*	*in* England
'Japan-in'	
nihon + ni (postposition head final)	*in* (preposition head first) + England
Verb phrase	
watashi-wa nihonjin *desu.* (verb phrase)	I *am* English
I-topic Japanese am	

Wide-ranging early studies on L1 acquisition across languages have found that, from the beginning of early syntax, the child is sensitive to the correct setting for the grammar of his/her L1 on this parameter of phrase structure directionality. In addition, L1 studies found that the child not only sets this parameter very early, but also draws deductive consequences from this parameter setting with respect to an independent factor of anaphora direction as summarised below (e.g. Lust *et al.*, 1996).

Deductive consequences of parameter-setting in the L1

In early child language, direction of anaphora is constrained in accord with the *principal branching direction* (PBD) of the specific language being acquired. If the PBD of the language they are acquiring is 'right', children establish anaphora in a mainly forward direction. If the PBD is 'left', they establish a backward direction of anaphora as unmarked (Lust & Mazuka, 1989: 665-684).

Subject information for the children tested is summarised in Table 4.1.

Table 4.1 Subject information

Children	Age range
L1 English children	3.06-5.07 (Lust, 1981)
L1 Japanese children	3.01-5.11 (Lust *et al.*, 1985; Lust, in preparation)

As shown in Figure 4.4 (next page), children acquiring English exhibit productive control of right-branching structures and treat a forward directionality of anaphora as unmarked. (This and all later figures represent average scores out of 3 sentences.) In contrast the experimental results for Japanese children show productive left-branching structures, and backward anaphora as well as forward (e.g. Lust & Mazuka, 1989; Lust *et al.*, 1996 for Chinese; cf. Lust, in preparation.) The results in Figure 4.4 were obtained through an elicited imitation task in which the child is asked to repeat stimulus sentences such as those illustrated below. As is demanded by this task, all sentences are equated in terms of length and number of syllables. The ability to reconstruct the target utterance productively and accurately provides a measure of a child's developing language specific grammar (Lust *et al.*, 1996).

Example sentences:

English:

(a) *Preposed (left branching)/Backward anaphora*

   While he was outside, John saw a fire truck

(b) *Postposed (right branching)/Forward anaphora*

   Jenna drank some juice while she was having lunch

Japanese:

(c) *Preposed (left branching)/Backward anaphora*

   Ocha-o ireru-to, oniisan-ga akubi-o shita

   (Tea pour when, brother yawn did)

(d) *Postposed (right branching)/Forward anaphora*
   (In Japanese, the configuration may not be actually 'right branching' in
   the same way as English; the general point is that the subordinate clause
   is on the right.)

   Mama-ga kasa-o otoshita-no, doa-o akeru-to

   (Mama umbrella dropped, door open-when)

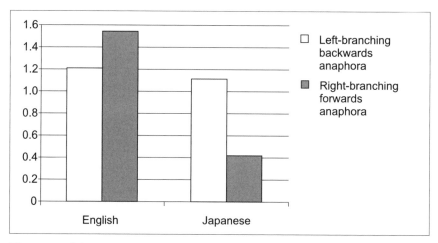

Figure 4.4 Mean correct production of RB and LB constructions by English
and Japanese Children (Correct means verbatim repetition of the target
sentence or no significant structural or semantic change.)

Table 4.2 Background subject information: L2 study (Flynn, 1983, 1987)

Language group			
L1	*Mean age*	*Mean length of ESL*	*Mean period in US*
Spanish (*n*=51)	24 years	6.33 years	0.50 years
Japanese (*n*=53)	30 years	8.50 years	1.25 years

Overall ESL proficiency level placements (University of Michigan test)						
Language group	*Beginning*		*Intermediate*		*Advanced*	
	n	**score**	*n*	**score**	*n*	**score**
Spanish	16	18	21	31	14	42

L2 acquisition

The role of this directionality parameter isolated in L1 acquisition was next investigated in adult L2 acquisition through a design that compared Japanese and Spanish learners' acquisition of ESL. As seen in Figure 4.3, Spanish (right branching) matches English on this parameter; Japanese (left branching) does not match English or Spanish. One hundred and four Japanese and Spanish adult L2 learners of English in matched samples, ranging from beginning to advanced ESL levels as measured by the Michigan Placement Test were empirically investigated. Background subject information for the individuals in these studies is shown in Table 4.2.

The Spanish and Japanese subjects were equated in terms of their ESL abilities both by the results of the Michigan Test and through the use of a covariate for general complex sentence formation in the statistical analyses (see Flynn, 1983, 1987; Flynn & Lust, 1990 for an extended discussion of the covariate factor).

This study evaluated both the adult L2 learners' production through an *elicited imitation* task and their comprehension through an *act-out* task on sentences exemplified in lists 1 and 2 below, using standardised experimental methods. The production sentences involved pre-and post-posing of an adverbial subordinate clause adjunct with respect to the main clause. In addition, they varied in terms of the presence or absence of some form of anaphora.

In sentences like 1(a) and 1(b) below, adjuncts were preposed to the main clause corresponding to left-branching sentence structures. In 1(c), the adjuncts were postposed to the main clause corresponding to right-branching structures. In addition, the stimulus sentences in the 1(ii) and 1(iii) sentences varied not only in terms of the preposing and postposing of the adjuncts, but also with respect to the instantiation of a lexical pronoun as in sentences 1(a)(ii) and 1(c)(ii), and a null pro-form as in sentences 1(a)(iii) and 1(c)(iii).

The sentences that most closely matched unmarked structures in Japanese L1, were LB, not RB. They involved null (not lexical) pronouns, such as 1(a)(iii) below.

1 Examples of stimulus sentences for L2 acquisition study: production

(a) *Preposed (left branching)*

(i) No anaphora

The worker called the owner when the engineer finished the plans.

(ii) Pronoun

When he entered the office, the janitor questioned the man.

(iii) Null

When Ø inspecting the room, the worker questioned the janitor.

(b) *Preposed/forward pronoun*

When the professor opened the package, he answered the man.

(c) *Postposed/(right branching)*

(i) No anaphora

The worker called the man when the engineer finished the plans.

(ii) Pronoun

The man answered the boss, when he installed the television.

(iii) Null

The lawyer questioned the doctor when Ø discussing the results.

The sentences used for the comprehension task are exemplified in list 2. They varied similarly in preposing and postposing of the adjunct to the main clause: preposed in 2(a); postposed in 2(b). These sentences varied additionally, as in production, with respect to the presence of a pronoun as in 2(a)(i) and 2(b)(i) or of a null pro-form as in 2(a)(ii) and 2(b)(i).

2 Examples of stimulus sentences: comprehension

(a) _Preposed_

(i) Pronoun

When _it_ moved up and down, the yellow circle pushed the blue square.

(ii) Null

When Ø turning around, the yellow triangle bumped the blue square.

(b) _Postposed_

(i) Pronoun

The yellow square touched the red triangle when _it_ turned around.

(ii) Null

The blue rectangle shoved the yellow square when Ø turning over.

All stimulus sentences were equalised in syllable length (15 syllables) and approximately in number of words (9–10). In addition, prior to testing, all learners who participated in the studies were given bilingual lists of the lexical items used in the stimulus sentences. Actual testing of the learners did not begin until they had demonstrated 100% comprehension of each lexical item. This was done in order to control for the fact that any differences or difficulties that the learners might have on the test sentences reflected knowledge of syntactic structure relevant to the sentences, and were not due to lexical deficits on the part of the learner.

Results

Previous work has argued, on the basis of our experimental results, that L2 acquisition is also, like L1, constrained by a phrase structure directionality parameter setting (Flynn, 1983, 1987). In that research, as reported in detail elsewhere (e.g. Flynn 1983, 1987; Epstein _et al._, 1996), in spite of the equivalence between the Japanese and Spanish learners as measured by the standardised ESL test and through the use of a covariate factor, dramatic differences were found between the Japanese and Spanish learners both in rate and patterns of acquisition on these experimental tests. Recall that the experimental tests were designed precisely to target parameter-setting effects. The Japanese speakers' L1 parameter setting for left-branching direction did not match English. Results from the L2 research described above showed that the Japanese learners of English evidenced a significantly reduced rate of acquisition in comparison to the Spanish speakers on their production and comprehension of sentences such as those in lists 1 and 2. That result could have been taken to suggest that adult L2 learners cannot reset a parameter or are incapable of accessing new parametric values because the adult is in a qualitatively different state with regard to UG than is a child acquiring an L1. It might even suggest that, consistent with the Maturation model above, the adult Japanese learner had to proceed differently from the child L1 learner in the course of language acquisition. Presumably the L2 learner might have transferred language structures from his/her L1 Japanese onto L2 English without first generating the grammar of English based on UG, the new target language.

When these data are considered more closely in new analyses, particularly developmentally, however, there is no suggestion that the Japanese speaker is transferring hypotheses about parameter values from the L1 to the L2. No evidence at any time indicates that the Japanese speaker does not know that the L2 differs from the L1 on this PBD parameter-value. There is also no evidence that the parameter setting takes extended time to be established.

Recall that both preposed/left-branching sentence structures and postposed/right-branching sentence structures as in 1 and 2 were tested. If Japanese speakers were transferring from the L1, one might predict that they would have an easier time with the preposed sentence structures (evidenced as a higher success rate in both production and comprehension). As discussed above, the preposed sentence structures involve left-branching adjuncts, and they are productively allowed by the phrase structure directionality of Japanese. If transfer from the L1 without consultation of the L2 were the case (i.e. if Japanese speakers had significantly more success on the preposed sentence structures than on the postposed structures) then this would make Japanese L2 acquisition unlike L1 acquisition of English. However, Figure 4.5, which shows Japanese and Spanish speakers' performance on the production of both preposed and postposed sentences without anaphora, illustrates that *overall* the Japanese have a much higher success for the English postposed right-branching structures than for the preposed left-branching sentence structures. Although the Japanese results in Figure 4.5 are depressed relative to the Spanish, they show the same pattern of right branching/left branching as the English L1 children illustrated in Figure 4.4 above. And, when the development Figures 4.6 and 4.7 are considered, results indicate that this pattern is

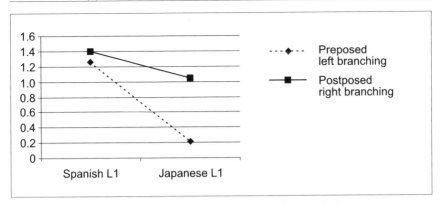

Figure 4.5 Japanese and Spanish acquisition of English L2: Mean correct production of RB and LB English structures

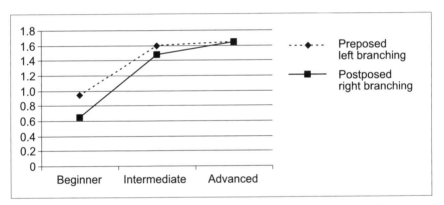

Figure 4.6 Spanish acquisition of English L2: Mean correct production of RB and LB English structures by developmental level

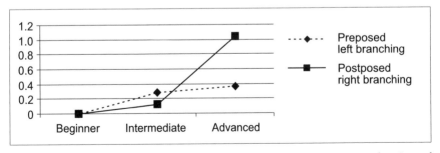

Figure 4.7 Japanese acquisition of English L2: Mean correct production of RB and LB English structures, by developmental level

continuous over L2 development for both the Spanish and the Japanese. At no level do the Japanese significantly prefer the left-branching to the right-branching sentence structures in production.

3 Examples of stimulus sentences:

(a) (RB) *Postposed/no anaphora*

The worker called the owner when the engineer finished the plans.

(b) (LB) *Preposed/no anaphora*

When the gentleman opened the package, the man answered the door.

In addition, the same pattern of results emerges for the Japanese speakers in their production of sentences varied in branching direction and additionally in pronoun anaphora direction. The results illustrated in Figure 4.8 indicate the same primacy for postposed, right-branching sentence structures even when these sentences systematically varied in direction of pronominal anaphora.

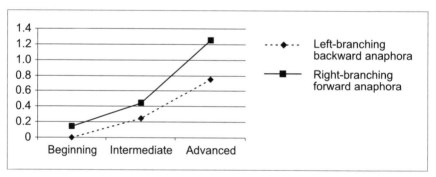

Figure 4.8 Japanese acquisition of English L2: Mean correct production: Preposed/backwards anaphora versus postposed/forwards anaphora by developmental levels

4 Examples of stimulus sentences:

(a) (LB) *Preposed/backward pronoun anaphora:*

When he entered the office, the janitor questioned the man.

(b) (RB) *Postposed/forward pronoun anaphora:*

The professor opened the package when he answered the man.

The results of the comprehension task illustrated in Figure 4.9 for the Japanese speakers on equivalent sentence structures to those tested in production also indicate the primacy of right-branching sentence structures. (Results for the advanced level indicate no significant differences in the speakers' abilities to interpret correctly either right-branching or left-branching sentence structures.) The developmental pattern for new and intermediate Japanese speakers resembled their production results (see Figures 4.6 and 4.8 above). Figure 4.9 indicates that there is no developmental level at which the Japanese learners are superior in their comprehension of preposed sentence structures with backward pronoun anaphora over their comprehension of postposed sentence structures with forward pronoun anaphora. In fact, as the figures show, Japanese L1 speakers are continuously more successful on comprehension of RB structures up to the final level, when these are equivalent.

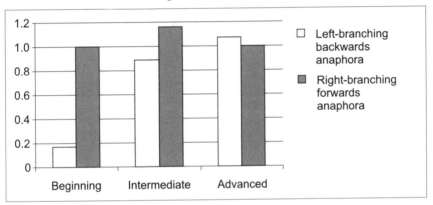

Figure 4.9 Mean correct for comprehension of RB and LB English structures with forward and backward anaphora by developmental level

5 Examples of stimulus sentences: comprehension

(a) (LB) *Preposed/backward pronoun anaphora*:

When *it* moved up and down, the yellow circle pushed the blue square.

(b) (RB) *Postposed/forward pronoun anaphora*:

The yellow square touched the red triangle when *it* turned around.

Returning to the production results, Figures 4.5, 4.7 and 4.8 illustrate the results for the Japanese production of English sentences that varied in preposing and postposing the adjunct. The sentences in list 4 also involved pronoun anaphora that varied systematically (forward and backwards) with the branching direction differences. The results for these sentences indicate that, at every developmental level, the Japanese learners show a preference for postposed (right-branching) sentence structures with forward pronoun anaphora over preposed sentence structures with backward pronoun anaphora. This pattern of results matches that for children learning English as their L1, as discussed above. These data suggest that there may be no period of time at which the Japanese speakers do not know that English as their target L2 is a right-branching language in parameter-setting. The results also suggest that the adult Japanese speaker, like the child, is drawing deductive consequences linking the directionality of phrase structure and anaphora direction in the target language.

Why then is Japanese L1 significantly depressed in performance versus Spanish L1 in these results? To answer this question, we are led to propose that what is often observed and labeled as a 'delay' in L2 acquisition may in fact not lie in problems with setting the value of a parameter, or even in the knowledge that there are deductive consequences that follow from a particular parameter setting. Rather the results might be a consequence of the grammatical 'work' involved in the realisation of deductive consequences in the construction of the target grammar. Such realisation requires the integration of a number of different factors in a specific language grammar. One piece of evidence in support of this speculation lies in the data illustrated in Figure 4.10. In this figure, it can be seen that, in spite of the Japanese speaker being capable of producing and comprehending sentences with forward pronominalisation as seen in the figures above, the most diffi-

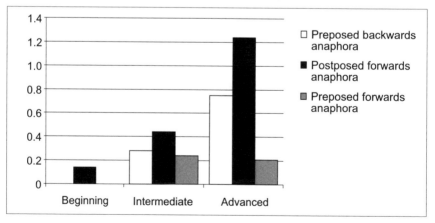

Figure 4.10 Japanese acquisition of English L2: Branching direction vs. anaphora direction: Mean correct in production by developmental level

cult sentence of all for these speakers to produce is a structure that involves a preposed, left-branching sentence structure with forward pronoun anaphora as in 6(a). It is well known that the grammar of Japanese productively allows preposed (left-branching) sentence structures with forward anaphora as exemplified in 6(c). Thus, the severe deficit in the Japanese speakers' production of this particular English sentence structure – preposed with forward anaphora as in 6(a) – seems to demonstrate quite convincingly that the Japanese speakers are not simply transferring grammatical knowledge from their L1 without first consulting the grammar of English, the target L2. The L2 learner, like the L1 learner, is building a system that must link a parameter (in this case a parameter of phrase structure) and its deductive consequences, e.g. in anaphora. If the Japanese speakers were not constructing the grammar of English but simply transferring their L1 grammar, it would be expected that sentences such as that in 6 (a) would be perhaps one of the easiest sentence structures for the Japanese to produce.

6 Examples of stimulus sentences

English

(a) (LB*) Preposed/forward anaphora*:

When the doctor received the results, he called the gentleman.

(b) (RB) *Postposed/forward anaphora*

The professor opened the package when he answered the man.

Japanese:

(c) (LB) *Preposed/forward anaphora:*

Taroo wa nyuusi no keitka o kiita toki Ø hahaoya ni denwa sita.

Taroo-Top entrance exam poss result acc heard when mother dat telephone did.

(When Taroo heard (found out) the result of the entrance exam, (he) called his mother.)

This specific integration of phrase structure directionality and anaphora direction cannot be pre-programmed in UG for a specific language; it must be constructed both for the L1 and the L2. We must thus attribute the delay that is found in the Japanese not to the parameter per se nor to parameter setting, but to the working out of the deductive consequences of such a parameter setting. The discrete principles and parameters of UG must be integrated in accord with a specific language grammar. This may be one example of 'mapping' UG to specific language grammar, necessary to both L2 and L1 acquisition.

Research such as this, along with the work of Martohardjono (1993) and Martohardjono and Gair (1993), allows us to analyse and dissociate specific principles or parameters of UG from language-specific grammars, and to investigate their potential role in adult L2 acquisition. Here the paper has not developed these data in great detail, but has attempted to exemplify the type of evidence, which arises in these domains, in support of our proposal at the beginning of the chapter.

Conclusions

Results such as these lead to the confirmation of our earlier hypothesis that the Strong Continuity model is a valid approximation of the language acquisition process. In addition they lead to a clarification of the definition of the term 'initial state'. These results lead to the recognition that the initial state is not absolute and it is not a temporal state. It does not mean, for example, 'The day that you are born'. It does not mean 'prior to *all* language experience and knowledge'. Rather the term 'initial state' is relative to the experience of a specific language.

Redefining the initial state

The initial state refers to the state of the mind/brain prior to experience with particular data and a particular new acquisition task. This state is 'initial' with regard to a particular acquisition task. To be in the initial state means that one has a set of finite discrete principles and these are available to be brought to bear on any language-specific phenomena to which one is exposed.

On this issue the proposal in this chapter differs critically from a maturation model of L1 acquisition, as well as from such a theory for L2 acquisition. On a maturation theory of language acquisition, it would be impossible for anyone ever to be in an initial state again with respect to language once this individual has acquired an L1. The initial state is viewed as a temporal construct in the maturation formulation. On our view, this application of the initial state is a misnomer.

This chapter does not attempt to explain in detail the real differences between L1 and L2 acquisition, that our research (as well as that of others) reveals, nor does it attempt to deny them. Such differences hold over and above the similarities/commonalties identified here. We have suggested a direction for explanation of these differences between L1 and L2 acquisition, namely in the integration of discrete principles and parameters of UG, which is necessary in the acquisition of specific language grammars. The integration of discrete principles and the *specific language grammars* cannot be biologically pre-programmed; rather the construction of a language specific grammar must lie in 'mapping' from UG to the specific target language being acquired. This paper intends here to underscore the claim that, whatever explains these differences (perhaps including performance systems related to the language faculty, see Chomsky, 1998), it is not differences in access or availability of UG for the L2 learner. Thus, it is hoped that the paper has clarified the pursuit of explanation of such differences as may exist. For example, evidence has been shown that, even while parameter-setting *does* have significant effects on L2 acquisition, it is *not* the case that parameter-setting takes extended time, that is to say more time than initial parameter-setting in L1 acquisition. The *setting* itself appears to be as quick and efficient in L2 acquisition as it is in L1 acquisition. It is this which is given by UG. In this paper, we also hope to have demonstrated how a principles and parameters approach to language acquisition has been instrumental in elucidating our understanding of both the L1 and L2 acquisition processes. Continued research meticulously comparing L1 and L2 acquisition promises further refinement and development of this approach to explanation of L2 acquisition, or L1.

Revisions in the Theory of UG: Minimalism[2]

The question that the *grammatical mapping* paradigm proposed here to account for the UG paradox raises is as follows: current revisions in linguistic theory, e.g. Chomsky (1995), in proposing a Minimalist Program, argue that 'The notion of grammatical construction is eliminated, and with it, construction-particular rules' (Chomsky, 1995: 170). Indeed, the status of 'specific language grammars' has been called into question. Can a *grammatical mapping* paradigm be maintained in the face of this current theory? It is suggested that current revisions in linguistic theory are quite closely compatible with the new approach to language acquisition, which is developed here. In fact, the two converge. For example, in this revised 'Minimalist' theory it is proposed that '... languages are based on simple principles that interact to form often intricate structures ... the language faculty is non-redundant, in that particular phenomena are not "overdetermined" by the principles of language ...' (Chomsky, 1993: 2; cf. Epstein *et al.*, 1996: 4). We suggest that this minimal postulation of autonomous, non-redundant principles provides the basis for the *grammatical mapping* that the learner must accomplish: i.e. the mapping consists of the integration of these UG principles in just the manner required by the language-specific grammar to be acquired. The integration of these principles in a specific language grammar is not given by the minimalist UG, just as the constructions themselves are not.

Within the emerging Minimalist Program, there now exist perhaps the clearest explicit proposals regarding what may well be considered the most fundamental and counter-intuitive assumption made within the generative framework, namely that there is only one human linguistic system, an apparently unique species-specific biological endowment. Within the subcomponent of the human language faculty called 'syntax' (or more recently, the 'computational component of the human language faculty'), Chomsky (1995) proposes quite explicit analyses within which cross-linguistic syntactic phenomena are unified, i.e. reduced to a single syntactic component, namely *'the'* human syntactic component. (For reviews, see Freidin, 1997; Abraham *et al.*, 1996.)

The central hypothesis that there is, in fundamental respects, only one human language, is however confronted with certain recalcitrant phenomena – namely, what is called 'crosslinguistic variation'. That is, human languages are apparently not totally identical to one another, although explicit linguistic inquiry has revealed, surprisingly, just how similar to one another different human languages are. The question that confronts us then, is: 'In what respects do/can human linguistic systems differ?' Chomsky advances the following hypothesis:

> The standard idealised model of language acquisition takes the initial state S_0 to be a function mapping experience (primary linguistic data, primary language data) to knowledge of a language. UG is concerned with the invariant principles of S_0 and the range of permissible variation. Variation must be determined by what is 'visible' to the child acquiring language, that is, by the primary language data. It is not surprising then, to find a degree of variation in the PF component, and in aspects of the lexicon: Saussurean arbitrariness (association of concepts with phonological matrices), properties of grammatical formatives (inflection etc.), and readily detectable properties that hold of lexical items generally. Variation in the overt syntax or LF [logical form] component would be more problematic, since evidence could only be quite indirect. A narrow conjecture is that there is no such variation: beyond PF [phonetic form] options and lexical arbitrariness...variation is limited to nonsubstantive parts of the lexicon and general properties of

lexical items. If so, there is only one computational system and one lexicon, apart from this limited kind of variety. (Chomsky, 1993)

Importantly, notice that the above perspective construes word-order phenomena as a matter of Phonological Form (PF) variability, not pure syntax. Thus, word order is hypothesised to vary (in limited ways) crosslinguistically, and this variation is variation in PF interpretation of hierarchical, but not phono-temporally ordered, invariant syntactic representations. This phono-temporal PF ordering might be implemented by a head parameter or along the lines presented in Kayne (1994)[3].

Turning now to the applicability of this Minimalist approach to L2 language acquisition, Epstein *et al.* (1997) have suggested that UG constrains L2 acquisition, just as it does L1 acquisition. Importantly, the attribution of UG to a learner does NOT entail that the learner will develop linguistically in a fashion identical to an L1 learner placed in a normal linguistic environment. To take an extreme but illustrative example, there is every reason to believe that a child born deaf, being human, has the cognitive linguistic capacities of a hearing child – i.e. the deaf child also has UG, the aforementioned function mapping primary language data into knowledge of language. Nonetheless, even though equipped with UG, the deaf child, if placed in the environment of a spoken language, will not develop linguistically in a fashion identical to the hearing child, even though both have UG. Language acquisition, including L2 acquisition, thus depends on more than just UG. By hypothesis, then, UG is necessary, but not sufficient for the acquisition of human language. The hypothesis that UG constrains adult L2 acquisition therefore does *not* entail that adult L2 acquisition will be developmentally identical in all respects to child L1 acquisition. Conversely, the 'mere' attribution of UG to adult L2 learners also does NOT preclude non-identical development between child L1 and adult L2 acquisition, as will be discussed below.

Interestingly, Chomsky (1996: 24) also suggests (in passing) that UG constrains L2 acquisition as well, as we suggested in our introduction above: '… someone studying English as a second language would only be confused by instruction about the real principles of grammar, these they already know, being human'.

One of the results we present here is that , in determining order in the target grammar, adult learners of an L2 language do not encounter difficulty that is detectably different from a child difficulty in L1. Such experimental results can be readily explained by attributing UG – i.e. human knowledge of language – to an adult L2 language learner. Developmental similarities between the child L1 and the adult L2 could be explained as follows. Both types of acquirers are human, and as such they are both endowed with UG, a species-specific function that takes primary language data as input and yields knowledge of language as output. Although directionality facts are not identical in all languages, human language learners (both L1 and L2) can acquire any such systems (unlike any other known organisms/objects in the universe). This is because of an interaction between the input, which reveals directionality 'visible' to the human acquirer, and UG, which maps the acoustic signal to knowledge of 'words' (phono-semantic pairs), to knowledge of words-in-order, to more general linguistic laws regarding ordering, accounting for the well-known 'creative aspect of language' – such laws/knowledge being radically distinct from the acoustic primary linguistic input that gave rise to them.

By attributing UG to adult L2 learning, and by positing no linguistically relevant (UG-based) developmental distinctions between adult L2 learners and child L1 learners with regard to the acquisition of knowledge of structural order, the experimental results described above are explained. If indeed the experimental results indicate no difference between the child L1 learner and the adult L2 learner with respect to the acquisition of directionality knowledge, then it would be unreasonable to posit differences between the child L1 learner and the adult L2 learner with regard to UG involved in the acquisition of knowledge of directionality. Of course, apparent identity between child L1 learning and adult L2 learning with respect to *this* aspect of acquisition as suggested in *these* particular experiments, does not warrant the firm conclusion that the adult L2 learner and child L1 learner are identical in all relevant linguistic respects. Rather, to the extent that differences are *not* indicated, we maintain the null hypothesis that the two are in relevant respects non-distinct with respect to the language faculty.

Notes

1. Some current approaches to 'maturation theory' in L1 acquisition propose that it is 'constructs' that develop and change, not 'principles' of UG (e.g. Borer & Wexler, 1987). However, if 'constructs' refer to specific language constructions, these have no direct theoretical status (in a current minimalist theory of UG) and this revision of the proposal in the Maturation model would make it equivalent to the Strong Continuity model.
2. It is important to note that the Minimalist Program is *not* a theory of language; rather, it is a program that seeks to consider some new questions about the language faculty. In this context, the Minimalist Program 'seeks to discover to what extent minimal conditions of adequacy suffice to determine the nature of the right theory [of language]' (Chomsky, 1998: 5). The minimalist program assumes two levels of representation – phonetic form and logical form. Logical

form interfaces with the intentional-conceptual cognitive systems that are involved in the interpretation of sentences. Phonetic form interfaces with the articulatory-perceptual systems that are responsible for the production of an utterance. More details can be found in Van Valin (2001: 204).

3. Current minimalist theory suggests directionality differences may not be represented by a phrase structure parameter (e.g. Chomsky, 1995; Kayne, 1994, 2000). We return to this issue in our final section. This variation in representation would not change the arguments in this chapter, as some formal cross-linguistic difference must be captured in this area (directional differences), if not by a phrase structure parameter, then by some other form of principled grammatical difference (cf. Lust, in preparation).

References

Abraham, W., Epstein, S.D., Thrainsson, H. and Zwart, J.W. (1996) Introduction. In W. Abraham, S.D. Epstein, H. Thrainsson and J.W. Zwart (eds) *Minimal Ideas: Syntactic Studies in the Minimalist Framework*. Philadelphia: Benjamins.

Borer, H. and Wexler, K. (1987) The maturation of syntax. In T. Roeper and E. Williams (eds) *Parameter Setting* (123–72). Dordrecht: Reidel.

Boser, K., Santelmann, L., Barbier, L. and Lust, B. (1995) Grammatical mapping from UG to language specific grammars: Deriving variation in the acquisition of German, Dutch and Swedish. In D. McLaughlin and S. McEwen (eds) *Proceedings of 1994 19th Annual Boston University Conference on Language Development* (pp. 30–142). Boston: Cascadilla Press.

Chomsky, N. (1965) *Aspects of the Theory of Syntax*. Cambridge, MA: MIT Press.

Chomsky, N. (1988) *Language and Problems of Knowledge*. Cambridge, MA: MIT Press.

Chomsky, N. (1991) Linguistics and cognitive science: Problems and mysteries. In A. Kasher (ed.) *The Chomskyan Turn*. Oxford: Blackwell.

Chomsky, N. (1993) A minimalist program for linguistic theory. In K. Hale and J. Keyser (eds) *The View from Building 20*. Cambridge, MA: MIT Press.

Chomsky, N. (1995) *The Minimalist Program*. Cambridge, MA: MIT Press.

Chomsky, N. (1996) *Powers and Prospects*. Boston, MA: South End Press.

Chomsky, N. (1998) Minimalist inquiries: The framework. *MIT Working Papers in Linguistics*. Cambridge, MA: MIT Press.

Cook, V. (1973) The comparison of language development in native children and foreign adults. *International Review of Applied Linguistics* 11, 13–28.

Epstein, S., Flynn, S. and Martohardjono, G. (1996) Second language acquisition: Theoretical and experimental issues in contemporary research. *Brain and Behavior Sciences* 19, 677–758.

Epstein, S., Flynn, S. and Martohardjono, G. (1998). The strong continuity hypothesis: Some evidence concerning functional categories in adult L2 acquisition. In S. Flynn, G. Martohardjono and W. O'Neil (eds) *The Generative Study of Second Language Acquisition*, Mahwah, NJ: Erlbaum.

Flynn, S. (1983) A study of the effects of principal branching direction in second language acquisition: The generalisation of a parameter of Universal Grammar from first to second language acquisition. PhD thesis, Cornell University.

Flynn, S. (1987) *A Parameter Setting Model of L2 Acquisition*. Dordrecht: Reidel.

Flynn, S. and Lust, B. (1990) A note in defense of parameter setting in L2 acquisition. *Language Learning* 40, 4119–449.
Freidin, R. (1997) Review of Chomsky 'The Minimalist Program'. *Language* 73 (3), 571–583.
Kayne, R. (1994) *The Antisymmetry of Syntax*. Cambridge, MA: MIT Press.
Kayne, R. (2000) *Parameters and Universals*. Oxford: Oxford University Press.
Lust, B. (1981) Constraint on anaphora in child language. In S. Tavakolian (ed.) *Language Acquisition and Linguistic Theory*. Cambridge, MA: MIT Press.
Lust, B. (1999) Universal Grammar: The Strong Continuity Hypothesis. In Bhatia, T. and W. Ritchie (eds) *Handbook of First Language Acquisition*. New York: Academic Press.
Lust, B. (in preparation) *Universal Grammar and the Initial State: Crosslinguistic Studies of Directionality*. MIT Press/Bradford Books.
Lust, B. and Chien, Y-C. (1984) The structure of coordination in first language acquisition of Mandarin Chinese: Evidence for a universal. *Cognition* 17, 49–83.
Lust, B., Chien, Y-C., Chiang, C-P. and Eisele, J. (1996) Chinese pronominals in UG. *Journal of East Asian Linguistics* 5, 1–47.
Lust, B., Flynn, S. and Foley, C. (1996) What children know about what they say: Elicited imitation as a research method. In D. McDonald, C. McKee and H. Cairns (eds) *Methods for Assessing Children's Syntax* (pp. 55–76). Cambridge, MA: MIT Press.
Lust, B. and Mazuka, R. (1989) Crosslinguistic studies of directionality in first language acquisition: The Japanese data, a response to O'Grady, Suzuki-wei and Cho 1986. *Journal of Child Language* 16, 665–684.
Lust, B., Wakayama, T. Snyder, W., Otani, K., Mazuka, R. and Oshima, S. (1985) Configurational factors in Japanese anaphora: Evidence from acquisition. Paper presented at the LSA Annual Meeting.
Martohardjono, G. (1993) Wh-movement in the acquisition of a second language: A cross-linguistic study of three languages with and without movement. PhD thesis, Cornell University.
Martohardjono, G. and Gair, J. (1993) Misapplied principles or principles misapplied? In F. Eckman (ed.) *Confluence: Linguistics, L2 Acquisition, Speech Pathology*. Amsterdam: John Benjamins.
Mazuka, R. (1996) Parameter setting before the first word. In J.L. Morgan and D. Demuth (eds) *From Signal to Syntax: An Overview*. Mahwah, NJ: Laurence Erlbaum.
Van Valin, R. (2001) *An Introduction to Syntax*. Cambridge: Cambridge University Press.

Introduction to Chapter 5
Development of L2 Functional Use, Clive Perdue

VIVIAN COOK

One of the best demonstrations of the independence of the L2 user from native speaker norms comes from the ESF (European Science Foundation) project on which this chapter draws. The aim of the ESF project was to see 'whether a learner variety is based on recognisable organisational principles, how these principles interact, and whether they also apply to fully-fledged languages' (Klein & Perdue 1992: 1).

SLA research in 1970s tried to show that L2 learners of English from different backgrounds shared common orders of acquisition and difficulty. Similar sequences for English grammatical morphemes were found among Spanish and Chinese children in the USA (Dulay & Burt 1974), among Japanese children in Japan (Makino, 1993), among Bengali children in London (Hannan, in progress), and many others. Much of this, however, concerned only the acquisition of English, which has its own peculiarities in terms of function words and grammatical inflections. The results were not necessarily true of the acquisition of all second languages, particularly those without inflectional morphology, such as Chinese; more crucially there was no real explanation for these sequences except as being a 'natural order'. The Multidimensional model, later called Processability Theory, postulated a universal sequence of stages that would be true for all L2 users by virtue of their common cognitive processes, starting with learners of German (Meisel *et al.*, 1981) and gradually expanding to include English and other languages (Pienemann, 1998). The ESF project similarly assumed that L2 learners 'organise their utterances and texts according to elementary principles of their human language capacity' (Klein & Perdue, 1997: 343), but interpreted these in accordance with the communication of meaning in discourse. Hence much of its work is concerned with what can be called grammatical meaning – the expression of time and tense, of relative importance of elements, etc. – thus linking more to the European linguistic tradition than to American structuralism.

A major virtue of the ESF project is the extension of the range of L1 and L2s within the same research project. The research is no longer only about the acquisition of L2 English by speakers of different L1s, but is based on six L1s and five L2s, making 10 pairs of L1 and L2, as given below. The surprising fact to emerge was not just additional information about the acquisition of five L2s, but a common pattern across the ten pairings: adult L2 learners have the same grammar regardless of which language they are acquiring and which language they speak as native speakers. The discovery of this 'basic variety' of L2 user language was then the solid support for a universal process of L2 acquisition, with the caveat that the L2s in the study were historically related, though the L1s were not. It is not just that L2 users are different from monolingual speakers because they are relating two specific languages; they devise grammars that are similar to each other regardless of the language involved but different from those of monolinguals.

References

Dulay, H. and Burt, M. (1974) Natural sequences in child second language acquisition. *Language Learning* 24, 37–53.

Hannan, M. (in progress) Morphological acquisition of English by Bengali speaking children in Tower Hamlets. PhD thesis, University of Essex.

Klein, W. and Perdue, C. (1997) The basic variety. Or: Couldn't natural languages be much simpler? *Second Language Research* 13 (4), 301–347.

Makino, T. (1993) *Perspectives on Second Language Acquisition*. Tokyo: Yumi Press.

Meisel, J., Clahsen, H. and Pienemann, M. (1981) On determining developmental stages in natural second language acquisition. *Studies in Second Language Acquisition* 3 (2), 109–135.

Pienemann, M. (1998) *Language Processing and Second-Language Development: Processability Theory*. Amsterdam: John Benjamins.

Chapter 5

Development of L2 Functional Use

CLIVE PERDUE

1 Introduction: 'Degenerate Language'?

It is not always immediately obvious to the friendly inquirer why it is that *untutored, second* language acquisition should be more interesting than the *tutored* kind, where results can at least be applied to teaching, or *first* language acquisition, where at least you are guaranteed that the learner succeeds in his or her task. Why look at almost incomprehensible strings of seemingly unrelated words produced by the struggling learner when you could be looking at well-formed sentences? My aim in this chapter is to provide a modest answer to such a question by looking at L2 use, and the answer is simply that the verbalisations of such learners are interesting because you can gain insights from them into the way grammars are organised.

Such grammars may even provide clues as to what all grammars, considered as instantiations of the human language capacity, may share. I believe this, but such a claim takes us too far afield for present purposes. I will merely attempt to show that even the most basic user of a second language produces utterances that are recurrent, highly structured, and not to be explained by a direct appeal to the grammar of the first language (L1) nor to that of the language being learned/used (the L2). The word 'direct' in the last sentence is important. Obviously I do not wish to imply that the L1 grammar, or the L2 input, do not influence the organisation of the learner's variety. They do, but other factors can – will – be shown to mediate in the way the learner's variety is organised. Thus any attempt to explain the organisation of the learner's variety at a given time, or over time, which appeals only to L1 and L2 factors is inadequate.

The reader will have noticed that in this introduction I have referred only to the learner's *production*, and I will stick with this restriction. The chapter will also look only at a very small part of the linguistic phenomena relevant to the L2 user/acquirer, namely the way in which utterances are structured and temporal relations expressed. I therefore have nothing in particular to say about phonology, nor the lexicon.

2 The Functional Approach

Functionally oriented linguistics traditionally holds that language is an instrument for human communication that can best be understood by an analysis of the interaction of its various levels of organisation – phonology, (morpho-)syntax, semantics – and its contexts of use. Leaving phonology aside, this description immediately implies that the grammar of a language involves two types of computation.

The first type deals with the well-formedness conditions on sentences: how minimal meaningful units are combined into larger lexical items and how these items combine to form larger constituents up to the level of the sentence ('sentence grammar'). Such rules describe, for example, the sentence category 'subject': 'the finite verb agrees in person and number with the subject' or, in a more modern variant, 'nominative case is licensed by AGR'. They also give distributional restrictions such as the following: 'a matrix sentence may contain only one finite verb'.

The second type deals with the conditions under which a sentence may be actualised as an utterance in the situational (or discourse) context. Amongst other things, the contextual information is specified which provides a referential value to the lexical meanings of deictic and anaphoric expressions. Such rules describe, for example, the discourse category 'topic': 'the topic of an utterance is identifiable for speaker and hearer, and is the entity about whom/which the speaker intends to increase the hearer's knowledge'. They also specify the temporal or aspectual value of the finite verb in context, as we shall see in section 4.2. This is what Klein (1994) calls 'structure-based context dependency', and what I will term the 'context relating' or 'anchoring' rules.

For the acquisitionist working in a functionalist perspective, this double computation involves seeking to explain how a learner comes to master both sentence-level and discourse-level organisational principles. In production it involves understanding the 'learner's problem of arranging words' (Klein & Perdue, 1989), i.e. the task of arranging the items of L2 vocabulary the learner has available at any given moment of the acquisition process into meaningful utterances, in context. From this starting point, it is clear that (at least) two bundles of factors are appealed to in an attempt to explain the acquisition process: the communicative and the formal.

Communicative factors

Communicative factors obviously push the learner to develop an L2 vocabulary. The individual lexical items may vary considerably from learner to learner in view of their personal circumstances, but the structure of the lexicon over time may show striking commonalities (see Klein & Perdue, 1997, and the references there).

Communicative factors also intervene in the expression of recurrent relational meanings between items of vocabulary that languages grammaticalise to a greater or lesser extent – for brevity I will call these '(grammatical) functions' – relations such as assertion and temporal anchoring. The way learners manage the temporal anchoring of their utterances is described in 4.2. Assertion is linked to temporal anchoring, as it is carried by the finite verb in English (cf. the difference between the assertion 'John *came* to the party', and the infinitive 'for John *to come* to the party'). Such functions are numerous (but not unlimited), and the ones I have mentioned involve the interaction of sentence grammar and context-relating rules. There is little reason to assume that they are all equally important for the learner when communicating. The relative communicative importance of expressing such functions is thus held to be a determining factor for acquisition. This problem was called 'ranking of functions' in Perdue (1984).

There is a third aspect to such communicative factors. If a speaker wishes to express a complex amount of information, then he or she is faced with what Levelt (1981) called the 'linearisation problem', that of arranging the information for production in temporal order, between utterances and within each utterance. For example, when Linde and Labov (1975) asked speakers to describe their apartments, these speakers had both to decide *which* features of the apartment to mention and the *order in which* these features should be mentioned. The latter problem represented their linearisation problem, which follows from the fact that spoken language is linear: one can produce only one bit of information at a time. Some of the principles underlying the speaker's linearisation of information will be discussed in more detail in section 3.

Formal factors

Languages develop devices to express grammatical functions to different degrees of specification - one speaks for example of 'aspect-prominent languages' as opposed to 'tense-prominent languages'. For instance, German is said to have no grammatical aspect; English has both (present and past) tense and aspect (it grammaticalises the progressive and the perfect), whereas Chinese has no tense, but a small set of aspectual particles. Different languages therefore give different formal priorities to functions that are nevertheless shared (temporal reference is accomplished in aspect-prominent languages, and vice versa). The learner who by virtue of his L1 competence understands how to apply these functions has to find some means of expressing them in the L2. (This problem was called 'alternatives of expression' in Perdue (1984). One may wonder, for example, how a learner of L2 English manages to express assertion before mastering the finite verb.) It is therefore necessary to understand which are the linguistic means used at first, and how the means used for expressing a particular function change – and possibly complexify – over time. Note that the grammatical organisation of the L1, or characteristics of the L2 input, individually or in tandem, may make certain linguistic means highly salient, and others less so.

All these considerations are reflected in the methodology adopted in functional investigations. For example, the learners whose production provides the examples discussed in section 4 were first studied in the European Science Foundation's project on second language acquisition by adult immigrants (Perdue, 1993), which adopted a resolutely functional approach. The project was longitudinal, cross-linguistic, and it dealt only with second language acquisition outside the classroom. The results were based on the productions of 40 adult learners of Dutch, English, French, German and Swedish (or a sub-set of these). All were recently arrived immigrants with legal status, and in daily contact with the language of their new social environment. They were observed and recorded over a period of about 30 months. In order to control systematically for L1 and L2 effects, languages were organised as shown in Figure 5.1.

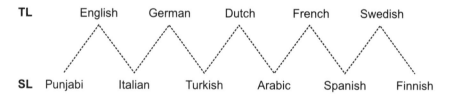

TL   English   German   Dutch   French   Swedish

SL Punjabi   Italian   Turkish   Arabic   Spanish   Finnish

Figure 5.1 The source language (L1) and target language (L2 or TL) combination

Various techniques of data collection were used; they were ordered into three data-collection cycles, such that all learners performed each task at least three times. The examples reported on below come from spontaneous conversation, but more often from complex verbal tasks (see section 3), that is, tasks that take many utterances to accomplish them, and where in principle one single speaker builds a coherent discourse. The tasks the examples come from are apartment descriptions as in the study by Linde and Labov (1975), picture descriptions, route descriptions, stage directions, retellings and personal narratives taken from linguistic interviews. Their coherence can be found in the way in which temporal and spatial information, and reference to different entities, is organised. In particular, they have a definable main structure; utterances of this main structure predictably apportion information between what are often called their topic component and their focus component. In these more constrained tasks, the methodological aim was to obtain stretches of connected texts of different types, with the linguistic context and extra-linguistic checks – the film to be retold, the picture to be described – favouring in-depth contextual interpretation of learners' utterances.

The longitudinal perspective is a central part of functional acquisitionist methodology. The analyst attempts to retrace over time how the learner succeeds, or does not succeed, in the communicative task he or she is engaged in, and this reconstruction allows one to identify what the learning problem was at any given moment during the acquisition process. The acquisitionist therefore looks first at the way the learner's linguistic repertoire is organised at a given moment, then at the way this repertoire is put to use in particular communicative tasks, and how the repertoire changes over time in respect to the same tasks. Acquisition and use – or rather, use and acquisition – are therefore not dissociated. The object of investigation is the L2 learner/user.

To recapitulate this section, the functional approach recognises both formal and communicative factors as determining the acquisition process. The cognitive and linguistic pre-disposition of the adult learner interacts with the formal characteristics of the L2 input in shaping the acquisition process, but this is not all: a second bundle of factors – communicative factors – also intervenes in pushing the learner to acquire the L2.

3 What an Adult Learner Can Initially Rely On

The functional approach thus attaches great relevance to the fact that the L2 learner is required to use the language in order to acquire it, and this poses the problem of what initially is useful knowledge. What does the adult absolute beginner bring to the learning task?

I assume that the beginner brings an articulatory and perceptual system in good working order and, with it, the ability to segment the speech stream and assign meaning to the segments. Apart from that, I suggest that this useful knowledge consists of an at least partial familiarity with the cognitive categories that universally receive grammatical expression in languages (the 'grammatical functions' described above), and also a knowledge of how information is organised in different types of discourse. That is all that can be generally assumed.

I also mentioned in section 1 that typological distance, or better, the perceived typological distance of the L2 from the L1 (Kellerman, 1977), may give some learners a head start. (We found in the ESF project, that the typological proximity of Spanish and French allowed the Hispanic learners to use relatively very early such closed-class items as the definite and indefinite articles and an array of prepositions. Such use was not observed in the Hispanic learners of the typologically more distant Swedish.) But this is not to answer the question of what is generally available.

Information organisation

Levelt (1981, and many other publications) has written at length about the speaker's linearisation problem of arranging the informational content to be expressed in temporal order. Utterances have to be placed in temporal order with respect to one another. These choices are in principle[1] part of the conceptualisation process: 'one should carefully distinguish between the selection of information to be expressed, the ordering of this information for expression, and the linguistic formulation of the information' (Levelt, 1981: 306). Levelt distinguishes between knowledge-based principles and process-related principles. The former are variants of the principle of *natural order*: order of mention reflects order of events, causes precede effects, source precedes goal, etc. The latter are variants of the principle of maximal connectivity: linearisation strategies to minimise the size and duration of memory load. In Levelt's classic experiment (Levelt, 1981), speakers had to describe arrays of differently coloured dots joined by straight lines. From certain dots there was a choice to be made as two lines branched in different directions, and both branches had to be described. Results showed clearly that speakers follow a connected path through the array, memorising the branching nodes. After describing one branch, they return to the most recent choice node to describe the other branch(es). This was done in such a way that the simplest branches (representing the least choices) were described first. This linearisation strategy was shown by Levelt to minimise memory load: it is fast and effective.

To the extent that both types of linearisation strategy intervene in the efficient retrieval of information on the part of the speaker, they may be seen as independent of particular cultures and languages[2]: *culture-neutral*. Stutterheim applies these considerations to the temporal organisation of texts:

> Specific text types imply a particular temporal organisation. These principles can be treated as *knowledge shared by speaker and hearer across languages*. Once the discourse type has been established, the hearer can draw inferences about the temporal relations between the reported 'events' if no explicit information is given. (Stutterheim, 1991: 399, emphasis added)

Such discourse-organisational strategies are generally available to the L2 learner right from the beginning. They are automated processes with no learning involved and, in principle, are fully transferable.

Are there similar principles that play a role within the utterance? I suggest that the learner who has managed to construct a small vocabulary (fifty words will do, see Dorriots, 1986) uses computational means which are usually *language-neutral,* to use Kellerman's (1977) term. The assumption is again that the computational means used reflect as closely as possible the temporal and/or topological organisation of the informational content to be expressed. The challenge then is to determine as precisely as possible what these principles are.

Here again, we may distinguish between knowledge-based and process-related principles.

In the results summarised in section 4.1, some L2 work was done (by Wolfgang Klein more than anyone; e.g. Klein, 1984) on the time-argument structure of predicates. Verbs have an argument structure, which imposes various constraints on the (type of) noun phrases that can, or must, go with the verb. Verbs also have an 'event structure': in traditional terms, they represent states, activities, achievements and accomplishments, that is, they possess intrinsic temporal characteristics. The idea is that the L2 learner-user may appeal to his or her knowledge of the temporal structure of the event in order to arrange the arguments around the corresponding verb. For example, for verbs denoting events that have dynamic temporal characteristics, the iconic way of portraying the event is to start at its beginning and finish at its end – the principle of natural order within the utterance, so to speak.

For process-related principles, Slobin's (1973) operating principles were a first step in this direction, and were usefully built on in L2 work by members of the ZISA group (e.g. Clahsen, 1984).

The idea of 'language neutral' should be clearly distinguished from the idea that a particular language has a basic word order. It should rather be the case that principles alluded to in the two previous paragraphs result in a set of phrasal patterns, each of which 'fits' a given informational context. We may illustrate this by a major finding from the ESF project (Klein and Perdue, 1997). We noted that, after some time, all 40 learners investigated developed a relatively stable system to express themselves which:

- seemed to be determined by the interaction of a small number of organisational principles;
- was largely (though not totally) independent of the specifics of source and target language organisation;

- was simple, versatile, and highly efficient for most communicative purposes.

This system we called the *basic variety*. For about one third of the learners investigated, acquisition ended on this structural level; some minor variation aside, they only increased their lexical repertoire and learned to make more fluent use of the basic variety. More specifically, it was found that learners of all the L2s, and with very different L1 backgrounds, regularly develop three main phrasal patterns, as follows (the numbering of the NPs corresponds to possible differences in their internal structure, described below):

(A) $NP_1 - V - (NP_2)(NP_2)$
(B) $NP_1 - Cop - NP_2/Adj/PP$
(C) $(Adv/PP) - V/Cop - NP_2$

The verbs in these patterns are uninflected. (More precisely, produced in a base form, or a form resembling the TL's infinitive or participle forms (as in Table 5.2). There are however no morphological *oppositions*. There is no functional verbal morphology, and indeed no productive morphology at all at this stage, therefore no tense, aspect, agreement, case, number, gender-marking. The range of closed-class items at this stage is moreover very small: one observes a few quantifiers, a word for negation, some overgeneralised prepositions and a rudimentary pronoun system comprising means to refer to speaker, hearer and a third person (functioning deictically and anaphorically). The range of possible NP structures varies with NP position in the pattern. In particular, NP_1 has a greater range of possibilities than the other positions. The most general structures are the following:

NP_1	NP_2
proper name	proper name
(det) noun	(det) noun
(strong) pronoun	Ø

This means that reference maintenance in connected text by pronominal means, or zero anaphor, is only possible in NP_1 position.

This system is simple and efficient, but clearly has severe expressive restrictions in relation to a fully-fledged language system. On the other hand, the form-function fit of the patterns in discourse emerges particularly clearly. In narrative texts, pattern A is used to encode main-structure (plot-line) events (Table 5.2), whereas pattern C with a lexical verb signals referential discontinuities in the plot-line (Table 5.3), and its copula variant, together with pattern B, is used for background information (Table 5.4).

(The following examples follow the ESF transcription conventions of giving the L1 first and indicating a silent pause by +; broad phonetic transcription is enclosed in square brackets [ ], that is to say sound sequences where orthography would impose an a priori analysis on the data; for more information see Perdue (1993)).

Table 5.2 Punjabi/English: Madan (retelling the bread-stealing scene from Chaplin's _Modern Times_) _Pattern A_

NP_1	V	NP_2	NP_2
girl	stealing	one shop	
one woman	coming back		
(after) woman	telling	shop gaffer	girl stealing
gaffer	telephoning	police	
police	coming		

Table 5.3 Italian/English: Andrea (retelling: _then the fire brigade arrived_) _Pattern C_

Adv	V	NP_2
after	come back	the brigade fire

Table 5.4 Italian/English: Santo (retelling: meta-discursive comment) _Pattern B_

PP	Cop	NP_2
in that moment	is	complication story

Table 5.5 Italian/English: Santo (picture description: _there's a chimney on the roof_)

PP	Cop	NP_2
over this house	have	the *camino*

In descriptive texts on the other hand, B and the copula variant of C supply the main structure, and A in this case provides background information. It is the fact that these form-function correspondences are indeed valid over the range of L1–L2 pairs analysed that motivates their being termed language neutral. (A crosslinguistic methodology thus represents for our purposes, a way of operationalising 'language neutral'. One observes what is attested in all learner languages vs. only some SL–TL pairings.)

Klein & Perdue (1992) found that there exists a stage of utterance organisation even before verb-argument structure comes into play, a so-called 'nominal utterance organisation' (NUO), which then develops into an organisation centred around the non-finite verb, i.e. the basic variety. Mastering verb-argument structure is in fact a major acquisitional task, but it then allows the learner to make use of the different types of valency which comes with the (non-finite) verb along dimensions such as agentivity, and the assigning of positions according to this ranking, as we shall see in 4.1 below. There is however no distinction made at this level between the finite and non-finite component of the verb, which is, of course, of fundamental importance in the Germanic and Romance TLs studied.

In NUO, utterances are very simple, consisting mainly of two (sometimes three) constituents formed by words corresponding to TL nouns, adverbs, particles, adjectives and participles. NUO lacks the structuring power of verbs, and could well be called 'pre-verbal utterance organisation'. Yet, a few recurrent semantic relations are nevertheless attested, one of which is directly relevant for section 4, namely, theme/relatum relationships.

'Theme' and 'relatum' are analytic notions for the referential domains of space and time. In both cases, a *theme* – entity or event – is related to some *relatum*, a space or time span (which can be filled by some entity or event). This is possible because both theme and relatum occupy a place in a referential domain – space or time – that is, in a structure characterised by a set of relations. 'Theme' and 'relatum' are used to capture this spatio-temporal correspondence. The spatial relation is termed the 'figure–ground' relation by Talmy (1985), and the temporal relation that between 'reference time' and 'event time' by Reichenbach (1947).

The following NUO examples are to be understood in a static context:

1 (a) Spanish/French: Gloria

   aujourd'hui ici + quatre familles

   (today here + four families)

   (b) Arabic/French: Abdel

   après + avec le police

   (after + with (= there was) the policeman)

   (c) Arabic/French: Zahra

   lifille + lisalledebains

   (the girl + the bathroom)

In 1(a) and (b) we have a case of referent introduction. In (a) the theme *quatre familles* is related to a deictic, spatio-temporal relatum; in (b) *police* is related to an anaphoric temporal relatum. In (c) the entity *girl* is mutually known, and localised: (c) answers a question such as *where is the girl?*

The following examples are to be understood in a dynamic context, answering a question such as *where is the man/woman going?*

2 (a) Arabic/Dutch: Fatima

  man ander stad

  (man (goes to) other town)

  (b) Polish/German: Janka

  dasfrau weg strasse

  (woman away (= goes to) street)

The theme *man/woman* is mutually known, and localised by a relatum at goal. This organisation: 'known theme before relatum at goal' is highly recurrent.

Utterances such as those in examples 1 and 2 are clearly primitive. At this stage, to convey their message learners have only the meaning of the few lexical items available, the situational context (and the inferencing capacity of the interlocutor), intonation and word order variation. Yet they are not pre-systematic, but rather pre-figure some of the relations between utterance constituents that development to the basic variety allows.

To summarise this section, we may say that, from the very beginning of the acquisition process, learners build up a repertoire that is put to use in context in remarkably similar ways across languages, in order to express recurrent communicative functions.[3]

4 Two examples

In section 3, I suggested that very early learner utterances provide a clear illustration of some correspondences between information structure and linguistic structure, since the learner relies on language- and culture-neutral knowledge sources that are initially available.

In this section, I illustrate this idea more concretely with two examples, one that concentrates on constraints within the utterance, and the other that appeals crucially to the situational or discourse context: verb-argument structure, and the expression of temporal relations, respectively. For the learner who has developed pattern (A) of section 2, repeated here:

(A) $NP_1 - V - (NP_2) (NP_2)$

the problem arises of how to organise the verb's arguments in relation to the verb itself, and the example will show how the semantic role relations between the arguments, together with the temporal characteristics of the event denoted by the verb, constrain the arrangement of the V and the NPs. A learner has to express temporal relations from his very first utterances as examples 1 (a) and (b) demonstrate, and the examples in 4.2 shows how this is achieved by different communicative means over the course of the acquisition process, and how the communicative limitations of a particular repertoire push the learner to further acquisition.

4.1 Verb-argument organisation

When a learner has successfully identified the TL verbs, one problem he or she has in arranging words in an utterance is to decide the order in which to produce the verb and its argument(s). I will restrict the discussion here to verbs with more than one argument, and try to show how Santo, an Italian learner of English, managed to produce some three-argument verbs during the 26 months during which he was observed. The two crucial examples are:

3 (Chaplin) give present for young children

4 (the one lady) speak the boss 'I see one young girl take you bread'

Both examples come from a film-retelling in the final weeks of data-collection, and belong to the plot-line, answering Labov's (1972) question 'What happened next?' The expressions in brackets in utterance-initial position are my specification of the referents. The utterances are taken from connected discourse with *Chaplin* and *the lady* highly presupposed topics, which Santo left implicit in the utterances he produced. In the English L2 production we examined, we (Huebner *et al.*, 1992) found that reference could be left implicit (justifying a 'zero anaphor') in a discourse context where reference was maintained to a referent from plot-line utterance to plot-line utterance, where the explicit referring expression was in NP_1, and where the semantic relation between verb and argument remained comparable. I now turn more generally to the semantic role relations we observed.

The 'control' constraint (Klein & Perdue, 1992)

The main crosslinguistic semantic constraint concerns the relationship between the arguments of verbs which associate more than one argument. For most of these verbs a semantic asymmetry is observed in that one NP referent has a 'higher' and the other(s) a 'lower' degree of control over the situation described. That NP-referent which is in control of, or intends to be in control of, the other entities in the situation is placed by learners in NP_1 position of pattern A. The constraint can be termed, for brevity:

S1 controller first

Strength of control ranges from clear agent–patient relations (*destroy, arrest*) to weaker asymmetries (*want, love*), so the NP with the more 'agentive' referent appears in NP_1. This NP-referent is most often human but, as human referents can also appear in NP_2 position (example 5(a)), it is semantic role properties, rather than intrinsic features of NPs, that are decisive in assigning position. The following examples are from an early film-retelling of Santo's (controller underlined):

5 (a) <u>the police</u> taking away Charlie Chaplin

   (b) <u>the police</u> drive the car

   (c) <u>Chaplin</u> have the bread

Santo adheres rigidly to the control constraint, which is a simpler organisational principle than TL-English, of course. One consequence is the absence from his production of 'reverse orientation' verbs such as *receive*, another is the difficulties he encounters when a conflict arises between reference maintenance and the 'controller' status of the referent, as in the following example:

6 and Charlie Chaplin + for + taking for same / taking away + for + so sorry + the Charlie Chaplin for + going together in prison the police.

The message Santo is trying to convey is: 'Chaplin wants to get taken back to prison'. The message is 'about' Chaplin, but *Chaplin* is not the controller of *take to prison* and Santo gets into trouble. After the metalinguistic apology 'so sorry' for his confusion, Santo reformulates with a one-argument verb 'going'.

Some verbs, notably verbs of saying and giving, take three arguments. Their lexical meaning involves two states – telic, or 'two-state' in Klein's (1994) terminology – a source state and a target state, and the control relation between arguments is different in each state. In example 3 – (Chaplin) *give present for young children* – there is a first state, a 'source' state, where Chaplin 'controls' the present, and is active in bringing about a distinct state, the 'goal' state. In the 'goal' state it is the children who 'control' the present. The 'controller first' constraint does not say which 'controller' should come first, and has to be supplemented by an additional constraint:

S2 Controller of source state outweighs controller of goal state

This constraint applies by analogy to example 4 – *(the one lady) speak the boss 'I see one young girl take you bread'* – which contains a verb of saying. There is a source state where the woman, but not the boss, has the information, and a goal state where the information is shared, and the source state controller comes first.

Difficulties arise with the use of such three-argument verbs, as neither S1 nor S2 explains where the third argument of the verb (the present, or the quoted speech) is placed. Furthermore, 'reverse orientation' verbs such as 'someone take something from somebody' are a predicted source of difficulty, as they go against constraint S2. This is one possible reason why *take* is never used by Santo with more than two arguments, thus complying with S1.

For quoted speech, Santo proceeds over the data collection period in two steps, which overlap temporally. In step one, the event is divided into two parts, and the first part corresponds to S1 (and S2):

7 (a) the police phone

(b) the one old woman speak the boss the shop

This frame is then completed by the quoted speech, introduced by Italian *dice*:

7 (a) the police phone *dice* coming in this address I take one person
       (= come to this address, I have made an arrest)

(b) the one old woman speak the boss the shop *dice* the young girl take the bread

and, once, by 'said':

8 (baker) phone the police said the one girl take my bread

In the final retelling, second step, the *dice* is absent from some, but not all examples. In these cases, the arguments are united under a single predication:

4 (the one lady) speak the boss 'I see one young girl take you bread'

For verbs of giving (3), the third argument is localised in the goal state by the controller 'children'; we observe a reflex of the 'theme before relatum at goal' constraint already operative at NUO (section 3), but such full constructions are very rare.

To conclude this discussion, we may say that Santo, who becomes a virtuoso basic variety speaker, builds up three-argument verb structures from his knowledge of the temporal characteristics of the corresponding events. The claim is that the target-like strings of examples 3 and 4 are not best analysed as a TL three-argument structure with bits of morphology missing, but as instances where the organisation of arguments around the verb reflect the time/space structure of the event: 'knowledge-based' organisational principles operating at utterance-level, in the terms of section 3. The claim is testable, and also predicts that dative alternation and locative alternation (and indirect object cliticisation in French) are not attestable at basic variety level. Santo will not produce:

9 (Chaplin) give *them* present

and a comparable learner of French will not produce:

10 Chaplin *leur* donne cadeau.

4.2 The expression of temporality

Right from the beginning of the acquisition process, it is necessary for an adult to contextualise the state of affairs talked about. This (temporal) relation can be inferred from discourse organisation principles, or simply left implicit, in which case the relation is by default contemporaneous with the moment of speech. We also saw in section 2 that the temporal relation of an utterance to the moment of speech or to another reference time can be specified by an utterance-initial adverb 1(a) and (b) and it is remarkable that adult learners very quickly acquire a stock of temporal adverbials, of position, but also of duration and frequency.

These initial means for expressing temporality are enriched at basic variety level by the fact that the verb-argument structure allows the expression of inherent lexical aspect (*Aktionsart*), as we have seen. However, as a defining characteristic of the basic variety is that utterances contain uninflected verbs, it completely lacks the usual grammatical means to express tense and aspect. Learners nevertheless manage to produce sophisticated temporal structures in their discourse with the means available, which allow the specification of some time span and certain relations between time spans. Following Klein (1994), we will call the time span about which the speaker wants to say something the 'topic time' (TT). TT is the time about which the speaker makes an assertion, in contrast to the time of situation (TSit), i.e. the time at which the situation talked about obtains. The notional category of tense then expresses the relation of TT to the deictically given time of utterance (TU), and the notional category of grammatical aspect expresses the relation between TT and TSit. (This tripartite distinction of TU, TT and TSit can be seen as an elaboration of Reichenbach's (1947) distinction between Speech time, Reference time, Event time. See Starren (2001) for a careful discussion.)

Starren (2001) uses the metaphor of the video camera to explain TT – it is the time the camera is 'shooting'. Imagine you are a witness in court, and the judge asks you, 'What did you see when you entered the room?' The crucial time span corresponds to your entering the room, and just this time span is filmed by the camera. You answer, 'A man was trying to open the safe. He looked Japanese.' The time span occupied by 'man try to open safe', and indeed the time span occupied by 'man look Japanese' – the 'situation times' – are considerable longer than it took you to enter the room. It would indeed be surprising if the man did not still look Japanese as you speak. But this was not what you were asked. The TT is your entering the room, and your, and the judge's, use of past tense puts this TT (but *not* necessarily the TSit) before the time of utterance: past tense. The time of the action of trying to open the safe, TSit, encompasses the TT : TT ⊃ TSit . This aspectual relation is imperfective, and explains the use of the past progressive aspect in your answer.

What pre-basic-variety learners do at the beginning of their discourse is to establish an initial TT either:

- implicitly, by taking over the time proposed by the interlocutor or using TU as a default case; or
- explicitly by means of an utterance-initial adverb as in 1(a).

This initial TT serves as a point of departure, and is maintained or shifted, depending on the type of discourse. If it is shifted (as in a narrative, for example), then this shifted time is marked by an initial anaphoric adverb (*then, after*), as in 1(b), or else follows on from discourse-organisational principles such as the principle of natural order (PNO)(Clark, 1973), whereby events are recounted in the order in which they occur.

With this organisation, the time of situation is always more or less simultaneous with TT, as there are no linguistic means allowing the learner to dissociate them. We return to this communicative restriction below.

As we have seen in examples 1(a) and (b) above, the utterance-initial adverb specifies the TT of the (rather minimally expressed) state of affairs of the utterance. Starren (2001) analyses the very early productions of Turkish and Moroccan learners of L2 Dutch or French from the ESF corpus, and finds a regular use of a *second* adverb of time, specifying the time span filled by the state of affairs, i.e. TSit:

11 (a) Turkish/Dutch (Mahmut):

altijd ik wakker om 8 uur

(always I wake up at 8 o'clock)

(b) Arabic/French (Zahra):

toujours moi [fe] la cuisine ce soir

(always me make the cooking this evening) (= 'in the evening')

12   Arabic/Dutch (Fatima):

vandaag ik altijd weg met auto

(today I always here and there with car)

13   Arabic/French (Abdel):

hier le capitaine bateau toujours [regarde]

(yesterday the captain the ship always look)

Starren's analysis of many such early utterances allows a distinction to be drawn between the aspectual values of habituality, continuity and iterativity, by the interplay of adverbs denoting TT and TSit. For habituality, as in 11(a), one time of situation *om 8 uur* is linked to a series of topic times within the TT *altijd*; or 1(b): for all the sub-intervals of *toujours*, 'I cook in the evening'. Example 13, which contains an activity verb, expresses continuity ('the time span *yesterday* is filled by the activity of supervising'). This example can be contrasted with example 12, where the particle *weg* conveys a bounded event, which provokes the iterative reading: a complex TSit expressed by *altijd* is linked to one TT span: *vandaag*.

Even at basic variety level, it is therefore possible to make some aspectual distinctions, by means of an adverb distribution that owes nothing to either SL or TL organisation. But Starren also shows that the major communicative limitation of this interplay of adverbs is that it does not alone suffice to dissociate TT and TSit. Learners thus cannot focus on the pre-state of an event (prospective: TT < TSit, English *going to*) or the post-state of an event (perfect: TT > TSit). In order to be able to do this, learners must go beyond the basic variety and develop a verbal morphology that allows for the independent specification of TT.

The overall picture that emerges from Starren's study is of a developing system that first allows temporal relations to be marked by discourse means and simple adverbs. It then passes through a stage where finer temporal distinctions can be expressed through the interplay of adverbs marking both TT and TSit, in conjunction with the internal temporal characteristics of the event denoted in the utterance, to the development of verbal morphology which alone allows TT and TSit to become dissociated, and grammatical aspect expressed.

This study may be compared to that of Benazzo (2000), who examined the use of additive and restrictive scope particles in English, French and German L2 in longitudinal data from the ESF corpus. She also looked closely at temporal adverbs expressing iteration and at temporal adverbs of contrast. Just as the temporal adverbs in Starren's study, these items are structurally not obligatory in an utterance, and have in common that they variably affect other constituents in an utterance in which they occur. They were found to be acquired in a fixed order, with additive and restrictive particles (*also, only* and translation equivalents) preceding the temporal items. For these latter, forms marking the iteration of an event (*again*, and equivalents) are used before temporal adverbs of contrast ('TACs': *already, still, no longer*). These latter are used only in post-basic varieties. The acquisitional sequence shared by learners of the three L2s is therefore:

additive > restrictive	iterative >	contrastive

Benazzo found that the placement and scopal properties of the items analysed correspond closely to the development from NUO, through the basic variety and beyond:

- learners of the same L2 use the same particles in the same way at each stage examined;
- at a given stage of utterance organisation, learners of all L2s show similar behaviour.

This is in itself a remarkable correspondence, and it has to do with the nature of the constituents that at each stage of development constitute the particle's domain of application.

Additive and restrictive particles characteristically quantify over entities, referred to by NPs. They can therefore be used independently of any verbal inflexion, and indeed of any verb, and their use is observed from NUO onwards.

Iterative particles characteristically express the repetition of an event, which happens again, at a later time interval. They quantify over events, referred to by V and its complements. To be repeated, an event has to be bounded (perfectively presented), and the expressive means for temporality of the basic variety allow this: TT and TSit coincide. This is why they appear at basic variety level, but not before. The central forms are *again, encore, noch (mal), nog,* but other more idiosyncratic forms are also used, as *autre fois* in the following example:

14 Spanish/French (Alberto):

(Charlot) [ale] à la prison autre fois

(Chaplin go to the prison another time)

These adverbs indicate that the event denoted by the utterance containing them is of the same type as that of a previously mentioned utterance; they quantify over that event and occur adjacent to the expression denoting it. In other words, their distribution is identical to that of the temporal adverbs modifying TSit which we have already seen in Starren's study.

But temporal adverbs of contrast relate *two* different time intervals (phases) of the same event. These time intervals have to be signalled, and for this it is necessary to master the relevant verbal morphology. In the following example of Lavinia, an Italian learner of English who, unlike Santo, develops beyond the basic variety:

15 Italian/English (Lavinia):

he's been already in the nursery

TT=TU > TSit, the use of *already* associates with the TSit ('be in the nursery'), and the finite *has* is necessary to specify the TT (One begins to understand why learners of L2 English have difficulty with the present perfect!) Another adverb of contrast – *still* – contrasts two temporal reference points: a state or event remains valid from one TT to a subsequent TT. In the utterance:

16 Italian/English (Lavinia):

(he) is still working

TT = TU ⊃ TSit, i.e. the event is presented imperfectively. The use of *still* associates this TT with a previous TT within the same TSit, and one needs the finite *is* to specify the TT. This is why these TACs are used productively only at post-basic-variety level.

There is one last remark to be made about this example: it is not the conceptual complexity of the adverbs that determines their order of acquisition. Precocious holophrastic use or direct repetitions of TACs would not run counter to the picture drawn here. We have observed the behaviour of the particles within a functioning system, and have seen that it is the overall organisation of the system that allows different particles to integrate into it at different stages.

5 Conclusion: Learner Language as a System in its Own Right

In this chapter I have tried to illustrate the functional approach to L2 use, drawing on data from the ESF second language data bank (Feldweg, 1993). This approach starts from language use, and analyses how an L2 user succeeds in understanding and being understood (with the obvious restriction for this paper that transcribed data is much more revealing about language production, rather than comprehension, processes). The approach also considers communication difficulty or failure as crucial evidence in understanding the workings of a learner variety at a particular time, and in understanding what may push the learner to further acquisition.

More specifically, the approach takes the view that there are a limited number of phrasal (morphosyntactic), semantic and context-relating (situational and discourse) organisational principles at work in learner languages, and that their *interaction* determines the actual organisation of a learner variety at a given time. The kind of interaction, and hence the specific contribution of a type of principle, varies with the proficiency level of the learner/user, and may vary as a function of the L1–L2 pairing. Acquisition may then be seen as a change in the interaction of the different principles over time.

I have tried to show that the very first verbalisations of the absolute beginner are already structured, that the adult's knowledge of how information is organised in coherent discourse is immediately useful, and that the organising principles initially at work do not subsequently disappear, but have their function modified as other organising principles are appropriated. In other words, I have tried to illustrate, albeit from a very limited number of examples, how learner varieties have a life of their own: they have to function under communicative pressure and are very selective as to what they incorporate, when.

The internal organisation of learner varieties is not that of the L1, nor that of the target language, nor a mixture of both. But the utterances they generate are linguistically as interesting as either.

Acknowledgements

I am grateful to the Max-Planck-Institut for Psycholinguistics in Nijmegen for the ideal working conditions I was offered during the writing of this article.

Notes

1. The caveat 'in principle' is necessary, as much subsequent work (e.g. Carroll & von Stutterheim, 1993) has examined more closely 'how far up' the process of message construction grammatical constraints operate. The less specific grammatical knowledge the speaker has available, the less immediate is the problem, which is why the crucial comparison for Carroll and von Stutterheim is between native speakers and very advanced L2 users. Levelt himself states: 'The grammar of a language may put certain boundary conditions on the order in which thoughts can be expressed, and the order of expression decided on will in turn limit the choice of appropriate grammatical forms' (Levelt, 1981).
2. The caveat here is that knowledge-based natural orders, depending on mutual knowledge between speaker and hearer, often can be culture-specific. This is well known. In the discussion following his paper, however, Levelt comments on the relevance of his model in a pidgin situation: 'In [this] situation the boundaries of mutual knowledge are very restricted, and I would suspect that a speaker would be particularly careful not to cross them' (Levelt, 1981: 315). Very early learners are if anything in a more extreme position than pidgin speakers, as lack of mutual knowledge is compounded by the inequality of the native/non-native interaction. Levelt's comment surely applies here, too.
3. It follows that language specifics come in later. For L1-based hypotheses, the conditions under which language-specific organisation will *not* be operative in the building up of a L2 grammar are probably threefold:
   (a) The particular aspect of the grammar is (unconsciously judged as – Kellerman, 1977) too specific for hypotheses to be entertained.
   (b) An aspect of the grammar encodes a grammatical function that is not (yet) communicatively relevant to the learner.
   (c) The learner's present L2 grammar is not (yet) capable of incorporating the particular aspect. As we shall see, certain classes of verbs (section 4.1), and a semantic class of adverbs (section 4.2) are absent from learner's production until such a stage as the learner's grammar is ready for them.

References

Benazzo, S. (2000) *L'acquisition des particules de portée en Français, Anglais et Allemand L2*. PhD thesis, Université Paris VIII.

Carroll, M. and von Stutterheim, Ch. (1993) The representation of spatial configurations in English and German and the grammatical structure of locative and anaphoric expressions. *Linguistics* 31, 1011–1041.

Clahsen, H. (1984) The acquisition of German word order: A test case for cognitive approaches to L2-development. In R. Andersen (ed.) *Second Languages: A Cross-Linguistic Perspective* (pp. 219–242). Rowley, MA: Newbury House.

Clark, E. (1973) How children describe time and order. In C. Ferguson and D. Slobin (eds) *Studies of Child Language Development*. New York: Holt, Rinehart and Winston.

Dorriots, B. (1986) How to succeed with only fifty words. *Göteborg Papers in Theoretical Linguistics* 52, 1–80.

Feldweg, H. (1993) Transcription, storage and retrieval of data. In C. Perdue (ed.) *Adult Language Acquisition. Cross-Linguistic Perspectives* (Vol. 1). Cambridge: Cambridge University Press.

Huebner, T., Carroll, M. and Perdue, C. (1992) The acquisition of English. In W. Klein and C. Perdue (eds) *Utterance Structure: Developing Grammars Again.* Amsterdam: Benjamins.

Kellerman, E. (1977) Towards a characterisation of the strategy of transfer in second language learning. *Interlanguage Studies Bulletin* 2, 58–145.

Klein, W. (1994) *Time in Language*. London and New York: Routledge.

Klein, W. and Perdue, C. (1989) The learner's problem of arranging words. In B. MacWhinney and E. Bates (eds) *The Crosslinguistic Study of Sentence Processing* (pp. 292–337). Cambridge: Cambridge University Press.

Klein, W. and Perdue, C. (1992) *Utterance Structure: Developing Grammars Again.* Amsterdam: Benjamins.

Klein, W. and Perdue, C. (1997) The basic variety. Or: Couldn't natural languages be much simpler? *Second Language Research* 13 (4), 301–347.

Labov, W. (1972) *Language in the Inner City.* Philadelphia: University of Pennsylvania Press.

Levelt, W. (1981) The speaker's linearisation problem. *Philological Transactions of the Royal Society of London* Series B 295, 305–15.

Linde, C. and Labov, W. (1975) Spatial networks as a site for the study of language and thought. *Language* 51 (4), 924–939.

Perdue, C. (ed.) (1984) *Second Language Acquisition by Adult Immigrants: A Field Manual.* Rowley, MA: Newbury House.

Perdue, C. (ed.) (1993) *Adult Language Acquisition. Cross-linguistic Perspectives* (2 vols). Cambridge: Cambridge University Press.

Reichenbach, R. (1947) *Elements of Symbolic Logic.* New York: Free Press.

Slobin, D. (1973) Cognitive prerequisites for the development of grammar. In C. Ferguson and D. Slobin (eds) *Studies of Child Language* Development (pp. 175–208). New York: Holt, Rinehart and Winston.

Starren, M. (2001) The expression of temporality in Dutch and French L2. PhD thesis, Brabants Universiteit.

Stutterheim, Ch. von (1991) Narrative and description: Temporal reference in second language acquisition. In T. Huebner and C. Ferguson (eds) *Crosscurrents in Second Language Acquisition and Linguistic Theory.* Amsterdam: Benjamins.

Talmy, L. (1985) Lexicalization patterns: Semantic structure in lexical forms. In T. Shopen (ed.) *Language Typology and Syntactic Description* (Vol. III). Cambridge: Cambridge University Press.

Introduction to Chapter 6
Cognitive Processes of L2 Users, Ellen Bialystok

VIVIAN COOK

The contribution by Ellen Bialystok raises several fundamental issues, not only about the L2 user but also about the nature of language and language acquisition.

- *The nature of language.* One of the perpetual debates in linguistics is between those who see language as internal mental 'rules', 'I-language' in Chomsky's terms (Chomsky, 1986), and those who see it as external utterances produced in interaction with other people, 'E-language'. Some (as in the Flynn and Lust chapter) try to describe the knowledge of language in the minds of L2 users; others (as in Pavlenko's chapter) look at the interactions of L2 users with other people. This divide in a sense corresponds to two personality types – the introvert who looks to the world inside his or her own mind, as with a Romantic poet such as Wordsworth, and the extravert who relies on the world outside, say classicism in literature, exemplified by Alexander Pope. Currently this schism seems to be phrased as the difference between emergentism, in which language is a by-product of interaction and development (MacWhinney, 1999), and Universal Grammar in which language is an unvarying grammar with only lexical properties contributed by the environment (Chomsky, 2000).
- *The relationship of language and thought.* Is there a distinct language faculty separate from the rest of the mind on Chomskyan lines, or is language integrated with the other cognitive aspects of a unitary mind, as Anderson (1993) suggests? The L2 user is a test case since cognition can be disengaged from language development (Cook, 1981): if L2 learners think in different ways from monolinguals, then thinking must be connected to language. One question is whether the actual concepts possessed by L2 users are the same as those of monolinguals. Acquiring another language might mean either acquiring a

new set of concepts in parallel alongside the first, or combining the two sets of concepts into one new set.

The model that Bialystok uses reconciles these two issues through the two dimensions of analysis of representational structure and control of attention. Analysis is the connection to actual knowledge of language – competence. Control is the connection to the processes of production and comprehension. Learners' performance varies in both dimensions. Some may have good knowledge but low control over some items; they know, say, how to do multiplication, but they make many mistakes when they do it. Or, as with an L2 user who writes 'Everytimes I concentrate to speak out, don't know why always had Chinese in my mind', they have complex structures but poor control over them. Others may have poor knowledge but good control: their only skill is adding-up but they always get the answer right; one L2 user writes 'I am a ~~gril~~ girl and my name is Joan and I am 11 yea old and I go to ... School and I live on 224 ... Road and I have one Brother' – simple structures but good control over them. It turns out that increased control of attention is what is affected in child L2 learners,and that decreased control goes with the ageing process.

References

Anderson, J. (1993) *Rules of the Mind*. Hillsdale, NJ: Lawrence Erlbaum.
Chomsky, N. (1986) *Knowledge of Language: Its Nature, Origin and Use*. New York: Praeger.
Chomsky, N. (2000) *The Architecture of Language*. New Delhi: Oxford University Press.
Cook, V.J. (1981) Some uses for second language learning research. *Annals of the New York Academy of Sciences* 379, 251-258.
MacWhinney, B. (ed.) (1999) *The Emergence of Language*. Hillsdale, NJ: Lawrence Erlbaum.

Chapter 6

Cognitive Processes of L2 Users

ELLEN BIALYSTOK

What is cognitive functioning like for people who know two languages? Are these processes altered in a mind that incorporates two linguistic systems? And if so, can traces of these altered processes be found in the ordinary cognitive behaviour of bilinguals? The questions themselves betray an assumption that ultimately determines the answer. For linguistic knowledge to impact on cognitive processes, the mind must present a configuration in which language and cognition freely interact. This assumption, however, is far from consensual, and represents a major divide between alternative conceptions of language and its place in the mind. For language and cognition to interact in this way, language must be governed, at least to some extent, by the same processes that guide other cognitive activities. Views of language that assume this mental architecture comprise the loosely connected set of functional linguistic theories. In contrast, formal linguistic theories set language apart in some measure from the rest of cognition. In these views, language is one of several specialised modules that functions autonomously, invoking dedicated processes and a special-ised knowledge base. These different conceptions can be represented sche-matically. Figure 6.1(a) depicts the mind as it would be organised in functional linguistic theories, indicating its centrality with other cognitive activities but enjoying no special status. Figure 6.1(b) depicts the mind as it would be construed by formal linguistic theories, where language is one of several specialised systems that co-exist in a mental space.

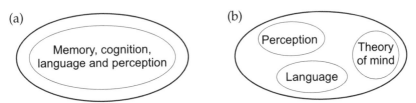

Figure 6.1 Structure of language and cognition in (a) functional theories and (b) formal theories

The debate between formal and functional linguistic theories is at the heart of a range of issues in linguistic and cognitive theorising. Most notable is its role in deciding between alternate conceptions of language acquisition (cf. Pinker, 1994 versus Tomasello, 1998). Equally crucial, however, is its impact on deciding whether knowing two languages has a generalised impact on cognition. Not only is the answer to this question determined by a position on the formal–functional debate, but the question itself can provide a forum for testing some of the more extreme claims of each position. If the formalists are right, then learning two languages in early childhood should have minimal, if any, impact on non-linguistic cognitive processing. Language evolves through the systems designed by biology to serve this function. Conversely, if the functionalists are right, then learning two languages in early childhood is an intensely cognitive activity and could be expected to alter processing in significant ways.

These conceptions of language, its development and its place in the mind also lead to different conceptions of what constitutes proficiency in a language. The criteria for defining proficiency become the basis for decisions regarding how language is learned, how it should be taught and what consequences might follow its acquisition. The difference between the theoretical orientations, therefore, is not simply a matter of academic debate but also carries practical consequences. Hence, if interactions between language and cognition in young bilinguals can help to adjudicate some of the issues in this dispute, the results would not only reveal the nature of cognitive processing for bilingual language users, but also provide a glimpse into something fundamental about the nature of language itself. The chapter begins with an overview of the two perspectives to explore the relation between language proficiency and cognitive processing. The second section describes research with bilingual children that demonstrates the influence that a second language has on their cognitive processing. Finally, speculations are proposed regarding the role of language learning in cognition.

Theories of Language Processing

The clearest divide between formal and functional theories is in their assertions about how language acquisition takes place. Therefore, examining the conjectures of each position on language acquisition helps to clarify the differences between them. As one moves from explanations based primarily on innate factors (formal theories) to those focusing on linguistic input (functional theories), the mechanisms for language acquisition drift outward. This movement shifts the balance of the explanatory force from endogenous factors residing in the mental and cognitive predispositions of the child, to exogenous ones encountered in the contingencies in the environment. It is simplistic to assume that either of these approaches alone could adequately account for the monumental task of mastering an entire language, but adherence to one of the theoretical perspectives commits one to a position regarding the priority of these competing factors. Because language is multifaceted, there is ultimately a role for myriad factors in its acquisition, and theorists can focus their accounts on those that appear most relevant. What happens, however, is that the resulting explanation of language acquisition tends to be an explanation of the acquisition of some portion of language. Not coincidentally, the apparently competing explanations of language acquisition from formal and functional theories place the linguistic features most conducive to their explanatory apparatus at the centre of language. To oversimplify, formal theories aim their explanations primarily at syntax and phonology and functional theories mainly address semantics and pragmatics.

The feature most essential to the distinction between the theoretical perspectives is the status of language as a domain of knowledge that is independent of other cognitive functions. In formal approaches, language is a relatively autonomous domain and carries its own universal structure, but, in functional conceptions, language is convergent with the rest of cognition. Therefore, if language acquisition is governed by a dedicated module, then the process of language acquisition, and to a large extent its outcome (that is, language proficiency), will be universal. In formal linguistic theories, language proficiency is the reflection of circumscribed and specialised knowledge that is an elaboration of an abstract template. This template is part of the inheritance of humans and develops with little need for social manipulation, provided children are placed in normally functioning environments where a community language is heard. It is frequently related to cognitive theories in which many such specialised modules co-exist, each with their own dedicated knowledge and procedural specifications.

For functional linguistic theories, language proficiency is the reflection of cognitive processes that extract regularities from the environment and record those generalities as knowledge. In this sense, linguistic knowledge is no different from other kinds of knowledge of the world – knowledge about the nature of objects and categories, for example – and becomes part of the child's knowledge. The mental representations for language are equivalent to the mental representations for any other aspect of children's knowledge of the world. Interaction is crucial for the accrual of this knowledge. Moreover, if language acquisition is an aspect of general cognitive development, regulated by the generic processes that guide children through the acquisition of conceptual knowledge and skill-development, then there is no reason to expect that any two language learning experiences will be the same. In sequential second-language acquisition, for example, children already know one language, and that knowledge, part of children's conceptual repertoire, is certain to influence the acquisition of another language.

Although theoretical perspectives differ on the innateness of language, the issue of innateness is largely a red herring; not much follows from either position and the debate can easily lead one away from distinctions that are more important. Both extreme views are untenable: to say that language is innate is not to say that knowledge of specific linguistic structures is innate, and to say that language is not innate is not to say that humans have no preconditioned bias to learn language in some form. This factor, therefore, shall not be pursued as a productive distinction between the perspectives.

Evaluating each of these perspectives individually reveals shortcomings for both views. The formal theories are excessively selective in the linguistic phenomena they attempt to explain. Although they easily deal with the emergence of structure, they are too complacent about the experiences that are necessary to trigger these insights. Specifically, the claim is that it is sufficient to hear language, presumably in an interactional setting, for the innate mechanisms to create linguistic principles. This conjecture understates the active involvement with which the child engages in language acquisition.

The main failure of functional approaches is that they leave unsolved the mystery of coincidence: how to explain the constraints that make natural languages similar to each other and children's progress in learning them so parallel. To a great extent, functionalists must place faith in the empiricist principles that transform patterns in the environment into mental structures, or knowledge. In construction grammar, for example, Tomasello (e.g. Tomasello, 1992; Tomasello & Brooks, 1999) locates children's early utterances in their knowledge of scenes and routines in which they have been engaged. From these individual concrete experiences, children extract commonalties, associate events with words and build up mental structure. Similarly, in connectionist approaches (e.g. Elman *et al.*, 1996), the concrete foundation is the lexicon. After passing a vocabulary threshold, structure begins to emerge in children's knowledge of language. But how does the correct structure get built up? Linguistic principles are not inherent in the knowledge of scenes or words, yet children manage to find just the right combinations of words and sounds. Moreover, they all do it in the same basic order at about the same age.

Some hybrid theories avoid the controversy by incorporating aspects of both theoretical traditions. An early acknowledgement of the need to approach language acquisition from both sides was submitted by Bruner (1983). He proposed that the language acquisition device (LAD), the engine of learning for generative linguistics, is accompanied by a language acquisition support system (LASS). The social environmental structures that bring the child to language assure that appropriate interactions take place, and present the information to the child's conceptual system in ways that are clearly interpretable and conducive to learning. Thus, Bruner acknowledged a role for both perspectives by making each responsible for a different aspect of language learning: the internal cognitive mechanism, LAD (cf. formal), and the external interactive mechanism, LASS (cf. functional) were jointly responsible for language acquisition.

Locke (1993) has proposed a different kind of interactionist account, called a 'biolinguistic' approach. The essential feature of his explanation is that language acquisition depends on two jointly crucial components of human information processing: a grammatical analysis module (GAM), and a specialisation in social cognition (SSC). His assumptions straddle both sides of the debate by incorporating features from each. Regarding independence, at least some of language, specifically phonetic processing and generative morphology, is modular and specialised, but language processing includes other domains as well. Regarding input, the environment is needed to shape the non-modular aspects of language but the core, including the SSC, is universal and automatic.

Finally, some recent proposals from the perspective of evolutionary cognition have attempted to situate language ability within a conception of the phylogenetic emergence of human intelligence. These explanations incorporate the assumptions of formal theories by making language continuous with other abilities that develop through the species; they incorporate the assumptions of functional theories by preserving a distinction between the language abilities of *Homo sapiens* and the precursors from which they evolved. Deacon (1997), for example, argues that language evolved from a general symbolic function that began to emerge in the prefrontal lobes about 2 million years ago. Although the theory leaves some rather large gaps around some technical linguistic issues, it has the appeal of embedding the innate basis of language in the human mind without requiring humans to be pre-wired for any *specific* knowledge about language. This point is further illustration that it is simplistic to consider nativism to be a binary feature of knowledge, that is, language is innate or it is not innate. Many conceptual foundations could give the appearance of innate language ability without themselves actually instantiating language.

These examples illustrate the danger of assuming that dichotomies can adequately describe theoretical options. Halliday (1994), for example, is a functional linguist who pays great attention to the formal structure of the language he describes. The point is that these classifications are useful because they identify the correlated constellations of features that describe positions that are significantly different from each other. The differences are significant because they share implications, notably for the present discussion, implications for language acquisition. The feature most relevant to these outcomes is the determination of language as an isolated module or as an extension of cognition.

The independence of language as an autonomous domain has strong implications for the way that language interfaces with cognition in the minds of bilinguals. Therefore, the question about the cognitive processes available to bilinguals, or the effect that a second language has on cognitive processing, depends crucially on the position taken in this debate. Deciding between formal and functional options is the key to determining the nature and possibility of cognitive effects of language learning. Since linguistic arguments do not easily declare a preferred option, evidence from cognition may shift the balance.

Identifying Cognitive Processes

One way of deciding on the relation between language structure and cognition is to explore the extent to which cognitive processes can account for the major phenomena in language acquisition and use. The intention here is not to decide the outcome of the debate but rather to set parameters that may eventually provide a fruitful resolution. Ultimately, language proficiency must include both formal structure and communicative application, it must evolve from a prepared mind and be nurtured by a supportive context, it must set clear standards of use and include disparate (but systematic) variations of the rules. We need a way of organising this multiplicity into a coherent statement about the human potential to learn and use language. If there is no agreement about what is included in language proficiency, then any explanation that attempts to probe some of the more profound mysteries of language will be incomplete.

A framework proposed in earlier work for considering the relation among different uses of language and their underlying cognitive requirements may provide a starting point (e.g. Bialystok, 1991, 2001). The framework uses two cognitive processes, analysis of representational structure and control of attention, to define the demands of various linguistic (and nonlinguistic) tasks. These processes increase in their power with development, enabling children to solve more difficult problems and to use language in complex ways. To the extent that they may also explain the development of language acquisition and use, language is placed under the jurisdiction of general cognitive processing.

The process of analysis refers to the level of explicit structure and organisation that is represented with knowledge. A significant change with development is that mental representations of knowledge become more explicit and more structured. Children increasingly are able to comprehend not only unrelated facts, but also the relationships between various concepts and ideas. In the early stages of development, knowledge is represented as implicit routines, embedded in concrete contexts, and unrelated to other representations that share some abstract similarity. For example, children's early knowledge of the alphabet is a memorised routine. As the routine becomes analysed, the child comes to understand that the routine is comprised of constituents (letters), that the constituents have individual functions (they signify sounds), that the functions have a computational significance (they can spell words), and that there are other systems (numbers) that work that way. The way in which children's knowledge of the letters is represented in each of these levels of understanding is different, and that difference indicates the explication and analysis that is applied to the initially implicit, unanalysed representation of the alphabet. As mental representations become analysed, knowledge can be organised around abstract categories and details retrieved independently of their contexts. These are essential characteristics for the development of thought.

Other theoretical perspectives have described this development in different terms but come to a similar conclusion. Karmiloff-Smith (1992), for example, points to representational redescription as the fundamental cognitive change for children, and Zelazo and Frye (1997) describe cognitive complexity as the mechanism for cognitive development. An important similarity in all these positions is that the evaluation of explicitness is relative: knowledge constantly undergoes a process of explication and elaboration that moves it gradually along a continuum of analytic representation. This processing component captures the need for complex linguistic behaviour (such as metalinguistic or literacy applications) to be based on knowledge that is more explicit or more formal than that needed for more ordinary linguistic performance (such as conversation).

Control of attention is the process that allows the child to direct attention to specific aspects of the environment or a mental representation as problems are solved in real time. The need for control is most apparent when a problem contains conflict or ambiguity. In such misleading situations, two or more mental representations may be constructed, each of which bears some relation to the problem. The correct solution typically requires attending to only one of these possible representations, thereby inhibiting or resisting attention to the other. This selective attention is more difficult if some habitual or salient response to the problem contradicts the optimal one and must be overruled. The tendency to attend to the (incorrect) competing representation may either simply slow down the problem solving or mislead the child to the incorrect solution.

Tipper and his colleagues (Tipper, 1992; Tipper & McLaren, 1990) have argued that attention is comprised of independent, and independently-developing components. Whereas inhibition develops slowly in childhood, selection and habituation are as well-formed for children as for adults. Other researchers, too, have documented the development of inhibition in young children and connected it to important changes in problem solving (Dagenbach & Carr, 1994; Dempster, 1992; Harnishfeger & Bjorklund, 1993). Therefore, the developmental aspect of the control process is likely rooted in the inhibition component of attention.

As with the process of analysis, the demands for control are continuous across problems (or situations of language use) and the ability to exercise it increases gradually in development. Most language use situations present some degree of ambiguity. Even the simple act of carrying on a conversation provides the speaker with at least two alternative signals to which attention can be paid: the use and structure of the formal symbol system and the set of meanings that the symbol system has been invoked to represent. These alternatives are scarcely noticed in conversational uses of language, since the meaning is so clearly the relevant level of representation and attention for language comprehension and production. Other uses of language, however, in particular those normally invoked as metalinguistic tasks, demand high levels of control in that misleading information is deliberately introduced into the problem. Higher levels of control are associated with processing that is more intentional (cf. Jacoby, 1991). Such intentional processing is the hallmark of higher forms of thought.

In normal development, children progress incrementally both in the analysis responsible for increasing the explicitness of representations and in the control responsible for selective attention and inhibition. Moreover, analysis and control are related: more explicit representations are more available to consciousness and thus more amenable to manipulation by such executive processes as attention and inhibition. Therefore, the methodological problem in investigating this conceptualisation is in disentangling the two processes. A factor analytic study by Ricciardelli (1993), however, confirmed that analysis and control contribute uniquely to the solution to metalinguistic tasks. Bilingualism presents an important forum for this research. If learning more than one language in childhood changed the evolution of one of these processes, then it would be possible to observe their developmental effects individually.

The advantage of this framework is that it sets out the links that may ultimately be the conduit between the learning and use of languages and the way that cognitive processing is carried out. The framework can remain neutral on some of the major questions that still divide the theoretical perspectives. For example, linguistic rules may begin as representations of innate abstractions or they may be accumulations of experiential associations. In either case, they will be subject to the evolution of structure imposed by analysis and to the limitations of attention necessitated by control. Further, the approach eliminates the need to make a forced choice between two opposing positions and compels us to consider a more complete set of factors in our conception of language learning. Allowing for a more nuanced explanation by removing false dichotomies and incorporating degrees of variation along specified dimensions will advance theorising around many questions (Bialystok, 1998). Finally, it provides a backdrop against which it is possible to examine not only whether language learning impacts on cognitive processing, but also how that impact is realised. The next question, then, is whether knowledge of languages alters the way cognitive processing takes place.

Evidence From Bilinguals

There has been a longstanding concern amongst researchers, educators and parents about what effect bilingualism might have on the intellectual development of children. Strong positions and passionate convictions have characterised the argument on both sides, leaving a balanced resolution difficult to find. Early research warned of devastating cognitive impairment if children were required to learn two languages, while later research promised accelerated learning and enhanced ability for children with the opportunity to become bilingual (review in Hakuta, 1986). With such polarisation, neither position can be expected to uniquely reveal the actual effect that bilingualism has on children's developing intelligence. The attempt in this section is to identify what aspects of cognition are affected by childhood bilingualism and to explain these areas of advantage (and no advantage). Instead of examining intelligence as a multidimensional construct, the approach is to focus on precisely-defined cognitive processes. The two processes that serve as the basis for this examination are analysis and control, delineated in the framework described above.

The examination of how bilingualism affects children's cognitive development is inherently complicated because it is confounded by the myriad factors that make bilingual situations and bilingual children different from each other. Children become bilingual for many reasons: immigration to a new country, extended family that speaks a traditional language, education in a language other than the language of the home, or temporary residence in another country. These circumstances are all normal, and lead children to routinely encounter other languages, and in many cases to achieve high levels of proficiency in those languages. However, these circumstances are correlated with other social and demographic factors that are relevant in defining the kind of children who are most likely to encounter each. The source of confounding is that these social and demographic factors themselves are instrumental in determining children's likely level of cognitive achievement. The factors include the following: the education level of the parents, the literacy environment that the child is exposed to, the nature and extent of the child's proficiency in the first (or home) language, the purposes for which the second language is used, the degree and nature of community support for that language, and the extent to which the child identifies with the group who speaks that language. These are crucial in determining both extent of language proficiency and level of cognitive development.

With this multiplicity of variables impinging on children' performance, how is it possible to isolate the role that bilingualism plays and assess its contribution independently? The present approach is to hold constant as many of these variables as possible and examine bilingual children only in a small band of social possibilities. In the studies described here, the bilingual children have been selected to be as similar as possible to the monolingual children to whom they are compared. All the children come from homes that are middle class, with high achievement expectations, and environments rich in literacy. Still, bilingual children are inherently different from monolingual children, and no amount of experimental control can eradicate that essential fact.

The research methodology in these studies is to use the analysis-control framework both for the development of the tasks and for the interpretation of the results. The attempt is to create problems that isolate, or at least bias the need for, only one of the two processes. Although it is never possible to eliminate the inevitable interaction between these two essential aspects of cognition, it is possible to make one of the processes more crucial in the solution to a specific problem. As far as possible, pairs of tasks that differ only in their bias for one or other of the processes are constructed. The studies summarised below are investigations of monolingual and bilingual children solving problems in each of three domains: language concepts (metalinguistic awareness), number concepts (cardinality), and problem solving. In each case, the tasks are designed to separate the role that analysis and control play in their solution so that children's progress with each process can be observed. One example from each domain will be described.

Language concepts

The primary example of a metalinguistic problem is grammaticality judgement. The problem can be adapted so that it becomes an instrument of assessing the development of analysis and control by biasing the demands required to solve specific items. A sentence such as *Why is the dog barking so loudly?* makes few demands on either the explicitness of representational structures or the control of attention required, and children easily recognise it as acceptable. The analysis demand is increased by introducing a grammatical error, such as *Why the dog is barking so loudly?* Children need to detect the violation in structure and respond that the sentence is unacceptable. The control demand is increased by introducing distracting information, such as *Why is the cat barking so loudly?* Children are trained to respond only to grammaticality, so they must accept this sentence as correct. That response is difficult because the error in meaning is a compelling magnet for their attention and they are drawing a conclusion that the sentence is unacceptable. In repeated studies, we have found that bilingual children can answer the high-control question (anomalous meaning, but grammatical) better than monolinguals, but that both groups are at the same level in responding to the high-analysis question (meaningful but ungrammatical) (Bialystok, 1986, 1988; Bialystok & Majumder, 1998). These results have been replicated in independent studies (Cromdal, 1999). The pattern has also been shown for other aspects of metalinguistic functioning, including word awareness (Bialystok, 1988) and concepts of print (Bialystok, 1997; Bialystok *et al.*, 2000). If a problem contains misleading information that must be ignored, such as the sentence meaning in the anomalous grammatical sentences, then monolinguals find it more difficult than bilinguals do to ignore that information and respond correctly.

Number concepts

The same pattern has been demonstrated in the acquisition of specific number concepts. Children have a difficult time in coming to understand cardinality, the idea that numbers have quantitative significance (Fuson, 1988; Gelman & Gallistel, 1978; Wynn, 1992). This concept addresses the symbolic basis of numbers that is most closely tied to the symbolic function of language: the number 'four' that children learn in an ordinal sequence has an invariant meaning of 'fourness' as a set size. We tested children's understanding of cardinality using two problems (Bialystok & Codd, 1997). In the towers task, children were shown two towers and asked to count the number of blocks in each and decide which tower had more blocks. The control demands were increased in half the items by building the taller tower out of fewer (but larger) blocks. In these incongruent items, children had to ignore the height and attend only to the number they had just counted. The congruent items could be solved simply by counting the number of blocks in the two towers, but the result of that counting was supported by the perceptual information from the height of the tower: the taller tower also had more blocks. Both groups performed the same (almost at ceiling) for the consistent items in which the counting and perceptual information led to the same judgement, but the bilingual children performed significantly better than the monolinguals in the inconsistent items in which the perceptual information was misleading and had to be ignored. In another problem, the sharing task, children shared a set of candies equally between two identical dolls. They were then asked to count the number of candies in the possession of the first doll, and then to say without counting how many candies the second doll had. Both tasks assessed children's understanding of cardinality, but only the towers task contained misleading information. Bilingual children solved the towers task better than monolinguals but both groups were at the same level in solving the sharing task.

Problem solving

The final example comes from a problem in conceptual sorting. The task is adapted from one developed by Zelazo and his colleagues (Zelazo & Jacques, 1996). Children are required to sort cards into two compartments, each marked by a target stimulus, for example, a red square and a blue circle. The set of cards contains instances of shape-colour combinations that reverse the pairings, in this case, blue squares and red circles. Children are first told to sort by one dimension, for example, colour, then asked to re-sort the same cards by the opposite dimension, shape. The finding is that pre-school children persist in sorting by the first dimension (colour) after they are given the second instructions (shape). Bilingual children, however, adapt to the new rule and solve this problem earlier than monolinguals do (Bialystok, 1999).

There are different possibilities for why children perseverate on the first set of rules. According to Zelazo and Frye (1997), children cannot solve the problem until they acquire sufficiently complex rule systems and reflective awareness of those rules. In contrast, our research has shown that the main impediment to using the new rule to correctly sort the cards the second time is in the requirement for inhibition. Children code the target stimuli according to the first rule system, in this case, the red thing and the blue thing. When the second rule system is explained, those descriptions become obsolete and must be revised, re-coding the targets as the square thing and the round thing. Having already represented the targets in one way, however, it is difficult for children to now think of the items as a square thing and a round thing. This re-interpretation of the targets requires inhibition of their original values, and that is difficult because the colours remain perceptually present even though they are now irrelevant. Some accounts have claimed that the problem is in the inhibition of the response, namely, the act of placing a particular card into a particular box. Our explanation is based on inhibition of the symbolic association that defines the box. There is no reason to believe that the physical response is problematic or that bilingual children have more control over these physical responses.

Across all these studies, the consistent finding is that bilingual children are more advanced than comparable monolinguals on tasks that require inhibition of attention to a misleading cue. The common feature in tasks for which there is a bilingual advantage is the presence of two pieces of competing information, only one of which must be attended to. This attention is the function of control, and bilingual children solve problems designed to assess control earlier and more successfully than monolingual children do. Tasks whose primary processing demand is on analysis of representations are not consistently solved better by bilingual children. Sometimes advantages occur on these tasks, but there are invariably special experiences involved that can be identified as the source of the bilingual advantage. In sum, the process of control of attention appears to develop more easily in bilingual children than in monolinguals. No persistent group difference is found for the development of analysis.

There are two conclusions to be drawn from this series of studies. The first is that there are significant changes in the way in which children carry out general cognitive processing as a function of having learned two languages. The second is that the impact is found in only one of the two processes set out in the analysis-control framework, affirming the distinctness of these processes and suggesting independent developmental courses for each. These conclusions are the basis for considering how to describe the cognitive processes of second-language users.

Language and Cognitive Processing

What could account for the acceleration of the control of attention in bilingual children? Current research on the organisation of two languages in the mind of adult bilinguals shows convincingly that both languages remain active during language processing in either language (Grainger & Dijkstra, 1992). This view is in contrast to earlier models that posited a 'switch' that activated only the relevant language (Macnamara & Kushnir, 1971). But, if both languages are active, then how do speakers maintain performance in only one language without suffering from intrusions by the other? One explanation is that there is constant inhibition of the non-relevant language (Green, 1998; Kroll & De Groot, 1997). In this case, bilingual children experience extensive practice of this function in the first few years of life, and this practice in inhibiting linguistic processing may carry over to processing in disparate cognitive domains.

If this explanation is correct, then there are two important implications. The first is an affirmation of the claim that control of processing, specifically inhibition of attention, is a central cognitive function whose jurisdiction includes linguistic processing. The second is a more subtle extension of this argument: not only is linguistic processing under the influence of the same processes that govern other cognitive functions, but also the influence is bi-directional. A particular language experience, namely, the acquisition of two languages in childhood, can fundamentally alter a cognitive process and the effects of this alteration can be found in children's ability to solve non-verbal problems.

The pattern of cognitive processing found for bilingual children mirrors the profile of cognitive processing in two other populations. First, the pattern of facilitation for bilingual children is the opposite of the pattern of deficit that is found for frontal lobe patients. Individuals with damage to the frontal cortex fail to solve the Wisconsin Card Sort Test (Burgess & Shallice, 1996). This test is similar to the card-sorting task, but is used with adult populations. Respondents must classify stimuli by some perceptual dimension, but at some point the target dimension changes and individuals need to understand that the change has taken place and switch their sorting criterion accordingly. Patients with frontal lobe damage are unable to switch, instead perseverating on the originally successful dimension. These patients also perform poorly on Stroop tests, have difficulty with sentence completion when there are misleading cues, experience perseveration in motor activity, and suffer disturbances in disinhibition and impulsivity (Kimberg *et al.*, 1997). In other words, frontal lobe patients are impaired in solving tasks that require selective attention and the ability to ignore misleading information: precisely the skills in which bilingual children excel. For frontal lobe patients, the impairment is attributed directly to the region of the frontal cortex that is responsible for the executive functions of attention and inhibition.

The second population that reveals reminiscent behavioural patterns is ageing adults who exhibit declines in cognitive processing. The subcomponents of attention, including selective attention and divided attention, that are favoured in the intellectual development of bilingual children have marked similarities to the attentional processes that deteriorate in normal ageing (McDowd & Shaw, 2000, for review). Among the components, however, inhibition is a salient and persistent victim of ageing. Hasher and Zacks (1988) propose a model of attention that includes both the excitatory mechanisms that are triggered by environmental stimuli and the inhibitory mechanisms that are required to suppress the activation of extraneous information. As inhibitory control declines, one becomes more reliant on the familiar, practised and salient routines that characterise automatic responses and less able to carry out intentional thought (Jacoby, 1991). Furthermore, without adequate inhibition, working memory becomes cluttered with irrelevant information and decreases the efficiency of cognitive processing (Hasher *et al.*, 1999). Dempster (1992) proposes a similar description of the function and decline of these inhibitory processes. The consequence of all these conceptions is that older adults have less control over the contents of working memory and therefore less executive control in general than younger adults have.

The parallels in the cognitive profiles of these diverse populations suggest a possible extension of the research on the cognitive processing of second language users. The pattern emerging from the disparate accounts indicates a continuous evolution of a few cognitive mechanisms that are systematically enhanced and diminished throughout the lifespan. There is now reasonable evidence for how bilingualism affects the development and functioning of these processes in childhood. The extension of this research would be to trace these trajectories across the lifespan and to determine whether bilingualism continues to be a significant factor in cognitive functioning. Specifically, it may be the case that the enhancement of control of attention persists into adulthood, and possibly provides a defence against some of the cognitive ravages of ageing.

The pattern of results from these diverse studies with monolingual and bilingual children leads to three general conclusions. First, the extent of the influence of early childhood bilingualism on significant aspects of cognitive development indicates that language and cognition cannot be isolated as independent modules in the child's developing language. Language development has ramifications for general cognition, so theories that partition cognitive domains into a set of non-interacting systems are incompatible with the empirical evidence. Language and cognitive development proceed through the same mechanisms, in response to the same experiences, and with considerable mutual influence on each other.

This conclusion rules out strong forms of at least one of the assumptions underlying formal linguistic theories. The assumption of the autonomy of a linguistic module is difficult to reconcile with a position in which language and a general cognitive process interact bidirectionally early in development. It is particularly troublesome for the strong formal view because this general cognitive process probably resides in the prefrontal cortex and is responsible for control over diverse non-verbal aspects of thought united only by their need for inhibition of attention.

Second, converging evidence points to the centrality of selective attention as one of the primary mechanisms in cognition. Selective attention is normally considered one of the components of the executive functions that guide cognition (e.g. Tipper, 1992) and its impairment under certain kinds of lesions to the brain, specifically in the frontal cortex, is reasonably well understood (e.g. Burgess & Shallice, 1996). The contribution of the research with bilingual children is to identify a specific experience that can enhance its development.

Finally, psychologists have begun looking to the brain to reveal the secrets of the mind. To this end, functional imaging has examined regions of the brain that are involved in different kinds of cognitive activities, different domains of thought and different types of mental processes. Some research with bilinguals has tried to seek evidence for the way two languages are represented. Specifically, do bilinguals have two separate representational areas for language, or just one (e.g. Kim *et al.*, 1997)? The research with bilingual children suggests a different kind of question that may be more significant. The direction would be to use the techniques of functional imaging to examine the function of the frontal cortex, the seat of inhibition. This region be different for bilinguals and may be differentially involved in specific types of thinking. Bilingualism is a significant experience, and we are only beginning to realise the extent of its impact.

References

Bialystok, E. (1986) Factors in the growth of linguistic awareness. *Child Development* 57, 498–510.

Bialystok, E. (1988) Levels of bilingualism and levels of linguistic awareness. *Developmental Psychology* 24, 560–567.

Bialystok, E. (1991) Metalinguistic dimensions of bilingual language proficiency. In E. Bialystok (ed.) *Language Processing in Bilingual Children* (pp. 113–140). Cambridge: Cambridge University Press.

Bialystok, E. (1997) Effects of bilingualism and biliteracy on children's emerging concepts of print. *Developmental Psychology* 33, 429–440.

Bialystok, E. (1998) Beyond binary options: Effects of two languages on the bilingual mind. *Studia Anglica Posnaniensia* 33, 47–60.

Bialystok, E. (1999) Cognitive complexity and attentional control in the bilingual mind. *Child Development* 70, 636–644.

Bialystok, E. (2001) *Bilingualism in Development: Language, Literacy, and Cognition.* Cambridge: Cambridge University Press.

Bialystok, E. and Codd, J. (1997) Cardinal limits: Evidence from language awareness and bilingualism for developing concepts of number. *Cognitive Development* 12, 85–106.

Bialystok, E. and Majumder, S. (1998) The relationship between bilingualism and the development of cognitive processes in problem-solving. *Applied Psycholinguistics* 19, 69–85.

Bialystok, E., Shenfield, T. and Codd, J. (2000) Languages, scripts, and the environment: Factors in developing concepts of print. *Developmental Psychology* 36, 66–76.

Bruner, J. (1983) *Child's Talk: Learning to Use Language.* New York: W.W. Norton.

Burgess, P.W. and Shallice, T. (1996) Response suppression, initiation and strategy use following frontal lobe lesions. *Neuropsychologia* 34, 263–272

Cromdal, J. (1999) Childhood bilingualism and metalinguistic skills: Analysis and control in young Swedish-English bilinguals. *Applied Psycholinguistics* 20, 1–20.

Dagenbach, D. and Carr, T. (1994) *Inhibitory Processes in Attention, Memory, and Language.* New York: Academic Press.

Deacon, T. (1997) *The Symbolic Species: The Co-evolution of Language and the Human Brain.* Harmondsworth: Penguin Press.

Dempster, F.N. (1992) The rise and fall of the inhibitory mechanism: Toward a unified theory of cognitive development and ageing. *Developmental Review* 12, 45–75.

Elman, J.L., Bates, E.A., Johnson, M.H., Karmiloff-Smith, A., Parisi, D. and Plunkett, K. (1996) *Rethinking Innateness: A Connectionist Perspective on Development.* Cambridge, MA: MIT Press.

Fuson, K.C. (1988) *Children's Counting and Concepts of Number.* New York: Springer-Verlag.

Gelman, R. and Gallistel, C.R. (1978) *The Child's Understanding of Number.* Cambridge, MA: Harvard University Press.

Grainger, J. and Dijkstra, A. (1992) On the representation and use of language information in bilinguals. In R.J. Harris (ed.) *Cognitive Processing in Bilinguals* (pp. 207–220). Amsterdam: Elsevier Science Publishers.

Green, D.W. (1998) Mental control of the bilingual lexico-semantic system. *Bilingualism: Language and Cognition* 1, 67–81.

Hakuta, K. (1986) *Mirror of Language: The Debate on Bilingualism.* New York: Basic Books.

Halliday, M.A.K. (1994) *An Introduction to Functional Grammar.* London: Edward Arnold.

Harnishfeger, K.K. and Bjorklund, D.F. (1993) The ontogeny of inhibition mechanisms: A renewed approach to cognitive development. In R. Pasnak and M. Howe (eds) *Emerging Themes in Cognitive Development* (Vol. 1) (pp. 28–49). New York: Springer Verlag.

Hasher, L. and Zacks, R.T. (1988) Working memory, comprehension, and ageing: A review and a new view. In G.H. Bower (ed.) *The Psychology of Learning and Motivation* (Vol. 22, pp. 193–225). San Diego: Academic Press.

Hasher, L., Zacks, R.T. and May, C.P. (1999) Inhibitory control, circadian arousal, and age. In D. Gopher and A. Koriat (eds) *Attention and Performance, XVII: Cognitive Regulation of Performance: Interaction of Theory and Application* (pp. 653–675). Cambridge, MA: MIT Press.

Jacoby, L.L. (1991) A process dissociation framework: Separating automatic from intentional uses of memory. *Journal of Memory and Language* 30, 513–541.

Karmiloff-Smith, A. (1992) *Beyond Modularity: A Developmental Perspective on Cognitive Science.* Cambridge, MA: MIT Press.

Kim, K.H.S., Relkin, N., Lee, K. and Hirsch, J. (1997) Distinct cortical areas associated with native and second languages. *Nature* 388, 171–174.

Kimberg, D.Y., D'Esposito, M. and Farah, M.J. (1997) Effects of bromocriptine on human subjects depend on working memory capacity. *Neuroreport* 8, 3581–3585.

Kroll, J.F. and De Groot, A.M.B. (1997) Lexical and conceptual memory in the bilingual: Mapping form to meaning in two languages In A.M.B. de Groot and J.F. Kroll (eds) *Tutorials in Bilingualism* (pp. 169–199). Mahwah, NJ: Erlbaum.

Locke, J.L. (1993) *The Child's Path to Spoken Language.* Cambridge, MA: Harvard University Press.

Macnamara, J. and Kushnir, S. (1971) Linguistic independence of bilinguals: The input switch. *Journal of Verbal Learning and Verbal Behavior* 10, 480–487.

McDowd, J.M. and Shaw, R.J. (2000) Attention and ageing: A functional perspective. In F.I.M. Craik and T.A. Salthouse (eds.) *The Handbook of Ageing and Cognition* (2nd edn, pp. 221–292). Mahwah, NJ: Erlbaum.

Pinker, S. (1994) *The Language Instinct.* New York: W. Morrow and Co.

Ricciardelli, L.A. (1993) Two components of metalinguistic awareness: Control of linguistic processing and analysis of linguistic knowledge. *Applied Psycholinguistics* 14, 349–367.

Tipper, S. (1992) Selection for actions: The role of inhibitory mechanisms. *Current Directions in Psychological Science* 1, 105–112.

Tipper, S.P. and McLaren, J. (1990) Evidence for efficient visual selectivity in children. In J.T. Enns (ed.) *The Development of Attention: Research and Theory* (pp. 197–210). Amsterdam: Elsevier Science Publishers.

Tomasello, M. (1992) *First Verbs: A Case Study of Early Grammatical Development.* Cambridge: Cambridge University Press.

Tomasello, M. (ed.) (1998) *The New Psychology of Language: Cognitive and Functional Approaches to Language Structure.* Mahwah, NJ: Erlbaum.

Tomasello, M. and Brooks, P.J. (1999). Early syntactic development: A construction grammar approach. In M. Barrett (ed.) *The Development of Language* (pp. 161–190). Hove: Psychology Press.

Wynn, K. (1992) Children's acquisition of the number words and the counting system. *Cognitive Psychology* 24, 220–251.

Zelazo, P.D. and Frye, D. (1997) Cognitive complexity and control: A theory of the development of deliberate reasoning and intentional action. In M. Stamenov (ed.) *Language Structure, Discourse, and the Access to Consciousness* (pp. 113–153). Amsterdam and Philadelphia: John Benjamins.

Zelazo, P.D. and Jacques, S. (1996) Children's rule use: Representation, reflection, and cognitive control. In R. Vasta (ed.) *Annals of Child Development* (Vol. 12, pp. 119–176). London: Jessica Kingsley Press.

Introduction to Chapter 7
Portrait of the Bilingual Child, Fred Genesee

VIVIAN COOK

In this chapter Genesee raises crucial issues about the simultaneous acquisition of two languages by young children. These issues have practical consequences for parents, who do not know whether knowing two languages advantages or disadvantages their children, and for teachers, who do not know how to handle this in their education. Two general questions arise:

- *Does learning a second language damage the young child?* A pamphlet still available for parents of Down syndrome children in England asserts: 'Bilingual families: for any child this is confusing – one language should be the main one to avoid confusion' (Streets, 1976, reprinted 1991). This captures the popular belief in monolingual-dominated societies that a second language introduces a clashing element into the young child's life, supported by Bloomfield for instance – 'this process retards the child's development' (Bloomfield, 1933: 55). Early research found that rural L2 user children in Wales were not only confused but scored ten points lower on IQ tests than monolinguals (Saer, 1922). From the 1960s the pendulum swung towards the positive advantages of L2 use, suggesting that earlier studies had *inter alia* involved children who differed in other factors than knowing a second language, typically advantaged middle-class versus disadvantaged immigrant minorities. Once the well-known effects of social and economic deprivation are eliminated from the analysis, L2 user children show advantages over monolinguals, seen for example in Bialystok's chapter. Lists of advantages include 'creativity' (Lambert *et al.*, 1973), verbal and non-verbal IQ (Peal & Lambert, 1962), literacy learning in the L1 (Yelland *et al.*, 1993), and a range of other factors given for example in Diaz (1985). Comparing children with and without second languages is always problematic. Grosjean (1998) lists six types of variation in bilingual

167

subjects: language history, language stability, functions of language, language proficiency, language modes, and biographical data (age, etc.). Above all, the L2 user perspective does not accept the implication that differences between L2 users and monolinguals mean deficiencies. It is not the comparison with monolinguals that matters so much as what L2 users, perhaps the majority of people in the world, can do in their own right, as Genesee shows firmly.

• *Are the two languages separate or combined in the young child?* This has traditionally been seen as a matter of whether the child has two separate languages or one – a choice between separation and integration poles of the integration continuum used in the background chapter, typically assuming that the more the languages can be kept apart the better. Hence the typical advice to parents since Ronjat (1913) is 'one parent, one language', even though other options have proved successful, depending on the relationship of the language in the home to the language outside (Harding & Riley, 1986). Some have interpreted the question developmentally; the child starts with an integrated system, which then splits in two. Oksaar (1971) for example studied a child who kept the pronunciation of Swedish and Estonian separate up to the age of three. Typical evidence is whether there are 'mixed language sentences'; De Houwer (1990) argued for separate English and Dutch grammatical systems in the child she was observing because of the low proportion of mixed sentences. The implication is that the child should be able to keep the languages completely apart, and that code-switching is part of the damage inflicted on the L2 child, not an inevitable part of L2 use. The importance of Genesee's position here is the recognition that the code-mixing of the L2 child is skilful and purposeful; as Gawlitzek-Maiwald and Tracy (1996) put it, code-mixing, is 'a sign of what the child CAN do'.

References

Bloomfield, L. (1933) *Language*. New York: Holt.
De Houwer, A. (1990) *The Acquisition of Two Languages from Birth: A Case Study.* Cambridge: Cambridge University Press.
Diaz, R.M. (1985) The intellectual power of bilingualism. *Quarterly Newsletter of the Laboratory of Comparative Human Cognition* 7 (1), 16–22.
Gawlitzek-Maiwald, I. and Tracy, R. (1996) Bilingual bootstrapping. *Linguistics* 34, 901–926.
Grosjean, F. (1998) Studying bilinguals: Methodological and conceptual issues. *Bilingualism: Language and Cognition* 1 (2), 131–149.

Harding, E. and Riley, P. (1986) *The Bilingual Family: A Handbook for Parents.* Cambridge: Cambridge University Press.

Lambert, W., Tucker, C.R. and d'Anglejan, A. (1973) Cognitive and attitudinal consequences of bilingual schooling. *Journal of Educational Psychology* 85 (2), 141–159.

Oksaar, E. (1971) Zum Spracherwerb des Kindes in Zweisprachiger Umgebung. *Folia Linguistica* 4, 330–358.

Peal, E. and Lambert, W. (1962) The relation of bilingualism to intelligence. *Psychological Monographs* 76 (27), 1–23.

Ronjat, J. (1913) *Le Développement du Langage Observé Chez un Enfant Bilingue.* Paris: Champion.

Saer, D.J. (1922) An inquiry into the effect of bilingualism upon the intelligence of young children. *Journal of Experimental Pedagogy* 6, 232–240 and 266–274.

Streets, L. (1976, reprinted 1991) *I Can Talk.* London: Down Syndrome Association.

Yelland, G.W., Pollard, J. and Mercuri, A. (1993) The metalinguistic benefits of limited contact with a second language. *Applied Psycholinguistics* 14, 423–444.

Chapter 7
Portrait of the Bilingual Child

FRED GENESEE

Researchers/theoreticians, professionals and laypersons alike often view the simultaneous acquisition of two languages during the pre-school years with reservation and outright apprehension because it is thought to exceed the language learning capacity of the young child and thus to incur potential costs, such as delayed or incomplete language development or even deviant development. Such views are often evident in communities and among individuals who themselves are monolingual. They are reinforced in the research community by the overwhelming attention paid to monolingual acquisition by researchers and in research journals and textbooks. Most linguistic and psycholinguistic theories of language acquisition are silent on the matter of bilingual acquisition, reinforcing the notion that monolingualism is the norm, and bilingualism is not. What is normal is usually regarded as risk-free; and by default bilingual acquisition is, thus, often viewed as extraordinary and potentially putting the individual at some kind of risk (Genesee, 1988). Demographically speaking, however, there is no reason to believe that bilingualism is in fact unusual; to the contrary, there may well be as many, or more, children who grow up bilingually as monolingually (Tucker, 1998).

This chapter will review current scientific evidence concerning the simultaneous acquisition of two languages during the first years of life with a view to evaluating these pessimistic views of bilingual acquisition. The focus will be on one aspect of bilingual acquisition, namely bilingual code-mixing. Bilingual code-mixing is the use of elements (phonological, lexical, and morpho-syntactic) from two languages in the same utterance or stretch of conversation. Code-mixing has been a primary focus of attention in this field of research and a significant source of misperception concerning bilingual development. It will be discussed in the following sections from multiple perspectives – cognitive, linguistic and communicative – and the interpretation of the evidence that is offered will challenge the view that simultaneous acquisition of two languages is burdensome and puts the learner at risk.

Before proceeding, it is important to point out that, while the focus in this chapter is on the simultaneous acquisition of two oral languages, bilingual first language acquisition can also refer to the acquisition of more than two languages – that is, multilingual acquisition (see Quay, 2001, for an example) and to the acquisition of signed as well as spoken languages (e.g. Petitto *et al.*, 2001; Richmond-Welty & Siple, 1999).

Cognitive Perspective

Young children in the process of learning two languages often use elements from both languages in the same utterance or stretch of conversation when they start speaking. This has been noted by many researchers and is often referred to as code-mixing or code switching (see Genesee, 1989, for a review). The mixed elements can include different aspects of language, including sounds, words, or grammatical structures (see Genesee, 1989). Let us look at a couple of examples. Using a word from one language while using the other language is the most common form of mixing among children. For example, a young Spanish/German bilingual boy speaking with his Spanish-speaking mother said, *Das no juegan. Das* is the German word for *that* and *no juegan* is Spanish for *do not play* (Redlinger & Park, 1980: 341). Using the syntactic (grammatical) patterns of one language while speaking another language is another form of mixing. Saunders (1982) reported that his five-year old German/English-speaking son said to his English-speaking mother, *Mum, I had my school jumper all day on* (p. 178). While German requires this word order, this construction is not grammatical in English.

Bilingual children's use of elements from both languages in the same utterance or conversation has often been interpreted to mean that their developing representations of the two languages are not neuro-cognitively differentiated (Redlinger & Park, 1980; Swain, 1977; Volterra & Taeschner, 1978; for contrary views, see Bergman, 1976, and Padilla & Liebman, 1975). From a cognitive perspective, this interpretation of code-mixing implies that the child possesses a single unified system and, therefore, is not actually bilingual yet. This perspective is often referred to as the unitary language system hypothesis (Genesee, 1989). Separation of the two languages, or true bilingualism, is argued to occur by about the age of three (Leopold, 1949), when rates of mixing often decrease and the child uses one language predominantly with speakers of each language. There are wide individual differences in the rates of code-mixing – an issue that I will refer to later. Volterra and Taeschner (1978) formulated the most detailed and explicit theory of bilingual differentiation with the lexicon differentiating first, followed by syntax.

Adult bilinguals also code-mix with one another; it is more common to use the term code-switching when referring to adult bilingual usage (Myers-Scotton, 1993; Poplack, 1980). I use the more neutral term *code-mixing* when referring to bilingual children's language usage so as not to presuppose that it shares the same functional and structural properties as adult bilingual code-switching. The precise functional and structural properties of child bilingual code-mixing and its similarity to adult usage remain to be determined. Research has shown that adult code-switching is sociolinguistically and grammatically constrained; that is, it is not random. Sociolinguistically, adult bilingual code-switching is shaped by characteristics of interlocutors, the situation and the purpose of communication. Adult bilinguals code-switch for a variety of meta-communicative purposes; for example, to mark ethnic identities or affiliations, to negotiate social roles and status, and to establish interpersonal intimacy or distance. It has also been shown that the social functions of adult code-switching are conditioned by community factors. Poplack (1987), for example, has noted differences in prevalence, form and purpose in French/English code-switching in the Ottawa–Hull region of Canada in comparison to Spanish/English code-switching in the Puerto Rican community of New York City. Grammatically speaking, most theoreticians believe that adult code-switching is grammatically constrained; I explore the matter of grammatical constraints on child code-mixing in a later section. The evidence indicates further that proficient adult bilinguals engage in relatively fluent, sophisticated and prevalent code-switching in comparison to less proficient bilinguals. In sum, code-switching is a useful, sophisticated and rule-governed feature of language use among adult bilinguals and is linked to bilingual competence. In contrast, child bilingual code-mixing has often been interpreted as a sign of incompetence and even confusion.

Early studies of child bilingual code-mixing often suffered from a number of methodological weaknesses that compromise their interpretation of their results. For example, Volterra and Taeschner's (1978) model was based on evidence consisting of single, isolated examples of code-mixing. They did not examine their children's overall rates of mixing so we have no way of knowing how prevalent it actually was. Other evidence suggests that intra-utterance mixing is quite low (less than 10% of the children's overall language productions), and thus cannot be construed as evidence of their overall language usage (Genesee *et al.*, 1995). Yet other studies reported children's rates of mixing as a percentage of their total language output, but they often failed to examine the children's language use in different language contexts – examining the child's rates of mixing with interlocutors who speak different languages is critical to ascertaining whether the child can differentiate their two languages. In addition, few early studies examined how often bilingual children did *not* mix; that is, how often they produced entire utterances in the language of their interlocutor. Excluding these utterances yields an incomplete and thus misleading picture of their language use. In short, owing to methodological shortcomings, the conclusions from many early studies can be called into question.

Recent evidence refutes earlier interpretations of children's code-mixing. In fact, it is now generally accepted that bilingual children can use their developing languages differentially and appropriately from the one-word stage onward, and certainly from the stage when there is evidence of syntax in their spoken language (De Houwer, 1990; Genesee, 1989; Goodz, 1994; Lanza, 1997; Meisel, 1994; Petitto *et al.*, 2001). In the first study that systematically examined child bilingual code-mixing in context, Genesee *et al.* (1995) observed English/French bilingual children from Montreal during naturalistic interactions with their parents in the home. The parents, who spoke different native languages, used primarily their native language with their children – the so-called 'one parent, one language' rule. Thus, the parents presented different language contexts. The children were observed on three separate occasions: once with their mothers alone; once with their fathers alone; and once with both parents present. By observing the children with each parent individually and when both parents were present, we were able to observe the children's ability to keep their languages separate in different language contexts. The children were between 22 and 26 months of age and were in the one-word and early two-word stage of language development. We examined not only the frequency of the children's mixing (within and between utterances), but also the frequency with which they used single-language utterances that were appropriate to each parent (e.g. French utterances with the French-speaking parent and English with the English-speaking parent).

Even at this young age, these children were able to use their two languages in a context-sensitive manner; they used substantially more French than English with their French-speaking parent, and substantially more English than French with their English-speaking parent. When the parents were together with the children, the children likewise used more of the father's language with the father than with the mother, and vice versa for the mother's language (see Figure 7.1). That these children used their two languages appropriately with each parent, whether alone or together, is incompatible with the unitary language system hypothesis – according

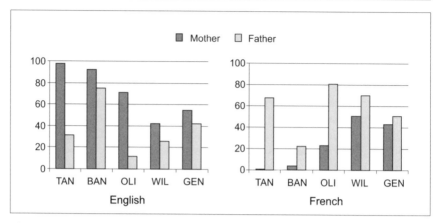

Figure 7.1 Children's use of French and English with parents together (mothers were English-speakers and fathers were French-speakers)

to this hypothesis, one would expect random use of each language, regardless of language context.

We conducted a follow-up study to examine the limits of young bilingual children's ability to use their developing languages appropriately (Genesee *et al.*, 1996). The initial study may have underestimated the ability of bilingual children to differentiate their languages because their parents, like the parents of many bilingual children, knew and sometimes used both languages with their children and thus they did not strictly require separation of the languages. Moreover, the differentiation that we observed might have reflected a process of associative learning whereby each child had come to associate certain words with each parent over time – French words with the French-speaking parent and English words with the English-speaking parent. True bilingual communicative competence entails the ability to adapt one's language use on-line in accordance with relevant characteristics of the situation, including the preferred or more proficient language of one's interlocutor. Thus, taken alone, our initial results would not reflect true communicative competence.

In order to examine these issues, we observed a number of additional French/English bilingual children during play sessions with monolingual strangers. The children had an average age of 24 months and their MLUs (mean length of utterance, measured in words) in French varied from 1.08 to 1.59 and in English from 1.33 to 1.66. These MLU values put these children in the one-word stage of development, according to Brown's (1973) guidelines. We selected strangers as conversational partners with the children on the assumption that evidence of differential language use on the part of the children with unfamiliar interlocutors would reinforce our argument that two-year-old bilinguals' languages are differentiated. It would also attest to true on-line communicative competence at an early stage of acquisition. The children would not have been able to associate the right language with this interlocutor, because this was the first time they had talked with her. We selected *monolingual* strangers in order to ascertain the children's ability to identify critical language characteristics of an interlocutor, despite having had minimal prior exposure with her. Since the language spoken by the stranger was the less proficient language of three of the four children, this was a particularly rigorous test of their abilities to accommodate the stranger.

Three of the four children gave evidence of on-line adjustments to the stranger by using more of the stranger's language with the stranger than they did with their parents and, in particular, the parent who spoke the same language as the stranger (usually the father). One of the children did not modify her language use appropriately with the stranger. Figure 7.2 presents results for two of the children, JES and JOE, who made the most clear-cut adjustments to the stranger. Also, three of the children used less of the language not known by the stranger with the stranger than they did with either parent. In short, these results indicated that the children were both extending their use of the stranger's language as much as possible and minimising their use of the language that the stranger did not know as much as possible. Thus, despite the fact that these three children had had no prior experience with this adult, and despite the fact that they were compelled to use their less proficient language with her, they not only used

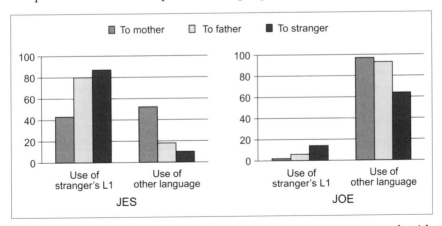

Figure 7.2 Children's use of their languages with a stranger and with parents

the appropriate language, they used it more frequently with the monolingual stranger than with the parent who also spoke that language. Many bilingual children appear to be more proficient in one of their languages relative to the other; proficiency is defined in different ways by different researchers, and can include MLU, relative number of word types and tokens, number of multimorphemic utterances in each language, and parental reports. It is often, although not always, associated with the amount of exposure to each language, with the more proficient language being the language of greater exposure. That they used a great deal of the language not known by the stranger simply reflects their proficiency in that language, a pattern that we observed even when the children were speaking with their parents; I will return to this issue later. The children did not all perform alike; one of the children (whose results are not included in Figure 7.2) did not appear to accommodate the stranger at all. This should not be surprising, given the well-documented and large individual differences among children in a variety of different aspects of language acquisition. There is no reason to believe that the development of communicative competence (bilingual or monolingual) is not subject to the same individual variation among children that is demonstrated in other aspects of language acquisition.

The research evidence reviewed in this section demonstrates clearly that, contrary to the unitary language system hypothesis, code-mixing is not symptomatic of linguistic fusion or confusion. Bilingual children in the one-word stage of development demonstrate that they can use their developing languages differentially and appropriately with interlocutors who use different languages. They demonstrate this ability even if they have had no prior experience with the interlocutor. These findings indicate that bilingual children develop the rudimentary sociolinguistic skills appropriate for bilingual usage from the outset, and that they possess the neurocognitive capacity to acquire and use two languages. In the next section, we examine the nature of their underlying linguistic systems directly.

Linguistic Perspective

Additional evidence that child bilingual code-mixing does not reflect the existence of an initial unitary language system comes from careful analyses of the linguistic development of children acquiring two languages. The issue here concerns the nature of the abstract knowledge (or competence) that underlies the bilingual child's language performance. Linguistically speaking, this knowledge is usually conceptualised as a system of structural constraints or principles that serve to organise the sounds, words and grammatical structures that comprise a language. The specific question here is whether young children exposed to two languages acquire abstract constraints (or 'rules') that from the outset are different for, and specific to, each of the languages being learned. Evidence that they do would be additional evidence for linguistic differentiation, and against fusion. There has been research on this question in early phonological production and sentential-grammar (or syntax); most research has focused on syntax, and so this will be the focus of the following discussion.

Were the unitary language system hypothesis true, from a syntax-theoretic perspective, one would expect one of three possibilities (see Meisel, 2000, for a more elaborate discussion of these possibilities):

(1) This system would be made up of the structural constraints that characterise one of the child's languages, and it would provide the basis for all of the child's early productions, regardless of language context – e.g. a French/English child would use the English Adj+Noun word order for adjective-noun constructions in both English and French, even though French uses a Noun+Adj order for most such constructions.

(2) This system would be comprised of syntactic constraints that are unrelated to either of the languages the child is acquiring – e.g. the same English-bilingual child would omit subject pronouns in all utterances in both languages, despite the fact that both languages require subject pronouns to be supplied in obligatory contexts.

(3) There would be a hybrid system comprised of syntactic constraints from both languages and it would be applied to all of the child's productions regardless of language context.

In fact, bilingual children have not demonstrated any of these possibilities. To the contrary, research has shown that bilingual children acquire language-specific and language-appropriate constraints in each language, for the most part. Paradis and Genesee (1996), for example, found that 2–3 year old French/English bilingual children:

(1) used finite verb forms earlier in French than in English – their French verbs were inflected for tense from 1;11 years (that is to say 1 year 11 months old) of age much more frequently (51% vs. 10%); than their English verbs at the same age:

(2) used subject pronouns in French exclusively with finite verbs (e.g. *il tombe* but not *il tomber*); but they used subject pronouns in English almost equally with both finite and non-finite verbs (e.g. *he talks* and *he talk*). These results are in accordance with the status of subject

pronouns as clitics (or agreement markers) in French but full NPs in English;
(3) appropriately placed negators after finite verbs in French (e.g. *je veux pas parler á Papa)*, but before lexical verbs in English (e.g. *I do not want it*).

These patterns characterise the performance of children acquiring these languages monolingually as well as monolingual adults. Moreover, the bilingual children acquired these patterns within the same age range as monolingual children. Methodologically, it is important to examine syntactic patterns that differ in monolingual child language as well as adult language because there are some patterns in early child language that appear to be virtually universal (e.g. omission of subject pronouns or determiner phrases) and thus are insensitive to differences between languages. Evidence of differentiated syntactic development has similarly been reported by De Houwer (1990) in an English/Dutch child (between 2;7 and 3;8 years of age), and Meisel (1986, 1989) in children acquiring French and Dutch (from 1;10 years of age).

At the same time, there is some evidence that specific aspects of certain language combinations may interact during bilingual development; in other words, the two grammars do not develop entirely autonomously as was reported above. Paradis and Genesee (1996: 3) define linguistic interaction as 'the systemic influence of the grammar of one language on the grammar of the other language during acquisition, causing differences in a bilingual's patterns or rates of development in comparison with a monolingual's'. We distinguish between accelerated and delayed acquisition and transfer as alternative forms of cross-linguistic interaction. While there is no evidence to date of significant delay or acceleration in bilingual development, as noted above, there is evidence of transfer in specific syntactic domains under certain circumstances. For example, Döpke (2000) reports that Australian children learning English and German simultaneously overgeneralised the Verb Object (V-O) order of English to German. German instantiates both VO (Verb-Object) and OV (Object-Verb) word orders depending on the complexity of the utterance. The VO order occurs in simple sentences such as *ich sehe dich* (I see you) SVO and the OV order in more complex sentence (e.g. *er kann dich sehen* (he can see you) S-AUX-OV. For example, they produced utterances of the type *S-AUX-VO: ich möchte tragen dich* (I want to carry you) which are never produced by monolingual German-speaking children. Working within the competition theory of language acquisition (Bates & MacWhinney, 1987), Döpke argued that the children were prone to overgeneralise the VO word order in their German because this order was reinforced in both the German and English simple sentences that they often hear. Hulk and Müller (2000: 229) have similarly argued that 'there has to be a certain overlap of the two systems at the surface level' for cross-linguistic syntactic influences to occur. Paradis (2000) also refers to structural overlap in the input as a possible explanation in cases of phonological transfer that she noted in the development of 2–3 year-old French/English bilinguals. Yip and Matthews (2000), along with Paradis, have proposed that proficiency may be an additional explanatory factor – more specifically, properties of the more proficient language may be incorporated inappropriately but temporarily into the less proficient language (see also Petersen, 1988). Proficiency alone is not sufficient to produce transfer, since at least one of Paradis and Genesee's French/ English subjects showed the same syntactic patterns as French-speaking children even though he was more proficient in English (see also Hulk & Müller, 2000, and Döpke, 2000).

It is important to note that these instances of cross-linguistic transfer are restricted. They pertain to specific aspects of the child's developing grammars, and they appear to occur only under certain linguistic circumstances – where there is overlap in the structures of the two languages for the analogous property and, possibly, when there is more proficiency in one language. Moreover, they are temporary since we know from research on adult bilinguals that, in the long run, bilingual children can (and most do) acquire the appropriate target language forms (White & Genesee, 1996). In short, these instances of transfer, while interesting, do not compromise the general conclusion that the syntactic systems of bilingual children are differentiated, and they are the same in most respects as those of monolingual children at the same stage of development.

Evidence for syntactic differentiation is most clear and, in fact, largely uncontroversial when bilingual children exhibit definite morpho-syntactic constructions in their language productions. However, children in the earliest stages of acquisition of some languages do not show clear knowledge of syntax. For example, inflectional morphology is absent and word order is simplified in children learning English during the one-word and two-word stages. There is some debate whether children have syntax during these stages of development. On the basis of a longitudinal study of a child acquiring English and Spanish, Deuchar and Quay (2000: 88) have argued that, while this child exhibited distinct and language-specific morpho-syntax from 1;11 onward, she possessed only 'a *single* rudimentary predicate-argument syntax' earlier in development (see Meisel, 2000, for a critique of this position). The question of syntactic differentiation in very young children acquiring two languages simultaneously begs a much more fundamental and thorny question; namely, whether children possess detailed innate knowledge concerning the syntactic properties of language from the outset (i.e. at birth). The alternative view is that such knowledge matures or is acquired as the child is exposed to and learns the target language. Clearly, one would not expect bilingual children to have differentiated syntactic systems during an early period in language development if syntax must mature or be acquired and, therefore, is not present from the outset. One way in which this fundamental issue could be addressed effectively is for researchers to examine bilingual children acquiring languages that give rise to early instantiations of language-specific syntactic properties, such as Inuktitut (Allen, 1996), along with a language that does not, such as English. Such cases could provide evidence of syntactic differentiation earlier than has been attested in the language combinations studied so far; we are currently in the process of conducting such a study.

Research on phonological development during the one-word stage could also provide evidence for linguistic differentiation even before the emergence of complex spoken language and overt syntactic constructions. In a re-analysis of longitudinal data from Leopold's daughter Hildegard, Paradis (1996) found that her phonological development followed 'different paths' in German and English from 1;6 years of age, during the earliest stages of productive language use (for a similar view, see Johnson & Lancaster, 1998; and for a contending view see Deuchar & Quay, 2000). Thus it appears that linguistic differentiation is present from the onset of the one-word stage.

In sum, contrary to the view that exposure to two languages from birth poses challenges to normal language development, the research results reviewed in this section indicate that children exposed to two languages from birth can acquire differentiated language-specific phonological and morpho-syntactic properties very early in development. Further evidence that bilingual acquisition does not pose extraordinary challenges to the developing child comes from studies reporting that bilingual children do not demonstrate delays in critical aspects of language development in comparison to monolingual children; some of these studies were referred to above. Cases of cross-linguistic transfer that have been reported to date are restricted to specific aspects of the grammars being learned and, importantly, they are constrained by the grammatical architecture of the two languages – in other words, they are not random.

Grammatical Constraints on Code-Mixing

I would like to explore the linguistic dimension of bilingual acquisition further, but with reference to the main focus of this chapter – *code-mixing*. The specific issue I would like to examine in this section concerns the grammatical organisation of bilingual children's early intra-utterance code-mixing – that is code-mixing that involves the use of elements (usually words) from both languages in the same utterance, e.g. *où car?* ('where car?' or 'where is the car?'). In question is whether intra-utterance mixing of elements in young bilingual children's early language occurs freely and thus violates the otherwise structural orderliness of language, or whether it is constrained in systematic ways. If we can show that child bilingual code-mixing is grammatically constrained, then we can argue that mixing is not symptomatic of incompetence because, like all other language phenomena that have been studied, it is organised according to certain linguistic principles. Moreover, if we can show that child bilingual code-mixing is organised according to the same principles that characterise adult code-mixing, then we can argue that bilingual children operate with essentially the same abstract grammatical knowledge as proficient adult bilinguals. And, finally, if we can show that child bilingual code-mixing is organised in accordance with the distinctive grammatical properties of the two languages being learned, we can then argue that they can co-ordinate their two grammars during on-line production according to the constraints that operate in each language. In other words, we could argue that the developing bilingual child not only possesses two grammars but can co-ordinate the two grammars to avoid linguistically illicit constructions. This would constitute a form of linguistic competence that sets bilingual children apart from monolingual children who lack such competence, because they possess only one grammar.

Grammatical constraints on code-switching in adult bilinguals have been the object of extensive investigation and theoretical speculation for some time, as noted earlier. When two languages are used in the same utterance, incompatibilities in the languages could arise due to differences in word order, inflectional morphology and syntactic sub-categorisation; these in turn can result in patterns of language use that are awkward or illicit. Indeed, the commonly held perception of code-switching is that it is a 'bastardised' (ungrammatical) form of language and, for this reason, parents and others often discourage their children from code-mixing. Contrary to this perception, it is generally agreed that adult bilingual code-switching is usually grammatical. Adult bilinguals code-switch selectively within utterances so that they avoid violating the grammatical constraints of each language. Until recently, there has been no systematic examination of the actual organisation of children's intra-utterance mixing and thus the misperception has prevailed that it is disorganised and symptomatic of low levels of language proficiency.

Several contending principles have been proposed to account for the constraints on adult code-switching (e.g. di Sciullo *et al.*, 1986; Myers-Scotton, 1993; Poplack, 1980). For example, in one of the earliest theories of bilingual code-mixing, Poplack (1980) proposed that there are two major principles that constrain intra-utterance code-mixing:

(1) Equivalence constraint. Code-switches will tend to occur at points in discourse where juxtaposition of L$_x$ and L$_y$ elements does not violate a syntactic rule of either language: that is, points around which the surface structures of two languages map onto each other' (Poplack, 1980). Code-switching will not occur around points where the surface structure of the two languages lack equivalence. For example, French/English bilinguals will avoid saying *I hid le* (I hid it), because object pronouns occur pre-verbally in French and post-verbally in English. However, they might say *I hid le bonbon* (I hid the candy), because both English and French have SVO word order.

(2) *Free morpheme constraint.* Codes may be switched after any constituent provided that constituent is not a bound morpheme; in other words, bound inflectional or derivational morphemes should not be mixed – for example, English/French bilinguals will avoid mixing verbal inflections from English with French lexical verbs: '*je mang-ing*' (I am eating).

Poplack and her colleagues have postulated an additional mechanism by which incompatibilities are avoided when two languages are used in the same utterance – namely, *nonce borrowing* (Poplack & Meecham, 1988). This mechanism applies to utterances in which the mixed element is a single lexical item, usually of a major form class, such as a noun or verb. According to Poplack (1988: 1179), 'nonce borrowing ... involves syntactic, morphological, and (possibly) phonological integration into a recipient language of an element from a donor language'. Nonces are like established loan words in that they preserve the monolinguality of the utterance. In contrast to established loan words, which occur frequently in community usage and, in fact, are regarded as bona fide lexical units in the recipient language, nonces occur infrequently and episodically in discourse. (Established loan words are words such as *rendezvous* which were originally French but have been adopted as full-fledged English words.) An example of nonce borrowing in French/English usage would be *Yesterday, I went to* the <u>centre-d'achat</u> (*shopping centre*) *and I bought a new suit*. Nonce borrowing deserves attention in the study of child bilingual code-mixing, because single content words are often the most commonly mixed units in bilingual children's mixing.

Because of the evidence found in studies of adults, we know that bilingual children ultimately acquire grammatical constraints on their code-mixing. The questions of concern here are whether there are grammatical constraints on child bilingual code-mixing, the nature of those constraints, and the age at which they are evidenced. Aside from their specific theoretical significance, these questions address the general issue of concern in this chapter –that bilingual acquisition is challenging and can compromise normal language development. Evidence for grammatical constraints on child code-mixing would argue for competence in coordinating two languages during on-line processing, much like that which has been attested in adult bilinguals. Evidence of grammatical constraints on child bilingual code-mixing would complement the evidence presented in the preceding section that bilingual child language is orderly and rule-governed, and thus would support the general conclusion that the neuro-cognitive capacities of humans support bilingual acquisition as well as monolingual acquisition.

Answering these questions is potentially problematic because, as noted earlier, there is no consensus among researchers who have examined adult code-mixing as to what the specific constraints are; and thus application of different adult models to child code-mixing could yield divergent findings. There is the added problem of mapping the constraint-models developed on the basis of adult bilingual competence onto bilingual child language, which may or may not be the same, although it is clearly en route to adult competence. Arguably, this is an issue for all studies of child language acquisition which are, for the most part, guided by theoretical models that are based on mature, adult language. There is a further complication that can arise from divergent patterns that might result from comparing mixing in languages that are typologically similar (such as English and French) versus those that are divergent (Inuktitut and English). Thus, triangulation of results based on different language combinations (including pairs that are typologically more or less divergent) and different constraint models is critical to answering the questions posed earlier.

Fortunately, there have been a number of studies recently that, collectively, meet these requirements, and there is a remarkable degree of consensus among them with respect to their general conclusions. To date, research has examined constraints on intra-utterance code-mixing by bilingual children learning the following language pairs: French and German

(Köppe, in press; Meisel, 1994), French and English (Genesee & Sauve, 2000; Paradis *et al.*, 2000); English and Norwegian (Lanza, 1997); English and Estonian (Vihman, 1998), and Inuktitut and English (Allen *et al.*, 1999). The constraint models of Poplack (1980) and of Myers-Scotton (1993) have formed the basis for most, although not all, analyses in studies on this topic (see Köppe, in press, and Meisel, 1994, who based their analysis on more general generativist principles). The Myers-Scotton and Poplack models differ substantially in the extent to which they refer to abstract, underlying grammatical constructs (such as system and content morphemes) versus surface level grammatical phenomena (such as word order and bound versus open class morphemes), respectively. Despite the diversity of language pairs and analytic frameworks that comprise this body of research, all researchers have concluded that child bilingual code-mixing is grammatically constrained. The operation of constraints based on abstract notions of grammatical knowledge, which are at the core of Myers-Scotton's Matrix Language Frame model, is most evident in bilingual children once they exhibit such knowledge in their actual language use (as marked by verb tense and agreement, for example), usually around 2;6 years of age and older, while the operation of constraints that reflect surface features of grammar (such as word order) are evident even earlier in development, prior to overt marking of abstract grammatical relations in the child's language, from the two-word/morpheme stage onward. Köppe (in press) has proposed a hybrid model, composed of linear, word order constraints during the early stages of production and abstract, hierarchically-organised constraints subsequently.

Research in our own laboratory that compares code-mixing in pairs of languages with radically different structural properties sheds further light on the sophistication of the young bilingual child's capacity to acquire and manage two distinct linguistic systems. We have compared the code-mixing of children acquiring English and French, as noted earlier, with that of children acquiring English and Inuktitut, the language of the Inuit in Northern Quebec (see Allen, 1996, for research on acquisition of Inuktitut as a first language). We based our analyses on Poplack's framework since it applies more easily to both early and later stages of acquisition. To fully understand our results, it is necessary to provide a brief comparative description of these language pairs.

English is a language of the Germanic branch of the Indo-European family. It is relatively sparse in its morphological inventory, particularly with respect to inflectional morphology; the morphology it does have follows a mildly synthetic pattern. That is, it consists primarily of suffixes (e.g. *in*attentive) and affixes (e.g. walk*ed*). Syntactic relations are indicated primarily through word order, with the basic word order being SVO. French, although a member of the Romance branch of the Indo-European family, shares many of the same characteristics as English. English and French provide relatively few structural contrasts and, most importantly, there are few discrepancies between the two languages that could cause violations of either of Poplack's constraints during code-mixing.

Inuktitut is a language of the Eskimo branch of the Eskimo-Aleut family. In contrast to English, it is extremely rich in its morphological inventory, which numbers some 400 derivational affixes and more than 1000 inflectional affixes. Though basic word order is SOV, word order is typically relatively free and differences in word order are linked to discourse phenomena rather than to syntactic relations. Syntax tends to be marked within the word, both through extensive inflectional morphology and through a variety of derivational affixes that change word class (polysynthesis). Thus, an utterance such as that which follows is quite typical for adult Inuktitut. Line (1) presents the utterance in its entirety; (2) breaks it down in to separate morphemes; (3) provides a linguistic gloss of it; and (4) provides an English gloss of the utterance.

(1) Illujuaraalummuulaursimannginamalittauq.
(2) illu-juaq-aluk-mut-uq-lauq-sima-nngit-nama-li-ttauq
(3) house-big-EMPH-ALL.SG-go-PAST-PERF-NEG-CSV.1sS-but-also
(4) 'But also, because I never went to the really big house.' (Dorais, 1988: 8)

This word begins with the noun root *illu* 'house', followed by two nominal modifiers and then the allative case marker *mut*. The next morpheme, *uq* 'go', turns the word into a verb, and is followed by two tense-aspect affixes, a negation affix, and then the verbal inflection *nama* (CSV.1sS). The final two affixes are enclitics. Thus, although this word begins as a noun, it changes into a verb; the meaning of an entire English sentence is conveyed through its 11 morphemes. In contrast to English and French, Inuktitut and English provide extensive contrasts in word order, and the rich inflectional and derivational morphology of Inuktitut is in sharp contrast to the paucity of such morphology in English.

The combination of Inuktitut and English provides a particularly interesting test case for examination of Poplack's constraints and the possible role of nonce borrowing in child bilingual code-mixing. Relevant to the Free Morpheme Constraint, this language pair is interesting because of Inuktitut's extraordinarily rich inflectional morphology and the fact that young monolingual Inuit children demonstrate knowledge and use of it as early as 2;0 years (Crago & Allen, 2001). In fact, almost all words in typical spoken Inuktitut are composed of two or more morphemes, and thus mixing of English and Inuktitut provides ample opportunity for violating the Free Morpheme Constraint. With respect to the Equivalence Constraint, English and Inuktitut also provide an interesting combination since, for most syntactic structures, they either have different word orders (e.g. in a prepositional phrase, English requires PREP-N order, while Inuktitut requires the reverse) or English licenses only one order and Inuktitut licenses alternative ordering of elements (e.g. in a verb phrase, English requires verb-object order while Inuktitut allows both verb-object and object-verb orders). Thus, there is ample opportunity to violate the word order (and morphological) characteristics of Inuktitut if it is mixed with English.

When we analysed the code-mixing of ten English/French bilingual children (from 1;10 to 3;08 years of age), we found that virtually all 429 code-mixed utterances that occurred in their language samples conformed to Poplack's Equivalence and Free Morpheme Constraints (Genesee & Sauve, 2000). In fact, the children generally avoided code-mixing in an utterance when it could violate either constraint. There were only four utterances that could be interpreted as violations of either constraint, for example:

(1) OLI: I'm gonna play with my <u>rose</u> bat (2;11 M)

   I am gonna play with my pink bat.

Utterance (1) is an example of a violation of the Equivalence Constraint because the French adjective *rose* would normally follow a noun in French, but it appears before this English noun.

(2) GEN: bross-<u>ing</u> dents (2;07 F)

   brushing (my) teeth

Utterance (2) is a violation of the Free Morpheme constraint, which prohibits affixing a bound morpheme from one language (*-ing* from English) to a free morpheme from another language.

In contrast, when we analysed the code-mixing of 6 Inuktitut/English children (2;1 to 3;3 years of age), we found many more instances (well over 50%) of mixing that could be interpreted as violations of each constraint (Allen *et al.*, 1999). However, when these utterances were examined more carefully, the vast majority could be interpreted as nonce borrowings; more specifically, they involved the insertion of single English words into utterances that followed Inuktitut patterns; for example:

(3) <u>movie</u>-mik rumajunga

    <u>movie</u>-mik ruma-junga

    movie (MOD.SG) want (PAR.1sS)

    'I want a movie'.

This utterance has Inuktitut word order and inflectional patterns and thus can be interpreted as an Inuktitut utterance with an English word (*movie*) that has been incorporated into it. In effect, the English word *movie* has temporarily been treated as if it were an Inuktitut word. Poplack has found that this is exactly how adult bilinguals who know similarly different languages (Finnish and English) code-mix (Poplack *et al.*, 1987). By comparing the performance of these two groups of bilingual children, we can see that they knew the structural properties of the two language systems they were acquiring, since each group was able to mix its two languages using different strategies that avoided violations of each language's grammatical constraints.

Taken together, these findings indicate that there is no fundamental difference between the constraints on child code-mixing and those that have been attested in adult bilingual code-switching. By inference, child code-mixing is not symptomatic of incompetence. The linguistic competence of bilingual children is revealed even more dramatically when we observe how they are able to adapt their mixing strategies to accommodate the particular characteristics of the linguistic systems they are learning. The English/French bilingual children demonstrated a different pattern of mixing from that of the English/Inuktitut bilingual children, and each group adopted a strategy that reflected the structural properties of the systems being acquired. Once again, then, we have evidence that the language faculty is unperturbed by the complex grammatical challenges posed by bilingual acquisition and use. To the contrary, the systematicity that characterises early monolingual acquisition, as well as early bilingual acquisition (as noted earlier), is also evident in the grammatical interactions that occur when the two languages co-occur in the same utterances when children code-mix. In short, young children not only have the underlying competence needed to acquire two distinct language systems, but also the competence to co-ordinate them online during code-mixing.

Communicative Perspective

A final source of evidence that contests the view that bilingual code-mixing reflects incompetence, confusion, or deficient language development comes from an examination of code-mixing within a communicative framework. Several pieces of evidence can be culled from research in our laboratory and from the work of others which indicate that, when bilingual children code-mix (within a single utterance or from one utterance to another), they are seeking to extend their communicative competence during a stage of development when they have incomplete proficiency in their two languages. To be more specific, arguably, a child who says 'un petit bird' (a little bird) when speaking with her French-speaking mother does not know the French word for 'bird' (*oiseau*) and, therefore, substitutes the English word to complete her utterance. We might refer to this as the *lexical bootstrapping* hypothesis to parallel Gawlitzek-Maiwald and Tracy's general notion of *bilingual bootstrapping* (Gawlitzek-Maiwald & Tracy, 1996). Indeed, on occasion, even fully proficient adult bilinguals do this when they experience a temporary block in accessing words in one language or when a more appropriate word or expression exists in the other language.

There is considerable evidence to support the lexical bootstrapping hypothesis of code-mixing in children (except, see Deuchar & Quay, 2000, for a counter example). First, we have found that young French/English bilingual children tend to code-mix more, within and across utterances, when they use their less proficient language (Genesee *et al.*, 1995). Figure 7.3 summarises the rates of intra-utterance code-mixing of the five children I discussed earlier when they used their more or their less proficient language. Four of the children code-mixed more often when using their less proficient language. One likely explanation of these results is that the children were filling in lexical gaps in that language. There is some direct evidence for this from a short-term intensive study we conducted to examine the vocabulary development of two bilingual children (Wolf *et al.*, 1995). We trained two sets of parents who were raising their children bilingually to keep detailed daily records of their children's language use during three consecutive weeks. The two children were in the one-word stage of development and had not yet acquired 50 words in total in both languages; FEL was 1;8 years old and had an MLU (mean length of utterance, measured in words) of 1.08 in English and 1.08 in French; and WAY was 2;0 years old and had an MLU of 1.55 in English and 1.39 in French. The parents were asked to record every word and utterance that their child produced (including its target form if it was not produced exactly like the target), the context in which the utterance was spoken (setting and addressees), and the child's intended meaning (according to the parents' interpretation). We selected children who were in the one-word stage in order to test the claim that young bilinguals do not learn translation equivalents initially because they have a single system and thus avoid learning words with synonymous meanings (Clark, 1987; Volterra & Taeschner, 1978). As well, it is possible to record the language of relatively immature language learners (prior to the acquisition of 50 words) because their stock of vocabulary and other language skills is quite limited. After the 50 word milestone, however, most children show such an accelerated rate of development and are so talkative that is impossible to record everything they say without special audio/video recording equipment. The dilemma is that the use of recording equipment is practical only during restricted times of the day and, yet, in order to obtain a comprehensive record of everything the child says, one must record all the time.

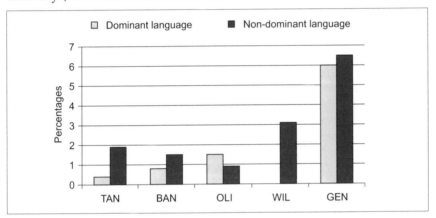

Figure 7.3 Rates of intra-utterance mixing with dominant and non-dominant language

We examined in detail the instances when each child used a word from the inappropriate language with each interlocutor (e.g. a French word with the English-speaking parent) to see whether the child knew the equivalent term in the appropriate language. The detailed records from the parents made this analysis possible. Our analyses indicated clearly that both children were much more likely to code-mix when they did not know the translation equivalent in the appropriate language. WAY did not know the equivalent word in the appropriate language for 94.7% of his code-mixed words, and FEL did not know the word in the appropriate language in 65.2% of his code-mixed words.

Using the corresponding word from the other language in these cases was a way for these children to extend their communicative competence by using the resources of both languages. It has been well documented that monolingual children overextend the use of certain words to referents that are not perfectly appropriate – the most widely cited, and embarrassing, example being children's use of the word *daddy* to refer to all adult males. Children usually stop doing this once they have larger vocabularies and thus have more appropriate terms for referring to specific referents – other male adults, in our example. One could argue that bilingual children who code-mix to fill lexical gaps are overextending in the same way as monolingual children except that they have the lexical resources of two languages to draw on. This interpretation is compatible with the finding that code-mixing often decreases with age (e.g. Redlinger & Park, 1980; Vihman, 1982). Presumably, as the child's stock of vocabulary and other linguistic resources in each language expands, borrowing becomes less necessary since the child is able to express him/herself completely in a single language. Interestingly, 34.83% of the time that FEL code-mixed, he knew the equivalent word in the appropriate language. Thus, filling lexical gaps is not the only explanation of code-mixing. Children and families often have favorite words from one language, and some concepts may not have exact translation equivalents in both languages, forcing speakers to use the 'inappropriate' language whenever they want to refer to that concept.

While these examples have been drawn from the lexical domain, evidence in support of the bootstrapping hypothesis has also been presented from morpho-syntactic domains. Gawlitzek-Maiwald and Tracy (1996) have argued that bilingual children use syntactic structures from their more developed language to bolster use of their less developed language, and Petersen (1988) has argued that inflectional morphology from the 'dominant language' can co-occur with free morphemes from the 'non-dominant language', but not vice versa. In other words, children use syntactic structures, including morphology, from their stronger language to bolster communication in their weaker language. This same phenomenon can also explain instances of inter-utterance code-mixing – switching languages from one utterance to the next. More specifically, children might switch from Language X to Language Y because they lack the syntactic resources they need to express themselves in Language X but not in Language Y.

The main point here is that a significant number of instances of code-mixing can be interpreted to reflect the child's developing communicative competence. In other words, it is a sign of resourcefulness, not incompetence. A particularly striking and even paradoxical example of this comes from our earlier 'stranger study'. It had been our initial expectation that bilingual children would code-mix less when talking with a monolingual stranger than when talking with their bilingual parents, because the stranger did not know both languages. However, we found exactly the opposite for three of the four children (Figure 7.4). We speculate that they

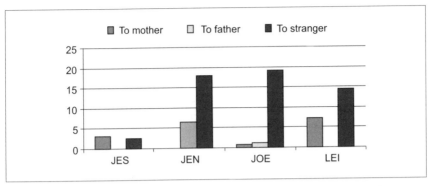

Figure 7.4 Rates of intra-utterance code-mixing with strangers and parents

mixed more with the stranger in order to extend as much as possible their limited proficiency in the language of the stranger. Remember that in three of the four cases the language known by the stranger was the less proficient language of three of the four children. Their proficiency in the language of the stranger was indeed very limited. For example, for JEN, only 3% of the total stock of different words (types) that she knew were in English (the language of the stranger), and for LEI only 12% of the different words she knew were in French (the language of the stranger). Code-mixing with the monolingual interlocutor may have been a way of using the stranger's language as much as possible at the same time as the children extended their communicative competence by inserting words from their other (stronger) language. Without the resources of the other language, the children would have been literally 'speechless' because their proficiency in the stranger's language was so limited.

Conclusions

In this chapter, I have reviewed evidence from studies of children in the early stages of acquiring two languages. I have focused on one particular aspect of acquisition, code-mixing, with a view to understanding the bilingual child's language acquisition in general. I focused on code-mixing because it is a distinctive and common language behaviour among bilingual children, one that sets them apart from monolingual children and one that is often thought to be indicative of the challenges or even problems that children face when they acquire two languages simultaneously. According to this view, bilingual acquisition poses challenges to the developing child that put the child at risk for delayed, incomplete or even deviant language development.

However, whether viewed from cognitive, linguistic or communicative perspectives, the evidence concerning code-mixing indicates quite consistently that acquisition of two languages simultaneously does not put children at risk of delayed, incomplete or deviant language development. First of all, we saw that code-mixing is not indicative of linguistic fusion, or confusion, contrary to some early speculations to this effect. Bilingual children in the one-word stage of development are able to use their developing languages differentially and appropriately in different language contexts, even with interlocutors with whom they have had no prior social experience. Such performance argues that young bilingual children have distinct neuro-cognitive representations of their developing languages early in development.

We then examined their linguistic development in detail and saw that most research indicates that bilingual children acquire distinct and language-specific phonological and syntactic patterns that match those of monolingual children, for the most part. Even isolated instances of transfer that occur in some cases do not challenge this general conclusion. In fact, we saw that transfer is systematic and reflects language-specific properties of the target languages. Child bilingual code-mixing, like adult code-switching, is not random but is systematic and constrained in accordance with the grammatical principles of the target languages. Thus, contrary to lay opinion, and even that of some scientists, the language that bilingual children acquire is not deviant. The linguistic competence that underlies their performance in both of their languages reveals the same underlying linguistic competence as that of monolinguals in most significant respects. Moreover, the systematic on-line coordination of two languages during code-mixing that most bilingual children engage in reveals a kind of linguistic competence that exceeds that which is demonstrated by monolinguals.

Finally, our examination of code-mixing from a communicative perspective indicates that it is a mechanism whereby bilingual children can extend their communicative competence during development, when their proficiency in language is not complete. We saw that when bilingual children code-mix they are drawing on all their linguistic resources to express themselves, much like monolingual children, except that bilingual children have the resources of two languages – in contrast to the monolingual child who has only one. Code-mixing for communicative purposes is a strategy that works because other people in the bilingual child's community are often bilingual; but it is a strategy that can easily be misinterpreted by those who are not bilingual.

In conclusion, bilingual code-mixing is a classic example of the all-too-frequent phenomenon of interpreting *differences* in language as *deficits*. Bilingual children clearly demonstrate different language behaviours in comparison to monolingual children; most noticeably, they mix elements from two languages in the same utterance or conversation. This has often been interpreted as a sign of incompetence or deficit, as noted earlier, arguably because monolingual behaviour has been used as the norm and monolinguals do not code-mix like this. Misinterpretation of child bilingual code-mixing may also be attributable, in part, to a lack of understanding of its actual functional and formal properties. The research presented in this chapter, along with other current work, is critical in dispelling the deficit view of code-mixing by providing detailed and in-depth evidence concerning its cognitive, linguistic and communicative features.

Acknowledgement

I would like to thank the Social Sciences and Humanities Research Council, Ottawa, Canada for funding that has made possible the research by me and my students cited in this chapter.

References

Allen, S.E.M. (1996) *Aspects of Argument Structure Acquisition in Inuktitut.* Amsterdam: John Benjamins.

Allen, S., Genesee, F., Fish, S. and Crago, M. (1999) Code-mixing in Inuktitut-English children. Paper presented at the Eighth International Congress for the Study of Child Language, San Sebastian, Spain.

Bates, E. and MacWhinney, B. (1987) Competition, variation, and language learning. In B. MacWhinney (ed.) *Mechanisms of Language Acquisition* (pp. 157–194). Hillsdale, NJ: Lawrence Erlbaum,

Bergman, C.R. (1976) Interference vs. independent development in infant bilingualism. In G.D. Keller, R.V. Taeschner and S. Viera (eds) *Bilingualism in the Bicentennial and Beyond* (pp. 86–96). New York: Bilingual Press/Editorial Bilingue.

Brown, R. (1973) *A First Language: The Early Stages.* Harmondsworth: Penguin.

Clark, E. (1987) The principle of contrast: A constraint on language acquisition. In B. MacWhinney (ed.) *Mechanisms of Language Acquisition* (pp. 1–33). Hillsdale, NJ: Lawrence Erlbaum,

Crago, M.B. and Allen, S.E.M. (2001) Early finiteness in Inuktitut: The role of language structure and input. *Language Acquisition* 9, 59–111.

De Houwer, A. (1990) *The Acquisition of Two Languages from Birth: A Case Study.* Cambridge: Cambridge University Press.

Deuchar, M., and Quay, S. (2000) *Bilingual Acquisition: Theoretical Implications of a Case Study.* Oxford: Oxford University Press.

di Sciullo, A-M., Muysken, P. and Singh, R. (1986) Government and code-mixing. *Journal of Linguistics* 22, 1–24.

Döpke, S. (2000) Generation of and retraction from cross-linguistically motivated structures in bilingual first language acquisition. In F. Genesee (guest ed.) *Bilingualism: Language and Cognition: Aspects of Bilingual Acquisition* 3 (3), 209–226. Cambridge: Cambridge University Press.

Dorais, .-J. (1988) *Tukilik: An Inuktitut Grammar for All*. Quebec, QC: Association Inuksiutiit Katimajiit.

Gawlitzek-Maiwald, I. and Tracy, R. (1996) Bilingual bootstrapping. *Linguistics* 34, 901–926.

Genesee, F. (1988) Bilingual development in preschool children. In D. Bishop and K. Mogford (eds) *Language Development in Exceptional Circumstances* (pp. 62–79). Edinburgh: Churchill Livingstone.

Genesee, F. (1989) Early bilingual development: One language or two? *Journal of Child Language* 16, 161–179.

Genesee, F., Boivin, I. and Nicoladis, E. (1996) Talking with strangers: A study of bilingual children's communicative competence. *Applied Psycholinguistics* 17, 427–442.

Genesee, F., Nicoladis, E. and Paradis, J. (1995) Language differentiation in preschool bilingual children. *Journal of Child Language* 22, 611–631.

Genesee, F. and Sauve, D. (2000) Grammatical constraints on child bilingual code-mixing. Paper presented at the Annual Conference of the American Association for Applied Linguistics, March 12, Vancouver

Goodz, N. (1994) Interactions between parents and children in bilingual families. In F. Genesee (ed.) *Educating Second Language Children* (pp. 61–81). New York: Cambridge University Press.

Hulk, A., and Müller, N. (2000) Bilingual first language acquisition at the interface between syntax and pragmatics. In F. Genesee (guest ed.) *Bilingualism, Language and Cognition: Aspects of Bilingual Acquisition* 3 (3), 227–244. Cambridge: Cambridge University Press.

Johnson, C. and Lancaster, P. (1998) The development of more than one phonology: A case study of a Norwegian–English child. *International Journal of Bilingualism* 2/3, 265–300.

Köppe, R. (in press) Is codeswitching acquired? In J. MacSwan (ed.) *Grammatical Theory and Bilingual Codeswitching*. Cambridge, MA: MIT Press.

Lanza, E. (1997) *Language Mixing in Infant Bilingualism: A Sociolinguistic Perspective.* Oxford: Clarendon Press.

Leopold, W. (1949) *Speech Development of a Bilingual Child: A Linguist's Record.* Evanston, IL: Northwestern University Press.

Meisel, J.M. (1986) Word order and case marking in early child language: Evidence from simultaneous acquisition of two first languages, French and German. *Linguistics* 24, 123–183.

Meisel, J.M. (1989) Early differentiation of languages in bilingual children. In K. Hyltenstam and L. Obler (eds) *Bilingualism Across the Life-span: In Health and Pathology* (pp. 13–40). Cambridge: Cambridge University Press.

Meisel, J.M. (1994) Code-switching in young bilingual children: The acquisition of grammatical constraints. *Studies in Second Language Acquisition* 16, 413–441.

Meisel, J.M. (2000) The simultaneous acquisition of two first languages: Early differentiation and subsequent development of grammars. In J. Cenoz and F. Genesee (eds) *Trends in Bilingual Acquisition* (pp.11–42). Amsterdam: John Benjamins.

Myers-Scotton, C. (1993) *Duelling Languages: Grammatical Structure in Codeswitching.* Oxford: Clarendon Press.

Padilla, A.M. and Liebman, E. (1975) Language acquisition in the bilingual child. *Bilingual Review* 2, 34–55.

Paradis, J. (1996) Phonological differentiation in a bilingual child: Hildegard revisited. In A. Stringfellow, D. Cahana-Amitay, E. Hughes and A. Zukowski (eds) *Proceedings of Boston University Conference on Language Development* 20 (pp. 528–539). Somerville, MA: Cascadilla Press.

Paradis, J. (2000) Beyond 'one system or two': Degrees of separation between the languages of French–English bilingual children. In S. Döpke (ed.) *Cross-linguistic Structures in Simultaneous Bilingualism.* Amsterdam/Philadelphia: John Benjamins.

Paradis, J. and Genesee, F. (1996) Syntactic acquisition in bilingual children: Autonomous or interdependent? *Studies in Second Language Acquisition* 18, 1–15.

Paradis, J., Nicoladis, E. and Genesee, F. (2000) Early emergence of structural constraints on code-mixing: Evidence from French-English bilingual children. In F. Genesee (guest ed.) *Bilingualism, Language and Cognition: Syntactic Aspects of Bilingual Acquisition* 3 (3), 245–262 Cambridge: Cambridge University Press.

Petitto, L.A., Katerelos, M., Levy, B.G., Gauna, K., Tetreault, K. and Ferraro, V. (2001). Bilingual signed and spoken language acquisition from birth: Implications for the mechanism underlying early bilingual language acquisition. *Journal of Child Language* 28, 453–496.

Petersen, J. (1988) Word-internal code-switching constraints in a bilingual child's grammar. *Linguistics* 26, 479–493.

Poplack, S. (1980) 'Sometimes I start a sentence in English y termino en Espanol': Toward a typology of code-switching. *Linguistics* 18, 581–618.

Poplack, S. (1987) Contrasting patterns of codeswitching in two communities. In J.E. Wande Anward, B. Nordberg, L. Steensland and M. Thelander (eds) *Aspects of Bilingualism: Proceedings from the Fourth Nordic Symposium on Bilingualism, 1984.* Upsala: Borgström.

Poplack, S. (1988) Code-switching. *Sociolinguistics: A Handbook of the Science of Language and Society* 2, 1174–1180.

Poplack, S. and Meecham, M. (1998) Introduction: How languages fit together in codemixing. In S. Poplack and M. Meecham (guest eds) *International Journal of Bilingualism: Instant Loans, Easy Conditions: The Productivity of Bilingual Borrowing* 2, 127–139.

Poplack, S., Wheeler, S. and Westwood, A. (1987) Distinguishing language contact phenomena: Evidence from Finnish-English bilingualism. In P. Lilius and M. Saari (eds) *The Nordic Languages and Modern Linguistics* (pp. 33–56). Helsinki: University of Helsinki Press.

Quay, S. (2001) Managing linguistic boundaries in early trilingual development. In J. Cenoz and F. Genesee (eds) *Trends in Bilingual Acquisition* (pp. 149–200). Amsterdam: John Benjamins.

Redlinger, W.E. and Park, T. (1980) Language mixing in young bilinguals. *Journal of Child Language* 7, 337–352.

Richmond-Welty, E.D. and Siple, P. (1999) Differentiating the use of gaze in bilingual-bimodal language acquisition: A comparison of two set of twins of deaf parents. *Journal of Child Language* 26, 321–338.

Saunders, G. (1982) *Bilingual Children: Guidance for the Family.* Clevedon: Multilingual Matters.

Swain, M. (1977) Bilingualism, monolingualism, and code acquisition. In W. Mackey and T. Andersson (eds) *Bilingualism in Early Childhood* (pp. 28–35). Rowley, MA: Newbury House.

Tucker, G.R. (1998) A global perspective on multilingualism and multilingual education. In J. Cenoz and F. Genesee (eds) *Beyond Bilingualism: Multilingualism and Multilingual Education* (pp. 3–15). Clevedon: Multilingual Matters.

Vihman, M. (1982) The acquisition of morphology by a bilingual child: A whole-word approach. *Applied Psycholinguistics* 3, 141–160.

Vihman, M. (1998) A developmental perspective on codeswitching: Conversations between a pair of bilingual siblings. *International Journal of Bilingualism* 2, 45–84.

Volterra, V. and Taeschner, T. (1978) The acquisition and development of language by bilingual children. *Journal of Child Language* 5, 311–326.

White, L. and Genesee, F. (1996) How native is near native? The issue of ultimate attainment in adult second language acquisition. *Second Language Research* 12, 233–265.

Wolf, L., Genesee, F. and Paradis, J. (1995) *The Nature of the Bilingual Child's Lexicon.* Unpublished research report, Psychology Department, McGill University, Montreal, Quebec.

Yip, V. and Matthews, S. (2000). Syntactic transfer in a Cantonese-English bilingual child. In F. Genesee (guest ed.) *Bilingualism, Language and Cognition: Aspects of Bilingual Acquisition* 3 (3), 193–209. Cambridge: Cambridge University Press.

Introduction to Chapter 8
The Neurolinguistics of L2 Users, Franco Fabbro

VIVIAN COOK

An important insight of the past few years is that the human brain may be changed by the experience it encounters. Learning and using two languages may therefore cause the brain of the L2 user to function differently from that of the monolingual in a number of ways, as Fabbro elucidates in this chapter. This is usually seen as a question whether the second language is stored in a different area of the brain from the first.

SLA (Second Language Acquisition) research over the years has generated masses of debate and speculation on the location of the second language in the brain. One approach to this question involves correlating different types of language loss in bilingual aphasia with the site of brain damage; if one language is lost but not the other, then this is prima facie evidence for it being stored in a different place. The other approach involves correlating the use of one language or another with various measures of localised brain activity; if one area of the brain 'lights up' when one language is used but not the other, this suggests that the languages are stored in different places.

Over a hundred and twenty years many case studies of bilingual aphasia have been built up. Unfortunately these mostly bear witness to the sheer variability between people and to the difficulties of linking language to brain locations. For example ten days after a road accident, a bilingual Moroccan could speak French but not Arabic; the next day Arabic but not French; the next day she went back to fluent French and poor Arabic; three months later she could speak both (Paradis, 1983). Such cases show the dangers in thinking simplistically of a language as a whole stored in a single place.

The approach via measurement of brain activity has been fruitful in recent years. Fabbro's chapter shows us how modern experimental techniques can begin to test the location of the different languages. Cabeza and Nyberg (2000) give an overall view of the results of these techniques. From a linguistic perspective, the view of language used in these studies is still fairly debatable, involving snags detailed in the chapter such as the difficulty of using slow measures to measure rapid language activity, or whether the 'internal speech' tested by Kim *et al.* (1997) is a proper measure of 'real' language use, being detached from any articulatory or comprehension process, or indeed any visible or audible aspect of language.

An inevitable subtheme in this area is the link between age and second language acquisition. The belief prevalent among both linguists and the general public is that children are better L2 learners than adults are. Some research indeed confirms this: Japanese users of English who learn English as children are much better at making the /1/-/r/ distinction in production than those who start as adults (Kasai, 2002). If there are differences between children and adults in the ease with which they acquire second languages, one of the many possible explanations may be differential brain storage, whether across the hemispheres of the brain (as the early SLA research believed), or within specific areas of the brain such as Broca's area (as some recent work claims). As yet though, as Perani *et al.* (1998) argue, it is hard to disentangle the role of age in these experiments from that of language experience.

References

Cabeza, R. and Nyberg, L. (2000) Imaging cognition II: An empirical review of 275 PET and fMRI studies. *Journal of Cognitive Neuroscience* 12, 1–47.
Kim, K.H.S., Relkin, N.R., Lee, K.M. and Hirsch, J. (1997) Distinct cortical areas associated with native and second languages. *Nature* 388, 171–174.
Kasai, C. (2002) The age effect in language acquisition: the production and discimination of English /1/ and /r/ by Japanese learners. PhD thesis, University of Essex.
Paradis, M. (1983) Epilogue. In M. Paradis (ed.) *Readings on Aphasia in Bilinguals and Polyglots*. Quebec: Didier.
Perani, D., Paulesu, E., Galles, N.S., Dupoux, E., Dehaene, S., Bettinardi, V., Cappa, S.F., Fazio, F. and Mehler, J. (1998) The bilingual brain: Proficiency and age of acquisition of the second language. *Brain* 12, 1841–1852.

Chapter 8

The Neurolinguistics of L2 Users

FRANCO FABBRO

One of the main questions of neurolinguistics is whether the two languages of a bilingual have a similar or different brain representation. At the micro-anatomical level – that is, at the level of neuronal circuits – it is reasonable to assume that the two languages are represented in completely or partially independent neuronal circuits. On the other hand, the question whether at the macroanatomical level the first language (L1) and the second language (L2) are represented in common or different cerebral structures is still under debate. Some of the main aspects that seem to influence the cerebral representation of the two languages are age and acquisition modality. Other important aspects concern the level of knowledge and use of the two languages. This chapter discusses some of the main findings of studies on the cerebral organisation of languages in bilinguals who acquired L2 subsequent to L1. To make it easier for the reader to visualise, Figures 8.1 and 8.2 give labeled diagrams of the relevant areas of the brain.

Recovery of L2 in Bilingual Aphasics

One way to study the cerebral organisation of L1 and L2 is to assess their recovery following a brain lesion. According to this approach, if the patient recovers both languages to the same extent, it can be assumed that they have the same macroanatomical representation. If the patient shows a differential recovery, then the hypothesis of a different cerebral representation and/or organisation may be advanced.

When bilinguals or polyglots suffer a brain injury affecting language areas, they may lose the ability to use all the languages they knew, and exhibit the same type of aphasia in all their languages. Subsequent recovery may be *parallel* in all languages. In some cases, aphasia affects only one of the languages known by the patient. In his study of 1895, Pitres was the first to draw attention to the fact that the dissociation of the languages affected by aphasia was not an exceptional phenomenon, but rather ordinary. Pitres described seven clinical cases of patients exhibiting *differential* recovery of the two languages they spoke. On the basis of the frequency of dissociation, Pitres put forward hypotheses on the causes that might determine a better recovery in one language. He suggested that patients tended to recover the language that was most familiar to them prior to the insult.

Pitres (1895) and other neurologists in the last century claimed that failure of a language to recover was not due to its loss, but rather to inhibitory effects caused by the lesion. Pitres had drawn this conclusion on the basis of a general assumption and some empirical studies. The general assumption was supported by several neurologists (including S. Freud, A. Pick, O. Pötzl, M. Minkowski, W. Penfield) and presupposed that all languages of a bilingual or a polyglot subject were localised in common language areas (Fabbro, 1999a, 1999b). This theory had developed in the wake of the scientific debate which started with R. Scoresby-Jackson in 1867 and continued throughout the second half of the nineteenth century. Scoresby-Jackson speculated that Broca's area (see Figure 8.1) was responsible for the representation of a subject's native language, whereas the portions anterior to Broca's area were responsible for foreign language acquisition (Scoresby-Jackson, 1867). This hypothesis was rejected following a post-mortem study of the brain of a polyglot, Sauerwein, who spoke 54 languages, both at poetry and prose level. In the brain of this exceptionally gifted individual Broca's area and the structures anterior to it were of normal extension and showed a perfectly normal development (Veyrac, 1931). It should be noted, however, that Scoresby-Jackson's contemporaries had not understood that he was referring to the capacity of the tissue adjacent to Broca's area to be neurofunctionally involved in processing of other languages vs. the native language. This fact does not necessarily imply an increase in the anatomic extension of structures adjacent to Broca's area.

A second element – derived from the empirical observation of bilingual aphasic patients – led Pitres to claim that the language that was not available was not lost, but only inhibited. Pitres had repeatedly noticed that these patients could progressively recover a language in a lapse of time shorter than that needed to acquire a foreign language, which meant that the disorder provoked by the lesion did not cause loss of the language, but only made it partially inaccessible. Pitres defined this disorder as 'inertia' of the cortical language centres, which manifested itself by the temporary extinguishing of the motor and sensory images used to understand and utter words and sentences. In his opinion, the cerebral organisation of language in polyglots was to be studied by adopting a *neurophysiological* approach, rather than a *neuroanatomical* approach, which was certainly more direct, but less effective. Swiss neurologist Mieczyslaw Minkowski supported Pitres' theories on polyglot aphasia and thus maintained that the linguistic deficits and the recovery patterns of bilingual aphasics could be explained on the basis of neurofunctional modalities, rather than anatomical modalities. In the wake of Pitres, Minkowski held the general assumption that it was not necessary to assume the existence of separate centres responsible for each language known by a subject. With respect to this point, he stated:

If we assume no spatially separate centers or areas in the cortex for the different languages, but instead assume that within the same area, the same elements are active, though in different combinations and interacting with a differential linguistic constellation, it is easy to explain the phenomena occurring in polyglot aphasia in terms of the interaction of such a large set of factors. (Minkowski, 1927: 229)

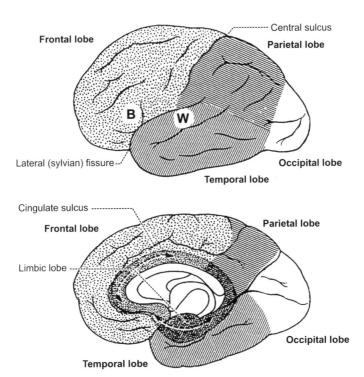

Figure 8.1 Lateral (top) and medial view (bottom) of the cerebral hemisphere, showing Broca's area (B) and Wernicke's area (W) (adapted from DeMyer, 1988)

A large number of neurologists in the past (Pitres, Freud, Minkowski, Pötzl) and also some contemporary scholars (Paradis) have suggested that, when a language is not available, this is not because its neural substrates have been physically destroyed, but because its system has been weakened (see Fabbro, 1999b). This weakening can be explained in terms of increased inhibition, raised activation threshold or unbalanced distribution of resources among the various languages (Green, 1986; Paradis, 1998). However, in some cases, stable dissociations in the recovery of the two languages observed in the *late phase* (beginning 6 months post-onset, and continuing for the rest of the patient's life) cannot be ascribed only to neurofunctional impairments, but also to the consequences of the destruction of cortical and/or subcortical neural substrates (Fabbro *et al.*, 1997; Fabbro, 1999b). In actual fact, dynamic phenomena have hardly ever been described in the late phase. This seems to suggest that after one or two years from onset, the recovery pattern remains stable as a result of pathological phenomena that are partly due to neurofunctional impairments and partly due to the loss of cerebral tissue originally involved in the organisation of linguistic functions.

In recent years I had the opportunity to assess 20 right-handed bilingual aphasics using the *Bilingual Aphasia Test* (BAT) (Paradis & Libben, 1987) in two versions, Friulian and Italian. All the patients presented with aphasia following a left hemisphere lesion. Seventeen patients were native Friulians and three patients were native Italians. All patients learnt their L2 between 5 and 7 years of age. Before the insult all patients used both languages in their everyday lives. Thirteen patients (65%) showed a similar impairment in both languages (*parallel recovery*), four (20%) showed a greater impairment of L2, while three (15%) showed a greater impairment of L1 (*differential recovery*) (Fabbro, 2001a; Fabbro & Frau, 2001). These percentages are in line with a recent review on language recovery in polyglot aphasics (Paradis, 2001). Several factors have been proposed to explain parallel language recovery vs. differential recovery in bilinguals. Neither the native language, nor the language most familiar to the patient at the time of the insult, nor the most socially useful or the most affectively loaded, nor even the language of the environment, recover first or best. Nor does it seem to be a matter of whether the two languages were acquired and used in the same context rather than different contexts, at different times of development (Paradis, 1977, 1989, 1998). Still, neither the type of aphasic syndrome nor the type of lesion (tumour, infarction or cerebral haemorrhage) nor the site of the lesion (cortical vs. subcortical, frontal lobe vs. temporal lobe, etc., see Figures 8.1 and 8.2) seem to be directly responsible for parallel language recovery vs. differential recovery. So far, empirical

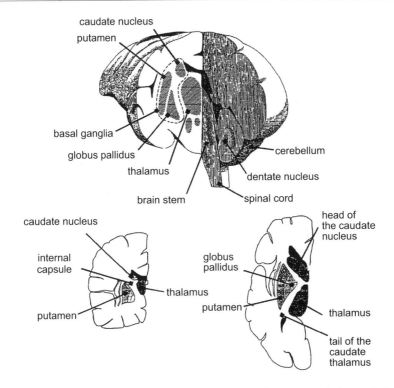

Figure 8.2 Subcortical structures subserving language (adapted from Fabbro 1999b)

studies have not provided tenable explanations for the presence of parallel recovery in some bilingual aphasic patients and of differential recovery in others.

Unexpected Recovery of L2

A few cases have been described of aphasic patients with 'unusual' recovery of one of the languages they knew premorbidly. Their peculiarity is that these patients had either never spoken or used this language for communicative purposes before (e.g. the so-called 'dead' languages such as classical Greek and Latin). In 1937, A. Gelb described the clinical case of an officer who became aphasic owing to a gunshot wound suffered during World War I. The lesion had affected the left frontal lobe and the patient had undergone a neurosurgical operation in order to medicate the internal wound. Afterwards, the patient was no longer able to speak, but could still silently read and understand philosophy books. Before the war the officer had been a professor of classical languages, and after the operation he noticed that not only could he still read, but he could still correctly express himself in Latin. He decided he would rehabilitate himself by mentally constructing sentences he wanted to utter in Latin and, later, by mentally translating them into German by the grammar-translation method. The patient recovered his mother tongue using a second dead language as mediating system. On this basis, Gelb concluded that aphasic syndromes tend to affect the most automatised (i.e. unconsciously used) languages more severely, whereas the foreign languages or dead languages are best preserved since they require conscious efforts and reflection (Gelb, 1937).

In the past I had the opportunity to study a peculiar case of recovery of the second language (Aglioti & Fabbro, 1993; Aglioti _et al._, 1996) in which the patient was not aware of being able to speak her L2 to the high standards she reached after the insult. The patient (EM), right-handed, aged 70, had the Veronese dialect – a variant of Venetian – as her mother tongue. Since infancy she had always spoken Veronese dialect within her family, with her husband, her children and her relatives. As a child she had attended elementary school for three years only, where she learnt to read and write Italian (L2). All her life long, beside housework, she cultivated and sold vegetables. Even during this activity she used Veronese exclusively. Before the insult her husband made sure that she spoke Italian at least 2 or 3 times a year. On these occasions, the patient said only a few words in Italian and switched back to her dialect. In November 1990 EM suffered an injury to the left hemisphere with consequent aphasia. She was admitted to hospital and remained completely mute for two weeks. Magnetic resonance imaging revealed a lesion localised in some left subcortical structures only (mainly the caudate nucleus and the putamen, see Figure 8.2).

When she did start speaking, much to her own and her family's amazement, she expressed herself in Italian instead of Veronese dialect, even though in the hospital ward the staff mainly spoke Veronese. When she was discharged from hospital a month after the insult, the patient's condition had improved: she understood both her dialect and Italian, but expressed herself only in Italian. When asked by the patient, doctors replied that this condition was temporary. EM had to use a new language to communicate with her family, which sounded rather artificial. EM expressed herself in Italian, whereas adults replied in Veronese dialect and her younger nephews in Italian. On these latter occasions, EM noticed that she understood Italian better than Veronese dialect. She had communication difficulties with her acquaintances and friends who addressed her in Veronese dialect, whereas she could reply only in Italian. These aphasic disorders were not understood by the patient's friends who thought she wanted to snub them by speaking Italian instead of their dialect as she had always done. A year after, since the situation had not improved, EM decided to apply to the speech therapy service of the University of Verona to rehabilitate Veronese, a language that to her was socially more important than Italian. Unlike most Venetians, when speaking Italian EM did not have a Venetian accent. On the contrary, her verbal output was characterised by a foreign accent. This phenomenon is known as 'foreign accent syndrome'; it is characterised by the onset – following an acquired lesion – of a strong foreign accent in the first language and is generally associated with a lesion to the basal ganglia (see Figure 8.2) (Cappa & Abutalebi, 1999). In this patient, the linguistic deficit in the mother tongue production was observed in spontaneous speech and in cross-linguistic translation tasks, which showed an asymmetrical paradoxical performance. Indeed, unlike neurologically intact subjects, EM presented more difficulties when translating into her mother tongue than into her second language. Another remarkable feature of EM's impairment is its stability over almost 10 years since the stroke.

Recent studies on long-term memory may provide an explanation why some patients exhibit a better recovery of the second language as opposed to the mother tongue, and hence unexpected recovery. The distinction between explicit and implicit memory is of crucial importance. Explicit memory refers to learnt knowledge of which subjects are aware, and consists of semantic memory and autobiographical memory. Implicit memory concerns learnt knowledge of which subjects are not aware, even though they use it. The two memory systems are organised in distinct brain structures. Implicit memory involves subcortical structures, such as the basal ganglia and the cerebellum, and specific cortical areas; explicit memory is represented diffusely in the cerebral cortex (see Ullman *et al.*, 1997). Paradis (1994) advanced the hypothesis that the mother tongue, being acquired unconsciously in informal contexts through constant repetition, is stored mainly in implicit memory systems. Therefore, the mother tongue seems to be organised mainly in the subcortical structures that account for language and in limited areas of the cerebral cortex. On the other hand, the second language (and hence all other languages of a polyglot) is acquired through explicit strategies, and seems to be more diffusely represented in the cerebral cortex. A case in point for languages being acquired and stored in the explicit memory systems is 'dead' languages. These are generally learnt at school, through reading, and their use requires a conscious knowledge of their grammar. However, many people also use conscious learning strategies based on explicit rules to learn modern languages, too. Since it has been claimed that aphasic syndromes mainly affect the implicit memory systems of language, it is no surprise that some bilingual aphasics show a better recovery of the languages that they spoke least well premorbidly, or that they recover those languages that they had mainly learnt and used through explicit strategies. In the case of EM, the lesion affected the basal ganglia of the left hemisphere, and the language least well known was recovered. We interpreted these results as a sign of a greater impairment of the implicit memory systems subserving the mother tongue and organised in deep cerebral structures. EM started speaking Italian (L2), because the cerebral lesion did not affect the cortex, and thus spared the second language, which is organised in the explicit memory systems (mainly in cortical structures).

Differences in age and manner of learning and language use seem to influence the way in which languages are stored in the brain. When a second language is learnt formally and mainly used at school, it apparently tends to be more widely represented in the cerebral cortex than the first language. However, if it is acquired informally (as usually happens with the first language) it is more likely to involve subcortical structures (basal ganglia and cerebellum) (cf. Paradis, 1994; Fabbro & Paradis, 1995; Fabbro *et al.*, 1997; Fabbro, 2000). Beside this interpretation, other hypotheses – not necessarily opposed to it – have been advanced. Numerous neuro-physiological studies stress the importance of the basal ganglia for the selection of series of behaviour patterns. Language may be considered as a series of behaviour patterns, too. Therefore, the basal ganglia of the left hemisphere may be mainly involved in the selection and activation of the native language (Abutalebi *et al.*, 2000). The degree of involvement of these structures in the production of a less automatised language, such as the second language, may be different from their degree of involvement in the production of the native language. Age and manner of acquisition or learning of L2 can therefore determine a greater or reduced involvement of implicit memory and subcortical structures (e.g. basal ganglia and cere-bellum) in the organisation of L2 vs. L1.

There are no data in the neurolinguistic literature in favour of the hypothesis whereby a prolonged (over years) and exclusive use of L2 causes changes to occur in the brain representation of this language. However, there have been anecdotal reports of people who, after learning and using their L2 almost exclusively, presented a strong foreign accent in their L1. For example, neuropsychologist Alfonso Caramazza speaks his first language, Italian, with a strong English accent. If this example is systematically and experimentally confirmed, it can be assumed that in some cases L2 interferes with the neuronal representation of L1 prosodic systems.

Lateralisation of Languages

In the late seventies, Albert and Obler (1978), in an attempt to explain a few cases of non-parallel recovery among their patients, suggested that bilinguals had a more symmetric representation of language in the two cerebral hemispheres than monolinguals. The hypothesis appealed to the scientific imagination of many researchers, who over the past 20 years have carried out studies on the cerebral organisation of language in bilinguals (Vaid & Hall, 1991). These studies were generally performed using typical techniques of experimental neuropsychology, namely dichotic listening, tachistoscopic technique and finger-tapping, but their results were rather controversial (Paradis, 1990). The analysis of a large number of cases of bilingual aphasics showed that the incidence of aphasia following a lesion to the *right* hemisphere (crossed aphasia) is as high in monolinguals as in bilinguals (Karanth & Rangamani, 1988).

However, it is known that the right hemisphere (also called the 'minor' hemisphere) is crucially involved in the processing of pragmatic aspects of language use (Chantraine *et al.*, 1998). Acquired lesions of the right hemisphere determine clear deficits in comprehension and production of humour, affect, and various aspects of the non-literal interpretation of utterances (Joanette *et al.*, 1990; Paradis, 1998). During the first stages of second-language learning, both in children and adults, the right hemisphere tends to be more involved in verbal communication processes because beginners try to compensate with pragmatic inferences for the lack of implicit linguistic competence in L2. The greater involvement of the right hemisphere during verbal communication in L2, however, does not necessarily imply a greater representation of language processes (phonology, morphology and syntax) in the right hemisphere (Paradis, 1998).

In conclusion, neurolinguistic studies suggest that the sheer linguistic aspects (phonology, morphology and syntax) of both L1 and L2 are organised in the language-dominant hemisphere (the left hemisphere). The hypothesis of a greater involvement of the right hemisphere in the organisation of L2 linguistic aspects has therefore not been confirmed.

Neural Structures Involved in Selection of Languages

Cerebral lesions may alter the capability of bilingual subjects to separate their languages and use each language in appropriate contexts. Many neurologists have supported the hypothesis of the existence of a centre that is responsible for the ability to switch between languages. Pötzl (1930) located the switching mechanism in the posterior boundary of the Sylvian fissure and in the neighbouring parietal region (see Figure 8.1). Leischner (1948) suggested that the bilingual switching mechanism was located in the supramarginal gyrus. According to these authors, a lesion to the switching mechanism causes a patient either to speak only one language or to repeatedly switch from language to language. Subsequent studies have made a distinction between pathological switching and pathological mixing phenomena (Paradis, 1977). Patients who show pathological mixing intermingle different languages within a single utterance (a self-contained segment of speech that stands on its own and conveys its own independent meaning). By contrast, patients affected by pathological switching alternate their languages across different utterances. Additional studies have established that pathological mixing typically occurs in bilingual aphasia and is mainly due to lesions in the parieto-temporal structures of the left hemisphere, whereas the nervous structures responsible for switching between languages have not been clearly described so far (Fabbro, 1999b). Recently we described a 56-year old bilingual patient (SJ) (L1 Friulian, L2 standard Italian) with a lesion to the left anterior cingulate and to the prefrontal lobe (see Figure 8.1) who presented with compulsive switching between languages in the absence of any other linguistic impairment (Fabbro *et al.*, 2000).

By using a systematic linguistic analysis, we have provided evidence for the important part played by anterior cingulate and prefrontal structures in switching between languages (Fabbro *et al.*, 2000). Moreover, this result remarkably implies that segmentation of utterances is not a mere theoretical linguistic concept, but has a neurological basis. As already maintained by the famous neurologist Hughlings Jackson in the nineteenth century, not only words but also utterances are represented in the brain as linguistic units (Hughlings Jackson, 1874). Another important question is whether the decision to speak one language rather than another is regulated by a specific cognitive system peculiar to bilingual subjects, or by a general system responsible for switching between various behavioural patterns. The decision to switch from a given pattern to another (for example, from sitting to walking), or from one linguistic register to another, or even from one language to another, may be regulated by the same general neural mechanism, which may be neurofunctionally separate and independent of the linguistic system. The lack of aphasic symptoms in the case we described suggests that the system responsible for switching between languages is independent of language, being part of a more general system underlying the selection of different behaviours.

Electrophysiological Studies

A series of studies carried out by Helen Neville and associates (Neville *et al.*, 1992; 1997; Weber-Fox & Neville, 1996) by means of electrophysiological techniques (event-related potentials, ERPs) revealed possible differences in the cerebral cortical organisation of languages according to the age of acquisition and learning strategies. In early bilinguals, closed-class words of both languages tend to be represented in the left frontal lobe, whereas open-class words tend to involve post-rolandic cortical structures. On the other hand, in bilinguals who learnt their second language after the so-called 'critical age' (about 7 years of age), closed-class words of L2 vs. L1 seem to be represented, not in left frontal areas but together with open-class words in post-rolandic areas.

Functional Neuroanatomy Studies

Over the past few years, many studies have used advanced functional neuroanatomical techniques such as Positron Emission Tomography (PET) and functional Magnetic Resonance Imaging (fMRI) to investigate language representation in the brain of bilingual subjects. PET involves the injection of slightly radioactive substances into the blood stream. These substances are used by the brain as sources of energy during the execution of sensory-motor or cognitive tasks. The first structures activated during the execution of a cognitive task take up the injected radioactive substances more than others. A computer processes this data by reconstructing and showing the cerebral structures that are most active during a task. Functional magnetic resonance imaging is a type of tomographic functional imaging that does not use radioactive compounds, and has a better spatial and time resolution than PET. It consists in recording local haemodynamic changes and in particular blood oxygenation during cognitive tasks. Thus, fMRI also measures the activation of cerebral structures during cognitive tasks in general and language tasks in particular. Their results raised much interest on the part of both the scientific community and the general public. These investigation techniques certainly present advantages, but they also show some limitations.

These limits depend on some important methodological issues, such as the following:

(a)   the time needed to study the cerebral representation of a function is expressed in seconds, whereas language processes are expressed in milliseconds;

(b)   subtractive comparisons between two activation tasks are often diffi-
      cult to interpret;
(c)   often results of neuroimaging studies do not correspond to clinical
      neuropsychological findings;
(d)   neuroimaging techniques do not allow one to determine whether acti-
      vation of a cerebral structure depends either on an increase in activa-
      tion processes or in neurophysiological inhibition processes; and,
      lastly,
(e)   brain activation was studied with tasks that are too complex (for
      example listening to stories) and whose linguistic and pragmatic
      nature is still scarcely known; these tasks generally simultaneously
      activate many linguistic, pragmatic and affective structures, thus
      making it difficult to interpret data.

PET and fMRI studies that investigated language organisation in the
brain of bilinguals will be discussed according to the linguistic stimuli that
were used: word processing; sentence processing; and short-story processing (Fabbro, 2001b).

Word processing

The first neuroimaging study on bilinguals was by Klein *et al.* (1995). In
English/French bilinguals, PET revealed a greater activation of the left
putamen (see Figure 8.2) during a word generation task in the language
that subjects knew less well. Recently, Klein *et al.* (1999) carried out another
PET study on Chinese/English bilinguals. All the subjects were native
Chinese who had acquired their L2 (English) in adolescence. Subjects
received verb-generation tasks. Despite the fact that subjects had learnt
English later in life, the two languages showed activation in the same cerebral structures (left inferior frontal, dorsolateral frontal, temporal and parietal cortices, and right cerebellum). In this study, the authors did not find
any difference in the activation of the two languages in the basal ganglia. In
their opinion, their results suggested a common macroscopic cortical representation for L1 and L2.

Chee, Tan *et al.* (1999b) used fMRI to study cerebral activation during
word stem completion tasks in Chinese (Mandarin)/English bilinguals.
The activated brain areas (left prefrontal region involving the inferior
frontal gyrus, the supplementary motor area and, bilaterally, occipital and
parietal regions) were the same in the two languages (despite their structural distance and different writing) for both early bilinguals (L2 learnt
before the age of 6) and late bilinguals (L2 learnt after the age of 12). The
authors hypothesised that cortical representation of words in bilinguals

involves – at the macroscopic level – the same cortical areas regardless of the age of acquisition of L2, and that cerebral asymmetries were the same for both languages and identical to those of monolinguals. Illes *et al.* (1999) used fMRI to investigate brain activation during semantic judgement tasks (concrete/abstract judgements) in eight late English/Spanish bilinguals. In all eight participants they found a similar cortical activation of the left inferior frontal gyrus for both languages (six participants also showed increased activation in the right inferior frontal gyrus for both languages), which led them to suggest that, in the bilingual brain at the macroanatomical level, there is a common neuronal system responsible for semantic processing in both languages.

These studies indicate that the lexicons of the L1 and the L2 are macroscopically represented in the same brain areas regardless of the age of acquisition. These results are in line both with theories supported by the first neurologists who investigated the bilingual brain (e.g. Pitres, 1895; Minkowski, 1927; Chelnov, 1948; all reprinted in Paradis, 1983), and with the most recent hypotheses on the different memory systems involved in language acquisition and learning (Paradis, 1994; Ulmann *et al.*, 1997). According to these hypotheses, lexicons of L1 and L2 – learnt after the so-called critical age – are stored in declarative memory systems that are represented in the left cortical associative areas subserving language functions.

Processing sentences

In an fMRI study, Kim *et al.* (1997) compared cortical areas activated during silent sentence generation tasks in L1 and L2 in early vs. late bilingual subjects. For both languages, they found a similar activation of Broca's and Wernicke's areas in early bilinguals, while in late bilinguals they found a similar activation of Wernicke's area but a significant difference in the activation of Broca's area between L1 and L2. In late bilinguals the authors found in the left Broca's area two distinct but adjacent centres, separated by approximately 8 mm, subserving language production in L1 vs. L2. They thus concluded that the anatomical separation of the two languages in Broca's area depended on their different acquisition age. The differences in functional organisation in Broca's area between early bilinguals and late bilinguals could also be correlated with L2 competence of late bilinguals. Unfortunately, the authors did not describe the phonologic skills (presence of foreign accent?) and syntactic skills (presence of syntactic errors?) of the late bilinguals. They reported only that these participants showed a high standard fluency in L2.

Chee, Caplan *et al.* (1999a) tried to replicate these results using fMRI to investigate cortical areas activated during a sentence processing task in fluent early Chinese (Mandarin)/English bilinguals. All the subjects were exposed to both English and Mandarin prior to the age of 6. Participants were asked to judge whether the visually presented sentences were 'true' or 'false'; for example: *The minister gave the speech* (true); *The reporter gave the speech* (false). The most activated areas were: the inferior and middle prefrontal cortex (more extensive on the left side), the left temporal region, the left angular gyrus, the anterior supplementary motor area (more activated on the left side), and the bilateral superior parietal and occipital regions, with no difference between the two languages. The authors concluded that, in early fluent bilinguals, common macroscopic areas were activated by syntactically complex English and Mandarin sentences. According to the authors, their results support the hypothesis of a 'one-store' model for linguistic representation of two languages in early fluent bilinguals. However, the fact that Chee, Caplan *et al.* (1999b) studied only proficient bilinguals exposed to both languages early in life does not allow us to exclude the possibility that the brain representation of languages in late bilinguals (with lower phonologic and syntactic skills in L2) is compatible with the so-called 'two-store' model.

Processing short stories

In their first study, Perani *et al.* (1996) used PET to study brain activation during story listening tasks in Italian (L1) and English (L2) in subjects with moderate command of the L2. While in L1 the most activated areas were the classical perisylvian language areas (inferior frontal gyrus, the superior and middle temporal gyri, the temporal pole, the angular gyrus) and the right cerebellum, in L2 the number of active language areas was significantly reduced. Only left and right superior and middle temporal areas remained active, with bilateral activation of the parahippocampal region. According to the authors, their results clearly supported the hypothesis of a partially different representation of the two languages in the brain.

Dehaene *et al.* (1997) carried out an fRMI study to explore brain activation during short story listening tasks in French (L1) and English (L2) in eight subjects with moderate command of L2. In L1, all subjects showed a remarkable consistency in the activation of the same areas of the left temporal lobe (superior temporal sulcus, superior and middle temporal gyri). In L2, however, the story-listening task activated networks that varied greatly from subject to subject (six subjects showed dispersed active pixels in the left temporal lobe, the remaining two only in the right temporal lobe). During a story processing task in L1, the average active volume (that is, the volume of nervous tissue that activates during story listening) of the *left* temporal lobe was significantly greater than that of the *right* temporal lobe (LTL = 1378 mm³; RTL = 456 mm³). In story processing in L2, the average active volume was considerably reduced but activation of the *left* temporal lobe was still significantly greater than that of the *right* temporal lobe (LTL = 666 mm³; RTL = 327 mm³). According to the authors, their results confirmed the hypothesis of a left hemisphere representation for L1, whereas late acquisition of a second language caused great variability in its cortical representation (from complete right lateralisation to standard left lateralisation for L2).

More recently, Perani *et al.* (1998) used PET to investigate brain activation during short story-listening tasks in two groups of bilinguals with high proficiency of L2 but with different ages of acquisition: High Proficiency Late Acquisition (HPLA) vs High Proficiency Early Acquisition (HPEA). The brain structures that were activated in both languages during the task were similar in both groups. In the HPLA group (L1 = Italian; L2 = late acquisition of English) listening to Italian stories activated foci in the left temporal lobe (temporal pole, superior temporal sulcus, middle temporal gyrus and hippocampal structures). Listening to English stories showed a similar activation pattern in the left temporal lobe and a bilateral activation of the hippocampal structures. No areas were found with a significantly different activation according to the language that participants were listening to. In the HPEA group (L1= Spanish or Catalan; L2= early acquisition of Catalan or Spanish) both languages activated bilateral foci in the temporal poles, in the hippocampal structures and the lingual gyrus, and in the left hemisphere the superior temporal sulcus, the inferior parietal lobule, the lingual/cuneus region and areas of the cerebellar vermis were activated. The direct comparison of L1 vs. L2 showed significantly different activations only in the right hemisphere (in the middle temporal gyrus for L1 and in the hippocampal structures and superior parietal lobe for L2). These results led the authors to conclude that representation of languages in the bilingual brain seems to be dependent on proficiency in the two languages and to be independent of the acquisition age.

As has already been said, interpreting results of functional anatomical studies with bilinguals performing short story listening tasks is very difficult. In fact, knowledge of the different linguistic and pragmatic levels involved in a story processing task is still scant. Therefore, the linguistic and pragmatic complexity of the task is most probably responsible for the complexity and the variety of the brain activation patterns shown by these studies. The choice of linguistic stimuli that are so complex and, at the same time, scarcely known, makes it difficult to study language representation in the brain of bilinguals.

Conclusions

One of the first methods used to study representation of L1 and L2 in the brain was to investigate bilingual aphasia. Some authors hypothesised that differential recovery indicated a different cerebral representation for the two languages (see Albert & Obler, 1978). Recent studies on bilingual aphasics showed that differential recovery seems to depend not so much on the macroanatomical representation of languages but on neurofunctional factors due to the brain lesion (Paradis, 1998; Fabbro, 1999a, 1999b).

Clinical neurolinguistic investigations have allowed one to better define the role of some cerebral structures in correct choice of words and sentences during verbal communication in a bilingual (Paradis, 1989). Pathological mixing (mixing of linguistic elements from various languages within a single sentence) is an aphasic symptom associated with the classical word-finding difficulties that are generally present in fluent aphasias (Fabbro, 1999b). Pathological switching (the tendency to switch from language to language in verbal production) seems to be due to pragmatic disorders of communication, which are independent of language as rightly suggested by Michel Paradis (1989), and are generally due to prefrontal lesions (Fabbro *et al.*, 2000).

An interesting working hypothesis by Paradis (1994) is that the acquisition or learning modality seems to determine a different participation of procedural memory systems vs. declarative memory systems. Procedural memory refers to implicit competence that underlies the performance of motor and cognitive skills and relates to internalised procedures and genuine behaviour programs, which eventually contribute to the automatic performance of the task. Declarative memory refers to everything that can be represented at the conscious level (Squire & Kandel, 2000). If L1 and L2 are acquired in informal contexts and both are at a high level of proficiency, their phonologic and morphosyntactic aspects are stored in procedural memory systems (see Kim *et al.*, 1997; Perani *et al.*, 1998; Chee *et al.*, 1999). On the other hand, traditional learning of L2 after the age of 7, along with limited proficiency in production, seems to involve the declarative memory systems to a greater extent. Furthermore, according to Paradis (1998), during the first stages of second-language learning (both in children and adults) the right hemisphere tends to be more involved in verbal communication processes because beginners attempt to use pragmatic inferences to compensate for the lack of implicit linguistic competence in L2. This might explain the greater bilateral activation of some hippocampal structures during the processing of short stories in individuals who have a moderate knowledge of L2 acquired in school contexts (Perani *et al.*, 1996; Dehaene *et al.*, 1997).

Neurophysiologic and neuroimaging studies evidenced a similar cerebral representation of L1 and L2 lexicons in both early and late bilinguals (Klein *et al.*, 1999; Chee *et al.*, 1999; Illes *et al.*, 1999). The representation of grammatical aspects of languages seems to be different between the two languages if L2 is acquired after the age of 7, and automatic processes and correctness are lower than those of the native language (Neville *et al.*, 1992; 1997; Weber-Fox & Neville, 1997; Kim *et al.*, 1997). These results are in line with a greater representation of the two lexicons in the declarative memory systems, whereas morphosyntactic aspects may be organised in different systems according to the acquisition vs. learning modality (Ullman *et al.*, 1997).

Lastly, a crucial aspect concerns the brain volume involved in processing of a complex task in the L1 vs. a language that is little known. Dehaene *et al.* (1997) showed that, during a story-listening task in L1, the proportion of activated brain volume is significantly higher than that activated during the same task in L2. Therefore, the greater the knowledge of a language, the greater the number of circuits activated during its processing. This important result is in line with studies on changes in the brain following the automatic learning of motor sequences (Karni *et al.*, 1995; Elbert *et al.*, 1995).

References

Abutalebi, J., Miozzo, A. and Cappa S.F. (2000) Do subcortical structures control 'language selection' in polyglots? Evidence from pathological language mixing. *Neurocase* 6, 51–56.

Aglioti, S., Beltramello, A., Girardi, F. and Fabbro F. (1996) Neurolinguistic and follow-up study of an unusual pattern of recovery from bilingual subcortical aphasia. *Brain* 119, 1551–1564.

Aglioti, S. and Fabbro, F. (1993) Paradoxical selective recovery in a bilingual aphasic following subcortical lesions. *NeuroReport* 4, 1359–1362.

Albert, M.L. and Obler, L.K. (1978) *The Bilingual Brain.* New York: Academic Press.

Cappa, S.F. and Abutalebi, J. (1999) Subcortical aphasia. In F. Fabbro (ed.) *Concise Encyclopedia of Language Pathology* (pp. 319–327). Oxford: Pergamon Press.

Chantraine Y., Joanette, Y. and Cardebat, D. (1998) Impairments of discourse-level representations and processes. In B. Stemmer and H.A. Whitaker (eds) *Handbook of Neurolinguistics* (pp. 262–75). San Diego: Academic Press.

Chee, M.W.L., Caplan, D., Soon, C.S., Sriram, N., Tan, E.W.L., Thiel, T. and Weekes, B. (1999a) Processing of visually presented sentences in Mandarin and English studied with fMRI. *Neuron* 23, 127–137.

Chee, M.W.L., Tan, E.W.L. and Thiel, T. (1999b) Mandarin and English single word processing studied with functional magnetic resonance imaging. *Journal of Neuroscience* 19, 3050–3056.

Chlenov, L.G. (1948) On aphasia in polyglots. In M. Paradis (ed.) (1983) *Readings on Aphasia in Bilinguals and Polyglots* (pp. 445–454). Montreal: Didier.

Dehaene, S., Dupoux, E., Mehler, J., Cohen, L., Paulesu, E., Perani, D., van de Mortele, P., Lehericy, S. and Le Bihan, D. (1997) Anatomical variability in the cortical representation of first and second language. *Neuroreport* 8, 3809–3815.

DeMyer, W. (1988) *Neuroanatomy*. New York: Wiley.

Elbert, T., Pantev, C., Wienbruch, C., Rockstroh, B. and Taub, E. (1995) Increased cortical representation of the fingers of the left hand in string players. *Science* 270, 305–307.

Fabbro, F. (1999a) Aphasia in multilinguals. In F. Fabbro (ed.) *Concise Encyclopedia of Language Pathology* (pp. 335–340). Oxford: Pergamon Press.

Fabbro, F. (1999b) *The Neurolinguistics of Bilingualism*. Hove: Psychology Press.

Fabbro, F. (2000) Introduction to language and cerebellum. *Journal of Neurolinguistics* 13, 83–94.

Fabbro, F. (2001a) The bilingual brain: 1. Bilingual aphasia. *Brain and Language* 79, 201–210.

Fabbro, F. (2001b) The bilingual brain: 2. Cerebral representation of languages *Brain and Language* 79, 211–222.

Fabbro, F. and Frau, G. (2001) Manifestations of aphasia in Friulian. *Journal of Neurolinguistics* 14, 255–279.

Fabbro, F. and Paradis, M. (1995) Differential impairments in four multilingual patients with subcortical lesions. In M. Paradis (ed.) *Aspects of Bilingual Aphasia* (pp. 139–176). Oxford: Pergamon Press.

Fabbro, F., Peru, A. and Skrap, M. (1997) Language disorders in bilingual patients after thalamic lesions. *Journal of Neurolinguistics* 10, 347–367.

Fabbro, F., Skrap, M. and Aglioti, S. (2000) Pathological switching between languages following frontal lesion in a bilingual patient. *Journal of Neurology, Neurosurgery and Psychiatry* 68, 650–652.

Gelb, A. (1937) On medical psychology and philosophical anthropology. In M. Paradis (ed.) (1983) *Readings on Aphasia in Bilinguals and Polyglots* (pp. 383–385). Montreal: Didier.

Green, D (1986) Control, activation, and resource: A framework and a model for the control of speech in bilinguals. *Brain and Language* 27, 210–223.

Hughlings Jackson, J. (1874) On the nature of the duality of the brain. In J. Taylor (ed.) (1958) *Selected Writings of John Hughlings Jackson* (pp. 129–145). New York: Basic Books.

Illes, J., Francis, W.S., Desmond, J.E., Gabrieli, J.D.E., Glover, G.H., Poldrack, R., Lee, C.J. and Wagner, A.D. (1999) Convergent cortical representation of semantic processing in bilinguals. *Brain and Language* 70, 347–363.

Joanette, Y., Goulet, P., Hannequin, D. (1990) *Right Hemisphere and Verbal Communication*. New York: Springer Verlag.

Karanth, P. and Rangamani, G.N. (1988) Crossed aphasia in multilinguals. *Brain and Language* 34, 169–180.

Karni, A., Meyer, G., Jezzard, P., Adams, M.M., Turner, R. and Ungerleider, L.G. (1995) Functional MRI evidence for adult motor cortex plasticity during motor skill learning. *Nature* 377, 155–158.

Klein, D., Milner, B., Zatorre, R.J., Zhao, V. and Nikelski, J. (1999) Cerebral organisation in bilinguals: A PET study of Chinese-English verb generation. *NeuroReport* 10, 2841–2846.

Klein, D., Zatorre R.J., Milner B., Meyer E. and Evans A.C. (1995) The neural substrates of bilingual language processing: Evidence from positron emission tomography. In M. Paradis (ed) *Aspects of Bilingual Aphasia* (pp. 23–36). Oxford: Pergamon Press.

Kim, K.H.S., Relkin, N.R., Lee, K.M. and Hirsch, J. (1997) Distinct cortical areas associated with native and second languages. *Nature* 388, 171–174.

Leischner, A. (1948) On the aphasia of multilinguals. In M. Paradis (ed.) (1983) *Readings on Aphasia in Bilinguals and Polyglots* (pp. 456–502). Montreal: Didier.

Minkowski, M. (1937). A clinical contribution to the study of polyglot aphasia especially with respect to Swiss-German. In M. Paradis (ed.) (1983) *Readings on Aphasia in Bilinguals and Polyglots* (pp. 205–232). Montreal: Didier.

Neville, H.J., Coffey, S.A., Lawson, D.S., Fischer, A., Emmorey, K. and Bellugi, U. (1997) Neural systems mediating American Sign Language: Effects of sensory experiences and age of acquisition. *Brain and Language* 57, 285–308.

Neville, H.J., Mills, D.L. and Lawson, D.S. (1992) Fractionating language: Different neural subsystems with different sensitive periods. *Cerebral Cortex* 2, 244–258.

Paradis, M. (1977) Bilingualism and aphasia. In H. Whitaker and H.A. Whitaker (eds) *Studies in Neurolinguistics* (Vol. 3, pp. 65–121). New York: Academic Press.

Paradis, M. (ed.) (1983) *Readings on Aphasia in Bilinguals and Polyglots*. Montreal: Didier.

Paradis, M. (1989) Bilingual and polyglot aphasia. In F. Boller and J. Grafman (eds.) *Handbook of Neuropsychology* (Vol. 2, pp. 117–40). Oxford: Elsevier.

Paradis, M. (1990) Language lateralisation in bilinguals: Enough already! *Brain and Language* 39, 576–586.

Paradis, M. (1994) Neurolinguistic aspects of implicit and explicit memory: Implications for bilingualism and SLA. In N. Ellis (ed.) *Implicit and Explicit Language Learning* (pp. 393–419). London: Academic Press.

Paradis, M. (1998a) Language and communication in multilinguals. In B. Stemmer and H.A. Whitaker (eds) *Handbook of Neurolinguistics* (pp. 418–31). San Diego: Academic Press.

Paradis, M. (1998b) *Pragmatics in Neurogenic Communication Disorders*. Oxford: Pergamon.

Paradis, M. (2001) Bilingual and polyglot aphasia. In R.S. Berndt (ed.) *Handbook of Neuropsychology* (2nd edn, pp. 69–91). Oxford: Elsevier Science.

Paradis, M. and Libben, G. (1987) *The Assessment of Bilingual Aphasia*. Hillsdale, NJ: Lawrence Erlbaum.

Perani, D., Dehaene, S., Grassi, F., Cohen, L., Cappa, S.F., Dupoux, E., Fazio, F. and Mehler, J. (1996) Brain processing of native and foreign languages. *Neuroreport* 7, 2439–2444.

Perani, D., Paulesu, E., Galles, N.S., Dupoux, E., Dehaene, S., Bettinardi, V., Cappa, S.F., Fazio, F. and Mehler, J. (1998) The bilingual brain. Proficiency and age of acquisition of the second language. *Brain* 121, 1841–1852.

Pitres, A. (1895) Aphasia in polyglots. In M. Paradis (ed.) (1983) *Readings on Aphasia in Bilinguals and Polyglots* (pp. 26–49). Montreal: Didier.

Pötzl, O. (1930) Aphasie und Mehrsprachigkeit. *Zeitschrift für die gesamte Neurologie und Psychiatrie* 12, 145–162.

Scoresby-Jackson, R.E. (1867) Case of aphasia with right hemiplegia. *Edinburgh Medical Journal* 12, 696–706.

Squire, L.R. and Kandel, E.R. (2000) *Memory from Mind to Molecules.* New York: Scientific American Library.

Ullman, M., Corkin S., Coppola, M., Hickok, G., Growdon, J.H., Koroshetz, W.J. and Pinker, S. (1997) A neural dissociation within language: Evidence that mental dictionary is part of declarative memory, and that grammatical rules are processed by the procedural system. *Journal of Cognitive Neuroscience 9,* 266–276.

Vaid, J. and Hall, D.G. (1991) Neuropsychological perspectives on bilingualism: Right, left, and centre. In A.G. Reynolds (ed.) *Bilingualism, Multiculturalism, and Second Language Learning* (pp. 81–112). Hillsdale, NJ: Erlbaum,

Veyrac, G.J. (1931). A study of aphasia in polyglot subjects. In M. Paradis (ed.) (1983) *Readings on Aphasia in Bilinguals and Polyglots* (pp. 320–338). Montreal: Didier.

Weber-Fox, C.M. and Neville, H.J. (1997) Maturational constraints on functional specialisations for language processing: ERP and behavioral evidence in bilingual speakers. *Journal of Cognitive Neuroscience 8,* 231–256.

Introduction to Chapter 9

Individual Differences in L2 Fluency: The Effect of Neurobiological Correlates, Jean-Marc Dewaele

VIVIAN COOK

A classic question in Second Language Acquisition (SLA) research is why some people pick up second languages quickly and easily, and others never become fluent up to their dying day, as any class of language students soon reveals. First language acquisition does not seem to have such extremes; the typical linguist's view is that all normal children acquire their first language, barring the 1.5% who suffer from Specific Linguistic Impairment. Nevertheless it is a commonplace observation for there to be variation in the speed and level of the second language attained.

Treated in the failure-driven monolingualist model (Cook, 1997), much SLA research sets out to describe what goes wrong with L2 acquisition. Unlike acquisition of the L1, L2 acquisition might depend on a special aptitude for language learning, on the strength and type of motivation, on the learning strategies chosen by the learners, on the linguistic environment that they encounter, on whether they have particular cognitive styles, and on many other factors. A summary is given in Skehan (1989). While L1 acquisition is oblivious to differences in the individual and the environment, L2 learning is not. Some of these factors reflect aspects of the educational situation in which taught L2 students find themselves, and are not specific to L2 acquisition.

The L2 user perspective changes the way in which L2 users are viewed by interpreting the question as a matter, not of why they differ from native speakers, but of why they differ from each other. The causes lie somewhere in the possible relationships between the two languages in the same mind: some people are forming more effective mental links than others; the issue is which factors lead to the most effective learning.

In the present chapter Jean-Marc Dewaele builds on this field in two ways. One is to link it to studies of fluency. An extensive literature inspired by the Kassel research of the 1980s (e.g. Dechert *et al.*, 1984) has investigated the temporal variables of speech – the speaker's speed, hesitation noises, pauses, etc., more recently turning to the links to conversational interaction (Wagner, 1998). Dewaele then treats fluency as a temporal variable between L2 users, as it would be in the L1, rather than as a sign of lack of 'success'.

He also goes a stage further back in the causation by looking behind personal qualities such as anxiety or introversion to the physical basis in the complex interactions of brain chemistry and the localisation of functions within the brain; the fault, dear Brutus, is not in our stars, but in our brains. An old topic has again been revitalised by looking at two languages in one mind and by using modern techniques for the study of the brain.

References

Cook, V.J. (1997) The consequences of bilingualism for cognitive processing. In A.M.B. de Groot and J.F. Kroll (eds) *Tutorials in Bilingualism: Psycholinguistic Perspectives* (pp. 279–300). Mahwah, NJ: Lawrence Erlbaum.

Dechert, H., Möhle, D. and Raupach, M. (1984) *Second Language Productions.* Tubingen: G. Narr.

Skehan, P. (1989) *Individual Differences in Second-Language Learning.* London: Edward Arnold.

Wagner, J. (1998) Silences in international communication. In D. Albrechtsen, B. Henriksen, I.M. Mees and E. Poulsen (eds) *Perspectives on Foreign and Second Language Pedagogy* (pp. 79–92). Odense: Odense University Press.

Chapter 9

Individual Differences in L2 Fluency: The Effect of Neurobiological Correlates

JEAN-MARC DEWAELE

Introduction

Research on individual differences in Second Language Acquisition (SLA) is usually concentrated on a number of social and psychological variables (such as motivation) that can affect the rate of *development* of a learner's L2 (see Hamers & Blanc, 2000 for a recent survey and Pavlenko, this volume) and also on individual differences in the actual use of an L2 learned through formal instruction (e.g. Busato *et al.*, 1999). The aim of this study is to identify possible neurobiological causes for *synchronic* variation in the fluency of L2 production, i.e. why does fluency in L2 production differ from one situation to another (intra- and inter-individual variation), and why does it differ between users who have been through a similar learning process in a formal setting (inter-individual variation)?

Fluency in L2

Any L2 user is also an L1 speaker, and the multitude of interacting factors that affect fluency in the L1 also determines fluency in the production of the L2 or Lx. In other words, inter- and intra-individual variation in fluency that exists when a speaker produces his or her L1, linked to variables like age, sex, social status, extraversion, communicative anxiety, tiredness, situation, audience, etc. (see Furnham, 1990; Matthews & Deary, 1998), also appears in that person's L2. None of these independent variables are language-specific, but some may have stronger effects on the individual speaking his or her L2. Anyone who has been through oral exams or public presentations in his or her L1 knows that nervousness and stress can have adverse effects on his or her fluency. However, exercise and experience (previous talk about the topic, discourse routines, jokes, appeals to common ground) help the L1 speaker to overcome this fear, alleviate the stress and be reasonably fluent. However, the same type of task in a less frequently used language might be daunting. The lower level of activation of the language (Green, 1998) probably means that the speaker will have to work harder to display a similar ease and fluency.

Towell and Dewaele (2001) analysed the development of fluency in twelve English L1 learners of French who had spent a six-month period in France. The results showed that fluency (as measured by speaking rates in story retelling and the rate of success in shadowing and recall tasks) increased significantly between time 1 (before the period abroad) and time 2 (after the period abroad), but still remained significantly below fluency values for these tasks when performed in the L1. A highly significant positive correlation was also found between L1 and L2 speaking rates. It was suggested that fluency in the L2 depends on the same neurological substrate as the one that determines fluency in the L1, hence the reflection of L1 interindividual differences in the L2.

Speakers in the process of L1 attrition who produce their L1 are likely to experience a situation not very dissimilar from that of infrequent L2 users. This difficulty is not necessarily linked to the content of the knowledge base (although it might be more limited in the case of beginning and intermediate L2 learners), but rather to accessibility and retrieval. Paradis (1997) argues that L2 production might involve a variable reliance on different long-term memory systems that could allow L2 users to be (very often) as fluent as native speakers. One such system is *explicit memory*, which refers to 'learnt knowledge of which individuals are aware and which they can imagine or verbally express on request or at will' (Fabbro, 1999: 96). The other is *implicit memory*, which refers 'to a type of learning or knowledge that depends on repeated execution of a task, even though the subject is not aware of the nature of implicit knowledge, has forgotten or cannot remember when he has learnt the task' (Fabbro, 1999: 98).

The greater effort needed to be fluent in less frequently used language(s) has both objective and subjective consequences: most importantly, speakers may be aware that they have to make a greater effort. This realisation will have different subjective effects on speakers according to their psychosocial identity, and will determine their willingness to communicate, their self-perceived competence, their self-confidence and their language anxiety (MacIntyre, 1999). When these factors are negative, they may contribute to a diversion of cognitive resources from the verbal tasks and thus hamper speech production.

Whereas L1 production and reception are largely automatic (Levelt, 1989; Levelt *et al.*, 1999), allowing the speaker to concentrate on content, L2 speech production and reception require the speaker to intervene regularly in the process. These interventions can be directed at different levels in the production process and may involve particular 'subtasks'. During the conceptualisation phase of Levelt's production model, the L2 speaker might need to decide whether a particular register is appropriate. Another intervention might be needed during the formulation phase: is the word or structure retrieved from the mental lexicon socio-pragmatically appropriate? Some crucial diacritic features attached to the activated lemma might be missing, requiring attention. The L2 speaker would need to solve these morphological or syntactical problems as quickly as possible. The pronunciation of some difficult phonemes might again need conscious intervention during articulation. Because of the ad hoc nature of these interventions, or their absence, L2 forms or structures might display patterns of free variation (Dewaele & Véronique, 2001) and high levels of inter-individual variation (Dewaele & Regan, 2002). One possible reason for the regular need of conscious control in L2 production is that the speaker relies more on declarative knowledge than on implicit competence (Paradis, 1997). L2 production is more controlled but can be speeded up, making it indistinguishable from L1 production (Segalowitz & Segalowitz, 1993; Paradis, 2000). The inability to maintain automatic production in the L2 at all times has also been attributed to incomplete proceduralisation or syntactic building procedures (Towell *et al.*, 1996; Temple, 2000), or to a lack of conceptual fluency, i.e. 'knowing how the target language reflects or encodes its concepts on the basis of metaphorical structuring and other cognitive mechanisms' (Kecskes & Papp, 2000: 10).

L2 production seems to be more demanding and puts more pressure on the working memory (WM). L2 users with a more limited short-term memory (STM) and WM are thus at a disadvantage (Paradis, 1997; Cook, 1997).

Stress also affects L2 production more than L1 production (Dornic, 1978; Dewaele & Furnham, 1999, 2000). Heightened stress might deplete the resources needed for speech production at a higher rate (Green, 1998) and affect general language processing mechanisms (Hamers & Blanc, 2000).

Fluency in language production is influenced by neurophysiological mechanisms (Jacobs & Schumann, 1992; Pulvermüller & Schumann, 1994; Perani *et al.*, 1996, 1998; Schumann, 2001). Neuro-imaging studies of language comprehension in bilinguals suggest that 'increasing language proficiency appears to be associated at the neural level with the engagement of a common network within the dedicated language areas' (Abutalebi *et al.*, 2001: 187).

It would be wrong, however, to view neurophysiology as the sole cause of differences in fluency. Numerous contextual and social factors interact with psychological and neurophysiological variables (MacIntyre *et al.*,

1998; Dörnyei & Kormos, 2000) which might in turn affect fluency. The linguist's work, as Grosjean (2001) puts it, is to isolate these factors and ascertain how they interact. This means keeping track of a very large number of possible independent variables that could be linked to fluency in the speech production of multilinguals (Grosjean, 1992, 1998).

After presenting the research questions of the present study, the next part of this chapter is devoted to the description of long-term memory (LTM), short-term memory (STM), working memory (WM) and their location in the brain. Then we outline the WM model developed by Alan Baddeley, juxtapose it to Levelt's psycholinguistic speech production model insofar as WM is concerned, and look at studies on WM and STM capacity in L1 verbal tasks. Next we survey research on the mechanisms and types of knowledge used in L1 and L2 speech processing, highlighting the crucial role of the STM and present the literature on individual differences in WM and STM. Parallels are drawn between findings from personality research, cognitive psychology, neuroanatomy, neurochemistry and L2 research on personality variables. Finally the main conclusions of the study identify four interrelated independent variables that affect speech production in the L2: the nature of knowledge representation in the L2 user, extraversion, anxiety and their link to WM and STM capacity and efficiency, and the perceived formality of a situation and the stress it generates.

Research questions

Our research questions are the following:

- How could STM capacity or efficiency be linked to fluency in the L2?
- Is there a relationship between anxiety and fluency?
- Does stress have similar effects on the fluency of all L2 users?

Long-Term and Short-Term Memory

The relationship between memory and language is rich and complex (Caspari & Parkinson, 2000). Speaking involves a constant use of both LTM and STM (Levelt, 1989; Fabbro, 1999, this volume). Levelt argues that at the macro- and micro-planning stage attention is constantly divided between the retrieval of information from LTM and the preparation of new messages. Search results are stored in WM. Both operations require a substantial memory search and differential allocation of attentional resources (Caspari & Parkinson, 2000). Fluent speech production thus requires:

(1) the presence and easy accessibility of the required information in LTM;

(2) efficient preparation of new messages (which need to be coherent and relevant in the interaction);
(3) a correct allocation of resources between both operations; and
(4) sufficient capacity in the STM (and WM) for it to act as a repository.

Swann *et al.* (1992) observed that an informal conversation in the L1 with a new acquaintance makes many demands on the interlocutors including: comprehension, smooth turn-taking, generating responses, remembering one's thoughts until one's turn, and actual production of the responses. These may all be considered as part of the general process of *conversation maintenance*. This process is considered to be an effortful controlled process (Gilbert *et al.*, 1988) rather than an automatic process. In describing the difference between automatic and controlled processes, Gilbert (1989: 194) stated that, '[controlled] processes require significant [working memory] resources and are therefore mutually debilitating; alphabetising words and reciting poetry are activities done quite well alone but quite poorly in tandem'. Thus, if a person's cognitive resources are depleted by the process of conversation maintenance, there may be insufficient resources to carry out the other tasks.

Recent research has focused on the properties of LTM and STM (Medina *et al.*, 1999) and on the mechanisms involved (Izquierdo *et al.*, 1999). Cansino *et al.* (1999) demonstrated that event-related potentials (ERPs) can accurately reflect STM and LTM procedures. To help the reader, brief explanations of some neurolinguistic terms are given in the Notes section towards the end of the chapter; more information will be found in Chapter 8, or in Bradford (1986) and DeMyer (1988).

Recent noninvasive neuro-imaging techniques have revealed that several brain structures are involved in memory processing (Perani, 1999). If individual differences in L2 production are linked to differences in the architecture and the functioning of STM and LTM, one needs to consider complex neuroanatomical and neurochemical evidence. STM, WM and LTM seem to be situated in various brain areas and to be regulated by various neurotransmitter systems (Izquierdo *et al.*, 1998) – neurotransmitters are described by Bradford (1986) as chemical target seekers.

The amygdala (part of the limbic system[1]) seems to modulate LTM storage processes but is not involved in WM (or STM) processing (Bianchin *et al.*, 1999; Izquierdo *et al.*, 1999). Recent research on memory systems in humans has concentrated on the neuro-anatomical and neuro-chemical links between areas of the brain involved in memory formation (Martin, 1996; Robbins & Everitt, 1995). These authors suggest that the reticular formation[2] in the brainstem, which is the anatomical source of differences between introverts and extraverts (Eysenck & Eysenck, 1985), controls certain cortical and subcortical areas of the brain that are central to higher cognitive functions. The pontine reticular nucleus projects to both the prefrontal cortex and the basal ganglia[3] (see Figure 8.2), modulating the release of the neurotransmitter dopamine[4] (Lieberman, 2000). The dorso-lateral prefrontal cortex plays a key role in WM as it maintains information and is involved in the preparation of actions (Cabeza & Nyberg, 1997; Lieberman, 2000; Pochon *et al.*, 2001). Meanwhile, the basal ganglia play a central role in procedural memory formation (Saint-Cyr & Taylor, 1992) – part of the implicit memory (Fabbro, 1999: 98). Both the dorsolateral prefrontal cortex and the basal ganglia depend on dopamine for normal functioning (Lieberman, 2000).

Some researchers have claimed that WM 'should not be considered a separate "box" for short-term storage that is structurally distinct from other memory or cognitive systems' (Miyake & Shah, 1999: 443) and reject results from neuro-imaging studies because, to the critics, 'such studies seem almost like a search for the "Holy Grail"' (Miyake & Shah, 1999: 445).

In answer to this type of criticism, Lieberman and Rosenthal (2001) agree that no system in the brain is an island, as each system has bi-directional connections with several others, but they point to research that proved that particular areas of the brain, or circuits including multiple areas, are differentially involved in different functions (Kosslyn & Koenig, 1992). Considering the impact of arousal on different neuro-cognitive systems separately and then looking at the reactivity of these systems to relevant social-emotional-cognitive tasks is therefore perfectly justified (Lieberman & Rosenthal, 2001).

Models of STM and WM

The most widely used model of working memory is that developed by Baddeley (1986), Gathercole and Baddeley (1993) and Baddeley and Logie (1999) (see Figure 9.1). WM is defined as a specialised cognitive system that is involved in 'temporary processing and storage of information' (Gathercole & Baddeley, 1993: 2). It contains three components: a central executive that processes information and supervises temporary memory systems including a phonologically based store (the phonological loop) and a visuo-spatial store (the visual sketchpad) (Baddeley & Logie, 1999: 28). The phonological loop consists itself of two separate subsystems or processes. These are a storage component, namely the phonological store that can hold information for about 2 seconds, and an articulatory sub-vocal rehearsal process. Information in the phonological store decays over

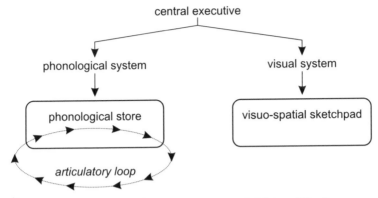

Figure 9.1 Baddeley's working memory model (simplified)

time, but this can be countered by active sub-vocal rehearsal which refreshes items within the store (Jarrold *et al.*, 2000).

Short-term memory plays a vital role in Levelt's (1989) model of speech production, although this is not a memory model as such. His idea that three autonomous processing components operate in the speech production process (the conceptualiser, the formulator and the articulator) is now widely accepted and these components have been integrated in models for L2 production (De Bot, 1992; Pienemann, 1998; Kecskes & Papp, 2000). The processing components work in parallel on different fragments of the message, which makes for a very efficient system (Levelt, 1989). The intermediate representations are stored in different facilities when they become available. The message, the parsed, internal speech and the preverbal messages are stored in the working memory which also monitors the speakers' own internal or overt speech (Levelt, 1989: 21). Bits of the surface structure are stored in the syntactic buffer and stretches of the articulatory plan are stored in the articulatory buffer for further execution as motor programs (Levelt, 1989: 28).

Baddeley's and Levelt's models are quite different in nature, and attempts by psycholinguists to marry the two (see for example Temple, 2000) have not been judged satisfactory so far (Paradis, personal communication). Levelt's model lacks the central executive component that directs operations in the WM, whereas the phonological loop in Baddeley's model implies a restriction in the type of information to be stored.

Fluent verbal comprehension and production in the L1 (and by extension the L2) is clearly linked to capacity in STM. Just and Carpenter (1992) showed that individual differences in WM capacity for language, related to the amount of activation, can account for qualitative and quantitative differences in several aspects of language comprehension. A larger WM capacity permits interaction between syntactic and pragmatic information and allows individuals to maintain multiple interpretations in cases of syntactic ambiguity. Emerson *et al.*'s (1999: 1301) study on individual differences in integrating and coordinating multiple sources of information (visuo-spatial and verbal) also lends support to the idea that a central construct (such as the central executive) with a limited capacity could create 'a possible bottleneck in which the visuo-spatial and verbal sources of information may compete for common resources involved in conversion when an overlap occurred'.

Rosen and Engle (1997) found that only high memory span participants could perform complex verbal tasks fluently while monitoring their output. The low memory span participants on the other hand committed more errors and 'did not have sufficient working memory capacity to allocate to all three of the retrieval components that required controlled attention' (Rosen & Engle, 1997: 224). Cowan *et al.* (1998: 158) conclude that rehearsal efficiency and STM retrieval efficiency determine an individual's memory span. This generally confirms an earlier study by Roodenrys *et al.* (1994). They found that accessibility and articulation rates of words retrieved from STM were determined by their frequency (high frequency words being articulated more quickly) and by the age at which the speaker had acquired the word (words acquired later in life being articulated more slowly). Individual differences are linked to the speed with which an individual can rehearse and produce items:

> On the one hand, the faster one rehearses, the more items one can refresh in the phonological store. In addition, the more rapidly one can output the to-be-remembered item in a verbal serial recall task, the less decay will degrade items that have yet to be verbally recalled. (Jarrold *et al.*, 2000: 234)

The authors refer to empirical studies where a relationship was found between overt speech rate and verbal STM span in order to support their claim that articulation speed is vital in serial verbal STM. However, inefficient or absent rehearsal of verbal material is not always the cause of STM deficit. Jarrold *et al.* (2000) found that neither their subjects with Down's syndrome (who suffer from relatively poor verbal STM) nor matched controls engaged in spontaneous sub-vocal rehearsal.

Differences in STM, more specifically in digit span, have been found to vary across languages. Chincotta and Underwood (1997) found that Chinese speakers had a larger digit span than speakers of English, Finnish, Greek, Spanish and Swedish, who did not differ among themselves.

However, under articulatory suppression, these differences were eliminated, and suppressed digit span was equivalent across the languages. The authors attribute these cross-linguistic differences in digit span to variation in the articulatory duration of digit names and the rate of sub-vocal rehearsal between languages.

Cheung *et al.* (2000) analysed cross-language variation in WM processing among Chinese/English bilinguals and concluded that both articulatory and non-articulatory processes contribute to the cross-language variation. They attribute the language effect to a difference in consonant-vowel structures of the items from the two languages. Their conclusion is that the phonological loop model is applicable to cross-language working memory processing.

STM in L1 and L2 Processing

Most research in L1 as well as L2 deals with the relationship of the phonological loop to *learning* rather than to processing (Gathercole & Baddeley, 1989, 1990; Service, 1992; Papagno & Vallar, 1995; Cheung, 1996; Baddeley *et al.*, 1998). There seems to be no reason to believe that there are fundamental differences in the architecture of the STM in L1 and L2 processing: 'the phonological basis of STM could be established on the same grounds in L2 processing as in L1 processing' (Cook, 1997: 284). Indeed, an adult L2 user does not have to recreate the system from scratch in STM. However, L2 users do seem to have an STM deficit compared to L1 users, and this deficit is more pronounced in beginners than in advanced learners (Brown & Hulme, 1992; Cook, 1977). Research into cross-linguistic STM spans showed that participants can hold fewer L2 items than L1 items in the STM (Cook, 1997). Chincotta and Underwood (1996) found that digit span is linked to levels of familiarity and practice in particular languages among bilinguals. Constant bilinguals (for whom the mother tongue was also the language of schooling) obtained faster reading rates and larger digit spans in their dominant language than compound bilinguals. This confirmed earlier research by Thorn and Gathercole (1999) who found that STM performance in English and French mirrored bilingual children's familiarity with these languages. The STM limitation for L2 users might also explain fluency differences in *decoding*: Laufer and Nation (2000) used a computerised vocabulary-recognition speed test to show that L2 users dominant in their L1 are much slower to recognise vocabulary meaning than native speakers. The L2 users were also found to form a heterogeneous group with regard to fluency, reflected in large variances of response times.

The main difficulty appears to be in identifying the source of the STM deficit, as it could be located in the central executive (Lieberman, 2000), in the phonological store or in the articulatory loop (Cook, 1997).

One major difference between L1 and L2 processing appears to be in the demands put on the STM that lead to radical rechanneling of resources. Paradis (1994) argues that, because of the incompleteness of the L2 users' knowledge-base or retrieval problems, less automatic processing is possible, which gives rise to a need for conscious intervention and monitoring. L2 users are also more likely to draw upon their declarative knowledge (which is located in the hippocampus[5] and anatomically related structures in the medial temporal lobe situated at the basis of the left hemisphere and diencephalon[6]) and less on their implicit knowledge (Paradis, 1994). Implicit knowledge consists of non-linguistic information, including imagery, schemas, motor programs, and auditory, tactile and somato-sensory representations, based on experiential world knowledge. It is generally stored in various brain systems outside the medial temporal lobe and diencephalon (implicit memory) and it is not vulnerable to aphasia (Paradis, 1994). Paradis (2000) insists on the fact that implicit competence is qualitatively very different from explicit knowledge. While the latter is conscious awareness of some data and of their explicit analysis, the former should be seen as a set of computational procedures, of which the speaker is unaware, that generates sentences (see also Fabbro, this volume). Paradis' suggestion that L2 users rely on different networks in the brain has also been defended independently by Perani *et al.* (1996). The researchers used PET (Positron Emission Tomography) scans to measure activation levels in the left hemispheric areas of the brain of Italian(L1)/English(L2) bilinguals during listening tasks and found that stories in Italian engaged the temporal lobes and temporoparietal cortex more extensively than L2 English. In the same vein, Dehaene *et al.* (1997) using functional MRI (Magnetic Resonance Imaging) found that, while L1 is mediated by a similar brain network in all subjects, there is great inter-individual variation in the networks mediating the L2. Using a similar approach, Kim *et al.* (1997) also found that in late learners, L1 and L2 were represented in spatially distinct parts of the left inferior frontal cortex. In a further study Perani *et al.* (1998) discovered that patterns of cortical activity in highly proficient bilinguals listening to stories in their L1 and L2 were comparable, whereas very different patterns emerged in low-proficiency subjects.

The fact that L2 users rely more on declarative knowledge, which can be accelerated (Segalowitz & Segalowitz, 1993; Segalowitz *et al.*, 1998), undoubtedly increases the load on the STM. This could account for the larger variation in fluency of relatively advanced L2 users compared to that of native speakers and learners at intermediate level (Largeau, 2000).

Indeed, as Paradis (2000: 8) points out, 'speeded-up control over explicit rules is not the same as automatic use of implicit competence'.

Paradis (1997) argues that a shortage of STM capacity in the L2 user hampers not only production but also reception of long or complex utterances. L2 speech production needs more WM, with attention directed at virtually every stage of processing (Cook, 1997; Temple, 1997; 2000). Temple (1997: 87) suggests that in L2 production WM 'is being used to store and coordinate fragments processed by the formulator, before the next stage of processing'. As the WM capacity is strictly limited (Gathercole & Baddeley, 1993), parallel processing breaks down and is replaced by serial processing with word-by-word or phrasal type of production (Temple, 1997: 2000). Intra-individual variation might thus be linked to L2 speakers' WM capacity as well as to their level of proficiency. Towell *et al.* (1996) and Towell and Dewaele (2001) have also argued that the ability to maintain automatic processing is crucial for fluent L2 production. Highly proficient L2 speakers would be more fluent because they rely more on proceduralised knowledge, which allows them to produce speech automatically. However, less proficient and less fluent L2 speakers would rely more heavily on declarative knowledge which is more costly in STM resources.

Some L2 verbal processing tasks may suffer more when speakers run out of STM resources. Dewaele and Furnham (2000) argue that speakers can prioritise particular sub-tasks by allocating extra resources drawn from elsewhere. It also possible, however, that a speaker has relatively little conscious choice for certain tasks. Caplan and Waters (1999), for example, found evidence that syntactic processing happens outside the dorsolateral prefrontal cortex where the WM is situated and that it escapes conscious attention.

In addition to limitations in STM capacity, the question arises as to whether any other factors might exacerbate the problems in the STM. Just and Carpenter (1992: 145) point to inefficient processing as a possible cause for an STM deficit, delays mean degradation of the data supplied between the components, thus, 'a slow or errorful component robs other processes not only of good data but also of resources'. Hirst and Kalmar (1987) argue that insufficient segregation of information generated by the components causes cross-talk that hampers the parallel processing. Jarrold *et al.*'s (2000) explanation of encoding difficulties as an alternative cause for apparent memory deficits in individuals with Down's syndrome could also be relevant for L2 users. 'If the information entering the phonological store is degraded in some way, then recall will necessarily be poor even if the phonological loop is essentially intact' (Jarrold *et al.*, 2000: 241). One could argue that in L2 processing some lemmas, when activated, may appear to

lack morphological or syntactic information, forcing the speaker to impro-
vise in order to find an acceptable alternative (Dewaele, 2001). This delay
would mean that the storage time of other items in the phonological loop
would be exceeded, interrupting production and forcing the speaker to
reconceptualise the preverbal message.

It is difficult however to pinpoint the cause of the STM deficit in L2
processing with certainty. Cook (1977) argued that slower articulation rates
mean that speakers can hold fewer items in the phonological store.
Chincotta and Underwood (1998) moderated the view that bilingual short-
term memory capacity is mediated exclusively by sub-vocal rehearsal and
indicated a contribution from language fluency and the strength of lexico-
semantic representations.

Segalowitz (1997: 103) points out that L2 speakers are required to
demonstrate, not only fluency, but also flexibility of processing: 'the ability
to shift attention from one stimulus dimension to another, as the occasion
requires, so as to remain sensitive to the pragmatic, social, semantic,
syntactic, and phonological cues one is receiving and sending'. The need
for flexibility is especially needed in situations where the speaker is already
struggling to maintain fluency. This flexibility could include the ability to
suppress irrelevant information and the control of relative activation levels
of two or more languages (Michael, 1999). An overstretched STM might
therefore lead to a breakdown in both fluency and flexibility. There seems
to be wide agreement amongst researchers that capacity in STM is an
important factor in L2 processing. However, Cochran *et al.* (1999) demonstrated that superior processing capacity is not necessarily linked to better
language learning among adults.

Individual Differences in STM

Extraversion

Eysenck's (1967) hypothesis that introversion–extraversion has a biological basis seems to have been widely accepted and confirmed by the
research community (Stenberg *et al.*, 1993; Fischer *et al.*, 1997; Furnham &
Heaven, 1998). However, this does not exclude interaction with social variables: introversion–extraversion is 'a truly psychological concept, slotting
in between phenomena at the biological and social levels and providing an
explanatory link between them' (Wilson, 1977: 213).

Differences in arousal levels would explain differences in behaviour and
preferences of extravert and introvert people. In the simplest terms,
extraverts are under-aroused, introverts over-aroused. As any individual
operates ideally with a moderate level of cortical arousal, extraverts

compensate for their sub-optimal arousal levels by tending towards more arousing tasks that involve greater sensory stimulation. The introverts' higher baseline levels (tonic) of cortical arousal as well as greater reactivity (phasic) to individual stimuli, means that they do not need this stimulation and will thus rather try to avoid over-arousing situations. When exposed to strong stimuli, introverts reach their tolerance levels much more quickly than extraverts do. The extraverts' low autonomic arousability and the insensitivity to punishment signals makes them more stress-resistant (Rawlings & Carnie, 1989). These processing characteristics 'assist them in dealing with high information flows (particularly of verbal stimuli) and time pressure' (Matthews & Dorn, 1995: 391). Extraverts thus seem better equipped than introverts to cope with speech production in stressful situations.

Recent research suggests that extraversion is related to brain systems associated with sensitivity to reward, particularly dopaminergic circuits, which also tend to increase motor activity (Matthews & Deary, 1998; Depue & Collins, 1999; Lieberman, 2000).

Psychological studies have consistently showed that extraverts are superior to introverts in STM (Howarth & Eysenck, 1965). M.W. Eysenck (1981: 204) found that introverts take longer than extraverts to retrieve information from long-term or permanent storage. One possible reason for this difference could be the over-arousal of the introverts, which would affect their parallel processing. Introverts would therefore be 'at a disadvantage in any task (...) involving the processing of several different items of information' (Eysenck, 1981: 203). Matthews (1992), using a free-recall experiment, confirmed earlier findings on extraverts' superior STM. The extraverts would be able to store more verbal information. Matthews and Dorn (1995: 384) argue that this low-level mechanism of passive, verbal storage could prove to be the main vehicle for extraverts' superiority in STM. The combination of the extraverts' speed of retrieval of information from memory and their higher degree of physiological stress resistance would explain their better performance in high-stimulation environments (Matthews & Deary, 1998).

The underlying causes for the reported differences in STM capacity/efficiency between introverts and extraverts are believed to be of a neurochemical nature.

A slight increase of dopamine in introverts, who already have higher levels of this neurotransmitter, might push them over the very narrow range of optimal innervation in the dorsolateral prefrontal cortex and impair performance (Lieberman, 2000). Lieberman used a memory-scanning task to tap the central executive component of WM and found that extraverts have better working memory skills than introverts (Lieberman, 2000: 484). Lieberman and Rosenthal (2001) argue that both dopamine and norepinephrine affect the functioning of the prefrontal cortex following an inverted U-pattern: 'too little or too much of either norepinephrine or dopamine disrupts attentional and working memory processes' (Lieberman & Rosenthal, 2001). This in turn could also delay the preparation of sequential actions based on the information stored in STM (Pochon *et al.*, 2001).

These neurochemical fluctuations can have social psychological consequences. Compared to extraverts, introverts have more difficulty in keeping several task-goals and contextual information active in the dorsolateral prefrontal cortex where they are neurally instantiated. Extraverts are better able than introverts to maintain and carry out two interpersonal goals, whereas introverts concentrate on the primary goal, neglecting the secondary one (Lieberman & Rosenthal, 2001).

High levels of dopamine in the dorsolateral prefrontal cortex might impair introverts' WM performance but it is probably an asset in the parts of the brain where learning takes place, namely the basal ganglia and the amygdala.[7]

Research has also focused on the link between cognitive processing speed and extraversion. Doucet and Stelmack (2000) analysed the biological basis of extraversion by using Event Related Potentials (ERPs) to explore cognitive and motor processes. They found that extraverts obtained faster movement times on reaction time and stimulus-response compatibility tasks, which the authors attribute to differences in fundamental, peripheral motor processes (Doucet & Stelmack, 2000: 963).

Dewaele and Furnham (2000) showed that correlations between extraversion scores of 25 Flemish university students producing French interlanguage (IL) in dyadic conversations with the researcher and the values of 6 linguistic variables reflecting style choice, fluency and accuracy were most pronounced in a formal, more stressful situation. The 25 Dutch L1 students, aged between 18 and 21, were continuous L1 users and had enjoyed formal instruction in the TL for more than 6 years. Their L2 could be described as high-intermediate to advanced. Sixteen subjects reported to make regular use of French outside the classroom. The extraverts were found to be have higher speech rates, less filled pauses, lower values of lexical richness and a higher proportion of semantic errors than the introverts, preferring more implicit/deictical speech styles and producing shorter utterances (based on the mean length of the three longest utterances). No significant correlations appeared between extraversion scores and morpho-lexical accuracy rates, however. These findings are very similar to those that emerged from psychological studies where task and situation were manipulated (Matthews & Deary, 1998). Complex tasks performed under stressful interpersonal conditions seem to differentiate extraverts and introverts more clearly.

Similarly, Socan and Bucik (1998) report that the correlation between extraversion and speed of information processing depends on the 'arousability' of the testing conditions.

One possible explanation advanced by the authors for these results is that introverts may be unable to maintain the same level of automaticity of speech production when they are under some sort of arousal/stress (being observed or tested). Moving from automatic to controlled processing overloads their working memory, hampering fluency, increasing the probability of making semantic errors and limiting their capacity to produce utterances of great length (cf. Caplan & Waters, 1999). By opting for very explicit speech styles, introverts have to perform more lexical searches of low-frequency (and low-activation) words that need more time to be accessed (Roodenrys *et al.*, 1994). The extraverts on the other hand, being better equipped to cope with interpersonal stress, are able to maintain most of their speeded-up controlled or automatic processing.

The higher degree of implicitness or context-dependence in the speech of extraverts could be linked to a better flexibility (Segalowitz, 1997) and/or a higher capacity in the spatio-visual sketchpad. One could argue that in order to anchor utterances in the spatio-temporal context, speakers need to keep an eye on the environment around them, and that the central executive must be convinced that the phonological loop has enough resources before redirecting some to the spatio-visual sketchpad. This might paradoxically lead to a saving in cognitive resources, as implicit speech is less costly (cf. supra). The introverts' more explicit style reinforced the interlocutors' impression that they were less involved in the conversation, and this correlated negatively with their oral exam grades (Dewaele & Sachdev, 2001).

Dewaele and Furnham (2000: 363) conclude that 'the stress of the formal situation could cause an excessive degree of arousal in the brain of the introverts, which would overload their STM and affect efficient incremental processing, hence a breakdown of fluency'. Lieberman and Rosenthal (2001) also argue that the extraverts' higher WM efficiency is the key to their more effective multi-tasking. Any additional burden on the WM will therefore limit the capacity to operate multiple task simultaneously.

The authors note that the closest identifiable neural concomitant of arousal in the brain is the monotonic increase in catecholamine activity[8] associated with increases in stress (Koob, 1999). Dopamine and norepinephrine, both catecholamines, increase production in response to stress (Arnsten, 1998). Norepinephrine levels relate to wakefulness indices and consolidation of memory processes (Bradford, 1986), while dopamine activation in basal ganglia is associated with positive emotionality (Depue & Collins, 1999; Lieberman, 2000). Lieberman and Rosenthal (2001) thus argue that both neurotransmitters have reasonable links to features associated with extraversion, and suggest that the two catecholamines vary together with extraversion, given that dopamine is the neurochemical precursor for norepinephrine.

Anxiety

Many theorists distinguish between state and trait anxiety (Furnham & Heaven, 1998). Whereas state anxiety is more transitory, trait anxiety is a relatively stable individual difference factor: 'As state anxiety is affected primarily by external stressors such as an imminent important examination, it follows that performance is more a function of state than of trait anxiety' (Furnham & Heaven, 1998: 80). Spence and Spence (1966) postulated that anxiety enhances performance on relatively simple tasks, but not on more complex tasks.

Eysenck and Eysenck (1985) developed and refined this view by proposing that anxiety has either a beneficial (i.e. motivational) effect or an inhibitory effect. Worry, considered as the cognitive component of anxiety, has been shown to have a negative impact on performance. The second component of anxiety is emotionality, which does not necessarily have negative effects on performance. We will focus on the cognitive factors in anxiety. According to some evidence, anxiety is composed of displeasure, high arousal and submissiveness. It can manifest itself as 'fear of failure' or 'test-taking anxiety' and both tend to be related to lower levels of achievement (Furnham & Heaven, 1998: 81).

Anxiety arousal is associated with distracting, self-related cognition such as excessive self-evaluation, worry over potential failure, and concern over the opinion of others. Anxious people tend to divide their attention between task-related cognition and self-related cognition, making cognitive performance less efficient (Fremont *et al.*, 1976; Tapasak *et al.*, 1978; Eysenck, 1979). Tobias (1986) developed this idea and showed that anxiety can cause paralysing thoughts that hamper information processing. This finding was recently confirmed by De Raad and Schouwenburg (1996), who found that subjects with high levels of test anxiety engaged in self-deprecatory thinking rather than focusing on the task at hand. When the processing demands were high, anxiety was found to have stronger inhibitory effects on verbal reasoning tasks than on spatial reasoning tasks

(Markham & Darke, 1991). The authors concluded that cognitive self-concern has different effects on the verbal and visual domains of the WM.

Recent research into the effects of anxiety on L1 verbal production tasks points to capacity problems in the WM as the main cause for impaired performance. Derakshan and M.W. Eysenck (1998), for example, found that the slowing of verbal reasoning performance of high-anxiety subjects (as measured by the Spielberger Trait Anxiety Inventory) under high memory load conditions was significantly greater than that of low-anxiety subjects. The authors suggest that anxious thoughts and feelings 'pre-empt some of the resources of working memory, and thus impair performance when the task demands on working memory are great' (Derakshan & Eysenck, 1998: 711).

Matthews and Deary (1998) reviewed the literature on the neuro-chemical causes of anxiety which seems to point to the involvement of norepinephrine in the adrenergic arousal. Low levels of norepinephrine seem to correspond to disinhibition and impulsivity. At low levels this catecholamine activity in the dopaminergic and noradrenergic systems 'may be rewarding and facilitating but at high levels may be associated with anxiety, distractibility, inhibition, and adrenergic arousal' (Matthews & Deary, 1998: 130).

A study by Vedhara *et al.* (2000) showed that lower levels of salivary cortisol are associated with enhanced STM capacity and attention, but not with auditory verbal WM. Surprisingly, the authors discovered that, while subjects (60 English university students) reported higher levels of per-ceived stress in an exam period, their cortisol levels were actually lower than in a non-exam period.

Some types of anxiety appear to be typical of L2 communication. In their exploratory study on the relations between language anxiety and other anxieties in speaking English L1 and French L2, MacIntyre and Gardner (1989) found two orthogonal factors which they labeled General Anxiety and Communicative Anxiety. The former factor included scales of Trait, State and Test Anxiety; the latter was defined by French Class, French Use, English Class and Audience anxieties. No relationship was found between General Anxiety and French vocabulary learning and production, but significant negative effects emerged in the learning of French L2 vocabu-lary. A similar effect appeared in tests for the written and oral production of similar items from LTM. A close analysis of the correlations between the individual anxiety scales and the language production measures revealed that the French anxiety scales were responsible for the effects observed for the Communicative Anxiety factor.

Similar results emerged from MacIntyre and Gardner's (1991b) study into the factor structure underlying 23 scales assessing both language anxiety and other forms of anxiety. French L2 tasks were judged to be more anxiety-provoking than English L1 tasks by 95 students who had had an average of eight years of courses in French as an L2 (MacIntyre & Gardner, 1991b: 518). Subjects with higher levels of language anxiety in the L2 (but not the L1) obtained significantly lower scores on a Digit Span test (a measure of STM) and on a Thing Category test (vocabulary production). The authors suggest that the impaired performance among more anxious students could be related to STM loss and problems in the long-term memory retrieval, both attributable to anxiety (MacIntyre & Gardner, 1991b: 530).

MacIntyre and Gardner (1994) proposed a 3-stage model of foreign-language anxiety. Foreign language students can experience fear at the input stage when they are presented with new information in the foreign language. This anxiety can have detrimental effects on their concentration and on their ability to encode the linguistic stimuli. Secondly, anxiety at the processing stage can debilitate cognitive operations performed on external stimuli and memory processes. The students may experience a reduced ability to understand messages and learn new vocabulary. Finally, anxiety at the output stage can interfere with the retrieval of previously learned material and might hinder the students' ability to produce the foreign language.

MacIntyre and Gardner (1994: 284) defined foreign-language anxiety as 'the feeling of tension and apprehension specifically associated with second language contexts, including speaking, listening, and learning'. They found that it 'tends to correlate with measures of performance in the second language but not in the native language' and conclude that the 'potential effects of language anxiety on cognitive processing in the second language may be pervasive, and may be quite subtle' (MacIntyre & Gardner, 1994: 301). More recently, Onwuegbuzie *et al.* (2000: 88) found further evidence of the 3-stage model of foreign-language anxiety that they defined as 'a form of situation-specific anxiety'. The authors fully agree with Young (1990) that foreign-language anxiety is both complex and multidimensional (see also Bailey *et al.*, 1999; Cheng *et al.*, 1999; Horwitz, 2001; MacIntyre & Gardner, 1991a).

Several researchers suggest that skill in one's native language (e.g. reading, vocabulary, group achievement) may affect anxiety levels in the foreign language (Ganschow & Sparks, 1996; Sparks *et al.*, 1998).

Anxiety can also have a stimulating effect in L2 production, according to MacIntyre and Gardner (1994). They point out that anxiety may facilitate verbal performance in cases where the increased effort more than compensates for the reduced efficiency of the cognitive processing. However, 'even when anxiety appears to facilitate or at least not impair performance, one must consider the degree of effort invested in that performance' (MacIntyre & Gardner, 1994: 285). One should not only consider the quality of performance, argue MacIntyre and Gardner (1994), but also the subtle effects of anxiety on specific task performance and on the cognitive activity that precedes performance.

A potentially crucial fact for our argument on individual differences in L2 production is the link that has emerged between introversion and anxiety in the catecholamine system. Excessive levels of dopamine and norepinephrine seem to impair performance. The cumulated effects of both dimensions could seriously affect fluency in L2 production. It is not surprising in this view that introverts have been found to be more anxious (Cheek & Buss, 1981; Gershuny *et al.*, 2000). M.W. Eysenck argues that the higher anxiety of introverts could further reduce the available processing capacity of working memory, 'This would explain why introverts take longer to access information ... from long-term memory or permanent storage' (Eysenck, 1981: 203).

Dewaele (2001) analysed the psychological and socio-demographic correlates of foreign-language anxiety in the French L2 and English L3 speech production of 100 Flemish students. The findings suggest that foreign-language anxiety is not a stable personality trait among experienced language learners. Both the societal and the individual contexts were found to determine levels of communicative anxiety. The perception of French as the former prestige language in Flanders and its function as a social marker were found to be linked to the participants' social class, which was, in turn, linked to levels of anxiety in French – but not in English. This social effect appeared to be a stronger predictor of communicative anxiety in French than three personality variables (extraversion, neuroticism and psychoticism[9]). However, psychoticism, extraversion and, to a lesser extent, neuroticism, did significantly predict levels of communicative anxiety in English L3 production. Students who scored high on the extraversion and psychoticism scales reported significant lower levels of communicative anxiety in English. Those who scored low on the neuroticism scale also tended to report lower levels of communicative anxiety in English. The same pattern emerged for communicative anxiety in French, but it was not significant. It was argued that the higher foreign-language anxiety of the introverts follows logically from the observation that they tend to be reserved, quiet and unassertive in contrast to the more outgoing and talkative extraverts (Furnham & Heaven, 1998). The extraverts' more optimistic side might limit their fear of speaking a foreign language. They were also found to possess higher levels of self-perceived competence in English, their L3. The extraverts' better STM might also explain their more relaxed attitude towards foreign language production. Their confidence in L2 communication could result from the fact that they never had to struggle to be fluent and flexible to the same extent as the introverts. Our study further showed that general trait anxiety, as measured by the neuroticism-scale (N-scale), and language anxiety might be considered as orthogonal dimensions, but that a moderate positive relationship exists between both. Speakers who scored higher on the N-scale (showing signs of anxiety, phobia, depression and hypochondriasis) also reported higher levels of language anxiety in English. This result contradicts earlier findings of the absence of a link between neuroticism/emotional stability and language anxiety (MacIntyre & Charos, 1996). Social and communicative demands of L2 interaction are not the only factors that drive language anxiety. A predisposition to trait anxiety, nervousness and neuroticism can reinforce the level of language anxiety (Dewaele, 2001).

Conclusion

Individual differences in the oral production of L2 users seem to be determined by at least three independent variables that interact with a fourth, namely the perceived formality of the situation and the stress that it generates. The first independent variable to affect processing is the nature of representation of linguistic knowledge in the bilingual memory, i.e. the amount of implicit versus explicit knowledge in the L2 and the degree of acceleration in the use of explicit knowledge. Speakers who have internalised large chunks of knowledge in the L2 through practice and exposure are able to use this implicit competence automatically and will continue to do so in stressful situations. One can assume that implicit competence encompasses conceptual fluency and automatic syntactic building procedures. Those who have a smaller amount of implicit competence in the L2, or no implicit competence at all, need to rely more on their declarative knowledge of the L2. This does permit highly fluent production, especially in case of speeded-up controlled processing. However, this almost native-like fluency can disappear once the situation becomes more demanding and cognitive resources are needed elsewhere. At that point the L2 user may revert to slower serial processing.

The reason for this 'breakdown' brings us to a second main cause for individual differences in fluency of oral L2 production, namely capacity and/or efficiency in the STM and WM. Heavy reliance on declarative knowledge requires an important amount of STM capacity. This could cause a STM overload in introvert L2 users. One possible explanation is that in some cases both 'slave systems' to the central executive, the phonological loop and visuo-spatial sketchpad, overload. This would mean that bits of linguistic information would have to queue before being processed, hence a slowdown in processing and in fluency. An alternative and complementary explanation is that the central executive itself overloads, impairing the efficiency of the STM and limiting the speaker's fluency and flexibility. When this occurs, linguistic information is stacked, like planes above a crowded airport. Research suggests that high levels of dopamine in the dorsolateral prefrontal cortex might be the cause of the overload. These dopamine levels seem to remain under the maximum limit in extravert L2 users, hence little disruption in the functioning of the STM and WM, and minimal reduction in flexibility and fluency. Extravert L2 users are thus able to allocate extra resources to task completion and message preparation. They can fully benefit from their visuo-spatial sketchpad to take into account cues from the context in order to readjust their speech pragmatically.

The third independent variable to affect L2 production is anxiety, and particularly communicative anxiety. This anxiety tends to co-occur with high stress, STM overload and breakdown in automatic processing. It does in fact exacerbate an already bad situation, as it diverts valuable resources from the task in hand. One could compare it to a fire spreading through an overstretched airport control centre. Anxiety seems to be linked to catecholamine activity, and norepinephrine in particular, which also seems to affect the capacity and/or efficiency of the STM. The combination of high anxiety and high introversion thus seems to reinforce the effects on speech production in the L2, especially in stressful interpersonal situations.

The anxious L2 user's fears may be reinforced by the realisation that, because of capacity problems, his or her speech might not be sufficiently fluent and flexible, and that this could lead to negative reactions by interlocutors. To sum up, it could be said that introvert and anxious L2 users have to overcome a double obstacle in order to produce fluent speech in the L2.

Acknowledgements

I would like to thank Vivian Cook, Zoltan Dörnyei and Aneta Pavlenko for their stimulating feedback on earlier versions of this paper.

Notes

1. The amygdala is part of the limbic system. It is a large nuclear mass located in the

temporal pole (DeMyer, 1988: 284). It augments or modulates several functions, rather than being a single centre with a single function (DeMeyer, 1988: 285).
2. The reticular formation consists of widely spaced neuronal perikarya loosely arranged into nuclear groups. It regulates mental activity (consciousness, attention span, alerting responses, and the sleep-wake cycle) (DeMyer, 1988: 171).
3. The basal ganglia refer to 'several closely grouped neuronal nuclei situated below and on each side of the cerebral cortex' (Bradford, 1986: 400).
4. Dopamine is a neurotransmitter system of major importance within the brain. It is involved in a range of apparently different brain mechanisms including central control of locomotion and neural processes generating motivational behavior, mood and emotion (Bradford, 1986: 414). Dopamine is the immediate biosynthetic precursor of norepinephrine (the latter is also known as noradrenaline) (Bradford, 1986: 155).
5. The hippocampal formation is primitive cortex, most of which, the hippocampus proper, is rolled into the floor of the temporal horn (DeMyer, 1988: 285). It is part of the circuitry involved in learning and recent memory. It may also have a chemoreceptor-endocrine function (DeMyer, 1988: 287).
6. One of four subdivisions of the brain (cerebrum, diencephalon, brainstem and cerebellum (DeMyer, 1988: 1). It comprises the epithalamus, thalamus and hypothalamus (DeMyer, 1988: 252).
7. The greater subcortical activation of the basal ganglia could explain the higher degree of procedural learning by introverts (Saint-Cyr & Taylor, 1992). Pulvermüller and Schumann (1994: 717) suggest that dopamine activity is linked to motivation, and related to neuronal activity in the amygdala. High levels of dopamine promote the acquisition of new linguistic material in the forebrain. It thus seems that introverts benefit from high dopamine levels in the learning process, as the amygdala is linked to LTM (Bianchin et al., 1999; Izquierdo *et al.,* 1999). One consistent finding in the literature is that introverts possess a better LTM and seem to possess a richer vocabulary (Dewaele & Furnham, 1999, 2000).
8. Catecholaminergic neurons control motor activity and mood (Bradford, 1986: 414).
9. Neuroticism (N) is the second major personality domain in Eysenck's model of personality. It could be described as a minor nervous disorder. Persons scoring high on this scale tend to suffer from 'anxiety, phobia, depression and hypochondriasis' (Furnham & Heaven, 1998: 326). Those with low scores on N can be described as calm, contented and unemotional. Psychoticism is the third major personality domain in Eysenck's model and measures tough-mindedness (Furnham & Heaven, 1998: 230). Persons scoring high on psychoticism 'tend to be hostile, cold, aggressive, and have poor personal interpersonal relations' (Furnham & Heaven, 1998; 327).

References

Abutalebi, J., Cappa, S.F. and Perani, D. (2001) The bilingual brain as revealed by functional neuro-imaging. *Bilingualism: Language & Cognition* 4 (2), 179–190.
Arnsten, A.F.T. (1998) Catecholamine modulation of prefrontal cortical cognitive function. *Trends in Cognitive Sciences* 2, 436–447.
Baddeley, A.D. (1986) *Working Memory.* Oxford: Clarendon Press.

Baddeley, A., Gathercole, S. and Papagno, C. (1998) The phonological loop as a language learning device. *Psychological Review* 105, 158–173.

Baddeley, A. and Logie, R.H. (1999) Working memory. The multiple-component model. In A. Miyake and P. Shah (eds) *Models of Working Memory. Mechanisms of Active Maintenance and Executive Control* (pp. 28–61). Cambridge: Cambridge University Press.

Bailey, P., Onwuegbuzie, A. and Daley, C.E. (2000) Using learning style to predict foreign language achievement at the college level. *System* 80, 125–133.

Bianchin, M., Mello e Souza, T., Medina, J.H. and Izquierdo, I. (1999) The amygdala is involved in the modulation of long-term memory, but not in working or short-term memory. *Neurobiology of Learning and Memory* 71 (2), 127–131.

Bradford, H.F. (1986) *Chemical Neurobiology. An Introduction to Neurochemistry.* New York: W.H. Freeman & Co.

Brown, G. and Hulme, C. (1992) Cognitive psychology and second language processing: The role of short-term memory. In R. Harris (ed.) *Cognitive Processing in Bilinguals* (pp. 105–121). Amsterdam: Elsevier.

Busato, V.V., Prins, F.J., Elshout, J.J. and Hamaker, C. (1999) The relation between learning styles, the Big Five personality traits and achievement motivation in higher education. *Personality and Individual Differences* 26 (1), 129–140.

Cabeza, R. and Nyberg, L. (1997) Imaging cognition: An empirical review of PET studies with normal subjects. *Journal of Cognitive Neuroscience* 9, 1–26.

Cansino, S., Ruiz, A. and Lopez-Alonso, V. (1999) What does the brain do while playing Scrabble? ERPs associated with short-long-term memory task. *International Journal of Psychophysiology* 31 (3), 261–274.

Caplan, D. and Waters, G.S. (1999) Verbal working memory and sentence comprehension. *Behavioral and Brain Sciences* 22 (1), 77–94.

Caspari, I. and Parkinson, S.R. (2000) Effects of memory impairment on discourse. *Journal of Neurolinguistics* 13, 15–36.

Cheek, J.M. and Buss, A.H. (1981) Shyness and sociability. *Journal of Personality and Social Psychology* 41 (2), 330–339.

Cheng, Y., Horwitz, E.K., and Schallert, D.L. (1999) Language anxiety: Differentiating writing and speaking components. *Language Learning* 49, 417–446.

Cheung, H. (1996) Nonword span as a unique predictor of second language vocabulary learning. *Developmental Psychology* 32, 867–873.

Cheung, H., Kemper, S. and Leung, E. (2000) A phonological account for the cross-language variation in working memory processing. *Psychological Record* 50, 373–386.

Chincotta, D. and Underwood, G. (1996) Mother tongue, language of schooling and bilingual digit span. *British Journal of Psychology* 87, 193–208.

Chincotta, D. and Underwood, G. (1997) Digit span and articulatory suppression: A cross-linguistic comparison. *European Journal of Cognitive Psychology* 9, 89–96.

Chincotta, D. and Underwood, G. (1998) Non temporal determinants of bilingual memory capacity: The role of long-term representations and fluency. *Bilingualism: Language and Cognition* 1, 117–130.

Cochran, B.P., McDonald, J.L. and Parault, S.J. (1999) Too smart for their own good: The disadvantage of a superior capacity for adult language learners. *Journal of Memory and Language* 41, 30–58.

Cook, V. (1977) Cognitive processes in second language learning. *International Review of Applied Linguistics* 15, 73–90.

Cook, V. (1997) The consequences of bilingualism for cognitive processing. In A.M.B. de Groot and J.F. Kroll (eds) *Tutorials in Bilingualism. Psycholinguistic Perspectives* (pp. 279–300). New Jersey: Lawrence Erlbaum.

Cowan, N., Wood, N., Wood, P., Keller, T., Nugent, L. and Keller, C. (1998) Two separate verbal processing rates contributing to short-term memory span. *Journal of Experimental Psychology: General* 127 (2), 141–160.

De Bot, K. (1992) A bilingual production model: Levelt's 'speaking' model adapted. *Applied Linguistics* 13 (1), 1–24.

De Raad, B. and Schouwenburg, H. (1996) Personality in learning and education: A review. *European Journal of Personality* 10, 303–336.

Dehaene, S., Dupoux, E. and Mehler, J. (1997) Anatomical variability in cortical representation of first and second languages. *Neuroreport* 8, 3809–3815.

DeMyer, W. (1988) *Neuroanatomy.* New York: John Wiley & Sons.

Depue, R.A. and Collins, P.F. (1999) Neurobiology of the structure of personality: Dopamine, facilitation of incentive motivation and extraversion. *Brain and Behavioral Sciences* 22 (3), 491–569.

Derakshan, N. and Eysenck, M.W. (1998) Working memory capacity in high trait-anxious and repressor groups. *Cognition and Emotion* 12 (5), 697–713.

Dewaele, J-M. (2001) Activation or inhibition? The interaction of L1, L2 and L3 on the language mode continuum. In J. Cenoz, B. Hufeisen and U. Jessner (eds) *Cross-linguistic Aspects of L3 Acquisition* (pp. 69–89). Clevedon: Multilingual Matters.

Dewaele, J-M. (2002) Psychological and socio-demographic correlates of communicative anxiety in L2 and L3 production. *The International Journal of Bilingualism.*

Dewaele, J-M. and Furnham, A. (1999) Extraversion: The unloved variable in applied linguistic research. *Language Learning* 49 (3), 509–544.

Dewaele, J-M. and Furnham, A. (2000) Personality and speech production: A pilot study of second language learners. *Personality and Individual Differences* 28, 355–365.

Dewaele, J-M. and Regan, V. (2002) Maîtriser la norme sociolinguistique en interlangue française: Le cas de l'omission variable de 'ne'. *Journal of French Language Studies.*

Dewaele, J-M. and Sachdev, I. (2001) Variable performance: From informal conversations to formal oral examinations. Unpublished manuscript, University of London.

Dewaele, J-M. and Véronique, D. (2001) Gender assignment and gender agreement in advanced French Interlanguage: A cross-sectional study. *Bilingualism: Language and Cognition* 4, 3.

Dornic, S. (1978) The bilingual's performance: Language dominance, stress and individual differences. In D. Gerver and H.W. Sinaiko (eds) *Language, Interpretation and Communication.* New York: Plenum Press.

Dörnyei, Z. and Kormos, J. (2000) The role of individual and social variables in oral task performance. *Language Teaching Research* 4, 275–300.

Doucet, C. and Stelmack, R.M. (2000) An event-related potential analysis of extraversion and individual differences in cognitive processing speed and response execution. *Journal of Personality and Social Psychology* 78 (5), 956–964.

Emerson, M.J., Miyake, A. and Rettinger, D.A. (1999) Individual differences in integrating and coordinating multiple sources of information. *Journal of Experimental Psychology: Learning, Memory, and Cognition* 25 (5), 1300–1321.
Eysenck, H.J. (1967) *The Biological Basis of Personality.* Springfield, IL: Thomas.
Eysenck, H.J. (1979) Anxiety, learning and memory: A reconceptualisation. *Journal of Research in Personality* 13, 363–385.
Eysenck, H.J. and Eysenck, M.W. (1985) *Personality and Individual Differences. A Natural Science Approach.* New York and London: Plenum Press.
Eysenck, M.W. (1981) Learning, memory and personality. In H.J. Eysenck (ed.) *A Model for Personality* (pp. 169–209). Berlin: Springer Verlag.
Fabbro, F. (1999) *The Neurolinguistics of Bilingualism. An Introduction.* Hove: Psychology Press, Francis and Taylor Group.
Fischer, H., Wik, G. and Fredrikson, M. (1997) Extraversion, neuroticism and brain function: A PET study of personality. *Personality and Individual Differences* 23, 345–352.
Fremont, T., Means, G.H., and Means, R.S. (1976) Anxiety as a function of task performance feedback and extraversion–introversion. *Psychological Reports* 27, 455–458.
Furnham, A. (1990) Language and personality. In H. Giles and W.P. Robinson (eds) *Handbook of Language and Social Psychology* (pp. 73–95). Chichester: John Wiley and Sons.
Furnham, A. and Heaven, P. (1998) *Personality and Social Behaviour.* London: Arnold.
Ganschow, L. and Sparks, R. (1996) Anxiety about foreign language learning among high school women. *Modern Language Journal* 80, 199–212.
Gathercole, S. and Baddeley, A. (1989) Evaluation of the role of phonological STM in the development of vocabulary in children: A longitudinal study. *Journal of Memory and Language* 28, 200–215.
Gathercole, S. and Baddeley, A. (1990) The role of phonological memory in vocabulary acquisition: A study of young children learning new words. *British Journal of Psychology* 81, 439–454.
Gathercole, S. and Baddeley, A. (1993) *Working Memory and Language.* Hove: Lawrence Erlbaum.
Gershuny, B.S., Sher, K.J., Rossy, L. and Bishop, A.K. (2000) Distinguishing manifestations of anxiety: How do personality traits of compulsive checkers differ from other anxious individuals? *Behaviour Research and Therapy* 38 (3), 229–241.
Gilbert, D.T. (1989) Thinking lightly about others: Automatic components of the social inference process. In J.S. Uleman and J.A. Bargh (eds) *Unintended Thought* (pp. 189–211). New York: Guilford.
Gilbert, D.T., Krull, D.S. and Pelham, B.W. (1988). Of thoughts unspoken and the self-regulation of behavior. *Journal of Personality and Social Psychology* 55, 685–694.
Green, D.W. (1998) Mental control of the bilingual lexico-semantic system. *Bilingualism: Language and Cognition* 1 (2), 67–81.
Grosjean, F. (1992) Another view of bilingualism. In R.J. Harris (ed.) *Cognitive Processing in Bilinguals* (pp. 51–62). Amsterdam: North-Holland.
Grosjean, F. (1998) Studying bilinguals: Methodological and conceptual issues. *Bilingualism: Language and Cognition* 1 (2), 131–149.

Grosjean, F. (2001) The bilingual's language modes. In J.L. Nicol (ed.) *One Mind, Two Languages: Bilingual Language Processing* (pp. 1–22). Oxford: Blackwell.

Hamers, J.F. and Blanc, M.H.A. (2000) *Bilinguality and Bilingualism* (2nd edn). Cambridge: Cambridge University Press.

Hirst, W. and Kalmar, D. (1987) Characterizing attentional resources. *Journal of Experimental Psychology: General* 116, 68–81.

Horwitz, E.K. (2001) Language anxiety and achievement. *Annual Review of Applied Linguistics* 21, 112–126.

Howarth, E. and Eysenck, H.J. (1965) Extraversion, arousal, and paired-associates recall. *Journal of Experimental Research in Personality* 3, 114–116.

Izquierdo, I., Izquierdo, L.A., Barros, D.M., Mello e Souza, T., de Souza, M.M., Quevedo, J., Rodrigues, C., Kauer-Sant'Anna, M., Madruga, M. and Medina, J.H. (1998) Differential involvement of cortical receptor mechanisms in working, short-term and long-term memory. *Behavioural Pharmacology* 9 (5–6), 421–427.

Izquierdo, I., Medina, J-H., Vianna, M.R.M., Izquierdo, L.A. and Barros, D.M. (1999) Separate mechanisms for short-and long-term memory. *Behavioural Brain Research* 103, 1–11.

Jacobs, B. and Schumann, J. (1992) Language acquisition and the neurosciences: Towards a more integrative perspective. *Applied Linguistics* 13 (3), 282–301.

Jarrold, C., Baddeley, A.D. and Hewes, A.K. (2000) Verbal short-term memory deficits in Down Syndrome: A consequence of problems in rehearsal? *Journal of Child Psychology and Psychiatry and Allied Disciplines* 41 (2), 223–244.

Just, M. and Carpenter, P. (1992) A capacity theory of comprehension: Individual differences in working memory. *Psychological Review* 99 (1), 122–149.

Kecskes, I. and Papp, T. (2000) *Foreign Language and Mother Tongue*. Hillsdale, NJ: Lawrence Erlbaum.

Kim, K.H., Relkin, N.R., Lee, K-M. and Hirsch, J. (1997) Distinct cortical areas associated with native and second languages. *Nature* 388, 171–74.

Koob, G. F. (1999) Corticotropin-releasing factor, norepinephrine, and stress. *Biological Psychiatry* 46, 1167–1180.

Kosslyn, S.M. and Koenig, O. (1992) *Wet Mind: The New Cognitive Neuroscience*. New York: Free Press.

Largeau, C. (2000) Apprendre et utiliser une règle en langue étrangère: la procéduralisation. Paper presented at the Instructed Second Language Colloquium, Free University of Brussels, August 2000.

Laufer, B. and Nation, P. (2000) Passive vocabulary size and speed of meaning recognition: Are they related? Unpublished manuscript, University of Tel-Aviv.

Levelt, W.J.M. (1989) *Speaking. From Intention to Articulation*. Cambridge, MA and London: ACL-MIT Press.

Levelt, W.J.M., Roelofs, A. and Meyer, A.S. (1999) A theory of lexical access in speech production. *Brain and Behavorial Sciences* 22, 1–75.

Lieberman, M.D. (2000) Introversion and working memory: Central executive differences. *Personality and Individual Differences* 28, 479–486.

Lieberman, M.D. and Rosenthal, R. (2001) Why introverts can't always tell who likes them: Social multi-tasking and non-verbal decoding. *Journal of Personality and Social Psychology* 80, 294–310.

MacIntyre, P.D. (1999) Language anxiety: A review of the research for language teachers. In D.J. Young (ed.) *Affect in Foreign Language and Second Language Teaching: A Practical Guide to Creating a Low-anxiety Classroom Atmosphere*. Boston: McGraw-Hill.

MacIntyre, P.D. and Charos, C. (1996) Personality, attitudes, and affect as predictors of second language communication. *Journal of Language and Social Psychology* 15, 3–26.

MacIntyre, P.D., Dörnyei, Z., Clément, R. and Noels, K.A. (1998) Conceptualizing willingness to communicate in a L2: A situational model of L2 confidence and affiliation. *Modern Language Journal* 82, 545–562.

MacIntyre, P.D. and Gardner, R.C. (1989) Anxiety and second language learning: Towards a theoretical clarification. *Language Learning* 39, 251–275.

MacIntyre, P.D. and Gardner, R.C. (1991a) Methods and results in the study of foreign language anxiety: A review of the literature. *Language Learning* 41, 25–57.

MacIntyre, P.D. and Gardner, R.C. (1991b) Language anxiety: Its relationship to other anxieties and to processing in native and second language. *Language Learning* 41, 513–534.

MacIntyre, P.D. and Gardner, R.C. (1994) The subtle effects of language anxiety on cognitive processing in the second language. *Language Learning* 44, 283–305.

Markham, R. and Darke, S. (1991) The effects of anxiety on verbal and spatial task performance. *Austrialian Journal of Psychology* 43, 107–111.

Matthews, G. (1992) Extraversion. In P.A. Smith and D.M. Jones (eds) *Handbook of Human Performance: Vol. 3 State and Trait* (pp. 95–126). London: Academic Press.

Matthews, G. and Deary, I. (1998) *Personality Traits*. Cambridge: Cambridge University Press.

Matthews, G. and Dorn, L. (1995) Cognitive and attentional processes in personality and intelligence. In D. H. Saklofske and M. Zeidner (eds) *International Handbook of Personality and Intelligence* (pp. 367–396). New York: Plenum Press.

Medina, J.H., Schroeder, N. and Izquierdo, I. (1999) Two different properties of short- and long-term memory. *Behavioural Brain Research* 103 (1), 119–121.

Michael, E. (1999). The consequences of individual differences in cognitive abilities for bilingual language processing. PhD dissertation, Pennsylvania State University.

Miyake, A. and Shah, P. (1999) Towards unified theories of working memory. Emerging general consensus, unresolved issues, and future research. In A. Miyake and P. Shah (eds) *Models of Working Memory. Mechanisms of Active Maintenance and Executive Control* (pp. 442–479). Cambridge: Cambridge University Press.

Onwuegbuzie, A., Bailey, P. and Daley, C.E. (1999) Factors associated with foreign language anxiety. *Applied Psycholinguistics* 20, 217–39.

Papagno, C. and Vallar, G. (1995) Verbal short-term memory and vocabulary learning in polyglots. *Quarterly Journal of Experimental Psychology* 48A, 98–107.

Paradis, M. (1994) Neurolinguistic aspects of implicit and explicit memory: Implications for bilingualism and SLA. In N. Ellis (ed.) *Implicit and Explicit Learning of Languages* (pp. 393–419). London, San Diego: Academic Press.

Paradis, M. (1997) The cognitive neuropsychology of bilingualism. In A.M.B. de Groot and J.F. Kroll (eds) *Tutorials in Bilingualism. Psycholinguistic Perspectives* (pp. 331–354). New Jersey: Lawrence Erlbaum.

Paradis, M. (2000) Awareness of observable input and output – not of linguistic competence. Paper presented at Odense University, Denmark, April 2000.

Perani, D. (1999) The functional basis of memory: PET mapping of the memory systems in humans. In L-G. Nilsson and H.J. Markovitsch (eds) *Cognitive Neuroscience of Memory* (pp. 55–78). Seattle: Hogrefe and Huber Publishers.

Perani, D., Dehaene, S., Grassi, F., Cohen, L., Cappa, S.F. and Dupoux, E. (1996) Brain processing of native and foreign languages. *Neuroreport 7*, 2439–2444.

Perani, D., Paulesu, E., Galles, N.S., Dupoux, E., Dehaene, S., Bettinardi, V., Cappa, S.F., Fazio, F. and Mehler, J. (1998) The bilingual brain: Proficiency and age of acquisition of the second language. *Brain 121*, 1841–1852.

Pienemann, M. (1998) *Language Processing and Second Language Development: Processability Theory*. Amsterdam: John Benjamins.

Pochon, J-B., Levy, R, Poline, J-B., Crozier, S., Lehericy, S., Pillon, B., Deweer, B., Le Bihan, D. and Dubois, B. (2001) The role of dorsolateral prefrontal cortex in the preparation of forthcoming actions: An fMRI study. *Cerebral Cortex 11*, 260–266.

Pulvermüller, F. and Schumann, J.S. (1994) Neurobiological mechanisms of language acquisition. *Language Learning 44* (4), 681–734.

Rawlings, D. and Carnie, D. (1989) The interaction of EPQ extraversion with WAIS subtest performance under timed and untimed conditions. *Personality and Individual Differences 10*, 453–458.

Robbins, T.W. and Everitt, B.J. (1995) Arousal systems and attention. In M.S. Gazzaniga (ed.) *Cognitive Neurosciences* (pp. 703–720). Cambridge, MA: MIT Press.

Roodenrys, S., Hulme, C., Alban, J. and Ellis, A. (1994) Effects of word frequency and age of acquisition on short-term memory span. *Memory and Cognition 22* (6), 695–701.

Rosen, V.M. and Engle, R.W. (1997) The role of working memory capacity in retrieval. *Journal of Experimental Psychology: General 126* (3), 211–227.

Saint-Cyr, J.A. and Taylor, A.E. (1992) The mobilization of procedural learning: The 'key signature' of the basal ganglia. In L.R. Squire and N. Butters (eds) *Neuropsychology of Memory* (2nd edn) (pp. 188–202). New York: The Guilford Press.

Schumann, J. (2001) Appraisal psychology, neurobiology and language. *Annual Review of Applied Linguistics 21*, 23–42.

Segalowitz, N.S. (1997) Individual differences in second language acquisition. In A.M.B. de Groot and J.F. Kroll (eds) *Tutorials in Bilingualism. Psycholinguistic Perspectives* (pp. 85– 112). New Jersey: Lawrence Erlbaum.

Segalowitz, N.S. and Segalowitz, S.J. (1993) Skilled performance, practice, and the differentiation of speed-up from automatisation effects: Avoidance from second language word recognition. *Applied Psycholinguistics 14*, 369–85.

Segalowitz, N., Segalowitz, S.J. and Wood, A.G. (1998) Assessing the development of automaticity in second language word recognition. *Applied Psycholinguistics 19*, 53–67.

Service, E. (1992) Phonology, working memory and foreign language learning. *Quarterly Journal of Experimental Psychology 45*A, 21–50.

Socan, G. and Bucik, V. (1998) Relationship between speed of information-processing and two major personality dimensions – extraversion and neuroticism. *Personality and Individual Differences 25*, 35–48.

Sparks, R-L., Artzer, M., Patton, J., Ganschow, L., Miller, K., Hordubay, D.J. and Walsh, G. (1998) Benefits of multisensory structured language instruction for at-risk foreign language learners: A comparison study of high school Spanish students. *Annals of Dyslexia* 48, 239–270.

Spence, J. and Spence, K. (1966) The motivational components of manifest anxiety: Drive and drive stimuli. In C.D. Spielberger (ed.) *Anxiety and Behavior* (pp. 291–326). London: Academic Press.

Stenberg, G., Wendt, P.E. and Risberg, J. (1993) Regional cerebral blood flow and extraversion. *Personality and Individual Differences* 15, 547–554.

Swann, W.B., Stein-Seroussi, A. and McNulty, S.W. (1992) Outcasts in a white-lie society: The enigmatic worlds of people with negative self-concepts. *Journal of Personality and Social Psychology* 62, 618–624.

Tapasak, R., Roodin, P.A. and Vaught, G.M. (1978) Effects of extraversion, anxiety, and sex on children's verbal fluency and coding task performance. *Journal of Psychology* 100, 49–55.

Temple, L. (1997) Memory and processing modes in language learner speech production. *Communication and Cognition* 30, 75–90.

Temple, L. (2000) Second language learner speech production. *Studia Linguistica* 54 (2), 288–297.

Thorn, A.S. and Gathercole, S.E. (1999) Language-specific knowledge and short-term memory in bilingual and non-bilingual children. *Quarterly Journal of Experimental Psychology: Human Experimental Psychology* 52A, 303–324.

Tobias, S. (1986) Anxiety and cognitive processing of instruction. In R. Schwarzer (ed.) *Self-related Cognition in Anxiety and Motivation* (pp. 35–54). Hillsdale, NJ: Lawrence Erlbaum.

Towell, R. and Dewaele, J-M. (2001) The development of fluency amongst 12 advanced learners of French. Paper presented at AAAL 2001, Saint Louis.

Towell, R., Hawkins, R. and Bazergui, N. (1996) The development of fluency in advanced learners of French. *Applied Linguistics* 17 (1), 84–119.

Vedhara, K., Hyde, J., Gilchrist, I-D., Tytherleigh, M. and Plummer, S. (2000) Acute stress, memory, attention and cortisol. *Psychoneuroendocrinology* 25, 535–549.

Wilson, G. (1977) Introversion/extraversion. In T. Blass (ed.) *Personality Variables in Social Behavior* (pp. 179–218). Hillsdale, NJ: Lawrence Erlbaum.

Young, D.J. (1990) An investigation of students' perspectives on anxiety and speaking. *Foreign Language Annals* 23, 539–553.

Introduction to Chapter 10

Language Attrition: Tests, Self-assessments and Perceptions, Kees de Bot and Madeleine Hulsen

VIVIAN COOK

Though it may be convenient to see the mind of the L2 user as static, the relationships between two languages in the mind are in reality dynamic. They change during the period of acquisition, during the period of language use and from moment to moment during the production of speech. The main theme of De Bot and Hulsen's chapter is, then, what happens over time to both languages in the L2 user's mind, looked at from the complementary perspectives of the observer and of the L2 user.

The various relationships outlined in the background chapter might be true for different stages in the development and loss of the learner's languages. In the separation relationship, the L1 may wither away as the L2 is used more pervasively. In interconnection relationships the effects are more diverse; most obviously elements of the L1 system 'transfer' to the L2, as attested in characteristic spelling mistakes of Japanese users of English such as *froppy disc*, *Engilish* and *priciples*. Less obviously elements of the L2 intrude on the L1; English people who know Japanese can be distinguished by their use of nodding for agreement (*aizuchi*) when talking English (Locastro, 1987). In integration models, both the L2 and the L1 effectively transform into a new system, which may in itself change over time; for instance Hebrew/English bilinguals exaggerate VOT differences for each language in production but use intermediate values between the two languages for perception (Obler, 1982).

The development of these relationships over time has been considered by many in terms of the 'loss' or 'attrition' of one or the other language rather than 'gain', as we see in the current chapter: L2 users may lose command of aspects of their first or their second language. After years of living in an L2 environment their first language dwindles away; when they pass their final examinations in a second language, they forget it for the rest of their lives. Language may also be lost after a trauma to the brain, as seen in Fabbro's chapter.

The relationships between languages apply at the level of society as well as that of the individual. In a society with two or more separate languages, one may disappear, emotively called 'language death', for example the virtual disappearance of Dyirbal in Australia within recent decades (Schmidt, 1985). Where there are interconnected languages, their links and uses may change, as in Hungarian speakers living in Austria who invent new Hungarian words, not knowing the actual Hungarian form (Gal, 1989). Or contact between two languages may result in a creole; some claim that the creolised features of modern English such as the dummy auxiliary *do* derive from its two hundred year co-existence with French (Domingue, 1977).

One intriguing question concerns what 'loss' means. The forms of the language might be truly lost from the mind or they might still be present but access to them is unavailable, demonstrated for example by people's abilities to speak languages under hypnosis that they have lost in their normal state of consciousness (Ås, 1962; Fromm, 1970). A second question is whether the route of language loss is the same as that for language acquisition in reverse – 'Last in, first out' (Cohen, 1975). The third question that De Bot and Hulsen invoke is whether anything useful can be done to prevent attrition by 'retraining'.

References

Ås, A. (1962) The recovery of a forgotten language knowledge through hypnotic age regression: A case report. *American Journal of Clinical Hypnotism* 5, 24–29.

Cohen, A. (1975) Forgetting a second language. *Language Learning* 25, 127–138.

Domingue, N. (1977) Middle English: another creole? *Journal of Creole Studies* 1(1), 89–100.

Fromm, E. (1970) Age regression with unexpected reappearance of a repressed childhood language. *International Journal of Clinical and Experimental Hypnosis* XVIII, 2, 79–88.

Gal, S. (1989) Lexical innovation and loss: The use and value of restricted Hungarian. In N. Dorian (ed.) *Investigating Obsolescence: Studies in Language Contraction and Death* (pp. 313–331). Cambridge: Cambridge University Press.

Locastro, V. (1987) Aizuchi: A Japanese conversational routine. In L.E. Smith (ed.) *Discourse across Cultures* (pp. 101–113). New York: Prentice Hall.

Obler, L. (1982) The parsimonious bilingual. In L. Obler and L. Menn (eds) *Exceptional Language and Linguistics*, New York: Academic Press.

Schmidt, A. (1985) *Young People's Dyirbal: An Example of Language Death from Australia*. Cambridge: Cambridge University Press.

Chapter 10

Language Attrition: Tests, Self-Assessments and Perceptions

KEES DE BOT AND MADELEINE HULSEN

Introduction

The portrait of the L2 user as it emerges from the present volume would not be complete without an account of what happens over time with the skills in L1 and L2. While privately we know very well that all the knowledge we acquired on all the subjects we have studied in our lifetimes tends to fade, research-wise we pretend that second or foreign language learners simply accumulate knowledge and skills, and that that knowledge is available whenever it is needed. Fifteen years of language attrition research in various countries all over the world have made it clear that the real picture is rather different: neither first languages nor second languages are immune to loss. With non-use they fade, and though they keep their place in our memory system, they become less accessible up to the point where the knowledge has sunk beyond reach and is for practical purposes lost.

There are various ways to make a portrait of someone. One is to make an 'objective' picture by measuring all relevant characteristics, the other is to have that individual him or herself inform us about what the really interesting characteristics are. It could be argued that a complete portrait involves both these perspectives: the objective, external one, and the subjective, internal one. In this article an attempt is made to portray the language loser or attriter by bringing together these two perspectives on language attrition as they emerge from different approaches and paradigms.

For the 'objective' perspective the picture is based on a number of quantitatively oriented empirical studies on first and second language attrition. In these studies, subjects are tested on their language skills at a given moment in time and the results are then compared to some point of reference in the past. In this approach subjects are really subjects, people that are being watched. The second, 'subjective' perspective makes use of more qualitatively oriented studies in which it is not the performance of subjects on language tests that is the main object, but individuals' self-observations and experiences presented in narratives.

These two lines of research have so far followed their own distinct tracks, and have sometimes been viewed as mutually exclusive rather than complementary. While the first, more quantitative approach has its origins in the Anglo-Saxon behaviourist tradition in the social sciences, the second, more qualitative approach is based on ethno-methodological traditions. There is a long-standing tradition of auto-biographical writings on processes of language acquisition and language loss (e.g. Davidson, 1994; Lvovich, 1997; Nabokov, 1966) that can be an important source of information, but that are themselves not part of any school or paradigm.

Defining Language Attrition

The overall concept of language *loss* is defined here as 'the decline of language proficiency of an individual or group of speakers' (De Bot & Weltens, 1985). This decline can be due to more or less natural (non-pathological) processes such as language contact, language change, and disuse of a language, but it can also be caused by pathological processes, for instance when language loss is caused by brain damage, aphasia or dementia. Another distinction that is frequently used in language loss research is the typology proposed by De Bot & Weltens (1985). Starting from a bilingual perspective of a first language (L1) and a second language (L2), and based on the question 'What is lost in what environment?', they distinguish four types of language loss (examples of the types are given in brackets):

(1) L1 loss in an L1 environment (language death, dialect death, e.g. Cornish in the UK).

(2) L1 loss in an L2 environment (L1 loss in migrants, dialect loss outside the community, e.g. the L1 of German immigrants in the US).

(3) L2 loss in an L1 environment (foreign language loss, L2 loss due to re-migration, e.g. the loss of French as a foreign language in the Netherlands).

(4) L2 loss in an L2 environment (L2 loss in ageing migrants, e.g. the loss of English in Dutch immigrants in Australia).

We will focus on research conducted on the second and third types of language loss (L1 loss in an L2 environment and L2 loss in an L2 environment), as these are most commonly investigated.

As illustrated in Figure 10.1, the term *loss* will be used as a general term in which two partially overlapping processes can be distinguished: *shift* and *attrition* (De Bot, 1998). The most important difference between these

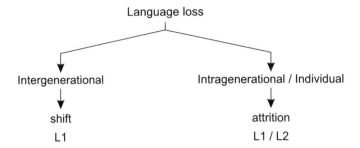

Figure 10.1 The relationship between language loss, shift and attrition

processes is that language shift is taken to refer to a decline of L1 proficiency at the group level, and that language attrition reflects a decrease in language proficiency at the individual level. Attrition can be used with respect to L1 attrition or L2 attrition, as both refer to processes that occur at the individual or intragenerational level.

A language in the process of *shift* is partially or completely replaced by another, usually more dominant, language. The functions of the language that is under threat, particularly in a migrant context, gradually become smaller, and the number of domains in which the language is used decreases. Eventually the non-dominant language is replaced by the dominant one in all language use domains and at all language levels (Pauwels, 1985). Although language shift can happen at the individual, or intragenerational level, the term language *shift* most frequently refers to an intergenerational process, in which a language is imperfectly transmitted from one generation to the next. In other words, from this perspective, language shift does not so much occur within a generation as between generations. In migrant contexts, the shift from the L1 to the L2 is often completed within three or four generations: the first generation is dominant in the L1 and less proficient in the L2, while the second generation consists of more or less stable bilinguals. By the third generation, the L2 has become dominant, while the fourth generation is monolingual in the L2 (Folmer, 1992).

Research into language *attrition*, the individual loss or decline of language skills, focuses on changes in the linguistic system of the L1 or L2 speaker. In the past, most research on language attrition has concentrated on the nature and outcome of these changes, in other words, on *what* happened to the language in question, while relatively little attention has been paid to *how* language attrition occurs and how reduced exposure to the L1 or the L2 affects the organisation of linguistic knowledge and the processing of information. However, a number of researchers (cf. Ammerlaan, 1996; D'Andrea, 1992; Grendel, 1993; Weltens, 1989; Hulsen, 2000) have shifted their attention towards a more psycholinguistic approach.

Language shift and language attrition are related in the sense that they can both lead to language-processing problems, e.g. a slowing down of the retrieval of lexical items, but the reasons for these problems are likely to be different. If second-generation migrants have trouble finding the right words in their L1, this may well be caused by *imperfect learning* (Verhoeven & Boeschoten, 1986) because of intergenerational language shift. However, failure to recall a word may also be due to insufficient exposure to the language (De Bot, 1998). An interesting question in language attrition research from the psycholinguistic perspective is whether these word-finding problems occur as a consequence of language attrition (Andersen, 1982), or whether, as mainstream psychological research on forgetting has suggested (Baddeley, 1990; Loftus & Loftus, 1976), it is a question of temporary unavailability. In other words, a failure to recollect specific words does not necessarily indicate 'permanent unavailability', or true attrition, but rather a temporary unavailability of the desired lexical items (Ammerlaan, 1996). Therefore, in the psycholinguistic approach, language attrition is viewed as a 'difficulty in retrieval rather than total loss' (Hakuta & D'Andrea, 1992: 72).

Language *maintenance* is the neutral or positive counterpart of language shift or attrition (Waas, 1996). As with language shift and attrition, language maintenance can occur at the group and individual level, although it usually refers to processes at the group and intergenerational level. The term language maintenance is therefore frequently used in conjunction with language shift. A number of models have been developed to explain the differences that exist between ethnic groups in the way they behave in language contact situations. Many scholars interested in language maintenance and shift have addressed the issue why some migrant or ethnic minority communities give up their language in favour of the L2, while others are able to maintain it for generations (Fishman, 1966, 1991; Giles, *et al.*, 1977; Haugen, 1969; Kloss, 1966). Sociological, sociolinguistic and sociopsychological aspects that have been related to language shift in order to attempt to explain *why* it takes place are, amongst others, sociopolitical attitudes, the relationship between language and identity, ethnolinguistic vitality, and social networks.

Sociocultural Perspectives on Language Attrition

More recently, Pavlenko and Lantolf (2000) have made an explicit link between biographical accounts of language attrition and sociocultural theory. They contrast the two lines of attrition research, particularly with reference to L1 loss by labeling them 'Third-person-accounts' (i.e. information on attrition processes as described by people other than the attriters themselves) and 'First-person-accounts' (i.e. information from the individuals who have themselves been in the process of losing their language). Pavlenko and Lantolf stress the importance of the participation metaphor as a complement to the acquisition metaphor. Following Sfard (1998), they indicate that:

> [The acquisition metaphor] compels us to think of knowledge as a commodity that is accumulated by the learner and to construe the mind as a repository where the learner hoards the commodity.... The participation metaphor, on the other hand, obliges us to think of learning as a process of becoming a member of a certain community. (Pavlenko & Lantolf, 2000: 155)

For L2 learners this means that becoming a part of the community using that language is the real activity and goal, not the acquisition of lexical items and grammatical rules. Obviously, for many foreign-language learners the foreign language community is restricted to the few hours in class and (in the European context in particular) some occasional contacts through the media or during holidays. For L2 learning, and specifically in settings of migration, there is a new community and language, and for some people there is a need to re-establish an identity. In her description of the struggle with his various languages of the German/English author Werner Landsburgh, Belz (2001) shows that he actually resists the formation of a new identity along with the learning of a second language, even while living in the foreign country for more than 30 years.

From the perspective of sociocultural theory and the participation metaphor, the processes of foreign language attrition and first language attrition are clearly different. For foreign languages, the identity that is linked to the first language setting and culture will hardly change with acquisition and attrition, while in most settings in which first language attrition takes place, moving out of the first language setting and into the second language setting has a profound effect. Interestingly, L1 attrition and L2 attrition may not be that different from the perspective of the acquisition metaphor, and most recent studies in attrition (see De Bot & Weltens, 1995 and Hansen, 2000 for overviews) have been carried out from this perspective. In those studies the focus is on 'things being learned and forgotten', and on storage and retrieval. The analogies used mostly come from an information-processing approach.

As Pavlenko and Lantolf (2000) indicate, the metaphors are complementary rather than mutually exclusive. The participation metaphor can handle the larger interactive context in which acquisition and attrition take place, while the acquisition metaphor can deal with the processing part that is largely inaccessible to introspection. Pavlenko and Lantolf base their analyses on the first-person narratives in a set of autobiographical accounts of migration experiences of American and French authors of Eastern European origin. They focus on the process of border crossing of those late bilinguals who moved to a new country as adolescents or young adults. The accounts show how the individuals move from a loss of identity and language to the emergence of a new identity and the new inner and outer language that goes with it (see Lantolf, 2000 and McCafferty, 1994 on inner speech). Following the tenets of sociocultural theory, the regulatory function on inner speech plays an important role in the accounts. Losing the inner voice in the first language is interpreted as a loss of identity, and only through the emergence of the inner voice in the other language can the new identity be constituted. Though Pavlenko and Lantolf do not explicitly mention this, they seem to imply that the inner voice has (or is) only one language, in other words the self as it presents itself through this inner voice is monolingual in nature. In none of the accounts they present do the languages in contact seem to merge; no interlanguage acts as a transitional form between the old and the new language. It is not clear to what extent this is more generally true. It is not unlikely that the autobiographers, all authors and scientists who depend on being able to use a language correctly to make a living, are biased towards seeing languages as real independent entities rather than as sets of words and rules that are constantly moving and highly individual. This sense of normativity is to a certain extent alien to a sociocultural perspective on language use as basically an interactional and interactionally-defined activity.

The aim of the present article is not to weigh the strengths and weaknesses of various scientific paradigms, but rather to find out how the confrontation of data generated by these different paradigms may further our understanding of language attrition. We will be looking at both L1 attrition and L2 attrition. We will try to relate our findings to those of Pavlenko and Lantolf.

Third-Person Accounts of Language Attrition

L2 attrition

The largest study of L2 attrition is Bahrick (1984), who looked at the retention of Spanish. In this cross-sectional study, skills in Spanish were tested in speakers who had learned the language up until 40 years prior to the time of testing, and who presented a range of proficiency levels as defined by amount of education in Spanish. Bahrick used a wide range of language proficiency tests. The data show that there is heavy attrition in the initial periods of non-use, and less attrition in subsequent years. Some of the language skills appeared to remain intact even after 25 years of non-use. This study provoked a comment by Neisser (1984) who concludes from Bahrick's data that there might be what he calls 'a critical threshold during learning', which implies that some knowledge that has been learned up to a certain level has become immune to forgetting. The idea of a critical threshold has become an important issue in later research on attrition, because it may serve as an explanation of some of the empirical findings.

Weltens (1988) reports on the loss of French competence by speakers of Dutch. In his research he introduced two independent variables: level of competence achieved, defined as the number of years of school-French, and period of disuse. The subjects were given a number of (receptive) phonological, lexical and grammar tests, and a questionnaire, which contained a number of self-assessment tests. The lexical tests were constructed in such a way that a possible influence of language contrast and frequency of occurrence could be measured independently: there were high and low frequency cognates and non-cognate words in the tests. The outcomes of this research can be summarised as follows. General receptive proficiency in French is not subject to attrition after four years of disuse, whereas some receptive aspects of grammar and vocabulary clearly are. For the first factor, level of competence achieved, it was shown that attrition is independent of training level. For the second factor, period of non-use, no significant differences between groups were found for lexical aspects, while there is significant attrition for grammar in the first interval of two years. Phonological skills, and listening and reading proficiency even increased significantly over time. The self-assessment tests and the morpho-syntactic tests revealed that there is substantial attrition in the first two years, which then levels off. Both language contrast and frequency played an important role: low frequency and linguistic contrast lead to attrition. Weltens (1988) gives a number of possible explanations for the discrepancy between his findings and those of others who did find substantial loss. The first is that his subjects had already reached the critical threshold mentioned earlier. This is in line with the hypothesis put forward by Pan and Berko-Gleason (1986: 204) that there might be a 'critical mass of language that, once acquired, makes loss unlikely'. A second explanation lies in the type of skills tested. The Weltens study was concerned with receptive skills only, and it is not inconceivable that productive skills are more easily lost than receptive skills (see Moorcroft & Gardner, 1987). A third explanation has to do with what 'period of non-use' actually means. It is very difficult, if not impossible, to get an accurate picture of the subjects' contacts with the language during what has been labeled the 'incubation period', and what the impact of these contacts has been. It is not clear whether very global measures of language contact provide us with the kind of information needed. Finally, it could be the case that the tests used are not really valid, in the sense that they allow for more processing time than is normally available in language use.

Studies on lexical access: Experimental studies

On the basis of the Weltens data, particularly the discrepancy between the test results and the outcomes of the self-evaluations, it was to be expected that real-time measurements would help clarify the process of attrition: knowledge is not lost, but cannot be found in time.

Grendel (1990, 1993) investigated orthographic and semantic aspects of word knowledge in Dutch students of French using the lexical decision paradigm. The aim of this study was to investigate both attrition of knowledge and the reactivation of that knowledge in an experimental setting. The data suggest that disuse of French does not lead to a decrease of specific orthographic or semantic skills but to a more general slowing down of the process of lexical access. Access to the lexicon is faster after training, no matter whether the training is concerned with orthographic skills or with semantic skills.

Hedgcock (1991) conducted one of the few studies on L2 attrition in the US when he looked at the loss of Spanish among college undergraduates. The study aimed at providing evidence for two versions of the regression hypothesis: 'last-learned = first forgotten' vs. 'best learned = last forgotten'. The students were tested at the end of their second term of Spanish, and four months later. Rather surprisingly, 'subjects improved their accuracy on 9 of the 14 items on the test: likewise, 16 of the 22 subjects also improved their overall performance from test 1 to test 2' (Hedgcock, 1991: 50).

Harley (1994) tested English Canadians who had learned French either through immersion or in core language courses in various parts of Canada. She found (as did Bahrick and Weltens) that a higher level of original proficiency is predictive of a higher level of retained knowledge. In her study,

Harley used 'Can-do scales' in which the subjects indicated on a 5-point or a 7-point scale to what extent they could perform a number of (increasingly complex) language activities (e.g. writing a personal letter, understanding native speakers on the phone, speaking about a complex issue). She also compared estimated level of proficiency now and at the end of formal training. The immersion group showed no real differences between these points in time but, interestingly, the core French graduates felt that their proficiency had actually improved. There was a moderate correlation between recency of contact with French and level of proficiency.

A major contribution to the sub-field of language attrition research comes from the work of Hansen (see Hansen 2000 and 2001 for overviews). She studied language attrition of English-speaking adults who went to countries such as Japan, China and Korea as missionaries. Part of their training was a rigorous program to learn the local language. Thousands of missionaries spent long stretches of time in these countries and acquired advanced skills in the local languages. After their return to the US, many of them discontinued the use of those languages, which makes them ideal subjects for language attrition research, as Hansen has shown. Under her guidance, a large number of projects have been carried out, in which various aspects of language attrition, and more recently, language re-learning, have been studied.

On the basis of the now-considerable amount of research on L2 attrition, Hansen (2000) draws a number of conclusions about what we now think we know about attrition. Out of all those studies the following trends emerge:

- There is an age advantage: contrary to what is generally assumed about language learning, older is better for retention. Young children tend to pick up the language fairly quickly, but also lose it in a short time.
- Knowledge that seems to be lost is still accessible when appropriate techniques are used, and relearning of previously learned knowledge is easier than acquiring completely new knowledge.
- There is also support for the 'regression hypothesis', which states that last learned is first forgotten.
- The higher the proficiency, the more is maintained, and for proficient learners there seems to be an initial plateau, which means that in the first few years of non-use, knowledge may still be stable and accessible.
- Finally, bilingual language use and code-switching are precursors of language attrition.

L1 attrition

There is a long tradition of research on L1 attrition. Languages are never lost in isolation, and L1 attrition typically comes as a by-product of language contact, particularly in migrant settings. As indicated earlier on, the settings of this type of attrition are different from those for L2 attrition. When two languages and their speakers come into contact, the smaller or less prestigious language is in danger. Migrants in many different settings seem to go through similar stages, from monolingualism in L1, through bilingualism with an increasing role for the host language, to mono-lingualism in that language (Paulston, 1994). A full description of the vast literature on L1 attrition is beyond the scope of this chapter – for overviews see Dorian (1989), Seliger & Vago (1991) and Fase *et al.* (1995). In fact, the distinction between L1 attrition and non-acquisition of the L1 is not always clear. The number of studies in which a proper point of reference is used (particularly research using longitudinal designs) is extremely limited, which is understandable given the problems of managing such long-term studies.

One of the seminal studies on L1 attrition is Clyne's (1967) study on German migrants in Australia. He interviewed a large number of recent arrivals and looked at specific aspects of their language skills. Later, he extended his research to include Dutch migrants (Clyne 1977). Using data from that earlier study as a point of reference, De Bot and Clyne (1994) looked at L1 attrition of Dutch migrants in Australia in a 16 year longitu-dinal study. Using different measures to assess various aspects of language, they found basically no signs of attrition over such a long period of time. They conclude that those migrants who manage to keep their first language in the first decade of their stay in the immigrant setting are likely to retain the language over a much longer period of time.

A recent trend in L1 attrition research that links it to developments in psycholinguistics is to look at speech data. Language production is a very complex activity that can be considered as a skill with a number of levels. In speech there are several clues to language production problems. Some errors are made and corrected, often very quickly. There is a considerable body of research on self-corrections in L1 and L2. Some errors are actually detected before they are produced or while they are produced. This will lead to various types of corrections. There are different types of speech markers: progressive (cut-offs, conversions) and regressive (repetitions, 'uh's and the like). Regressive speech markers evidence errors that have already (totally or partially) been produced. They are probably detected by the external feedback loop, while progressive speech markers show that errors have been detected (or other problems have been encountered) before they are articulated. In attrition, there may be less attention left for monitoring because production is effortful, the internal system that serves as a basis for the comparison on output and intention may have deteriorated, there may be more errors, and the speaker may need more time and may use specific strategies to gain time. De Bot and Keulen (1994) looked at progressive and regressive markers in the spontaneous speech data of 20 of the subjects from the De Bot and Clyne (1994) study. The data from this study show that for this group the efficiency of the production process has not decreased over time. There are few errors, and the amount of correction does not change over time. This is in contrast with Hansen's (2000) data on Japanese L2: their data show a difference in hesitation phenomena and fluency between groups differing in length of stay in the foreign country.

The literature on L1 attrition seems to suggest that attrition may not always occur within generations, at any rate not in the first generation of migrants. Waas (1996) looked at language attrition in German migrants who had been in Australia for less than 10 years. Many of her informants showed clear signs of attrition after such a relatively short period of migration. The findings of the Waas study seem to suggest that there may be attrition in the first decade, but other data show that the language skills that are still present after this period are fairly stable. Maintenance efforts should therefore be concentrated in the first decade after migration because, later on, the residual knowledge is likely to remain at the same level.

Hulsen (2000) presents data from three generations of Dutch migrants in New Zealand. In order to explain differences in attrition between generations and individuals within generations, she collected various types of data. An attempt was made to link sociolinguistic factors (attitudes, language use, ethnolinguistic vitality, social networks) with psycholinguistic processing variables. The combination of questionnaire data for the sociolinguistic variables and on-line techniques for language processing (picture naming and picture word matching) showed that the sociolinguistic differences between groups and individuals have an impact on speed of processing. With less contact with the L1, it takes longer to name a picture or to match a name with a picture. Hulsen's suggestion is that processes of language attrition can best be understood by looking at the interaction between sociolinguistic factors (particularly those that are linked to amount of L1 use) and processing mechanism. First language attrition is typically a downward spiral in which a lower level of skills leads to less use, and less use leads to a decline in skills.

Self evaluations

In research on language attrition, there is a tradition of using various forms of self-assessment. In a way such self assessments can be viewed as data in between first-person and third-person accounts. They reflect how individuals see their own language proficiency and changes in it in a more or less standardised way. Here we can already observe the discrepancy between data from language proficiency tests and self-assessments. For foreign language attrition, various projects (Grendel, 1993; Weltens, 1988) show that, while subjects consistently report a decline in their self-assessments, the attrition evidenced in the other proficiency measures on lexicon and grammar is far lower or even absent. So far, explanations of this gap have been sought in a failure to accurately measure the outcomes of on-line processes of language production and perception. The self-assessments refer to the subjects' feeling that they are not able to come up with the right word or construction in time in ongoing processes of production and perception, while the test formats typically used allow the subjects plenty of time to search and construct.

Interestingly, in contrast to studies of L2 loss, research into L1 loss (particularly studies that have included more experimental techniques) seem to show a more positive relation between self-evaluations and language proficiency. In an investigation of L1 loss in first generation German/Australian migrants, Waas (1996) found that her informants' evaluations of 'past' and 'present' L1 proficiency were in line with language attrition found in more objective measures, although the relationship was not analysed statistically. Yagmur (1997) found significant (though rather low) correlations ($r = 0.31$ and 0.38) between 'perceived loss' and actual language proficiency of first generation Turkish-Australian migrants measured with a verbal fluency (fruit naming) task and an oral relativisation test. In addition, Lemmon and Goggin (1989), whose study was not specifically aimed at language loss but investigated the relationship between bilingualism and cognitive ability, found that self-ratings of L1 proficiency correlated very highly ($r = 0.84$) with proficiency in the L1 of Spanish/English bilinguals, which was measured in a psycholinguistic picture naming task testing productive language skills. Hulsen (2000) also found extremely high correlations between the self-assessments of L1 skills of three generations of Dutch/New Zealand migrants and their scores on a picture-naming task.

First-person accounts

There are very few informative first-person accounts from the studies on L2 attrition. From informal conversations with their subjects, Weltens and

Grendel quote the following statements from their research on the attrition of French as a second language:

(1) The results of the investigation will probably show that speaking in French has also to do with courage. I have much more courage now than I had 19 years ago.

(2) I now have the courage to speak French and my knowledge has been adapted to actual practice. The proficiency in French, however, has decreased.

These quotes show that part of the explanation for not finding attrition in many studies is that sociopsychological factors are not normally included in the research design. In none of the other studies on L2 attrition is this kind of (highly informative) information provided.

There is much more conversational data from L1 research. In projects such as those reported by De Bot and Clyne (1994), Ammerlaan (1996), Waas (1996), Johri (1998), Hulsen (2000) and Schmid (2000), part of the interviews were actually on individuals' experiences with L1 and L2. Here we will concentrate on a number of specific topics that are related to the issues discussed earlier in this chapter. The first has to do with the migrants' perceptions of the languages used.

The following quote is from two second-generation Dutch migrants in New Zealand:

(3) I get a wee bit embarrassed sometimes [when I speak it] because when I hear it in my head, it sounds to me like I'm still at a 6 year old level, so, but I'd love to learn to speak it, like, a lot better (Johri, 1998: 32).

The interesting point here is the reference to what is probably inner speech in the Vygotskyan sense, which apparently has stopped developing over the years owing to lack of practice and contact. The L1 also takes time and effort to be reactivated:

(4) Yes [I like to hear Dutch], if the opportunity is there, I actually find very difficult here to speak Dutch, even if they are Dutch people because you're so used to it, somebody, you know if you meet some-body, you're so used to speak English to them that if they start talking Dutch I'm always a bit taken back and I have to force myself to talk Dutch, there's just that you have to translate the words back in Dutch, while if you do that for a few days, or say half an hour or so, after that you're all right, but I know that when I start talking Dutch, the first half an hour I have a terrible English accent because you really have to force yourself to, and after half an hour I'm all right, but that's prob-

ably because we don't have any Dutch friends and I've got a brother-in-law here who is Dutch, but his wife is Greek so we all speak English in their house too. (First-generation migrant. Johri, 1998: 8)

There is insecurity about the language that the migrants use, and an awareness of how dated it is:

(5) Nee, nee de meeste immigranten spreken dezelfde taal die ze stillds ... / die ze praatten toen ze Holland verlieten of dat nou in 1955 is geweest of in 1970 en daar zijn ze allemaal op stil blijven staan. De meesten uh hebben ove / zijn overgegaan op Engels en um ja ik denk toch dat ze allemaal ja zo'n beetje half ... half-half zitten: geen helemaal Hollands en niet helemaal Engels ook niet. (First-generation female, Dutch/New Zealand. Hulsen, unpublished data)

(No, no, most immigrants speak the same language ... they spoke when they left the Netherlands, no matter whether that was in 1955 or 1970 and at that point they all remained. Most of them have switched to English and uhm yes, I think they are sort of half ... in between: not completely Dutch and not completely English either.)

(6) Het Nederlands is niet veranderd, maar het is stil blijven staan. Je hebt geen woorden meer / geen nieuwe woorden meer geleerd in het Nederlands. En eigenlijk ben je stil blijven staan in de jaren zestig en later toen we drie jaar in Holland gewoond hebben heb je natuurlijk wat woorden overgenomen, maar zeventig toch ook niet meer. En ik denk toch wel dat de Nederlandse taal veranderd is. Dat moet wel haast in zoveel jaar ... / in twintig jaar ... / in vijfentwintig jaar en dus denk ik dat als wij nu Nederlands spreken dat je toch maar in een bepaald kringetje rond blijft draaien. (First-generation female, Dutch/New Zealand. Hulsen, unpublished data)

(The Dutch language hasn't changed, but is has come to a stand-still. You haven't got the words anymore, have not acquired new words in Dutch. And in fact you you've remained in the sixties and later when we lived in Holland for three years, you took over some words of course, but (those of the) seventies not any more. And I do think that the Dutch language has changed. It must have in so many years / ...in twenty years... in twenty-five years, so I think that when we speak Dutch now, that you keep turning in a specific little circle.)

It could be, as Lantolf (personal communication) argues, that, if inner speech is social in nature, the inner speech of these migrants couldn't develop after their childhood, because they hardly hear the language in social life.

In addition to *what* is said in these examples, *the way it is said* is also relevant. While the speaker in (5) and (6) clearly has problems expressing herself in Dutch, and many constructions show signs of English, the speaker in (7) still sees Dutch as the most adequate language:

(7) Je voelt je veel makkelijk ... eh ... je voelt je ... ik voel met veel gemakkelijker in het Nederlands, veel, ik kan me beter uitdrukken, ik kan beter precies zeggen wat ik bedoel. (First-generation Dutch in Australia. De Bot & Clyne, 1994)

(You feel very comfortable ... you feel ... I feel much more comfortable in Dutch, very, I can express myself better, I am better able to say precisely what I mean.)

The other issue that comes back time and again in the interviews is the insecurity about the language use and the mixing of the two languages:

(8) Soms dan gooi je d'r Nederlandse woorden doorheen als je Engels spreekt of je gooit er Engelse woorden doorheen als je Nederlands spreekt. [...] Sommige dingen are easily, more easily expressed in Engels en andere woorden more easily expressed in Dutch you see. (First-generation male, Dutch/New Zealand. Hulsen, 2000)

(Sometimes you throw in Dutch words when speaking English or you throw in English words when speaking Dutch. Some things are easily, more easily expressed in English and other words more easily expressed in Dutch you see.)

(9) Soms is het gemakkelijker het eerste woord dat naar je hoofd komt, zeg je meestal. 't Is luiigheid, soms, soms word ik zo kwaad op me eigen. Vooral als we visite hebben, denk ik, waarom kan ik nou niet of honderd procent Hollands praten of honderd procent Engels, en ik ken 't, maar 't is echt inspannen... . Een jaar was me nieuw jaar resolutie, ik ging Hollands praten of ik ging Engels praten, maar het lukte niet. Je hebt echt een taaltje van je eigen. (First-generation male, Dutch/Australian. De Bot & Clyne, 1994)

(Sometimes it's easier, the first word that comes to your head/mind, you say mostly. It's laziness, sometimes, sometimes I get so mad at myself. Especially when we have people visiting, I think, why is it that I cannot speak 100% Dutch or 100% English, and I can do it, but it takes a real effort. One year my New Year's resolution was, I was going to speak either Dutch or English, but I didn't succeed. You really have your own little language.)

For some migrants the borders between the two languages seem to be disappearing, both in how they talk about it, and in the way they talk, as can be observed in (10) and (11).

(10) [...] ik gebruik 't Engels en 't Hollands net naar ... hoe 't me uitkomt. Ik bedoel voor mij is d'r geen ... scheidingslijn. Gewoon 't Engels is gewoon een aanvulling op 't Hollands en 't Hollands is / is ... een aanvullling op 't uh / op / op 't Engels. (Hulsen, unpublished data)

(I use English and Dutch just as ... it suits me. I mean, for me there is no ... borderline. English is simply supplementing Dutch and Dutch is / is ... supplementing English.)

(11) Ja, there was a lot of life and I did zelf, want we hadden zeven children, dat kostten de money, hé en de lonen waren not zo high... maar ja, als je come here you have to take everything wat je kan pakken. (First-generation female, Dutch/Australian. De Bot & Clyne, 1994)

(Yes, there was a lot of life and I did it myself, because we had seven children, that costed money, right, and the wages were not so high... but yes, when you come here you have to take everything that you can get.)

According to insiders, this last speaker uses this mixed variety to both Dutch and English people. Attempts to make her speak more 'pure' English in a picture-description task failed in the sense that there was no difference in terms of language separation.

The notions of effort in keeping the two languages apart and reduced accessibility of words are also voiced repeatedly:

(12) Interviewer: Spreekt u meestal Nederlands thuis of Engels? Nou, Ik zou maar zeggen een mengelmoesje. Ja, als we met z'n tweetjes zijn, soms komt een woord veel makkelijker in 't Engels dan 't Hollandse woord, en dan gebruik je dat, maar ook weer andersom. (First-generation female, Dutch/Australian. De Bot & Clyne, 1994)

(Do you speak Dutch at home most of the time or English?)
(Well, I would say a sort of mix. Yes, when we are just with the two of us, sometimes a word comes easier in English than the Dutch word and then you use it, but also the other way around.)

(13) Well what I noticed is that people [the Dutch] have told me that I mmm ... speak slowly [in Dutch] and the reason for that is that I often have to think, yes, that I umm not like in English simply go on 'chatter-chatter-chatter'. (First-generation Dutch/Australian. Ammerlaan, 1996: 241)

This mixing of languages leads quite often to a reduced awareness of the choice of languages:

(14) Interviewer: En bij jullie thuis spreken jullie een mengelmoesje, hè? Geloof het wel, Ik weet het eigenlijk zelf niet wat we daar spreken. (Second-generation female, Dutch/Australian. De Bot & Clyne, 1994)

(Interviewer: And at home you speak sort of a mix, right?
I think so, but I don't know myself what language we use there, really.)

In the Pavlenko and Lantolf accounts, anger and frustration about the loss of the first language and the problems acquiring English abound. However, there are only a few signs of that in the transcripts we have been looking at.

(15) (a) Ik vind het heel moeilijk om met die twee talen te copen. (First-generation male, Dutch/New Zealand. Hulsen, 2000)

(I find it very difficult to cope with those two languages.)

(b) Interviewer: What do you do when you normally don't know a Dutch word?

In normal ... lang-? When I'm using the language? Then I use English. ... I combine Dutch and English I guess, and I obviously do ... cannot really bloody stand it ... No.' (First generation, Dutch/Australian. Ammerlaan, 1996: 213)

One speaker complains about the fact that she had to move from one school to another, but she does not complain about the language:

(16) We hadden een jaartje (Engels) gehad, geloof ik in de vijfde of zesde klas... Ik had genoeg geleerd om niet naar de Engelse les op de boot te gaan. (Second- generation female, Dutch/Australian. De Bot & Clyne, 1994)

(We had had a year of English at school, in fifth of sixth grade... I had learned enough so I didn't have to go to English classes at the boat.)

When asked about difficulties in different language skills, she indicates that she prefers writing over speaking:

(17) Ik schrijf liever dan dat ik 't spreek. Het is makkelijke, het gaat makkelijker. Dan heb je tijd om wat na te denken.

(I prefer writing in Dutch over speaking it, it's easier. Then you have time to think about it.)

This also seems to reflect the processing difficulties in speaking mentioned earlier.

One of Waas's subjects reported to have serious difficulties in speaking her L1 German when in a German-speaking country after many years in Australia:

(18) ... dass ich mich anhöre wie eine Engländerin die gut Deutsch gelernt hat... also, ich, meine Muttersprache kommt nicht durch, in andern Worten. (German/Australian. Waas, 1996)

[...that I sound like an English woman who has learnt German well... so, I, my mother tongue doesn't come through, in other words.)

Interestingly, the expression *kommt nicht durch* is a literal translation of English, in German it should be *hört man nicht aus*. Later on in the interview the subject mentioned that she spent three days in her family's house before she felt capable of functioning in German again.

Schmid (2000) quotes one of her subjects, a German Jewish woman who fled Germany as a child at the beginning of World War II and lost her parents in the genocide, who was unable to speak German when she visited the country after the war.

(19) I was physically *unable* to speak German [...]. When I visited Germany for 3 or 4 days in 1949 – I – found myself unable to utter one word of German although the Frontierguard was a dear old man. I had to speak French in order to answer his questions! (Schmid, 2000: 169)

It is likely that psychological causes and traumatic experiences blocked access to the German language in this case, although other speakers did not report such extreme problems, despite limited use of German and negative attitudes towards the language. Schmid stresses the importance of attitudes towards the language and the speech community in L1 maintenance and loss.

Concluding Remarks

In this chapter an attempt has been made to bring together different types of data on language attrition.

The 'first-person'accounts presented do not seem to support Pavlenko and Lantolf's suggestions that crossing cultural and linguistic boundaries involves a more or less complete shift from L1 to L2 unless this shift is related to very traumatic experiences, as in the case of Werner Landsburgh (Belz, 2001). The accounts suggest that, particularly for the first and second generation, the language variety used both internally and externally is a mixed one. This mixed variety is felt to be a natural one, and various accounts show that the mixing of languages is a completely unconscious process that speakers do not actively monitor. Availability and accessibility of words and rules seem to be more important than formal adherence to a particular language. Also, in contrast to the accounts presented by Pavlenko & Lantolf (2000), the individual narratives presented suggest that the loss of the first language is not felt as a loss of identity, and many individuals do not even seem to see it as a real problem. Intentions to maintain the language and to transmit it to the next generation are rather half-hearted, and have not led to much real activity in terms of sending children to heritage language classes or even to real efforts to consistently use the language at home. Maybe the gap between the accounts of the professional writers with a Eastern European background and the Western Europeans with a variety of educational and occupational backgrounds explains the difference between these findings. It is obvious, though, that the different kinds of data presented each make their own contribution to the picture of the language loser, and that the picture is far from homogeneous. As Pavlenko and Lantolf indicate, the process of transition from L1 to L2 is very unusual and may occur only in the rare cases of 'hyperliterates' they looked at. Differences in language background, educational level, attitudes towards L1 and L2 and professional activity have their effect on how the loss of a language is perceived. The factor of age at the time of migration may also have played a role – most migrants discussed in this chapter moved as adults. For children or adolescents the break with the home country may be more dramatic in terms of identity (Kouritzin, 1999). The first-person accounts also show that, in first-language attrition, studying the L1 in its canonical or standardised form is probably not the most appropriate way to proceed. The variety of the L1 used in the migrant settings is part of a continuum between the two languages in contact, and not a defective version of the official language. This makes the discussion on the point of reference in language attrition research even more complicated than it already is.

For L2 attrition, so far there are more third-person accounts than first-person accounts. The pain of losing a second language has not been the subject of autobiographical accounts to the same degree as the loss of the first language. The sociocultural differences between L1 and L2 attrition as mentioned earlier may account for this, but for our understanding of the process of L2 attrition the addition of rich narrative data is really needed.

There is also a paradox in directly comparing first-person and third-person accounts, since such a comparison calls for systematic gathering of relevant reports, which goes against the non-interventionist view that is typical of qualitative research of this type. One of the original motives for language-attrition research was to enhance our understanding of the process in order to prevent attrition from happening and, if it did occur, to redeem it through adequate re-learning techniques. Until we have more first-person accounts of the processes, this step will be hard to take.

To what extent does all this information lead to a coherent picture of the L2 user who is in the process of losing an L1 or L2? As for L2 acquisition, what emerges is not a single picture, but maybe a group portrait with many individuals showing vastly different traits. These range from a total indifference to maintaining the L1 to a total dedication to maintaining it against the stream, and from actively trying to maintain the L2 by using it whenever possible to almost intentionally avoiding using it in order to forget it as quickly as possible.

Acknowledgements

The authors are indebted to Vivian Cook, Jim Lantolf and Aneta Pavlenko for their comments on an earlier version of this chapter.

References

Ammerlan, T. (1996) 'You get a bit wobbly...' Exploring bilingual retrieval processes in the context of first language attrition. PhD thesis, University of Nijmegen.

Andersen, R. (1982) Determining the linguistic attributes of language attrition. In R. Lambert and B. Freed (eds) *The Loss of Language Skills* (pp. 83–118). Rowley, MA: Newbury House.

Baddeley, A. (1990) *Human Memory: Theory and Practice*. Hove: Erlbaum.

Bahrick, H. (1984) Fifty years of second language attrition: Implications for programmatic research. *Modern Language Journal* 68, 105–118.

Belz, J.A. (2001) The differential loss and gain of identity in late bilinguals. Internal paper, Department of German, Penn State University

Clyne, M. (1967) *Transference and Triggering*. The Hague: Martinus Nijhoff.

Clyne, M. (1977) Nieuw Nederlands or Double Dutch. *Dutch Studies* 3, 1–20.

Davidson, C. (1994) *36 views of Mount Fuji. On Finding Myself in Japan*. New York: Penguin.

De Bot, K. (1998) The psycholinguistics of language loss. In G. Extra and L. Verhoeven (eds) *Bilingualism and Migration* (pp. 345–361). Berlin: Mouton de Gruyter.

De Bot, K. and Clyne, M. (1994) A 16-year longitudinal study of language attrition in Dutch immigrants in Australia. *Journal of Multilingual and Multicultural Development* 15 (1), 17–28.

De Bot, K. and Keulen, A. (1994) Nederlands in Australië: een longitudinaal onderzoek naar taalbehoud. *Gramma/TTT* 3 (93), 219–234.

De Bot, K. and Weltens, B. (1985) Taalverlies: Beschrijven versus verklaren. *Handelingen van het 38e Nederlands Filologencongres*, 51–61.

De Bot, K. and Weltens, B. (1995) Foreign language attrition. *Annual Review of Applied Linguistics* 15, 151–166.

Dorian, N. (1989) *Investigating Obsolescence: Studies in Language Contraction and Death*. Cambridge: Cambridge University Press.

Fase, W., Jaspaert, K. and Kroon, S. (eds) (1995) *The State of Minority Languages: European Studies on Multilingualism* 5. Lisse: Swets & Zeitlinger.

Fishman, J.A. (1966) *Language Loyalty in the United States*. The Hague: Mouton.

Fishman, J.A (1991) *Reversing Language Shift*. Clevedon: Multilingual Matters.

Folmer, J. (1992) Dutch immigrants in New Zealand: A case study of language shift and language loss. *Australian Review of Applied Linguistics* 15 (2), 1–18.

Giles, H., Bourhis, R. and Taylor, D. (1977) Towards a theory of language in ethnic group relations. In H. Giles (ed.) *Language, Ethnicity and Intergroup Relations* (pp. 307–348). New York: Academic Press.

Grendel, M. (1990) Verlies en herstel van Franse woordkennis. *Gramma* 14 (2), 127–137.

Grendel, M. (1993) Verlies en herstel van lexicale kennis. PhD thesis, University of Nijmegen. Enschede: CopyPrint 2000.

Hakuta, K. and D'Andrea, D. (1992) Some properties of bilingual maintenance and loss in Mexican background high-school students. *Applied Linguistics* 13 (1), 72–99.

Hansen, L. (2000) Language attrition in contexts of Japanese bilingualism. In M. Noguchi and S. Fotos (eds) *Studies in Japanese Bilingualism*. Clevedon: Multilingual Matters.

Hansen, L. (2001) Language attrition: The fate of the start. *Annual Review of Applied Linguistics*, 22.

Harley, B. (1994) Maintaining French as a second language in adulthood. *Canadian Modern Language Review* 50 (4), 688–713.

Haugen, E. (1969) *The Norwegian Language in America: A Study in Bilingual Behavior*. Bloomington: Indiana University Press.

Hedgcock, J. (1991) Foreign language retention and attrition: A study of regression models. *Foreign Language Annals* 24, 43–55.

Hulsen, M. (2000) Language loss and language processing: Three generations of Dutch migrants in New Zealand. PhD thesis, University of Nijmegen.

Johri, R. (1998) Stuck in the middle or clued up on both? Language and identity among Korean, Dutch and Samoan immigrants in Dunedin. PhD thesis, University of Otago.

Kloss, H. (1966) German-American language maintenance efforts. In J. Fishman (ed.) *Language Loyalty in the United States*. The Hague: Mouton.

Kouritzin, S. (1999) *Face(t)s of First Language Loss*. Mahwah, NJ: Lawrence Erlbaum.

Lantolf, J. (2000) Introducing sociocultural theory. In J. Lantolf (ed.) *Sociocultural Theory and Second Language Learning*. Oxford: Oxford University Press.

Lemmon, C. and Goggin, J. (1989) The measurement of bilingualism and its relationship to cognitive ability. *Applied Psycholinguistics* 10, 133–155.

Loftus, G.R. & Loftus, E.F. (1976) *Human Memory: The Processing of Information*. Hillsdale: Erlbaum.

Lvovich, N. (1997) *The Multilingual Self: An Inquiry into Language Learning*. Mahwah: Routledge.

McCafferty, S. (1994) Adult second language learner's use of private speech: A review of studies. *The Modern Language Journal* 78 (4), 591–622.

Moorcroft, R. and Gardner, R. (1987) Linguistic factors in second language loss. *Language Learning* 37, 327–340.

Nabokov, V. (1966) *Speak, Memory: An Autobiography Revisited.* New York: Putnam.

Neisser, U. (1984) Interpreting Harry Bahrick's discovery: What confers immunity against forgetting? *Journal of Experimental Psychology: General* 113, 32–35.

Pan, B. and Berko-Gleason, J. (1986) The study of language loss: Models and hypotheses for an emerging discipline. *Applied Psycholinguistics* 7, 193–206.

Paulston, C.B. (1994) *Linguistic Minorities in Multilingual Settings.* Amsterdam, John Benjamins.

Pavlenko, A. and Lantolf, J. (2000) Second language learning as participation and the (re)construction of selves. In J. Lantolf (ed.) *Sociocultural Theory and Second Language Learning* (pp. 155-177). Oxford: Oxford University Press.

Pauwels, A. (1985) The role of mixed marriages in language shift in the Dutch communities. In M. Clyne (ed.) *Australia, Meeting Place of Languages* (pp. 39–55). Canberra: Pacific Linguistics.

Schmid, M. (2000) First language attrition, use, and maintenance. The case of German Jews in anglophone countries. PhD thesis, University of Düsseldorf.

Seliger, H. and Vago, R. (1991) (eds) *First Language Attrition: Structural and Theoretical Perspectives.* Cambridge: Cambridge University Press.

Sfard, A. (1998) On two metaphors for learning and the dangers of choosing just one. *Educational Researcher* 27, 4–13.

Verhoeven, L. and Boeschoten, R. (1986) First language acquisition in a second language submersion environment. *Applied Psycholinguistics* 7, 241–256.

Waas, M. (1996) *Language Attrition Downunder.* Frankfurt a/M: Peter Lang.

Weltens, B. (1988) The attrition of French as a foreign language. PhD thesis, University of Nijmegen. Dordrecht/Providence: Foris Publications.

Weltens, B. (1989) *The Attrition of French as a Foreign Language.* Dordrecht/Provence: Foris Publications.

Yagmur, K. (1997) First language attrition among Turkish migrants in Sydney. PhD thesis, University of Nijmegen.

Introduction to Chapter 11

Poststructuralist Approaches to the Study of Social Factors in Second Language Learning and Use, Aneta Pavlenko

VIVIAN COOK

'All the world's a stage ... and one man in his time plays many parts.' In everyday life we switch parts continually from parent to child, from employee to colleague to boss, from student to teacher, from driver to pedestrian, from spectator to skier, not just evolving through Shakespeare's seven stages but continuously switching parts all the time. The questions for SLA research have mainly been seen as whether people can acquire these parts in a second language, whether they can switch parts adequately in the second language, whether there is a distinctive L2 part that they have to play, and how successfully they can fit in to society. Thus L2 users rapidly acquire gender-specific aspects of English pronunciation (Adamson & Regan, 1991), accommodate to the perceived race of the interlocutor (Young, 1988), are treated in specific ways by native speakers (Arthur *et al.*, 1980), and have problems in maintaining cultural identity and relationships with other groups (Berry, 1998).

One problem with this approach is the balance between the individual and the group. It is easy to treat people solely in terms of one of the groups to which they belong; I object to being called an asthmatic, rather than a person who suffers from asthma. People are not just women or lawyers or parents or heterosexuals, but women and lawyers and parents and heterosexuals ... and all the other parts they play every day; they are simultaneously members of many groups. Everyday language use means one person combining many roles and simultaneously presenting relevant aspects of each; acquiring a language means creating and maintaining all these roles for ourselves within the context of situation. Looking only at the L2 parts of the L2 user is inadequate; they are complete people, some of whose parts are played in one language or the other, some in both at once.

Some physically-related parts can be avoided or altered with difficulty: the effects of age or asthma are hard to deny, race or gender difficult to change, parenthood not cancellable. Yet even these groups are culturally mediated; the ways that age or sexuality are expressed, the duties of parenthood, the status of particular races. Other parts, however, derive from the way that we have accommodated to and been assimilated by the society in which we find ourselves. To go back to Shakespeare, the whining schoolboy, the lover sighing like a furnace, the justice in fair round belly, all reflect the negotiation of the individual with the social environment to create social identities. A person creates his or her identities as well as being confined by them.

The approach seen in Aneta Pavlenko's chapter reflects then a radical break with earlier SLA research in concentrating on identity in flux. L2 users were often seen as having a fixed set of characteristics as part of the group of L2 users, not as having control over themselves, responding to the pressures around them and having multiple group memberships; variation in linguistic output was seen as failure rather than the normal skill of all speakers in all languages. The poststructuralist approach fits well with the L2 user perspective by starting, not from the native speaker, but from the identities that individuals create for themselves in a second language– how L2 users invest in themselves.

References

Adamson, H. and Regan, V. (1991) The acquisition of community norms by Asian immigrants learning English as a second language: A preliminary study. *Studies in Second Language Acquisition* 13 (1), 1–22.

Arthur, B., Weiner, M., Culver, J., Young, L. and Thomas, D. (1980) The register of impersonal discourse to foreigners: Verbal adjustments to foreign accent. In D. Larsen-Freeman (ed.) *Discourse Analysis in Second Language Research* (pp. 111–124). Rowley, MA: Newbury House.

Berry, J.W. (1998) Official multiculturalism. In J. Edwards (ed.) *Language in Canada* (pp. 84–101). Cambridge: Cambridge University Press.

Young, R. (1988) Variation and the interlanguage hypothesis. *Studies in Second Language Acquisition* 10, 281–302.

Chapter 11

Poststructuralist Approaches to the Study of Social Factors in Second Language Learning and Use

ANETA PAVLENKO

Introduction

While syntactic and psycholinguistic aspects of second language (L2) learning and use are the subject of many competing theories, up until recently social aspects of L2 learning and use have been both under-represented and under-theorised in the literature on second language acquisition (SLA). Some influential SLA volumes and texts (e.g. Archibald, 2000; Ritchie & Bhatia, 1996; Sharwood Smith, 1994) do not even include a separate chapter on social factors. Others present the reader with a laundry list of unrelated social and individual factors or, at best, with a discussion of Schumann's acculturation hypothesis and related sociopsychological studies (e.g. Gass & Selinker, 1994; Spolsky, 1989; for more comprehensive coverage see: Ellis, 1994; Larsen-Freeman & Long, 1991; Mitchell & Myles, 1998). This lack of attention to and interest in social factors is not surprising if we consider the fact that SLA as a field continues to be influenced by the Chomskian view of language as biologically innate rather than a social phenomenon. As a result, until recently, the bulk of research concentrated on the learner's 'black box' and only peripheral attention was paid to 'external factors', which were seen at best as affecting the type and amount of input that goes into the 'box'.

The last decade brought in several new developments in which scholars drew on contemporary poststructuralist theory to understand social influences on L2 learning. The goal of this chapter is to reflect upon the importance of these recent developments for SLA theory from the L2 user perspective. I will start my discussion by outlining the early attempts to theorise social factors in SLA in a sociopsychological paradigm, for three reasons. First of all, it is important to acknowledge that poststructuralist approaches did build on the previous research, even if most of it was criticised for oversimplification. Second, it is equally important to see the criticisms that were raised, in order to examine whether poststructuralist research fares any better. And, third, it is useful to understand the differences between the two approaches, since at times scholars in both frameworks appeal to the same terms, such as 'identity', but use them in very different ways.

Sociopsychological Approaches to L2 Learning and Use

The pioneering studies of sociopsychological variables in L2 learning by Gardner and Lambert (1959, 1972) demonstrated that a positive, statistically significant, relationship could be established between motivation, positive attitudes towards the L2 and its speakers, and the mastery of those aspects of the L2 that are less susceptible to conscious manipulation, such as phonology. Over time, more variables (such as age, gender, ethnicity and social class) were added to the list of sociopsychological factors, culminating in Schumann's (1978, 1986) attempt to theorise the influence of social factors on L2 learning outcomes in his acculturation hypothesis. Schumann's hypothesis suggests that the degree to which the learner (particularly the adult immigrant) acculturates to the target language (TL) group controls the degree to which the learner acquires the TL. In this view, differential language learning outcomes are explained in terms of psychological and social distance between adult learners and the TL group. Another attempt to theorise social factors in L2 learning is Gardner's (1979, 1985) socioeducational model. This model focuses on L2 learning in educational environments and views the learning process both as the acquisition of 'symbolic elements of a different ethnolinguistic community' (Gardner, 1979: 193) and as a re-evaluation of one's self-image and self-identification. The model posits that the social and cultural milieu in which learners grow up determines their beliefs about language and culture (attitude toward the whole learning situation) and, consequently, the extent to which they wish to identify with the TL culture (integrativeness).

Another strand of sociopsychological inquiry examined the relationship between L2 learning and ethnic group membership, drawing on Tajfel's (1974, 1981) theory of social identity. Tajfel viewed social identity as derived from group membership and suggested that, when individuals see their present social identity as less than satisfactory, they may attempt – at times successfully, at times not – to change their group membership in order to view themselves more positively. Based on this view, Giles *et al.* (1977), Giles and Byrne (1982), and Giles and Johnson (1987) developed a theory of ethnolinguistic identity which considers language to be a salient marker of ethnic identity and group membership. These researchers suggested that members of groups where the in-group identification is weak, in-group vitality low, in-group boundaries open and identification with other groups strong, may assimilate and learn the L2 rapidly. In contrast, members of groups whose ethnolinguistic vitality is high (for instance, strong in-group identification, hard in-group boundaries, etc.) may fear assimilation and achieve a low level of proficiency in the L2, which is seen by them as a threat to their ethnic identity.

While studies conducted within the sociopsychological paradigm did provide some empirical support for the claims made (with the exception of Schumann's acculturation hypothesis), not only did other empirical studies refute the claims, but several critics also raised theoretical objections to sociopsychological approaches, pointing to a number of biases and reductionist assumptions (for example: Husband & Saifullah-Khan, 1982; Norton Peirce, 1995; Syed & Burnett, 1999). I will now outline some of these objections.

(1)   It was suggested that the monolingual and monocultural bias underlying the sociopsychological approaches leads them to conceptualise the world as consisting of homogeneous and monolingual cultures, or in-groups and out-groups, and of individuals who move from one group to another. This monolingual bias is most evident in the unidirectional perspective which posits the necessity to abandon one's first language and culture in order to learn the second language and acculturate to the TL group, whether this abandonment is termed 'acculturation' or 'integrative attitude'. As such, sociopsychological approaches do not lend themselves readily to accounting for L2 users who may be members of multiple communities, and do not reflect the complexity of the modern global and multilingual world, where more than a half of the inhabitants are not only either bilingual or multilingual but also members of multiple ethnic, social and cultural communities.

(2)   A related problem is the assumption that, in the process of learning a second, or any additional language, L2 learners aspire to acculturate to or to join a particular group. While this may work for particular immigrant settings, in the global picture nothing could be further from the truth, as millions of people learn and use additional languages without giving a thought to those who could be considered a TL group. Taking the example of English in Liberia, Breitborde (1998) found that for the Kru in Monrovia English is becoming a symbol of civilisation and of their own ethnic identity, whereby its use distinguishes them positively from the other ethnic groups. At no point,

however, do these urban Africans think about approximating a group of 'native speakers' of English; rather, they are themselves rapidly becoming native speakers of a new nativised variety of English.

(3) A further problem is the adoption of a reductionist, static and homogeneous view of culture that appears 'to be referring to two specific, identifiable, perpetual cultures – a native culture and a host culture' (Syed & Burnett, 1999: 48). Such an approach does not take into consideration the on-going cultural change in which some cultural patterns (such as those belonging to American popular culture) may be exercising their impact worldwide through the use of the media and the internet. Nor does it consider the bi- or multi-directionality of change whereby various cultures and subcultures continuously influence each other, with host societies also transformed by incoming members.

(4) Another important objection to sociopsychological approaches is the lack of explanatory validity or even insight offered concerning the social causes of particular attitudes, motivations and beliefs. At best, inter-group theorists present us with constructs such as 'identity', 'in-group membership', 'self-identification' or 'accommodation', considering them to be explanatory, whereas in reality these constructs are themselves in need of explanation. For example, Sachdev and Wright (1996) suggest that an in-group self-categorisation by English children causes their negative attitudes toward a variety of Asian languages. What is, however, at the root of that self-identification? What are the ways in which society influences and shapes language attitudes and values?

(5) The causal, unidirectional and stable nature attributed to such constructs as motivation, attitudes, or social distance also creates a problem. As Gass and Selinker (1994), Norton Peirce (1995), and others point out, motivation and social contexts continuously shape and reshape each other, and initial success may prompt a greater investment in the target language, just as a series of failures may result in a diminished learning motivation.

(6) The clear separation assumed in sociopsychological approaches (as well as in much SLA literature in general) between social factors and the individual, or psychological, factors creates a further problem. In reality, many individual factors, such as age, gender or ethnicity, are also socially constituted, so that the understanding and implications of being Jewish or Arab, young or old, female or male are not the same across communities and cultures. Similarly, such seemingly internal and psychological factors as attitudes, motivation or language learning beliefs have clear social origins and are shaped and reshaped by the

contexts in which the learners find themselves. Norton Peirce (1995) argues that early SLA theorists were not successful in dealing with the relationship between the L2 learner and the social world precisely because they lacked a comprehensive theory of social identity that would integrate the learner and the learning context.

(7) With regard to methodology, serious questions were raised about the validity of questionnaires, the key method used in most socio-psychological studies. It was not clear what exactly was measured by the multiple questionnaires that attempted to quantify language atti-tudes, motivation, acculturation or language proficiency, in particular, when the latter was reduced to self-evaluation. Moreover, it was not clear if questionnaires took adequate account of intervening variables such as the interviewees' desire to look good in the eyes of the researchers.

(8) Many critics also pointed out that most of the studies within the sociopsychological paradigm have been carried out in English-speaking environments in the US, UK and Canada. In other words, they were carried out in environments where most often there was one clearly dominant language and culture (with the exception of some bilingual contexts in Canada). When more research is carried out in other contexts, it may paint a very different picture of the social worlds of L2 users.

(9) The key weakness of the sociopsychological approaches is, however, the idealised and decontextualised nature attributed to language learning, which is presented as an individual endeavour, prompted by motivation and positive attitudes, and hindered by negative attitudes and perceptions. This view led Spolsky (1989: 132) to claim that 'the social context is not directly involved in setting specific conditions for language learning'. In reality, however, no amount of motivation can counteract racism and discrimination, just as no amount of positive attitude can substitute for access to linguistic resources such as educa-tional establishments, work places, or programmes and services espe-cially designed for immigrants and other potential L2 users. The social context, thus, is directly involved in setting positive or negative condi-tions for L2 learning.

To sum up, I have argued that sociopsychological approaches to SLA do not allow us to theorise social contexts of L2 learning and use, mainly because they neglect 'the historical and structural processes ... which set the parameters of social boundaries' (Williams, 1992: 218). A strong explanatory theory of social contexts in SLA needs to consider the issues of power and domination in the relationships between majority and minority groups, as well as to find ways of relating the social to the linguistic. As Cameron repeatedly argued, to assume that people behave in certain ways because they are members of certain groups is a correlational fallacy, because the purported explanation is in reality nothing but a descriptive statement:

> The 'language reflects society' account implies that social structures somehow exist before language, which simply 'reflects' or 'expresses' the more fundamental categories of the social. Arguably however we need a far more complex model that treats language as *part of* the social, interacting with other modes of behaviour and just as important as any of them. (Cameron, 1990: 81–82)

Poststructuralist Approaches to L2 Learning and Use

In this section, I will review poststructuralist attempts to theorise social aspects of L2 learning and use. The beginning of poststructuralist inquiry in SLA can be traced to Pennycook's call for a critical applied linguistics for the 1990s, where he argued for the 'need to rethink language acquisition in its social, cultural, and political contexts, taking into account gender, race, and other relations of power as well as the notion of the subject as multiple and formed within different discourses' (Pennycook, 1990: 26). His call was answered in 1995, when Norton Peirce's (1995) study of L2 learning investment of immigrant women in Canada and Rampton's (1995) investigation of code crossing in the multilingual and multicultural UK pioneered new approaches, new questions, new agendas and new terminology in the study of L2 learning and use. Their ground-breaking studies were soon followed by theoretical treatments that attempted to reconceptualise SLA within the poststructuralist framework and by empirical examinations of L2 learning and use conducted in the poststructuralist spirit, both of which will be discussed in this section.

While the terms poststructuralism, postmodernism or critical inquiry serve as an umbrella for various theoretical approaches that have been adopted by different researchers, for purposes of clarity and simplicity this chapter focuses, not on the differences between these various strands (real as they may be), but on the similarities that they share. I see all these approaches as having a common focus on language as the locus of social organisation, power and individual consciousness. Thus, in this chapter, *poststructuralism* is understood broadly as an attempt to investigate and to theorise the role of language in construction and reproduction of social relations, and the role of social dynamics in the processes of additional language learning and use. At the centre of the poststructuralist theory of

SLA are the view of language as symbolic capital and the site of identity construction (Bourdieu, 1991; Gal, 1989; Weedon, 1987), the view of language acquisition as language socialisation (Ochs, 1993; Wenger, 1998) and the view of L2 users as agents whose multiple identities are dynamic and fluid (Lantolf & Pavlenko, 2001; McKay & Wong, 1996; Norton Peirce, 1995; Pavlenko, 2000). This theory allows us to examine how linguistic, social, cultural, gender and ethnic identities of L2 users, on the one hand, structure access to linguistic resources and interactional opportunities and, on the other, are constituted and reconstituted in the process of L2 learning and use. In what follows, I will discuss three key aspects of poststructuralist approaches to the study of social factors in SLA: the view of language, the view of learning and the view of L2 learners.

Language as symbolic capital and a site of identity construction

This section outlines ways in which language is theorised in the poststructuralist framework: as a collection of discourses, as symbolic capital and as a site of identity construction and negotiation. I will also discuss how these views allow us to theorise L2 learning outcomes.

The view of language in the poststructuralist paradigm differs significantly from that espoused in other theoretical frameworks. Going beyond the traditional views of language as consisting of grammar, phonology and the lexicon, or of language as an ethnic identity marker, poststructuralism views language as an array of discourses imbued with meaning. In other words, while the traditional view of language assumes a chain of signs without a subject, produced and seen from an 'objective' position or from nowhere in particular, 'discourses' are viewed as 'practices which form the objects of which they speak' (Foucault, 1972: 49) and serve to reproduce, maintain or challenge existing power and knowledge structures. Discourses may develop around specific topics, such as gender, class or linguistic competence, and compete with each other, creating distinct and often incompatible versions of reality.

Poststructuralist inquiry underscores the idea that not all languages, discourses or registers are equal in the linguistic marketplace: some are 'more equal than others'. Many poststructuralist linguists build on Bourdieu's (1991) view of linguistic practices as a form of symbolic capital, which can be converted into economic and social capital. In this view, the value of a particular linguistic variety (such as a standard or a vernacular form), or a particular linguistic practice (such as literacy) derives from its ability to provide access to more prestigious forms of education and desired positions in the workforce or on the social mobility ladder. The view of language as symbolic capital has a significant advantage over the notion of 'instrumental motivation', as it allows us to link the individual and the social, tracing the process by which particular linguistic varieties and practices become imbued with values or devalued in the linguistic marketplace. Current research suggests that the key role in the process of value assignment is played by the socioeconomic factors and by ways in which institutional practices legitimise or stigmatise various language varieties. Several recent studies analyse the ideologies underlying representations of languages and ethnicities in discourse, unmasking racist underpinnings of particular scientific, media and educational discourses that discriminate against minority and non-native speakers (Gal, 1989; Heller, 1999; Lippi-Green, 1997; McKay & Wong, 1996). Lippi-Green's (1997) work in particular exposes a number of ways in which ideological underpinnings function in institutional practices, including Disney films which consistently portray positive and attractive characters as speakers of socially mainstream varieties of English and negative characters as speakers of stigmatised varieties. Her study also demonstrates real-world consequences of monolingual biases that create fruitful conditions for job and other forms of discrimination to work against speakers of particular language varieties and speakers with 'accents' that others claim difficult or impossible to comprehend. In this way, poststructuralist work recasts the notion of language attitudes as language ideologies, highlighting their socially derived and dynamic nature, and enabling social critique, resistance and change.

Language in the poststructuralist framework is viewed not only as symbolic capital but also as a site of identity construction. *Identities* are seen as constructed by and in discourses that supply the terms by which identities are expressed (identity performance) and assign differential values to different identities or subject positions. Subject positions, in turn, refer to the intersection of factors that position individuals as single welfare mothers, Chicana lesbians, inner-city youth or middle-class accountants, and entail age, gender, sexuality, class and race, as well as other factors that influence the ways in which we are perceived by others. The subject position is not a stable entity, however: individuals may be collaborating in as well as resisting their own positioning and are continuously involved in the processes of producing and positioning selves and others (Davies & Harré, 1990). Multilingual contexts are particularly fraught with the tensions of identity politics whereby many individuals experience a perpetual conflict between self-chosen identities and others' attempts to position them differently. Thus, it is not surprising that some scholars view all instances of language use in multilingual contexts as 'acts of identity' (Le Page & Tabouret-Keller, 1985; Tabouret-Keller, 1997).

The view of language as a site of identity construction has important implications for theorising L2 learning outcomes. Poststructuralist scholarship views the outcomes as influenced by individuals' identities in two important ways. On the one hand, as will be demonstrated in the discussion of language socialisation, L2 users' subject positions, in particular race, ethnicity, class and gender, mediate their access to linguistic resources available in the L2. On the other hand, as will be discussed later, their agencies and investments in language learning and use are shaped by the range of identities available to them in the L2. At times, the L2 discourses available to L2 users may provide them with unique means of self-representation that prompt them to cross boundaries and assimilate to the new communities or to become members of multiple communities. In other contexts, L2 learners may opt for constructing new and mixed linguistic identities. Yet in other situations, the L2 users may see the new subject positions as unacceptable or incompatible with those they occupied previously. This conflict often occurs in immigrant contexts, where mature adults may suddenly find themselves positioned as incompetent workers or parents (Blackledge, 2000; Norton, 2000). In this case, their desire to acquire the symbolic capital afforded by the new language may be in conflict with their resistance to the range of identities offered to them by that language. This situation may negatively influence any attempts at learning, and learners may limit their L2 learning to the basic proficiency level and refuse to modify their behaviour and reconstruct their identities. Or they may stop attending language classes despite the fact that they realise the importance and value of the new language. Woolard (1985), Gal (1989) and Heller (1992) suggest that, in order to theorise the apparent contradiction between accommodation and resistance to symbolic hegemony, we need to revise and expand Bourdieu's (1991) view of language and to acknowledge that in many contexts minority language speakers resist symbolic domination. Similarly, poststructuralist SLA scholarship points out that, in cases where legitimate identities cannot be fashioned through the second language, L2 learning may be halted despite the high symbolic value of the L2.

The view of language outlined above has clear implications for linguistic competence, which has to entail more than competence in phonology, morphosyntax, lexicon or pragmatics. Norton Peirce (1995) and Miller (1999, 2000) point out that Bourdieu's (1991) view of linguistic competence as 'the power to impose reception' allows us to expand the notion of L2 competence to include 'the right to speak' or, in Miller's terms, 'audibility', which is crucial for a successful learning outcome.

In sum, I suggest that the poststructuralist view of language allows for a more nuanced, complex and context-sensitive understanding of contemporary multilingual realities in which all language users have at their disposal multiple means of expressing themselves. Recasting the notion of language attitudes as ideologies allows researchers to examine the discursive construction and functioning of ideologies, to link individual attitudes and belief systems to larger societal processes, and to argue against particular ideologies of language and selfhood seen as biased, racist, discriminatory and harmful. Recasting the notion of identity from unitary and stable into multiple and dynamic allows researchers to examine how identity options afforded by the L2 influence learners' choices and learning trajectories. Finally, the view of language as simultaneously a form of symbolic capital and a site of identity construction allows researchers to theorise conflicts inherent in L2 learning and use, and to expand the notion of L2 competence to include 'the right to speak' and 'the power to impose reception'.

L2 learning as language socialisation

Just as they view language as a social phenomenon and L2 users as socially constituted beings, poststructuralist approaches reconceptualise L2 learning as an intrinsically social – rather than simply cognitive – process of socialisation into specific communities of practice, also referred to as 'situated learning' (Lave & Wenger, 1991; Ochs, 1993; Wenger, 1998). Many researchers argue that 'second language socialisation' is a more accurate description of the process by which individuals not only internalise a particular body of knowledge but become culturally competent members of a particular community (Bremer *et al.*, 1996). At the same time, it is not a one-way process of blind accommodation, but one in which positionings are negotiated between novices and more competent members of a particular community. This section focuses on describing two areas in the study of L2 socialisation: (a) examination of language ideologies and institutional practices that may facilitate or block access to linguistic and interactional resources, and (b) investigation of the process of internalisation of particular discourses available for appropriation by newcomers.

The fact that interaction is crucial for L2 learning has long been accepted in the field of SLA, and became the cornerstone of interactionist approaches to the study of L2 learning. Poststructuralist inquiry confirms the importance of interaction, at the same time finding a number of faults with how interaction has been conceived. Many scholars criticise interactionist approaches for the lack of sensitivity to social contexts and participants' concerns (Firth & Wagner, 1997), for 'premature and over-simplistic attempts at generalisation within and across learners groups' (Mitchell & Myles, 1998: 188), and, most importantly, for equating access to interactional opportunities with motivation (Norton Peirce, 1995). They point out that, to date, interaction in mainstream SLA research has been explored mainly in language classrooms, rather than in non-instructional settings, and through quasi-experimental designs, rather than natural observation. Longitudinal ethnographic studies conducted in the poststructuralist spirit suggest that no amount of classroom instruction can replace spontaneous interaction in the target language (Miller, 1999, 2000; Moore, 1999; Norton Peirce, 1995). Most importantly, poststructuralist inquiry underscores the idea that unlimited access to linguistic resources and interactional opportunities should not be taken for granted in the study of SLA. It also demonstrates that this access is mediated by the L2 users' gender, race, ethnicity, age, class, social status and linguistic background (for further discussion, see Pavlenko, 2000).

To begin with, some target language speakers may simply refuse to interact with L2 users, perceived by them as incompetent communicators. For instance, a Bosnian ESL student in Australia states: 'So all these Australian people, they are nice but like, now they really won't, you know, talk to you' (Miller, 1999: 157). Her feelings are echoed by a Japanese student learning English in Canada: '... we want desperately to get into the mainstream, but we can't because Canadians don't allow us and also because we know that they look down on us and despise us' (Kanno, 2000a: 7). One of her Canadian classmates even yelled at her: 'Are you deaf or ESL?' (Kanno & Applebaum, 1995: 43). This linguistic gatekeeping is not restricted to English-speaking contexts: as Siegal (1996) points out, Japanese may refuse to interact with non-Asians in Japanese; moreover, even when they do so, they may not provide the necessary feedback about instances of inappropriate pragmatic usage.

Miller's (2000) ethnographic study of ESL students' socialisation into the mainstream in an Australian high school demonstrates that opportunities for interaction may also be mediated by race. It appears that white, often fair-haired, Bosnian ESL students assimilate quickly, appropriating a range of discourses in English and establishing friendships with the English-speaking students, while dark-haired Chinese-speaking students remain isolated from the mainstream. The Chinese speakers in the study felt discriminated against, because in their perception neither their peers nor their teachers acknowledged their legitimacy as L2 users of English in the same way that they acknowledged the legitimacy of their European immigrant classmates, who physically resemble Australians. One of the students, Nora, wrote in her diary: 'I just don't know why the teachers always likes fornigner, they always like white skin, gold hairs?' (Miller, 2000: 87). Race in conjunction with gender appears to have limited the interactional opportunities of Misheila, an African-American student on a study trip to Spain (Talburt & Stewart, 1999). She found herself consistently singled out and sexually harassed by Spanish men, and this, in turn, provoked a negative reaction in her toward Spanish and its speakers. Polanyi (1995), Siegal (1996) and Twombly (1995) describe similar reactions to behaviour that is perceived as sexual harassment in female American students studying abroad, respectively, in Russia, Japan and Costa Rica. Polanyi (1995) links sexual harassment to American women's growing reluctance to interact with Russians and to their subsequent low performance on the Russian Oral Proficiency test, on which male students, who did not experience similar problems, outperformed the females.

Other ways in which identities structure interactional opportunities for L2 users include age, social status and class. Age appears to have limited opportunities for social interaction for Antonio, an older ESL learner from Salvador, who was surrounded by much younger kids in an Australian high school (Miller, 1999). Low social status was found to disempower immigrants in Europe and Canada, limiting their opportunities to interact with interested and friendly interlocutors (Bremer *et al.*, 1996; Heller, 1999; Norton Peirce, 1995). Heller (1999) emphasises that most of the time the factors mediating access to linguistic resources act in combination. Her own ethnographic study of a French-language school in Ontario demonstrates that the most underprivileged students are older female immigrants who have most difficulty gaining access to English. Willett (1995) underscores the notion that class and gender mediate opportunities even for the youngest L2 learners. She studied L2 socialisation of four 7-year old ESL children in a mainstream classroom, and found that the combined effects of differences in boys' and girls' peer cultures and the seating arrangements (which were designed to keep the boys apart but allowed the girls to sit together) favoured the three female learners. The friendship between three ESL girls allowed them to collaborate and support each other, thus earning a high status in the girls' subculture and the status of 'good learners' in the eyes of the teacher. In contrast, the working-class Mexican-American boy, Xavier, was seated separately from other boys in the classroom and was not allowed to get out of his seat to get help from his bilingual friends. As a result, he had to rely on adults for help, thus earning the status of a needy child, unable to work independently. The school personnel also explicitly stated that children from the *barrio* like Xavier were semilingual and that their parents were unable to help their children academically. As a result, though all four children scored the same on the Bilingual Syntax Measure, the three girls were allowed to exit from the ESL class because of their reputation as independent workers and middle-class students, while Xavier was forced to continue with ESL instruction.

Recent studies paint a comprehensive picture of gatekeeping in educational contexts, which ranges from preferences for white European immigrant students (McKay & Wong, 1996; Miller, 2000), to insufficient feedback (Siegal, 1996), to physical arrangements in classrooms and cafeterias that separate students by gender, race, language or ethnic background (Kanno, 2000a; McKay & Wong, 1996; Miller, 2000; Toohey, 1998; Willett, 1995). Moore's (1999) ethnographic study of French language education in a Cameroonian village points to another possible source of gatekeeping, located in the discontinuity between community beliefs about language learning and use and classroom practices. The village in question is multilingual, and productive competence in five or six languages is not unusual. This multilingual competence is considered normal and essential by the villagers, who use the communicative resources of their multiple languages in context-appropriate ways, which at times may include code-switching. Neither aptitude nor age are considered to be a factor in second language learning, and SLA is viewed simply as a function of exposure and use. As a result of being exposed to multiple languages from birth, local children bring with them to the classroom considerable experience with second language learning and use, and a great motivation to learn French, seen as the language of socioeconomic advancement in francophone Africa. In interviews with the researcher, the students stressed that opportunities to use the language informally with more expert family members and peers, to ask questions, to make errors and to fall back on a stronger language are crucial for successful language learning. At the same time, their French language instruction minimises opportunities for informal interaction, prohibits the use of any other language but French and does not provide the students with sufficient opportunities for participation and interaction. As a result, students rarely succeed in learning French, and teachers blame their failure on low motivation and lack of parental commitment.

Gatekeeping practices in encounters between majority and minority speakers are examined in depth by Bremer *et al.* (1996). They describe the results of a longitudinal study, funded by the European Science Foundation, of adult L2 learning by migrant workers in several Western European countries (another part of this project is described by Perdue in Chapter 5 of this volume). In the study, the authors focus on unequal institutional encounters between TL speakers and L2 users, and identify a number of explicit and implicit linguistic strategies employed by TL speakers for gatekeeping purposes. In some cases, majority speakers refuse to acknowledge immigrant L2 users as legitimate speakers. Such is the case of a Chilean immigrant in France, Berta, who reported an interaction with the surgeon who had operated on her daughter after an accident at school. As she arrived at the hospital past visiting time, the surgeon told her that she should leave at once, and did not tell her anything about her daughter's health. Berta interpreted his behaviour as a refusal to consider her as a legitimate speaker and as the mother of the injured child. Frustrated and emotional, she was unable to find French words to protest against such behaviour.

More subtle linguistic strategies were used by the job counsellors in a number of counselling sessions with immigrant interlocutors. These counsellors either spoke too rapidly, or, when speaking slowly, produced long and complex sentences, with no clear pauses or other prosodic cues. They also produced several indirect questions and requests that did not facilitate understanding by the interlocutors with low levels of L2 proficiency. The authors argued that more attention should be paid to power relations between the interlocutors and to the role played by native speakers in miscommunication in encounters between native speakers and non-natives. Put together, the above studies suggest that access to linguistic resources is crucial for successful L2 learning and use. Kouritzin (2000) notes insightfully that this access cannot be simplistically reduced to availability of language classes and other linguistic resources. Her own and Norton's (2000, 2001) examinations of various social contexts in which L2 learning and interaction between immigrant women and Canadians take place demonstrate that even intensive instruction in various aspects of TL is of little value when opportunities to interact with TL speakers are limited.

More recently, a few researchers have also inquired which discourses of a particular community are available for self-representation and for appropriation by beginners in childhood (Orellana, 1994; Willett, 1995) and in adulthood (Pavlenko, 1998; Pavlenko & Lantolf, 2000). In doing so they were guided by Bakhtinian notions of heteroglossia and appropriation that allow for L2 learning to be seen, not only as a process of creative construction of interlanguage, but also as a process of internalisation of others' voices and of 'bending' of these voices to the speakers' own purposes (Norton & Toohey, in press). The analysis by Pavlenko (1998) and Pavlenko and Lantolf (2000) of autobiographies of adults who became writers and scholars in their L2 demonstrates that many of these L2 users describe their L2 learning as the process of appropriation and internalisation of the voices of those around them, often friends and close partners.

The process of appropriation is not limited to adults, as argued in Orellana's (1994) ethnographic study of three 3-year-old Spanish-speaking children who recently moved to the US and started attending a bilingual kindergarten. She found that, while the children spoke Spanish to each other most of the time, they switched to English in play-acting activities whenever they pretended to be someone else or impersonated characters from popular children's culture, such as Mickey Mouse, Peter Pan, the Little Mermaid, Superman, Supergirl, Spiderman, the Ninja Turtles and Barbie. One of the children, Carlos, also stated (in Spanish) that when he grows up he will speak only English because ... *los Ninja Turtles hablan ingles* ('the Ninja Turtles speak English'). Like no other research, Orellana's study ingeniously demonstrates how symbolic dominance is transmitted by society to its youngest members: 'English is the language of the strongest and most invincible creatures in these children's world' (Orellana, 1994: 188). Appropriating the voices of superheroes allows these children to represent powerful identities, thus, initiating the process of 'becoming the other' in a society that doesn't value bilingualism or the Spanish language. This study clearly shows the social consequences of the media constructions of language and identity analysed in Lippi-Green's (1997) study.

Willett (1995) shows that, while the ESL children she studied also engaged in linguistic experimentation, many of the utterances in their first year of English study can be traced back to regular classroom phrases used by their teachers, teachers' aides and peers fluent in English and to the text used in the classroom. The language these students internalise is also unique to their own positioning within the community. Thus, Xavier first acquired the highly public and sometimes crude language that other boys used to respond to teachers' elicitations, while the girls never repeated the crude utterances used by the boys. Together, these studies suggest that even the youngest learners don't internalise random linguistic items, rather they attend to and appropriate the most powerful discourses in their immediate environment. Toohey's (1998) work puts an interesting spin on the story of appropriation, however, demonstrating that in some contexts children may be discouraged from and even punished for appropriation of others' words, based on the monologic ideology of language, which views words as individually owned rather than as communal resources.

To sum up, I argue that poststructuralist studies, which see L2 learning as a process of socialisation rather than creative construction or inter-language development, provide new ways of framing the interaction between social contexts and learning processes, which can be productively combined with more linguistically and cognitively oriented interactionist approaches in SLA. In particular, they point to the importance of considering how access to linguistic and interactional resources is mediated by non-native speaker status, race, gender, class, age and social status, and to ways in which discourses appropriated by L2 learners are linked to power and authority.

L2 users as agents

Finally, poststructuralist inquiry in SLA not only reframes the view of language and the learning process, but also reconceptualises the view of the learners. Previously viewed as only minimally social recipients of input and producers of output, poststructuralist L2 users are individual agents whose multiple identities are subject to change over time. Norton Peirce succinctly summarises the shift from the sociopsychological to post-structuralist view of individual L2 users:

> whereas humanist conceptions of the individual – and most definitions of the individual in SLA research – presuppose that every person has an essential, unique, fixed, and coherent core (introvert/extravert; motivated/unmotivated; field dependent/field independent), post-structuralism depicts the individual as diverse, contradictory, and dynamic; multiple rather than unitary, decentered rather than center-ed. (Norton Peirce, 1995: 15)

The present section, therefore, will first outline the differences between the two views of language learners and then discuss ways in which 'agency' and 'investment' have come to replace 'motivation' in the study of L2 learning outcomes.

Two main differences distinguish poststructuralist conceptualisations of L2 users from those offered in the sociopsychological paradigm. To begin with, poststructuralism allows the researchers to conceptualise and examine identities that are much more complex than simply those of L1 and TL speakers. A good example of this complexity can be found in Japanese returnees, known as *kikokushijo*. These are students who return to Japan after a prolonged sojourn abroad and oftentimes display verbal and non-verbal behaviours that are perceived as different from the norm. For instance, in Japanese situations where a careful and subtle gauging of everyone's preference is the preferred mode of creating a group consensus, they may state their preferences clearly and explicitly. Similarly, when everyone is quietly writing down the teacher's words, they may be actively raising hands, asking questions, and voicing opinions. A closer examina-tion shows, however, that it is an oversimplification to say that *kikokushijo* became Westernised. In a longitudinal narrative study, Kanno (2000a, 2000b) followed the linguistic and cultural development of four *kikokushijo* students first in Canada, and later during the readjustment period in Japan through frequent interviews, letters, and e-mail exchanges. She found that the students' relationship with their languages was much more complex than the one captured in the native language vs. target language dichotomy.

Both in Canada and in Japan the students saw the majority language as a form of symbolic capital that ensured their participation in the local society while their minority language served as an emblem of their uniqueness. Thus, in the North American context most students thought of their English as a handicap that positioned them as secondary citizens. In turn, in Japan they found themselves to be by far the best speakers of English around and, as a result, redefined their relationship with English: 'they started to claim ownership over English and the sociocultural world that goes with it. In Japan, English became *their* language' (Kanno, 2000a: 11). Kanno's work underscores the importance of considering a range of language learning trajectories in order to capture the complexity of L2 users' dynamic relationship with their multiple languages. It also demonstrates once again how the views of language as a form of symbolic capital and as a site of identity construction could be combined to explain the conflicts in the process of L2 learning and socialisation.

The second feature that distinguishes the two approaches is the role assigned to human agency. While various sociopsychological theories view L2 learners as members of homogeneous groups and as passive recipients of input and output, poststructuralist L2 users are portrayed as agents in charge of their own learning. Human agency is the key factor in their learning: in many cases they may decide to learn the second, or any additional, language only to the extent that it allows them to be proficient, without the consequences of losing the old and adopting the new ways of being in the world (Lantolf & Pavlenko, 2001). An individual's will and choice are only part of the story, however, as agencies are always co-constructed. First, they are shaped by particular sociocultural environments, and, second, they are co-constructed with those around the L2 users; thus, individuals may act upon their wishes only if their present environments allow for such agency. As Bremer *et al.* (1996) clearly demonstrate, no matter how much some migrant workers in Western Europe may want to practice their L2 in conversational interaction, if their attempts are continuously rejected, they will not be able to learn the language this way.

McKay and Wong's (1996) study underscores the dynamic nature of agency whereby investments are selective and may shift over time. In a two-year-long ethnographic study, the researchers traced the linguistic and social development of four Mandarin-speaking students in a Californian junior high school. They found that, while all four students realised the importance of learning English, they had invested differently in different linguistic areas, and shifted their investment over time. For instance, Michael, who achieved significant gains in oral fluency, did not invest similarly in written English, and, as a result, was held back from the mainstream classes. The researchers suggest that, as an excellent athlete and a popular friend (to both Chinese and non-Chinese), Michael was satisfied in his search for self-representation and did not feel further compelled to perfect his academic writing skills. In contrast, Brad, who initially appeared invested in all four skills, did not manage to develop identities that allowed him to feel competent, appreciated and valued as a social being. As a result, he suffered a downward trajectory in his English learning and started misbehaving in and out of school. McKay and Wong's (1996) study is exemplary in that the researchers managed to link a very detailed discussion of discourses that shaped the agencies and investments of the four students with the discussion of the students' linguistic development assessed through oral and writing samples. In a similar vein, Heller's (1999) ethnography explores how the discourses of *francophonie internationale*, class and gender shape institutional practices and language learning outcomes in a Canadian school. Because the new vision of French positions it as a valuable form of linguistic capital rather than as a dimension of individual identity, it is academically successful middle-class males who are most likely to become bilingual in the way envisaged by school. In contrast, working-class speakers of vernacular Canadian French are marginalised by the discourses of *francophonie internationale* and oftentimes stop speaking French at school altogether.

The view of agency as both individual and social is in agreement with the general shift in poststructuralist SLA inquiry from the notions of individual 'attitudes', 'motivation' and 'personality' to socially constituted 'ideologies', 'investment', 'agency' and 'identity'. Norton Peirce (1995), who pioneered this shift, provided several examples of how the notion of 'investment' can capture the complexity of the students' sociocultural histories that was not easily captured through the construct of motivation. While instrumental motivation is a fixed personality trait, investment refers to the complex, socially and historically constructed and dynamic relationship of the learners to the target language and their sometimes ambivalent desire to learn and to practice it (Norton Peirce, 1995; Norton, 2000). The learners hope that this investment may yield a return and give them access, not only to material resources, such as capital goods, real estate and overall financial success, but also to symbolic resources such as education, literature, media or friendships. Thus, instead of asking whether the L2 user has instrumental or integrative motivation, we can start asking more nuanced questions about the ways in which the L2 user's investment in a particular language was shaped, and the ways in which it is being reshaped by his or her present engagement with the language and its speakers.

In sum, the poststructuralist view of L2 users favours the notion of co-

constructed agency as crucial in explaining language learning outcomes. The notions of agency and investment are also seen as dynamic. Thus, as time goes by, the L2 users' investment in their L2 may change, at times leading to higher investment and successful appropriation of new discourses (Norton, 2000; Pavlenko, 1998; Pavlenko & Lantolf, 2000), and at other times to withdrawal and plateauing or even attrition (Heller, 1999; McKay & Wong, 1996; Norton, 2001).

Advantages of poststructuralist approaches

In this section, I will argue that, compared with the sociopsychological approaches, poststructuralist approaches provide a more context-sensitive way of theorising social impact on L2 learning and use. They also appear to avoid a number of problems and biases discussed earlier:

(1)   Predicated on the acknowledgment of multiplicity, poststructuralist approaches appear to be well equipped for theorising social aspects of SLA, as they allow SLA researchers to avoid monolingual and monocultural biases, to examine the multilingual reality of the contemporary world, and to see all individuals as users of multiple linguistic resources and as members of multiple communities of practice. Thus, researchers can fruitfully examine complex situations in which transient L2 users move between different contexts or create hybrid identities, rather than 'stay put' in the TL environment and assimilate to the TL group.

(2)   Moving away from ethnocentric and multicultural biases toward diversity and multiplicity allows researchers to examine L2 users as legitimate speakers in their own right, rather than as failed native-speakers. A perfect example is Japanese returnees or *kikokushijo* (Kanno, 2000a, 2000b), who do not easily fit into the simplistic NS/NNS dichotomies painted by earlier research and, like other bilinguals and L2 users, cannot and should not be judged by monolingual and monocultural yardsticks.

(3)   While sociopsychological approaches theorise cultures as singular and stable, and individuals as making transitions and acculturating to the dominant culture, poststructuralist approaches recognise complex stratification in all societies and communities and acknowledge a range of, possibly multicultural, communities in which L2 users may seek membership. At times, these multiple memberships may coexist rather than be mutually exclusive as posited in the sociopsychological paradigm. This approach also recognises that, in the process of L2 learning, L2 users may be creating new and distinct linguistic and

ethnic identities, or even communities, that had not existed previously and where for a while no one may be a 'native speaker' of a particular language variety. As such, they allow researchers to ask new and more specific questions about particular communities that L2 users may have, seek, or resist memberships in.

(4) The use of social theory contributes towards the interpretive validity of poststructuralist scholarship. No longer satisfied with the deterministic statement that 'individuals use language to express their social identity', poststructuralist research demonstrates that languages delineate and constitute identities of the speakers, at times even despite the speakers' intentions. Bourdieu's (1991) view of language provides a powerful theoretical framework that allows the SLA researchers to examine and explain the functioning of various language ideologies and social processes that shape individual beliefs and behaviours. In doing so, they theorise social context in ways that were lacking in the previous studies of motivation and attitudes. Recasting language attitudes and language learning beliefs as ideologies, poststructuralist inquiry provides an array of answers to questions that went unanswered in the sociopsychological inquiry, in particular, illuminating the socially constructed nature of beliefs previously seen as individual. Thus, the negative attitudes of English schoolchildren toward Asian languages that were elicited in Sachdev and Wright's (1996) study would no longer be explained through a fuzzy and ultimately non-explanatory self-identification construct. Rather, they would be explained through the ways in which everyday social practices in Britain (particularly the media and educational environments), present Asian languages as inferior, and position their speakers as illegitimate and incompetent members of the white middle-class society (Blackledge, 2000; Leung *et al.*, 1997; Rampton, 1995: 325 on images of British Asian pupils in educational texts). Poststructuralist theory also allows us to account for ambiguities and complexities in the learning process. For instance, it explains the pushes and pulls that may exist between an L1 seen as linked to the user's preferred identity and the L2 seen as symbolic capital but also as imposing an identity that the user resists. The concerns with authority and the speaker's right to speak and the power to impose reception allow the researchers to theorise not only crossings between speech communities, but, more generally, acquisition of new discourses by all language users, especially disempowered and minority members who may be struggling for access to discourses of power and legitimacy. As such, poststructuralist approaches allow us to explain

not only regularities in L2 learning and use but also irregularities that at times appear as challenges to particular meanings and resistance to particular practices.

(5) Recasting motivation as investment allows the researchers to examine how individual investments are shaped and reshaped in particular social contexts. Several studies discussed above demonstrate that individual learners in the same social contexts may have distinct experiences as a result of power relations of gender, race and class, which, in turn, may shape different investments, learning trajectories and, ultimately, outcomes. The notion of investment is also sensitive to the fact that different learners invest selectively in different skills.

(6) By no longer assuming a conventional distinction between the social and the individual, poststructuralist approaches theorise ways in which individual subject positions are implicated in societal relations of power. This attention to the links between the social and the individual has led to the development of new approaches to linguistic interaction that see access to linguistic resources as problematic, and examine various gatekeeping ideologies and practices linked to ethnicity, gender, class and race.

(7) Poststructuralist approaches also provide the field of SLA with alternative methodologies for examining L2 learning and use. Unlike sociopsychological studies, which favoured surveys, questionnaires and quasi-experimental designs, poststructuralist investigations favour longitudinal ethnographic studies that examine both the learner language itself and the social contexts of its learning and use. Poststructuralist enquiry significantly expands the SLA repertoire and provides crucial data on learners' actual verbal and non-verbal behaviours in instructional and non-instructional contexts. Three aspects of these methodological approaches are particularly appealing: (a) the insistence on collecting real and, most importantly, longitudinal data; (b) the insistence on the 'emic', that is to say, participant-relevant, view of phenomena, as a result of which the L2 learners' and users' voices and opinions, gathered through interviews and the study of diaries and autobiographies, are heard on a par with those of the researchers; (c) the broadening of the scope of enquiry that at present takes place, not only in English-speaking contexts with one clearly dominant language, but all over the world where additional languages are learned and used – Eastern and Western Europe (Bremer *et al.*, 1996; Polanyi, 1995; Talburt & Stewart, 1999), Asia (Kanno, 2000a, 2000b; Siegal, 1996), and Africa (Breitborde, 1998; Moore, 1999).

(8) The extension of poststructuralist enquiry in language learning and

use to non-Western contexts has resulted in the acknowledgment that seeing L2 learning as a problem is a uniquely Western phenomenon whereas multilingual inhabitants of the Northwestern Amazon, India or the Cameroon may see learning of additional languages as completely unproblematic (see Moore, 1999). Adults in these contexts continue learning additional languages throughout their lives; neither age nor aptitude are considered important factors in the learning process. The key to success is seen in plentiful interactional opportunities, while the desired outcome is multi-competence rather than idealised 'native-speakerness'.

(9) Predicated on a powerful social theory that links socioeconomic and sociopolitical environments with language learning and use, poststructuralist enquiry views social contexts as crucial in understanding L2 learning, and treats language as part of what constitutes these contexts rather than as a separate and independent set of structures. The two-way relationship between language and identity recognises that languages serve to produce, reproduce, transform and perform identities, and that linguistic, gender, racial, ethnic and class identities, in turn, affect the access to linguistic resources and interactional opportunities, and, ultimately, L2 learning outcomes.

Conclusion

To conclude, I have argued that poststructuralist approaches represent a more theoretically advanced way of looking at the social contexts of L2 learning and use. At the same time, I acknowledge that these approaches may not be appropriate for those who view L2 learning as a unified and homogeneous phenomenon that can be explained away by one general theory. The enhanced explanatory value offered by poststructuralist attention to linguistic practices and power relations is balanced out by the fact that poststructuralist theory does not make predictive statements. It thus does not aim to identify a constellation of factors that may predict that, if A, B and C take place, the individual X will become native-like (*sic!*) in language Y. Instead, the researchers working in this paradigm acknowledge that, while they may recognise certain factors that shape human agency, agency in itself is dynamic, and the course of history is unpredictable. Thus, events taking place a year or two down the road may influence the processes of L2 learning and use in ways that no theory is able to predict. Instead, many poststructuralist scholars engage in identifying socioeconomic and sociopolitical factors that impede and/or favour multilingualism and multiculturalism. They advocate language and educational policies that ensure equal access to linguistic and educational resources, promote multilingualism without imposing 'acculturation' or 'native-like' ability, and raise consciousness about shared responsibility for understanding in cross-cultural encounters between minority and majority speakers (Bremer *et al.*, 1996; Heller, 1999; Leung *et al.*, 1997; Lippi-Green, 1997; Miller, 2000; Norton, 2000, 2001). This socially engaged scholarship resonates with contemporary poststructuralist educational theory and informs many innovative approaches to educational and language policy (Kanno, 2000a; Leung *et al.*, 1997; Rampton, 1995), to critical language pedagogy (Norton Peirce, 1995; Toohey, 1998) and to curricular innovation in L2 and FL classrooms (Kanno & Applebaum, 1995; Moore, 1999; Rampton, 1995; Talburt & Stewart, 1999).

Similarly, poststructuralist approaches that focus on individuals as social actors, rather than on the process of language development, may be of little use to those who, in the words of Roberts (1996: 24) 'assume that it is possible and worthwhile to isolate some aspects of language, and isolate language use from the language user, in order to trace through the acquisition of a particular feature'. As approaches concerned with the social aspects of L2 learning, they do not attempt to account for all aspects of SLA. There is no reason, however, why these approaches cannot be successfully combined with more cognitively and linguistically oriented analyses of L2 learning and use in a way that has already been masterfully accomplished by Bremer *et al.* (1996), McKay and Wong (1996) and Polanyi (1995). They are particularly compatible with the multi-competence perspective, as they paint a complex picture of L2 learning and use in which L2 users are portrayed as investing in bi- or multilingualism, rather than in ubiquitous TL development.

Finally, I would like to emphasise that at no point do poststructuralist researchers want to create a hegemony and replace all other paradigms, as this would contradict the basic premises of poststructuralism, predicated on multiplicity and sensitivity to power relations. Rather, to use Lantolf's (1996) metaphor, poststructuralist approaches will bloom best when surrounded by other flowers in the garden of theory and practice, giving rise to present and future debates and controversies.

References

Archibald, J. (ed.) (2000) *Second Language Acquisition and Linguistic Theory.* Oxford: Blackwell.

Blackledge, A. (2000) *Literacy, Power, and Social Justice.* Stoke-on-Trent: Trentham Books.

Bourdieu, P. (1991) *Language and Symbolic Power.* Cambridge: Polity Press.

Breitborde, L. (1998) *Speaking and Social Identity: English in the Lives of Urban Africans.* Berlin: Mouton De Gruyter.

Bremer, K., Roberts, C., Vasseur, M-T., Simonot, M. and Broeder. P. (1996) *Achieving Understanding: Discourse in Intercultural Encounters*. London: Longman.

Cameron, D. (1990) Demythologising sociolinguistics: Why language does not reflect society. In J. Joseph and T. Taylor (eds) *Ideologies of Language* (pp. 79–93). London: Routledge.

Davies, B. and Harré, R. (1990) Positioning: The discursive production of selves. *Journal for the Theory of Social Behaviour* 20, 1, 43–63.

Ellis, R. (1994) *The Study of Second Language Acquisition*. Oxford: Oxford University Press.

Firth, A. and Wagner, J. (1997) On discourse, communication, and (some) fundamental concepts in SLA research. *Modern Language Journal* 81 (3), 285–300.

Foucault, M. (1972) *The Archaeology of Knowledge*. London: Tavistock.

Gal, S. (1989) Language and political economy. *Annual Review of Anthropology* 18, 345–367.

Gardner, R. (1979) Social psychological aspects of second language acquisition. In H. Giles and R. St Clair (eds) *Language and Social Psychology*. Oxford: Blackwell.

Gardner, R. (1985) *Social Psychology and Second Language Learning: Attitudes and Motivation*. London: Edward Arnold.

Gardner, R. and Lambert, W. (1959) Motivational variables in second-language acquisition. *Canadian Journal of Psychology* 13, 266–272.

Gardner, R. and Lambert, W. (1972) *Attitudes and Motivation in Second Language Learning*. Rowley, MA: Newbury House.

Gass, S. and Selinker, L. (1994) *Second Language Acquisition: An Introductory Course*. Hillsdale, NJ: Lawrence Erlbaum.

Giles, H., Bourhis, R. and Taylor, D. (1977) Toward a theory of language in ethnic group relations. In H. Giles (ed.) *Language, Ethnicity, and Intergroup Relations*. London: Academic Press.

Giles, H. and Byrne, J. (1982) An intergroup approach to second language acquisition. *Journal of Language and Social Psychology* 5, 291–302.

Giles, H. and Johnson, P. (1987) Ethnolinguistic identity theory: A social psychological approach to language maintenance. *International Journal of the Sociology of Language* 68, 69–99.

Heller, M. (1992) The politics of codeswitching and language choice. *Journal of Multilingual and Multicultural Development* 13 (1), 123–142.

Heller, M. (1999) *Linguistic Minorities and Modernity: A Sociolinguistic Ethnography*. London: Longman.

Husband, C. and Saifullah-Khan, V. (1982) The viability of ethnolinguistic vitality: Some creative doubts. *Journal of Multilingual and Multicultural Development* 3, 195–205.

Kanno, Y. (2000a) Bilingualism and identity: The stories of Japanese returnees. *International Journal of Bilingual Education and Bilingualism* 3 (1), 1–18.

Kanno, Y. (2000b) Kikokushijo as bicultural. *International Journal of Intercultural Relations* 24, 361–382.

Kanno, Y. and Applebaum, S. (1995) ESL students speak up: Their stories of how we are doing. *TESL Canada Journal* 12 (2), 32–49.

Kouritzin, S. (2000) Immigrant mothers redefine access to ESL classes: Contradiction and ambivalence. *Journal of Multilingual and Multicultural Development* 21 (1), 14-32.

Lantolf, J. (1996) SLA theory building: 'Letting all the flowers bloom!' *Language Learning* 46 (4) 713–749.

Lantolf, J. and Pavlenko, A. (2001) (S)econd (L)anguage (A)ctivity Theory: Understanding second language learners as people. In: M. Breen (ed.) *Learner Contributions to Language Learning: New Directions in Research* (pp. 141–158). London: Longman.

Larsen-Freeman, D. and Long, M. (1991) *Introduction to Second Language Acquisition Research*. London: Longman.

Lave, J. and Wenger, E. (1991) *Situated Learning: Legitimate Peripheral Participation*. Cambridge: Cambridge University Press.

Le Page, R. and Tabouret-Keller, A. (1985) *Acts of Identity: Creole-based Aproaches to Language and Ethnicity*. Cambridge: Cambridge University Press.

Leung, C., Harris, R. and Rampton, B. (1997) The idealised native speaker, reified ethnicities, and classroom realities. *TESOL Quarterly* 31 (3), 543-560.

Lippi-Green, R. (1997) *English with an Accent: Language, Ideology, and Discrimination in the United States*. London: Routledge.

McKay, S. and Wong, S. (1996) Multiple discourses, multiple identities: Investment and agency in second-language learning among Chinese adolescent immigrant students. *Harvard Educational Review* 66 (3), 577–608.

Miller, J. (1999) Becoming audible: Social identity and second language use. *Journal of Intercultural Studies* 20 (2), 149–165.

Miller, J. (2000) Language use, identity, and social interaction: Migrant students in Australia. *Research on Language and Social Interaction* 33 (1), 69–100.

Mitchell, R. and Myles, F. (1998) *Second Language Learning Theories*. London: Arnold.

Moore, L. (1999) Language socialisation research and French language education in Africa: A Cameroonian case study. *Canadian Modern Language Review* 56 (2), 329–350.

Norton Peirce, B. (1995) Social identity, investment, and language learning. *TESOL Quarterly* 29 (1), 9–31.

Norton, B. (2000) *Identity and Language Learning: Gender, Ethnicity, and Educational Change*. London: Longman.

Norton, B. (2001) Non-participation, imagined communities, and the language classroom. In M. Breen (ed.) *Learner Contributions to Language Learning: New Directions in Research* (pp. 159–171). London: Longman.

Norton, B. and Toohey, K. (in press) Identity and language learning. In R. Kaplan (ed.) *Handbook of Applied Linguistics*. Oxford: Oxford University Press.

Ochs, E. (1993) Constructing social identity: A language socialisation perspective. *Research on Language and Social Interaction* 26 (3), 287–306.

Orellana, M. (1994) Appropriating the voice of the superheroes: Three preschoolers' bilingual language uses in play. *Early Childhood Research Quarterly* 9, 171–193.

Pavlenko, A. (1998) Second language learning by adults: Testimonies of bilingual writers. *Issues in Applied Linguistics* 9 (1), 3–19.

Pavlenko, A. (2000) Access to linguistic resources: Key variable in second language learning. *Estudios de Sociolinguistica* 1 (2), 85–105.

Pavlenko, A. and Lantolf, J. (2000) Second language learning as participation and the (re) construction of selves. In J.P. Lantolf (ed.) *Sociocultural Theory and Second Language Learning* (pp.157–180). Oxford: Oxford University Press.

Pennycook, A. (1990) Toward a critical applied linguistics for the 1990s. *Issues in Applied Linguistics* 1, 8–28.

Polanyi, L. (1995) Language learning and living abroad: Stories from the field. In B. Freed (ed.) *Second Language Acquisition in a Study Abroad Context* (pp. 271–291). Amsterdam/Philadelphia: John Benjamins Publishing Company,

Rampton, B. (1995) *Crossing: Language and Ethnicity among Adolescents.* London: Longman.

Ritchie, W. and Bhatia, T. (eds) (1996) *Handbook of Second Language Acquisition.* New York: Academic Press.

Roberts, C. (1996) Taking stock: Contexts and reflections. In K. Bremer, C. Roberts, M-T. Vasseur, M. Simonot and P. Broeder *Achieving Understanding: Discourse in Intercultural Encounters* (pp. 207–238). London: Longman.

Sachdev, I. and Wright, A. (1996) Social influence and language learning: An experimental study. *Journal of Language and Social Psychology* 15 (3), 230–245.

Schumann, J. (1978) The acculturation model for second language acquisition. In R. Gingras (ed.) *Second Language Acquisition and Foreign Language Teaching* (pp. 27–50). Washington, DC: Center for Applied Linguistics.

Schumann, J. (1986) Research on the acculturation model for second language acquisition. *Journal of Multilingual and Multicultural Development* 7 (5), 379–392.

Sharwood Smith, M. (1994) *Second Language Learning: Theoretical Foundations.* London: Longman.

Siegal, M. (1996) The role of learner subjectivity in second language sociolinguistic competency: Western women learning Japanese. *Applied Linguistics* 17, 356–382.

Spolsky, B. (1989) *Conditions for Second Language Learning.* Oxford: Oxford University Press.

Syed, Z. and Burnett, A. (1999) Acculturation, identity, and language: Implications for language minority education. In K. Davis (ed.) *Foreign Language Teaching and Language Minority Education (Technical Report No. 19)* (pp. 41–63). Honolulu: University of Hawaii, Second Language Teaching and Curriculum Center.

Tabouret-Keller, A. (1997) Language and identity. In F. Coulmas (ed.) *The Handbook of Sociolinguistics* (pp. 315–326). Oxford: Blackwell.

Tajfel, H. (1974) Social identity and intergroup behavior. *Social Science Information* 13, 65–93.

Tajfel, H. (1981) *Human Groups and Social Categories.* Cambridge: Cambridge University Press.

Talburt, S. and Stewart, M. (1999) What's the subject of Study Abroad? Race, gender, and 'Living Culture'. *The Modern Language Journal* 83 (2), 163–175.

Toohey, K. (1998) 'Breaking them up, taking them away': ESL students in Grade 1. *TESOL Quarterly* 32 (1), 61–84.

Twombly, S. (1995) *Piropos* and friendships: Gender and culture clash in study abroad. *Frontiers: The Interdisciplinary Journal of Study Abroad* 1, 1–27.

Weedon, C. (1987) *Feminist Practice and Poststructuralist Theory.* London: Blackwell.

Wenger, E. (1998) *Communities of Practice: Learning, Meaning, and Identity.* Cambridge: Cambridge University Press.

Willett, J. (1995) Becoming first graders in an L2: An ethnographic study of L2 socialisation. *TESOL Quarterly* 29 (3), 473–503.

Williams, G. (1992) *Sociolinguistics: A Sociological Critique.* London: Routledge.

Woolard, K. (1985) Language variation and cultural hegemony: Toward an integration of sociolinguistic and social theory. *American Ethnologist* 12, 738–748.

Introduction to Chapter 12

Second Language Learners' Rights, Francisco Gomes de Matos

VIVIAN COOK

One of the crucial points made in this book is that L2 users matter. They are real people in the real world, whose lives, minds, religious beliefs, careers and social relationships can be profoundly affected by their knowledge and use of a second language. People may be liberated by their second language; Steve Biko insisted for example on English as the language of the Black People's Convention in South Africa (Biko, 1978). Or they may be enslaved and deprived of their own reality by having to use a language other than their own. At one time or another:

> Children were forbidden to speak Basque in Spain, Navajo in the USA, or Kurdish in Turkey; Koreans in Japanese-occupied territories had to adopt Japanese names; the Turkish minority in Bulgaria had to use Bulgarian names. Indeed deaf children have often been made to sit on their hands in class to prevent them using sign language. (Cook, 2001: 163)

In some ways this was acknowledged in the 1990s debate about the use of English as an economic tool (Phillipson, 1992). A language can be used by its native speakers to exert power over L2 users through trade, through making it the language of scientific discourse, through the internet, through international bodies, through television films, just as globalised commerce can result in a Starbucks on every corner and a Coke in every café. This has practical spin-offs for business; the billion students of English represent a gold mine for the producers of teaching materials; income from learned journals exported from the UK in 1999 came to £508 million (Department for Culture, Media and Sport, 2001). For the individual there may be straightforward economic gains to using a second language (Breton, 1998); in hard cash, 'knowledge of the second official language improved the earnings of French-speaking women by 10.2%' in 1991 (Christofides & Swidinsky, 1998).

One of the under-currents in the background chapter was the notion that L2 users have not been treated fairly. Monolingually-dominant societies have talked only of the problems of multiple languages, not of the advantages. Even SLA research has mostly seen L2 users as deficient rather than as people in their own right. The chapter by Francisco Gomes de Matos reminds us of the learners' rights to be treated in education as independent human beings and to have their voices heard about what is done to them, extending down to the very teaching and learning techniques they encounter. Language teaching is far more than a skill of simple communication on a par with keyboard skills, but can affect every aspect of people's social and cognitive lives.

References

Biko, S. (1978) *I Write What I Like.* London: The Bowerdan Press.

Breton, A. (ed.) (1998) *Economic Approaches to Language and Bilingualism.* Canada: Canadian Heritage. Online document: http://www.pch.gc.ca/offlangoff/perspectives/english/economic/index.html.

Christofides, L. and Swidinsky, R. (1998) *Bilingualism and Earnings: A Study Based on 1971, 1981 and 1991 Census Data.* Ottawa: Official Languages Branch, Department of Canadian Heritage.

Cook, V.J. (2001) *Second Language Learning and Language Teaching* (3rd edn). London: Edward Arnold.

Department for Culture, Media and Sport (2001) Publishing in *Creative Industries Mapping Document 2001.* Online document: http://www.culture.gov.uk/creative/mapp_publish.htm.

Phillipson, R. (1992) *Linguistic Imperialism.* Oxford: Oxford University Press.

Chapter 12
Second Language Learners' Rights

FRANCISCO GOMES DE MATOS

Background to Linguistic Rights

One way of writing the history of ideas in second language education is to describe the rise and influence of key concepts focused on learners, such as abilities, creativity, values and many more. Up until the early 1980s, however, a key concept that was conspicuously absent from the literature on L2 learning was learners' rights (Gomes de Matos, 1986). Let us begin with its underlying conceptual foundation, namely, linguistic rights.

The idea of linguistic human rights is not new – it can be found in several traditions from different parts of the world in 'formal treaty-based language rights' drafted before 1815 (Skutnabb-Kangas, 2000: 507) – and some attention to language has been given in 'nearly one-third of the world's constitutions' (Blaustein & Epstein, 1986: 9). It was, however, the proclamation by the United Nations of the *Universal Declaration of Human Rights* (UDHR) in 1948 that provided the prime inspiration to a movement for a *Universal Declaration of Linguistic Rights* (UDLR). This document was proclaimed in Barcelona in 1996, nearly 50 years after the UDHR, a unique landmark in humankind's history of moral and ethical advances (UDLR, 1996).

Among the pioneering explorations of linguistic rights in the 1980s leading to the UDLR, we need to mention the following:

- *1984.* This year saw the publication of an article making a case for a universal declaration of individual linguistic rights and suggesting a 20-item list, which featured the person's right to learn a second language (Gomes de Matos, 1984a). This was followed by *A Plea for a Language Rights Declaration* in a newsletter then co-sponsored by FIPLV (World Federation of Modern Language Teachers) and UNESCO (Gomes de Matos, 1984b). An International Academy of Language Law (academyturi@attglobal.net) was established in Montreal, bringing together jurists, linguists, social scientists and language educators.

- *1987.* David Crystal, when mentioning the *Plea* in the Preface to his encyclopedia, states that 'All people have the right to use their mother tongue, to learn a second language ...' and he cogently stresses that 'Only concentrated public attention on the issues will promote the recognition of such rights' (Crystal, 1997: vii). An international Seminar on Human Rights and Cultural Rights took place in Recife, Brazil, co-sponsored by AIMAV, UNESCO and the Federal University of Pernambuco. The outcome of the seminar was *The Declaration of Recife*, which recommended that 'steps be taken by the United Nations to adopt and implement a Universal Declaration of Linguistic Rights'.

Since then, the interest in learners' rights has kept growing – as a web search or a glance at the programmes of World Congresses such as AILA, FIPLV and TESOL will rapidly reveal. In particular readers are referred to two articles published in the early 90s (Gomes de Matos, 1991 and 1994). The parallel development of a linguistic-rights awareness is documented in Skutnabb-Kangas (2000: 505–511).

The Rights of L2 Students

The above summary gives some idea of how linguistic rights began to attract international attention, especially among linguists and jurists, but an equally important, parallel development also took place at the same time: initial explorations of educational linguistics rights, in particular the rights of L2 learners.

First let us characterise 'rights' as used in the phrase 'second language learners' rights'. In this context a 'right' is a *quality* that L2 learners are entitled to by virtue of one or more of their individual characteristics and by the virtue of the conditions in which learning/teaching takes place. A right is balanced by a corresponding responsibility. Thus, a 'right' is more than simply that which learners may claim as justly true (the kind of broad definition given by dictionaries). Learners' rights include both individual characteristics and the educational ecosystem in which such rights can be exercised by learners, and asserted or assured by teachers or educational communities. The very labeling of specific rights (e.g. language learners' right to language play) can be reacted to in various ways, for instance, as something that 'sounds reasonable'. 'It being a right for the learner would make it I suppose an obligation for the teacher' (Guy Cook, personal communication, November, 2000).

To put it another way, defining learners' rights as something to which they have an educational claim is inherently circular. Rather, a right is characterised as having features such as a quality / a benefit / a humanising experiencing / cooperation. In such a spirit, when learners say 'I have the right to ...', they may mean either 'I have the right to experience this' or 'I have the right to use this or that (because of my condition as a learner in such and such a learning context)'.

In brief then a L2 learner's right involves:

(1) a new *experiencing* of a cognitive, cultural, educational or linguistic nature;
(2) a new *benefit* (especially a tangible one, such as access to dictionaries and other reference works, VCRs, computers, etc.);
(3) a *humanising* quality (the outcome of a cooperatively-negotiated classroom policy of mutual rights and responsibilities).

In short, a learner's right is a new humanising quality experienced by a person as a result of an educational decision or policy.

For this discussion we need to make a crucial distinction between humanism and humanising. The traditional concept of 'humanism' since the Renaissance has emphasised human welfare, values and dignity; the concept of 'humanising' centres on human linguistic rights, justice and communicative peace. Thus *humanist* teachers such as Comenius and Marcel, who emphasise individual respect for the learner, are different from *humanising* teachers such as Curran, Gattegno, Moskowitz and Stevick, who emphasise individual respect for the learner. They in turn are different from those engaged in the UNESCO-FIPLV LINGUAPAX Programme (described for example in Crystal, 1999), which started in 1987. This programme aims at integrating language education and peace education, while stressing human rights, democracy, justice, solidarity and intercultural understanding so as to help build and sustain a culture of peace through the teaching of first, second and further languages. In short, while there have been many 'humanist' teachers, 'humaniser' teachers are a slowly but steadily growing phenomenon, partly motivated by the rise of the awareness of linguistic rights which, in the case of language education, dates from the early eighties. Contrasting the two movements (humanism and humanising), and the corresponding 'agents' (humanist and humaniser) helps our understanding of the changes in the history of language education and of the important roles of language educators. For a psychological view on 'the humanisation of the other', see Deutsch (2000).

Having discussed the learner's rights, something should be added on the other side of the coin: the learner's responsibilities. The very moment a learner exercises his or her right to do something, he or she should be imbued with the corresponding responsibility. For instance, if students in my Brazilian Portuguese class tell me 'I have the right to look up new words in my dictionary during text production practice', they should be conscious of the responsibility of sharing such aids with classmates unequipped with a reference tool. I recall a student of mine asking me if 'the right to rewrite a text, prior to being given a grade on such composition' exempted him from telling me how he went about improving his production. This is a reminder to us language educators that promoting an awareness of rights and responsibilities should be one of the priorities in our first interaction with learners. After all, a truly humanising language education is aimed at cultivating both rights and obligations concurrently. To teach that rights and responsibilities are interdependent and to see that this holistic perspective is accepted and put into practice is part of our job as 'humanisers'.

The L2 learner should contribute to a harmonious communicatively-peaceful interaction in the classroom:

- providing assistance to classmates in need of linguistic and cultural peer cooperation;
- sharing personal language-learning aids with classmates (a dictionary, for example, in many developing countries is typically the property of a very few, sometimes only one student);
- performing his or her tasks as committedly and seriously as possible;
- providing feedback to his or her teacher on the quality of the teaching performance as well as on the quality of his or her own learning investment;
- and, last but not least, complying with the classroom charter of learners' and teacher's rights and responsibilities, using human-dignifying-and-edifying vocabulary.

This dimension of vocabulary learning is both under-taught and under-researched, which is why I coined the term 'positivisers' for adjectives that refer to constructive, positive features in human personality and performance. The tradition of teaching vocabulary thematically or in semantic groupings has not yet discovered that, if we are to help L2 learners use a language humanisingly, they should be guided how to select words and phrases that humanise both themselves as users and their interactive partners. The responsibility to learn how to use a language humanisingly should be one of the fundamental rights of all language users and essential in the preparation of L2 learners. This is, in fact, an instance in which both a right and a responsibility are involved.

As characterised in this chapter, a learner's right is thus a comprehensive notion, concerned with what the literature on Language Education and

Applied Linguistics has variously called 'processes of learning', 'process-based syllabuses' and 'learning strategies' (Oxford, 1990; Cohen, 1998). It goes well beyond the learner's cognitive manifestations of his or her language faculty (processes) or strategic ways of learning a language (strategies). In short, the notion of 'learner's right' should be understood, analysed, and implemented in its own right: as a new kind of humanising language-learning experience, inspired by insights from human rights, justice, peace and democracy. Process- and strategy-centred perspectives are important in the development of traditions in Language Education, but are here seen as part of the broader 'learner rights perspective'. They should be cultivated by those sharing the conviction that, as language educators, it is our major responsibility to enhance humanising uses of second languages for communicative peace (Gomes de Matos, 2000c) rather than merely a 'thoughtful (socially responsible) language use' (see Kern, 2000). The point to be stressed is that, in the history of ideas in language education, systematic sustained attention to learners' needs, processes and strategies, while very important, should be complemented by a new focus on learners' rights, so as to further humanise what learners and teachers do in classrooms and in other ecosystems where they interact.

Recognition of Learners' Rights

Limitations of space preclude extensive discussion here about when and how recognition of learners' linguistics rights started in the English-language-using literature on second language education. However, mention should be made of two works that have implicitly recognised that key concept, and have proved inspiring for this hitherto-neglected dimension in our field: (1) Freire's acclaimed Pedagogy of the Oppressed (Freire, 1970) and (2) a pioneering contribution to humanised language teaching by Moskowitz (1978).

Beginning with Freire's approach, how can learners be expected to become 'readers of the world' (cf. Freire's oft-cited phrase 'reading the world'), without being able to exercise their rights and fulfill their responsibilities? Up until Freire's cogent pleas for educational, economic and political oppression to be replaced by liberating, human-dignifying approaches and by the need for both recognition and implementation of learners' autonomy (Freire, 1996), educational attention and initiatives seemed to be focused on learning *about* rights and responsibilities rather than on ways to implement what I call 'linguistic/ communicative rights and responsibilities' – within language education in general and second language education in particular. Thus Freirean insights have inspired me to view learners' rights as something not only educationally or socio-politically desirable but also necessary, as part of that indispensable theoretical-practical foundation on which classroom interactions can be humanisingly experienced. In brief but memorable meetings with Paulo Freire in Recife I had the chance of sharing some of my extended applications of 'reading the world', through my proposed concept of 'reading the world for communicative peace through the responsible exercise of rights'. His words of encouragement led me to push on, by exploring frontiers beyond language education proper (Gomes de Matos, 2000b).

Turning to Moskowitz, when I read her book (Moskowitz, 1978) with its suggestive exemplification of how to apply humanistic techniques in L2 education, I realised that by integrating Freire's theoretically-provocative insights and the Temple University methodologist's plea for humanising interactions in classrooms, I would be able to continue in my search for what, from the early 90s I would call 'humanisation', instead of 'humanism'. Moskowitz's keenly pragmatic advice struck a chord and made me realise that learners' rights (especially of a linguistic and intercultural nature) would have to be dealt with in very specific terms if effective concrete steps were to be taken by language educators in implementing a language-learners'-rights philosophy of action in classrooms and other related contexts. In this spirit, I have been probing and disseminating ideas on ways to apply such rights through workshops for Brazilian teachers, especially at Associação Brasil América in Recife (www.abaweb.org). My experience as a language teacher educator (Portuguese and English) has shown that school strategies for building learners' rights should start from elementary school and proceed through university education. Promoting the development of Second Language Learners' Rights calls for universal, cooperative efforts. In my case, the ideas of Freire and Moskowitz have inspired me not only to apply but also to expand the range of such rights.

One of the very first articles dealing with the importance of L2 learners' linguistic rights was published in a Brazilian journal based in São Paulo (Gomes de Matos, 1984c). This argued that approaches to language teaching should add learners' rights to the then-prevalent concepts, among which learners' needs and interests were prominent. Revealingly for historians of contemporary language teaching, that text was primarily addressed to L2 teachers in public and private secondary schools and universities and in specialised language teaching organisations such as the Yázigi Institute of Languages, whose Center for Applied Linguistics sponsored the journal.

A slightly expanded treatment of L2 learners' rights in English appeared in a newsletter aimed at language planners (Gomes de Matos, 1985). In the same year Hammerly's nine-page *Bill of Rights for Language Learners* appeared as a pioneering appendix to his book (Hammerly, 1985: 211–220), in which he discusses educational-linguistic rights that 'are often violated in language programs'. In his conclusion, the Canadian author justifies his contribution by clarifying that 'It is hoped that the above discussion has not sounded too dogmatic – a danger when proposing something as legal-sounding as *rights*. Underlying this proposal is my bias in favour of enlightened eclecticism in language teaching' (Hammerly, 1985: 220). Whereas Hammerly's perception of learners' rights was grounded on methodological considerations, I have been inspired by the Human Rights traditions, reflecting a professional background in languages (Portuguese/ English), linguistics and law. It was not until 1986, however, that a plea for L2 linguistic rights was made in a newsletter for teachers of English to speakers of other languages (Gomes de Matos, 1986). This widely disseminated plea began to be echoed by second language educators, such as Grant (1987) and Ellis and Sinclair (1989). Gomes de Matos (1994) extends the concept by reporting how Brazilian secondary students learning French formulate their own rights – an exercise in educational linguistic democracy that could well be tried out by L2 teachers everywhere.

Recognition of L2 learners' rights was not only found among ESL teachers but also attracted a more diversified community, as attested by the fact that FIPLV published my 1984 *Plea* and by its own state-of-the-art publication (Batley *et al.*, 1993), which discussed language policies for the world in the twenty-first century in the light of such key concepts as linguistic rights, international cooperation and peace.

A Typology of Learners' Rights

Human rights can proceed from general to specific types, thus: civic rights, cultural rights, economic rights, social rights, and political rights exemplify the five well-known generic categories. On the other hand, the right to vote, the right to participate in the cultural life of one's community, the right to a fair salary, the right to language education, and the right to a fair trial illustrate specific realisations of human rights. Similarly, learners' rights can be categorised from comprehensive to specific types: examples of the former would be the cultural, educational, and linguistic rights of mother-tongue learners, teachers and teacher-trainers. Given the focus of this chapter on L2 learners' rights, an open-ended listing will be presented, on the basis of 12 criteria. Readers are urged to reflect on this classification, while making it relevant to the educational-linguistic-cultural contexts in their countries.

(1) *Learners' age*: Teachers should consider the specific age-related rights of children, teenagers, adults, senior citisens, and so on.

(2) *Performance level*: Teachers should respect the rights of different levels of students, whether beginners, intermediate, advanced, very advanced, or whatever.

(3) *Participation*: Teachers should consider if they are dealing with learners individually, in mini-groups, or as a classroom community.

(4) *Role*: Teachers should acknowledge learners' rights as listeners, speakers, readers, writers, viewers, test takers (examinees).

(5) *Language and cultural background*: Teachers should respect specific nationalities and their respective languages, for example Brazilian learners' rights as speakers of Portuguese and as members of the Brazilian culture, and the rights of bilinguals and multilinguals.

(6) *Language component*: Depending on their view of language, teachers might concentrate on learners' pronunciation, vocabulary, grammatical, pragmatic, spelling rights.

(7) *Strategy*: By considering the kind of strategy that learners prefer, teachers would respect the learner's right to do something in writing, rather than only by speaking (as authoritarian teachers sometimes prescribe) and the learner's right to paraphrase rather than use the expected construction (textbook-induced answers sometimes lead teachers to expect one and only one construction, thus violating a learner's right to be creative in the second language).

(8) *Personality*: Teachers could consider and, more importantly, respect and uphold learners' rights to be introverted or extraverted in class. The typical police warning 'you have the right to remain silent' also applies to classroom interaction, but, alas it is often violated, when teachers insist that a learner say something, even against his or her own will! The late, ever-inspiring, pioneering Wilga Rivers (1968) warns against the neglect of the student's right to silence, partly on the grounds that a lot of 'skill-using-improving' takes place via the processing of auditory and written symbols and not only through speaking.

(9) *Classroom communication:* These are the most visible, the easiest type of rights to exemplify, since violations seem to occur in classrooms all over the world. Consider, for instance, a learner's right to be heard by the whole class: how often is it assured by the teacher? Why? Why not? When there is a private dialogue between teacher and a particular student and the rest of the class can't hear the exchange, a violation of a classroom communicative right is taking place. How well prepared are we as language educators to assure learners of such rights as the

right to hear all that is relevantly said in class? Traditional seating arrangements by rows conspire against the establishment of a pedagogically indispensable face-to-face interaction in classrooms that emphase language use for communication.

(10) *Use of resources:* Learners have the right to use a dictionary while producing a written text in class, or taking a second language test (applicants for admission to an MA Program at the Federal University of Pernambuco's Graduate Programme in Letters, for instance, have the right to use a bilingual dictionary).

(11) *Language-teaching environment:* We could speak of classroom learners' rights, home or work-based learners' rights, rights of autonomous learners (in self-access centres or facilities)

(12) *Disabilities or illnesses of learners:* This often-neglected type of right is a special challenge to language policy makers and to language educators. It is the case, for example, of blind, deaf, dyslexic persons, as well as of brain-damaged bilinguals. Do students with low language aptitude have the right to be exempted from the foreign language requirement in some degrees?

Learners' Pronunciation, Grammatical and Vocabulary Rights: Some Examples

Having outlined twelve possibilities for dealing with L2 learners' rights, according to a learner-centred typology, I will now illustrate some specific types of learners' rights that I have been exploring, both theoretically and applicationally. I have explored the latter by applying the ideas in a university context (I teach Portuguese to speakers of other languages) and in meetings with teachers of English, especially at Associação Brasil-América (Brazil-America Association). The Associação Brasil-América is a Binational Centre in Recife, and is the first ELT organisation in Brazil where I introduced the concept of learners' linguistic and intercultural rights in the mid-1980s. Before exemplifying the kinds of rights that learners can – or more humanisingly, *should* have – it is well to reiterate that, though *rights* and *responsibilities* are interdependent, for limitations of space only the former are dealt with here. Interested readers are urged to take on the dual challenge of creating suitable conditions for implementing both qualities.

While the criterion-based typology presented at the beginning of the chapter reflects the theoretically broad range of learners' rights, the more detailed typologies to be presented now are meant to illustrate specific types of (predominantly) classroom-centred uses of learner rights. In moving from criterion-focused rights (*proficiency-oriented*, for instance) to classroom-oriented rights (a beginner's right to exposure to systematic vocabulary input, for instance), readers are urged to think of teachers as humanising translators of 'theory' into 'practical procedures'. It is as if 'knowledge of rights' were to become 'knowledge of the use of such rights'. By relating the earlier typology to later listings of rights, readers will be able to see how the theoretical notion of learners' rights can be applied.

Learners' pronunciation rights

(1) The right to be taught how to use transcriptions in dictionaries.
(2) The right to be sensitised to variation in speech.
(3) The right to have contextually realistic practice materials.
(4) The right to have access to recordings and transcripts of lectures and conversations.
(5) The right to have access to equipment (e.g. a language lab) that enables learners to compare their own production with that of native or non-native speakers.
(6) The right to be corrected in a positive, tactful manner.
(7) The right to receive explicit phonetic instruction.
(8) The right to be exposed to exemplary models, but also – in agreement with the late Kenneth Pike (personal communication) – the right to be exposed to different dialects).

Learners' vocabulary rights

Do teachers assure their students of their semantic rights to learn to use lexical items:

(1) Systematically, in lexical sets, or as word families, or through concept mapping, etc?
(2) Contextually, that is, in typical situations in which the vocabulary is used?
(3) Realistically – as far as data on frequency of use is concerned – so that more commonly used lexical items can be prioritised? A related semantic right would be the learners' right to haves access to dictionaries providing such guidance, as for instance the *Collins COBUILD English Dictionary* (1995).
(4) Appropriately, as regards information on word appropriateness, through usage labels such as formal, slightly formal, informal, slang (rude or taboo), as provided, for instance, by the *Cambridge Dictionary of American English* (2000)?
(5) Humanisingly, by being sensitised to the constructive, human-digni-

fying power of words and by being helped to make use of such hitherto little-explored vocabulary?

Learners' grammatical rights

Do I assure my learners of their right to:

(1) Ask for and receive clear, grammatical explanations on the interconnected dimensions of form, meaning and use? (Celce-Murcia & Larsen-Freeman, 1999)
(2) Know what their teacher's perception of grammar is, especially how pedagogically, descriptively, prescriptively, eclectically or communicatively oriented it is?
(3) Receive constructive, humanising feedback on their grammatical errors, with an emphasis on appropriateness, acceptability and grammaticality, rather than only on correctness?
(4) Learn to develop as grammatically secure L2 learners?
(5) Learn how to go on building up and refining their grammatical proficiency as autonomous learners?
(6 Learn grammar 'as related to the study of texts and responsive to social purposes?' (Carter, 1997)
(7) Receive a glossary of the key grammatical terms that their teacher will use in the course?
(8) Receive not only discursive but visual explanations, given that 'Human experience is now more visual and visualised that ever before' (Mirzoeff, 1999)? (For a recent example of 'Visual Grammar' in a textbook series, see Gammidge, 1998.)

The above examples have been taken from Gomes de Matos and Celce Murcia (1998), Gomes de Matos (1999) and Gomes de Matos (2000e). For an up-date on learners' pronunciation rights – views by language educators and linguists from several countries – see Gomes de Matos (2000e).

Expanding the range of second language learners' rights

Learners' rights are a challenging and thought-provoking subject – especially if one considers that, although some traditions in L2 education have been characterised as humanistic (see the entry on humanistic approaches in Johnson & Johnson, 1998), a systematic human-rights-based Pedagogy of Second Language Education is still in its infancy. This is despite noteworthy related efforts such as the UNESCO-FIPLV Linguapax Project and my own *Plea for Humanisation* (Gomes de Matos, 1996), which has been reiterated at events such as the FIPLV XIX World Congress in Recife in 1997 and the TESOL Convention in Vancouver, 2000.

That learners' rights can have their range explored can be easily shown, once one's typological creativity is duly exercised, on the basis of personal experience or under the inspiration of varied works in the specialised literature. The following paragraphs give just three examples of expanded types of rights. Researchers in applied linguistics and L2 education are urged to further probe this hitherto little-explored multidimensional domain within what I prefer to call 'humanised second language education', since in this case, language educators are seen as 'humanisers', as detailed earlier.

Expanded type 1: Learners' right as Internet users

As educators, let's ask ourselves if our learners have the right to learn to communicate on the Internet and to identify and use high-frequency (creative) spellings – such as 'ASAP' for 'as soon as possible'.

Expanded type 2: Learners' rights as text comprehenders and producers

Are we, in our classroom ecosystems, able to assure learners of their right to use both verbal and visual representational modes or to learn how to translate verbal-only messages into multimedia messages, or further still to learn to process verbal and visual representations more effectively and, last but not least, to learn the principles and practices of computer literacy, so as to navigate on the Web and make the most of what is offered to L2 learners? (For an inspiring source of related rights, see Windeatt *et al.*, 2000.)

Expanded type 3: Learners' rights as testees or examinees

How would we fare, as second-language educators, when it comes to these rights? Even with the pioneering, painstaking, praiseworthy effort of the International Language Testing Association's recent Code of Ethics, much is to be done if we are to become humanising testers and examiners in the deepest sense of the term. Do our learners – as testees – have the right to know to what extent the test reflects an error-oriented, a non-judgemental, or an eclectic evaluative approach or if the evaluation tool will focus predominantly on tasks and contents that were actually experienced in class? In short, do learners-as-examinees have the right to know if the form-meanings-uses found in the test are similar to those practiced in class? For more examples, see Gomes de Matos (2000b).

Teacher Education/training and Learners' Rights: A Look at the Twenty-First Century

In the macro-issue of L2 learners' rights, what priority actions could be anticipated for the early and mid-21st century in different educational, cultural, linguistic, psychological, political and social contexts all over the world? How can such an exercise in foretelling the future pay off for the universal community of learners, teachers and teacher–educators in a spirit of cooperation across cultures? Given the still-exploratory condition of such rights – within the gradually but steadily advancing movement in favor of linguistic human rights – how can the potentially humanising force of a learners' rights Theory-and-Practice be incorporated into teacher training programs? Granted that there may be limits to such rights, because of the power of corresponding responsibilities and other factors, what kinds of scenarios or landscapes can be envisaged for the next decades? What could a curriculum in democratic, communicative citizenship look like, as far as L2 learners' rights are concerned and why? For an overview of a broader topic – a humanising literacy curriculum (see Corson, 1999).

To help language educators, curriculum planners and policy makers as agents of human rights, democracy and peace, those who wish to influence the future need should not only consider how this chapter's central issue could be discussed in congresses, seminar, workshops and other kinds of awareness-consciousness-raising events. More importantly, to help them plan for the early decades of the new millennium, here is an open-ended checklist inspired by the commitment to making deeply humanising changes happen in twenty-first century classrooms. The sequence of key questions is meant to suggest possibilities, and it is not hierarchically organised. Complementary checklists can also be created on factors that will not be dealt with here.

A 'how-to' checklist

(1) How can language learners' rights-awareness campaigns be designed, implemented and sustained in schools at all decision-making levels? Given the significance of shared negotiation in the classroom, how can teachers 'give voice to students in the management of their learning', as Breen and Littlejohn (2000) cogently remind us?

(2) How can learners, teachers, and teacher–educators, materials writers, curriculum planners, etc. be prepared for acting effectively for their strategic roles as promoters of learners' rights and responsibilities?

(3) How can information be disseminated, clearly and objectively, through the media so that the community at large learns about learn-

ers' rights as an additional democratic prerogative to be assured to all students, regardless of age, cognitive maturity, language-culture-ethnic origin, socioeconomic and physical condition, etc?

(4) How can educational, (inter)cultural, and linguistic rights of L2 learners be included in university undergraduate and graduate programmes, such as those in Second Language Education (acquisition/learning), Applied Linguistics, etc?

(5) How could data banks be organised (both within educational organisations and among them) so as to document and disseminate relevant information on causes and consequences of a learners' rights policy for schools, or more, specifically, on violations of such rights and on case-based studies of how specific problems were identified, diagnosed and solved?

(6) How can new, innovative, interdisciplinary methodologies be proposed and applied for research in planning-and-policy concerning the influence of learners' rights in both learner and teacher performance, humanisation, etc?

(7) How can the respectable traditions in L2 education be further humanised, through the approach advocated here and other ways of learning–teaching second languages for communicating constructively? How can the principle that 'communicating well is communicating for the well-being of humankind' be integrated into linguistic humanising practices in classrooms where learners' and teachers' rights are recognised and respected?

(8) How can today's teacher–learner contracts and the like make way for deeply transforming actions enhancing the need for educating for the communicative rights and responsibilities of human beings?

Let us give one brief demonstration of how learners may formulate rights in the classroom. Two 13-year-old Brazilian learners of French were asked by their teacher 'What rights would you like me to assure you of in your French language class?' They replied: 'I'd like to have the right to communicate with French students, through an exchange between students' associations' and 'I'd like to be able to have the right to learn another language (English) upon conclusion of this grade'. The pairing of teacher-formulated and student-generated 'rights', of either group, can prove educationally inspiring to language educators and to those in charge of teacher education programs. Indeed, have we language teachers been documenting what our learners would consider to be their rights (linguistic, intercultural, etc.) as well as their responsibilities? Why (not)? Have we been going beyond such documentation to implementing rights in our classrooms? What effects could such decision-making have on learning conditions?

Establishing learners' rights and responsibilities calls for a spirit, a feeling of mutual trust, respect, and sharing in the classroom, between students and teacher. If we accept that communicating is an act of sharing, then it follows that classroom-decision making on such crucial issues as 'rights and responsibilities' is an equally shared enterprise. The formulation of such rights and responsibilities calls for an awareness that the classroom is first and foremost a 'humanising community', to be shared, cared for and sustained by its dwellers. The establishment of rights and responsibilities for both learners and teachers – expressing the former without the latter would be a distortion, to say the least – calls for these preparatory steps, presented through checklists such as the following. As a language educator:

(1) How well do I know my students, and how well do they know me, in terms of systems of beliefs, attitudes, etc? What do I know about their characteristics (age, literacy background, previous 'conditions of learning', especially prior L2 learning, etc.)?

(2) How can we learn more about each other – in the very first class interaction? What strategy should we use for gathering 'biographical information' on the classroom community members? What would be the indispensable minimum individual bio-data for the group to discuss the desirability of implementing learners' and teacher's rights and responsibilities in class?

(3) How could the group be initially prepared for discussing such rights and responsibilities? In a Brazilian cultural context, for instance, a warm-up phase could consist of a discussion of 'consumer rights' (often mentioned by the media). Minimal information on 'human rights', the core family, for example: civic-political-social-political-cultural rights would be mentioned and Article 19 (UDHR), on 'the right to freedom of opinion and expression' could be presented and related to the new notion of 'linguistic/communicative rights'. I have been achieving this by introducing the concept of 'linguistic rights' to language teachers, the overwhelming majority of whom have never heard or read the 1948 Universal Declaration of Human Rights. In short, planning how to establish learners' and teacher's rights and responsibilities in a classroom calls for a carefully-designed lesson plan on how to show that linguistic rights are a new (generic) member in the family of human rights and, as such, can be represented by very

specific types of rights, such as mother tongue users' rights, L2 users' rights, etc.

(4) In conducting activities aimed at rights and responsibilities awareness (conscientisation, as Paulo Freire would put it), the notions of learners' interests, preferences, and needs would be related to rights and responsibilities. A discussion could be centred on why the former are necessary, but insufficient, for assuring the functioning of classroom interaction as a responsible, humanising community. Twentieth century Second Language Education went through stages centred first on expected learners' goals (teachers' manuals everywhere seem to have been written on the basis of such 'expectancies of learner performance'), then on presumed learners' needs (the Needs Analysis emphasis in the 70s is testimony to that). They then focused on learners' strategies (the growing number of learner-generated or teacher-motivated strategies is a remarkable development of the last two decades), and more recently on learners' negotiated participation (Breen & Littlejohn, 2000). The last example shows that there is under way an approximation to what I would call a 'learners' rights and responsibilities' consciousness. In short, as regards L2 teachers being prepared to fulfil their roles as classroom humanisers, I am optimistic that the twenty-first century will be an age in which the systematic, cooperatively planned, implementation of learners' and teachers' rights and responsibilities will fundamentally alter and improve the way in which human beings learn to use second languages.

An 'ideal humanising classroom community' would be one in which:

(1) Learners and teacher would have agreed on a charter (a document, whatever name given to it) that stated their respective rights and responsibilities as L2 learners and teachers (note that Hammerly (1985) features a Bill of Rights for language learners, but not for teachers).

(2) Learners would know how to appeal against the teacher's (seemingly unfair) decisions (in this case, learners would know what types of evidence to submit to appeal against a decision that he or she did not agree with – such as seemingly questionable 'test scores'). In short, by the middle of the twenty-first century, I foresee L2 learners as having rights and responsibilities duly expressed (at a school level, at least), and implemented, especially 'educational, linguistic, and intercultural rights' – a vision of major humanising transformations ahead. Similarly, students and teachers will know what their responsibilities are.

In dealing with learners' rights, it is well to remember that, since they are value-and-belief-laden, teachers, teacher educators, school administrators, language education policy makers and others in the community may have different reactions to such educational-linguistic-cultural prerogatives. Reactions may be displayed in a continuum ranging from acceptance to rejection. In between we would find indifference, partial resistance and scepticism. The latter type of attitude is found especially among those who argue that, by granting a student a particular right, we are necessarily committing ourselves to an obligation or a responsibility and that such 'privilege' could have an undesirable cost, as regards teacher-decision-making in the classroom. I have heard this type of doubting comment from teachers and from teacher–educators and agreeing with them on the first part of their reasoning – after all, every right is linked to a corresponding responsibility whether by the benefactor of the right or by the person who grants such right. However, I must question their resistance to the humanising practice we have advocated, since it seems to show that 'undesirable cost' means 'not being ready to share such decision-making with learners' or, to put it more directly, 'not wanting to turn the classroom into a democratically-managed, humanising community'.

To end on an optimistic tone: judging by the emerging interest in the issue of Learners' Rights Studies, and by its gradual, but steady rate of growth, this domain of educational-linguistic-political action is to expand in the course of the twenty-furst century. I hope that the facts and reflections shared here will contribute, no matter how modestly, to making persons and institutions perceive L2 learners' rights not simply as an issue, but also as an indispensable, humanising component in language education. It may be that by 2010 or so the rights of L2 learners will be included in the accumulated wisdom of the right ways of learning. When learners' (and teachers') rights find their permanent place in the educational sun, our challengingly fascinating mission of co-educating human beings to learn a second language will help us become true 'humanisers' who carry on, enhance and transcend what 'humanists' achieved before us.

Acknowledgement

I would like to thank Vivian Cook for his friendly, untiring and insightful editing, especially for his comments, which have made my manuscript hopefully more processable, and for having enhanced my self-image as a non-native user of English. I am also grateful to my friend and colleague Ana Falcão for her expertise in the electronic preparation of my text for publication.

References

Batley, E., Candelier, M., Hermann-Brennecke, G. and Szepe, G. (1993) *Language Policies for the World of the Twenty-First Century.* Paris: Unesco.

Blaustein, A.P. and Epstein, D.B. (1986) *Resolving Language Conflicts: A Study of the World's Constitutions.* Washington, DC: US English.

Breen, M.P. and Littlejohn, A. (eds) (2000) *Classroom-decision Making: Negotiation and Process Syllabuses in Practice.* Cambridge: Cambridge University Press.

Cambridge Dictionary of American English (2000). Cambridge: Cambridge University Press.

Carter, R. (1997) *Investigating English Discourse.* London: Routledge.

Celce-Murcia, M. and Larsen-Freeman, D. (1999) *The Grammar Book: An ESL/EFL Teacher's Course.* Boston: Heinle & Heinle.

COBUILD English Dictionary (1995). London: Harper Collins.

Cohen, A. (1998) *Strategies for Learning and Using Languages.* London: Longman.

Corson, D. (1999) *Language Policy in Schools: A Resource for Teachers and Administrators.* Mahwah, New Jersey: Lawrence Erlbaum.

Crystal, D. (1997) *The Cambridge Encyclopedia of Language* (2nd edn). Cambridge: Cambridge University Press.

Crystal, D. (1999) *Penguin Dictionary of Language* (2nd edn). London: Penguin.

Deutsch, M. (2000) Justice and conflict. In M. Deutsch and P. Robinson (eds) *The Handbook of Conflict Resolution: Theory and Practice.* San Francisco: Jossey-Bass.

Ellis, G. and Sinclair, B. (1989) *Learning to Learn English. A Course in Learning Training. Teacher's Book.* Cambridge: Cambridge University Press.

Freire, P. (1970) *Pedagogia do Oprimido.* Rio de Janeiro: Editora Paz e Terra. (Published in English in 1972, by Penguin.)

Freire, P. (1996) *Pedagogia da Autonomia* (Pedagogy of Autonomy) (15th edn). São Paulo: Terra e Paz.

Gammidge, M. (1998) *Grammar Work: Student´s Book 1.* Cambridge: Cambridge University Press.

Gomes de Matos, F. (1984a) *Por uma Declaração dos Direitos Lingüísticos Individuais.* Petrópolis: Revista de Cultura Vozes, Março.

Gomes de Matos, F. (1984b) A plea for a language rights declaration. *FIPLV World News,* April. Paris: FIPLV/UNESCO (Alsed Programme).

Gomes de Matos, F. (1984c) *A Importância dos Aireitos Lingüísticos do Aprendi: Interação – A Revista do Professor* (June–July). Sao Paulo: Instituto de Idiomas Yázigi.

Gomes de Matos, F. (1985) The linguistic rights of language learners. *Language Planning Newsletter,* August.

Gomes de Matos, F. (1986) A gap in ESL pedagogy: Learners' rights. *TESOL Newsletter,* April.

Gomes de Matos, F. (1991) Learners' rights: Probing a new frontier in language teaching. In *Grenzenloses Sprachenlerner: Festschrift fur Reinhold Freudenstein* (pp. 270–275). Berlin: Cornelsen and Oxford University Press.

Gomes de Matos, F. (1994) A thesis 20 years on: Principles of linguistics and the theory-praxis of the rights of language learners. In L. Barbara and M. Scott (eds) *Reflections on Language Learning: In Honour of Antonieta Celani* (pp. 105–109). Clevedon: Multilingual Matters.

Gomes de Matos, F. (1996) Human rights and the history of language teaching: A plea for humanization. *FIPLV WORLD News*, April.

Gomes de Matos, F. (1999) Learners' vocabulary rights. *BRAZ-TESOL Newsletter*, December.

Gomes de Matos, F. (2000a) Learners' grammatical rights. *Materials Writers Interest Section Newsletter*, January, 3.

Gomes de Matos, F. (2000b) Learners' rights as test takers: A checklist. *New Routes in ELT*. São Paulo: DISAL (Distribuidores de Livros Associados).

Gomes de Matos, F. (2000c) Harmonizing and humanizing political discourse: The contribution of peace linguists. *Peace & Conflict: Journal of Peace Psychology* 6 (4) December, 339–344.

Gomes de Matos, F. (2000d) Introduction: Learner centred concepts. Special issue of *Speak Out* (IATEFL Pronunciation Group) 25, 44–49.

Gomes de Matos, F. (2000e) Learners' rights revisited. Special issue on The Americas, *Speak Out, IATEFL Newsletter* (Pronunciation SIG).

Gomes de Matos, F. and Celce-Murcia, M. (1998) Learners' pronunciation rights: A checklist. *BRAZ-TESOL Newsletter*, September, 14–15.

Grant, N. (1987) *Making the Most of your Textbook*. London: Longman.

Hammerly, H. (1985) *An Integrated Theory of Language Teaching and its Practical Consequences*. Blaine, Washington: Second Language Publications.

Johnson, K. and Johnson, H. (1998) *Encyclopedic Dictionary of Applied Linguistics. A Handbook for Language Teaching*. Oxford: Blackwell.

Kern, R. (2000) *Literacy and Language Teaching*. Oxford: Oxford University Press.

Mirzoeff, N. (1999) *Introduction to Visual Studies*. London: Routledge.

Moskowitz, G. (1978) *Caring and Sharing in the FL Class: A Sourcebook on Humanistic Techniques*. Rowley, MA: Newbury House.

Oxford, R. (1990) *Language Learning Strategies: What Every Teacher Should Know*. Rowley, MA: Newbury House.

Rivers, W. (1968) *Teaching Foreign Language Skills*. Chicago: University of Chicago Press.

Sinclair, J. (1992) *Introduction to Collins COBUILD English Usage*. London: Harper Collins.

Skutnabb-Kangas, T. (2000) *Linguistic Genocide in Education or Worldwide Diversity and Human Rights?* Mahwah, NJ: Erlbaum.

UDLR (1996) *Universal Declaration of Linguistic Rights*. Barcelona: Ciemen and Pen Club. On-line at: http://www.linguistic-declaration.org/index-gb.htm.

Windeatt, S., Hardisty, D. and Eastment, D. (2000) *The Internet*. Oxford: Oxford University Press.

Introduction to Chapter 13

Language Teaching Methodology and the L2 User Perspective, Vivian Cook

VIVIAN COOK

The aim of most of this book is to describe L2 users as they are. This chapter, however, looks at how some L2 users are created through language teaching; it is concerned with students being prepared to be L2 users, not with L2 users in general. It looks at some of the consequences for teaching of taking the rights of L2 users to be L2 users seriously, building on a series of papers (Cook, 1998, 1999a, 1999b, 2001, to appear), on Chapter 1 and on several of the other chapters.

The pioneers in second language acquisition (SLA) research such as Pit Corder, Robert Lado and Rod Ellis often came from a teaching background and saw the field *inter alia* as a vehicle for improving language teaching. A typical introduction to SLA claims that 'One of the fundamental goals of SLA research is to facilitate and expedite the SLA process' (Larsen-Freeman & Long, 1991: 6). However SLA research rapidly tried to establish its autonomy from teaching, to the extent that Newmeyer and Weinberger (1988: 42) thought that concern with pedagogy 'has slowed down the development of second language acquisition as an independent discipline'. SLA research in a sense fell for linguistics on the rebound from language teaching; some researchers treat second language acquisition primarily as a source of data for testing linguistics descriptions and theories rather than as being interesting in its own right, or indeed as something with practical implications for teaching.

SLA research can come into contact with language teaching in many dimensions, via syllabuses that specify *what* should be taught, methodology that says *how* it should be taught, course books that instantiate syllabuses and methods, examinations and tests that measure how well the goals are achieved, education programmes for the students and the teachers themselves, and so on. This chapter primarily emphasises the consequences of the L2 user perspective on the teaching syllabus and methodology.

References

Cook, V.J. (1998) Relating SLA research to language teaching materials. *Canadian Journal of Applied Linguistics* 1 (1/2), 9–27. On-line at: http://www.aclacaal.org/.

Cook, V.J. (1999a) Going beyond the native speaker in language teaching. *TESOL Quarterly* 33 (2), 185–209.

Cook, V.J. (1999b) Creating L2 users. *Jurnal Kurikulum* 1 (2), Curriculum Development Centre Kuala Lumpur. On-line document: http://www.ppk.kpm.my/abstract_bil2_99_vivian.htm.

Cook, V.J. (2001) Using the first language in the classroom. *Canadian Modern Language Review* 57 (3), 402–423.

Cook, V.J. (to appear) Materials for adult beginners. In B. Tomlinson (ed.) *Issues in Materials Design*. London: Continuum Press.

Larsen-Freeman, D. and Long, M. (1991) *An Introduction to Second Language Acquisition Research*. London & New York: Longman.

Newmeyer, F.J. and Weinberger, S.H. (1988) The ontogenesis of the field of second language language research. In S. Flynn and W. O'Neil (eds) *Linguistic Theory in Second Language Acquisition* (pp. 34–45). Dordrecht: Kluwer.

Chapter 13

Language Teaching Methodology and the L2 User Perspective

VIVIAN COOK

The adoption of a view based on the independence of the L2 user has radical implications for language teaching. This chapter focuses particularly on the distinct roles and uses of language that the students have and on the effects that a second language has upon the person learning it. First, however, we need to see something of the climate of language teaching today as reflected in its teaching methods and goals.

The Twentieth Century Language Teaching Consensus

Throughout the twentieth century, much language teaching was unified around the tenets of the late nineteenth century Reform Movement (Howatt, 1984). Diverse teaching methods shared assumptions that were seldom questioned and only rarely discussed in public. Among those listed in Cook (2001a) are:

- the supremacy of the spoken language over the written language;
- the avoidance of the first language in the classroom;
- the pointlessness of discussing grammar explicitly in teaching;
- the presentation of language through dialogues and texts rather than decontextualised sentences.

Whether the overall paradigm was called direct method, situational teaching, audiolingualism, audiovisualism, communicative language teaching or task-based learning, there was a consensus among twentieth century language teaching about certain general aspects of language and language learning embodied in these assumptions. The only assumption to have been relaxed in recent years is the avoidance of explicit grammar, now justified by FonF or Focus on Form (Long, 1991), which uses it as a follow-up to communicative activities rather than as the main point of the lesson. A late addition to this set of assumptions originating from the audio-visual methods of the 1940s was the division of language into the four skills of listening, speaking, reading and writing. This division has served ever since, not only as a basis for dividing up the tasks of teaching, but also as the sequence for teaching the skills – passive (listening and reading) before active (speaking and writing), spoken (listening and speaking) before written (reading and writing).

At every period a few mavericks went against this consensus, including the Reading Method used in the USA in the 1920s (Coleman, 1929), the use of Free Voluntary Reading as a form of comprehensible input (Krashen, 1993), or Dodson's Bilingual Method. The last-named was used in Wales in the 1960s (Dodson, 1967) and employed the L1 to convey the meaning of sentences of the L2. In some ways these common assumptions necessarily reflect the official face of language teaching rather than what actually happens in the classroom. Teachers probably transgress each of them every day of their working lives. Nevertheless they represented the mainstream public face of most language teaching throughout the twentieth century, which continues to be the official policy for classrooms around the globe. For example, the emphasis on L2 in the classroom is found in the Quebec English syllabus '... l'apprentissage de l'anglais ... exige que ... l'anglais soit la langue d'usage' (Ministère de l'Education, 2000), the English curriculum in Cuba emphasises 'The principle of the primacy of spoken language' (Cuban Ministry of Education, 1999), and the UK National Curriculum for Modern Languages (DfEE, 1999) uses the sequence of the four skills: 'During key stage 3 pupils begin to understand, speak, read and write at least one modern foreign language.' All these examples officially stand by the consensus.

The only consistent anti-movement was the academic teaching of languages through grammar explanation and translation, which has survived underground in many classrooms despite official censures. Coleman (1996) found that the grammar/translation method 'was clearly the most popular approach to language teaching in the universities' when he entered university teaching in England. While the grammar/translation paradigm is usually called 'traditional' language teaching, the true twentieth century tradition was this consensus of nineteenth century assumptions from the Reform Movement, as all-pervasive and restrictive as any operating system sold by Microsoft.

These shared assumptions still allowed for brand differentiation between teaching methods. Emphasise the importance of language use and you get the communicative method; prioritise the listening skill and you get the Natural Approach; add some behaviourist ideas of learning and you get audiolingualism; give the student tasks to carry out and you get task-based learning. Important as such differences may be, a visitor from a previous century might have been struck by the similarity between these classrooms. An English coursebook from 1910 says 'It is assumed throughout that the teacher ... uses the language of his audience as little as possible, his success being judged by the rarity of his lapses into the foreign tongue' (Thorley, 1918: p.vii). Eighty years later the UK National Curriculum in 1990 asserts 'The natural use of the target language for virtually all communication is a sure sign of a good modern language course' (DES, 1990: 58). The central assumptions changed little in the twentieth century, with the exceptions of FonF and the continual twilight existence of the grammar/translation method. As a rule, at the beginning of the twenty-first century, language teaching classrooms are still supposed to emphasise the spoken language, to avoid the first language and grammatical explanation and to practice language in whole dialogues rather than in isolated fragments – however different actual classroom practice may be.

Though largely implicit in the discussion, the goal set for students was mostly to get as close as possible to monolingual native speakers. The situations they encountered in books were those based on monolingual native speakers; the teachers that were most acceptable were native speakers: the monolingual native speaker rules OK? 'After all, the ultimate goal – perhaps unattainable for some – is, nonetheless, to "sound like a native speaker" in all aspects of the language' (González-Nueno, 1997: 261). The independent-grammars assumption put forward by SLA researchers in the 1970s had to some extent freed teaching methodology from audiolingual beliefs: the communicative method relied on the learners creating grammars of their own through language exchanges in the classroom. But the grammars they had to create were supposed to be like those of native speakers, not unique things of their own, as illustrated in the background chapter.

Multiple Goals of Language Teaching

Language teaching sets out to achieve an implicit or explicit set of goals, whether for the students or for the society (Cook, 2001a). A second language may be taught *inter alia* as:

- a vehicle to self-development, as in Community Language Learning;
- a method of training new cognitive processes, as in the rationale for the teaching of Latin;
- a way-in to the mother tongue;
- an entrée to the culture of another group;
- a form of religious observance, as in the use of Arabic, Hebrew or Latin, or indeed, in some parts of the world, English;

- a means of enabling people to communicate with those who speak another language.

To these can be added:

- a way of promoting intercultural understanding and peace (seen in the chapter by Gomes de Matos).

Most language teaching tries to cover a selection of these goals. For example the UK national guidelines for language teaching (HMSO, 1995) include most of the above goals. Some syllabuses go further; English in Malaysia is intended to encourage the virtues of 'good citizenship, moral values and the Malaysian way of life' (Kementarian Pendidikan Malaysia, 1987). Apart perhaps from communication, most of these goals do not necessitate comparison with the native speaker, but are concerned with the educational values of the second language for the learner.

A crucial distinction must be made between *external* and *internal* goals of language teaching (Cook, 1983, 2001a). External goals relate to actual L2 use outside the classroom: being able to buy a coffee when you go on holiday to a foreign country, being able to negotiate contracts with foreign businesspeople, being able to provide legal advice to minority groups in your own country, and so on. Internal goals relate to the educational aims of the classroom itself: having better attitudes towards speakers of other languages, being able to carry out projects in groups, helping with mental illness, and many others. Both external and internal goals are officially recognised in most syllabuses for language teaching. The UK National Curriculum includes external goals such as developing 'the ability to use the language effectively for the purposes of practical communication' and internal goals such as promoting 'learning of skills of more general application (e.g. analysis, memorising, drawing of inferences)' (DES, 1990). A crucial internal goal is the Freirean use of language teaching as a vehicle for politicisation of the oppressed (Wallerstein, 1983).

The diversity of teaching goals is stressed here because of the emphasis in the twentieth century consensus on external goals of 'behaving' in the L2 environment (whether in audiolingual situations or in communicative exchanges), rather than the internal goals of better cultural attitudes or greater cognitive flexibility. Ellis (1996: 74), for example, assumes that 'LP [language pedagogy] is concerned with the ability to use language in communicative situations'; in other words the point of language teaching is to help the students communicate. Nevertheless, in many educational systems, communication is only one among many overt or covert goals, often a subsidiary or far-distant goal; few students of English in Japan, for instance, can realistically expect to use the language for spoken communication. A model of the L2 user is relevant for teaching goals that envisage students either taking part in external L2 use situations or being transformed internally by the contact with another language. It has little relevance to, say, a student who wants to acquire an academic knowledge of the structure and semantics of another language.

The Nature of the L2 User

This section takes certain features of the L2 user perspective, most of which are encountered elsewhere in this book, and looks at the extent to which they relate to the twentieth century consensus in language teaching.

(A) L2 students have the right to become L2 users

The starting point is the right of L2 users to be L2 users, argued in Chapter 1 and in the chapter by Gomes de Matos (Chapter 12). Much in teaching has tugged the L2 student towards the native speaker, a construct that has political and ethical overtones of the power of natives over non-natives (Holliday, 1994; Phillipson, 1992). This is not to deny that, because of the institutionalised values put on native speakers in the West, such attitudes are widespread nor that it is an inevitable part of the human condition to judge others by what they are not. But there is no reason why any serious area of scientific study such as SLA research should accept value judgements based on discrimination against one group.

If L2 learners feel that the chief measure of L2 success is passing for native, few are going to meet it. Both teachers and students become frustrated by setting themselves what is in effect an impossible target, ugly ducklings regretting they will never become ducks without appreciating that they are really cygnets. Halliday (1968: 165), speaking of dialects, said, 'A speaker who is made ashamed of his own language habits suffers a basic injury as a human being: to make anyone, especially a child, feel so ashamed is as indefensible as to make him feel ashamed of the colour of his skin'. Yet L2 users have continually been made ashamed by their inability to meet the native-based aims of language teaching. Though it is hard to generalise for the multiplicity of global contexts for language teaching, teaching has rarely explicitly suggested that there are targets other than native speakers to aim at.

The next four sections essentially interpret the statements about the L2 user made in Chapter 1 (in the 'Characteristics of L2 Users' section) in terms of language teaching.

(B) The L2 user has other uses for language than the monolingual

One of the lessons from the other chapters is that L2 users use language differently from monolinguals. Many L2 users, for example, use translation in their lives. The twentieth century consensus of language teaching largely excluded translation from the classroom, partly because teaching supported avoidance of the L1, partly because it needed to distance itself from the scorned grammar/translation method. Yet there is no necessary connection between using translation in the classroom and having translation as an end-goal of teaching. A belief that translation does not work as a teaching technique is not incompatible with accepting that some students wish to be translators. As Malakoff and Hakuta (1991: 163) say, 'translation provides an easy avenue to enhance linguistic awareness and pride in bilingualism'.

The twentieth century consensus also ignored the nature of the L2 user situation in general. L2 uses seldom correspond completely to L1 uses. An L2 user is often an intermediary between two cultures and two peoples. The jobs for which people need second languages in the developed world often reflect this, whether the travel rep at a holiday resort or the executive forced to use English at a high level in an international company. It would be impossible to live in multilingual countries such as Pakistan or the Cameroon without using more than one language. These L2 users are not people trying to imitate the behaviours of native speakers; and indeed they may never have met a native speaker; they are L2 users carrying out their ordinary lives through several languages.

One of the chief characteristics of L2 users is that they code-switch from one language to another in mid-speech in order to carry out a range of social and psychological functions to do with the social roles of the participants, the topics they are talking about, and so on. Code-switching proper is possible only when both participants are aware that they share the same two languages. Potentially the classroom is a code-switching situation par excellence since the students all know two languages. The twentieth century teaching consensus however tried to discourage code-switching in the classroom (Cook, 2001b). The usually-unstated belief is that students would fare better if they kept to the second language, i.e. a coordinate relationship in which the languages in the mind are kept in separate compartments. The L2 user perspective suggests, however, that in general teachers should recognise the classroom as an L2 user situation. In particular, they should develop the systematic use of the L1 in the classroom alongside the L2 as a reflection of the realities of the classroom situation, as an aid to learning and as a model for the world outside. The exceptions in practice are multilingual classes in which the students do not share the same first language, say many adult EFL classes in England. In this case code-switching is obviously excluded from teaching because the participants do not share the same two languages, particularly when monolingual native speaker teachers are preferred.

(C) The L2 users' knowledge of the second language is not identical to that of a native speaker

Language teaching has mostly assumed that the language to be taught should be that of native speakers, whether pronunciation, grammar or vocabulary. Vocabulary is selected for teaching on the basis of its frequency in native speech, not in L2 user speech or even in speech addressed to L2 users. Grammatical structures for teaching are selected from the description of native speech or writing, not that of L2 users. While the examples of native speech and writing that are presented to the student are often simplified, native-like speech is required from the outset, even if in a suitably simplified form (Cook, 1970). In other words, students are usually supposed to say *I live in France* not *Me live France* in the classroom. Success in external goals is measured against the perceived norms of the native speaker. Only a vanishing small percentage of students ever come close to the 'success' of duplicating native attainment.

(D) The L2 users' knowledge of their first language is not the same as that of a monolingual

A characteristic of L2 users that is now fairly well attested is the difference between their knowledge of their first language and that of monolingual native speakers. So far as language teaching is concerned, this may have little relevance. Effects on the first language are of interest only in so far as they contribute to the general 'civilising' goals mentioned below. Knowing about another language helps one both with one's first language and with knowing about the nature of language itself, for example the ability to 'understand and apply patterns, rules and exceptions in language forms and structures' (DES, 1990). At best, students may feel reassured to learn that they are not alone if their L1 competence is changing.

(E) L2 users have different minds from monolinguals

As we have seen in several of the chapters, the L2 user thinks in different ways from the monolingual. The relationship to teaching has for once little to do with the twentieth century teaching consensus but harks back to earlier beliefs about the civilising values of learning a second language. One of the attributes of an English eighteenth-century gentleman was the ability to speak other languages, usually French, and this is still perhaps visible in the twentieth century in, say, T.S. Eliot's use of quotations in other languages.

> London Bridge is falling down
> *Poi s'ascose nel foco che gli affina*
> *Quando fiam uti chelidon*—O swallow swallow
> *Le Prince d'Aquitaine á la tour aboli* (T.S. Eliot, *The Waste Land*, V)

(Indeed students of mine with L1 Italian and French have difficulties with these quotations!) Learning a second language improved the status and mental powers of the elite, even if it was dangerous for those of lesser status such as immigrants. Hence a twentieth century justification for teaching Latin was still 'brain-training'; powers of thought are sharpened by the rigorous discipline of mastering another language, particularly through formal traditional grammar. This goal of cognitive improvement still surfaces in some educational systems. The alternative 'civilising' goal of greater cultural awareness is again frequently mentioned in language-teaching syllabuses. In Japan, for instance, it is seen as 'an interest in language and culture' (Tokyo, 1990), in the UK as the ability 'to recognise cultural attitudes as expressed in language and learn the use of social conventions' (HMSO, 1995), and in Malaysia as producing 'courage, honesty, charity and unity' (Kementarian Pendidikan Malaysia, 1987).

Yet the internal goals seldom figured overtly in twentieth century teaching except in a broad sense. Instead it consistently emphasised external goals, whether the ability to behave in situations of the audio-lingual or situational methods or the ability to communicate of the commu-nicative methods. Language teaching was seen as social or physical activity rather than as mental activity; students want to learn to interact and to communicate, not to think better. On the surface, task-based learning and strategy-based learning seem to go further towards recognising that students have minds. Yet both have effectively concentrated on the use of tasks and strategies for their own sake, not for their pay-off in increased cognitive flexibility. The L2 user perspective reminds us that teaching is concerned with changing students' minds, hopefully for the better.

Application of L2 user concepts to teaching

Let us now try to put forward some concrete proposals for language teaching based on the concepts of the L2 user proposed above.

The external goals of language teaching should be related to the L2 user, not to the native speaker

As we have seen, language teaching has usually stressed external goals at the expense of internal goals. Audiolingual teaching emphasised speaking automatically in situations (Lado, 1964), communicative language teaching emphasised the exchange of information and the building of social relationships (Littlewood, 1981). These goals were identified with the native speaker's use of language. Task-based learning on the other hand has had no particular external goals; while it has seen its job as developing the classroom use of language, it has not tackled the general civilising aspects of language teaching in education.

If L2 users have the right to be themselves (A), to use language differently from monolinguals (B), and to have different knowledge of the second language from that of monolingual native speakers (C), it is impossible to maintain external goals based only on the native speaker. Instead the students should aim at being proficient L2 users. At present there are no adequate descriptions of successful L2 user goals. It may of course be that no single L2 user goal will suffice but that, rather like English for Specific Purposes, teachers need in principle to specify where, when and why each student needs to use the second language before settling on their goals. But the logic is nevertheless that teachers should aim at getting people to use the second language effectively.

One consequence is that teaching should help the students with L2 uses of language, most obviously translation and code-switching, as we saw above. If these are normal activities for L2 users, students deserve to be helped to carry them out by teaching. Teaching methods that have employed translation, such as the *Bilingual Method* (Dodson, 1967), and code-switching, such as the *New Concurrent Approach* (Jacobson & Faltis, 1990), have, however, related these to learning rather than to the learner's final goals. There is a difference between using them as codebreaking processes in learning and using them for decoding language as part of final behaviour. While not all L2 users need these bilingual skills, they nevertheless form valid external goals for some students. What is valid for all students is the idea that L2 use differs from L1 use to some degree.

The crucial implication for education is ensuring that the standards against which L2 users are measured should be L2 user standards, not L1 native speaker standards. Success should be measured by the ability to use the second language effectively. The Institute of Linguists examinations show one way of achieving this by using tests that depend on the conjunction of both the second language and the first (Institute of Linguists, 1988).

For example a recent intermediate Italian exam makes the student act as a journalist working for a religious newspaper that has received an Italian newspaper article; the student has to summarise the relevant points for the editor. Both languages are relevant to the task, yet translation itself is not involved. The student is being tested as an L2 user, capable of bridging two languages, rather than on the level of their second language alone.

This is not of course to say that abandoning the native speaker standard would be easy to do. Rather than the single standard of the native speaker against which the L2 user can be measured, there may have to be multiple standards to accommodate the variety of L2 users. In English for Specific Purposes (ESP), the language to be taught is related to the specific roles that learners assume in later life. Doctors are taken through the five stages of the medical consultation (Kurtz & Silverman, 1996) so that they can carry out the interactions necessary to their roles, and waiters are given the types of language function they need for serving customers (Bung, 1973). Similarly the language used to create L2 users could in principle be based on the description of the perceived needs of the learner. This is easier to do when the learner is mature and has a specific career in mind, less easy when the learner is a child with no idea of what they will be doing later in life. Jenkins (2000) has indeed provided a Lingua Franca Core phonological syllabus for English based on the comprehensibility of non-natives to non-natives, abandoning the native speaker model. While native speakers can continue to provide a convenient common denominator, they should not provide the core target that the students are aiming at. Whatever their age and experience, the students will become L2 users, not native speakers.

Role models should be those of successful L2 users, not low-level L2 users or native L1 users

If students are to be persuaded to become L2 users, they need to be presented with proper role models of L2 users to emulate. Let us see how some recent coursebooks live up to this idea, taking three adult beginners coursebooks: English *Atlas 1* (Nunan, 1995), Italian *Ci Siamo* (Guarnuccio & Guarnuccio, 1997) and French *Libre Echange* (Courtillon & de Salins, 1995). Out of 200 named characters in these books, fifteen are clearly identified as non-native. One is a language teacher, one an entertainer, one a TV presenter, four are students, the rest are not specified. It may be that other characters are intended to be non-native speakers because of their non-native sounding names, for example Tomoko (*Atlas*) and Helmut (*Libre Echange*). If this is indeed the case, course writers need to be reminded that it is not warranted to deduce that someone called Tomoko is non-English simply from the name. A-level examination scripts in Scotland now have the candidates' names removed, as students with non-English names were being given lower marks than the rest. Not that it could be really said that the native characters have more interesting jobs – students (19), teachers (4), waiters (3), civil servants (3), doctors (3), receptionists (3), sailors (3), and an assortment of walk-on tobacconists, ticket-sellers, shop assistants, journalists, lace-makers and one interpreter. As for the celebrities that are mentioned, these consist of film stars (Emma Thompson), explorers (Jacques Cousteau) and tennis-players (Martina Hingis), whose abilities in a second language are immaterial – even if in fact the last two are clearly highly efficient L2 users. Where are the bilingual heroes and villains such as Albert Einstein, Geoffrey Chaucer or Robert Maxwell?

The role models that are presented to the students are thus largely those of natives. L2 users are never shown using the target language as a second language except as tourists or students who ask the way in the street, decipher a restaurant menu, or try to get a train from one place to another. They are supplicants to native speakers, not people in their own right who are successful because of their command of a second language.

This argument re-ignites the controversy in language teaching over whether native-speaker teachers should be preferred over non-natives. Much language teaching still sees a native speaker teacher as the ideal. Typical examples found on the Web are the Alliance Française claiming French 'taught by French nationals' or the Eurolingua Institute saying 'All Eurolingua tutors are fully-qualified teachers and native speakers, experienced in teaching their mother tongue as a foreign language'. English universities fill most of their modern language teaching posts with native speakers. In other words, the primary role model in many classrooms is someone who speaks the language as a native, not as an L2 user. If the target is indeed to become like a native, this may be ideal.

But, if the proper goal is the L2 user, native speaker teachers have no intrinsic advantages. On the one hand they are not using an acceptable L2 form of the language; on the other they do not necessarily have the ability to use two languages, and so have not experienced learning a second language for themselves. Indeed their inability to speak the students' first languages may be a poor advertisement for success in L2 learning; one hears anecdotes about students instructing the teacher in aspects of their first language with which he or she is not familiar. Only in a world where native speakers take precedence do native speaker teachers have any advantage. Otherwise they are only one of the many groups that the L2 user may have to deal with in the world. A non-native teacher may set the students a more feasible goal since, as Kramsch (1998: 9) puts it, 'non-native teachers and students alike are intimidated by the native-speaker norm'.

Students may prefer the more achievable model of the fallible non-native speaker.

The aspects of language that are taught should have an L2 element

The aspects of language that are taught should also in principle reflect the nature of L2 use. Native speakers speak differently when they detect a non-native speaker. At one extreme this may be foreigner-talk; my overseas students all claim to have encountered the stereotypical extra loudness and careful diction, even if few are treated to the classic *Me Tarzan, you Jane* simplification. At a straightforward practical level, students need to encounter situations in which non-native speakers are represented so that they can learn to deal with native speaker alteration in the company of non-native speakers.

The same is true of the L2 situations that are employed. Teaching normally presents a situation involving native speakers in the target country. When there are non-native speakers present in a course book, they are usually in the customer role in a service situation in a restaurant, hotel etc. The native speakers are notably also monolingual, never showing any knowledge of another language, and seldom belonging to any minority group – come to England and you might expect to meet only RP speakers. The few exceptions in the textbooks are essentially sops to discrimination, since, other than having non-white faces or non-native names, they behave identically to the rest of the cast, and give no sign of being L2 users.

Students need to be shown the richness of L2 use. Rather than a few L2 users stumbling through conversations with powerful native speakers, they need to encounter the language of people who use the language effectively as a second language, who, because they speak two languages, can say things that monolingual native speakers can never say.

Language teaching should emphasise the internal educational goals in the changes in the individual L2 user

As we have argued, language teaching in the twentieth century mostly disregarded internal goals, despite their presence in official syllabuses. Public pronouncements on the audiolingual or communicative methods stressed the usefulness of social use of the second language. An exception to some extent is task-based learning, in which students try to achieve the goals of fluency, accuracy and complexity (Skehan, 1998). Task-based learning uses internal goals relevant to the goals of teaching in the process syllabus tradition of Prabhu (1987); these link to the internal L2 user goals of helping the person's thinking, even if they are seldom expressed as such.

But these can be called L2 *student* goals rather than L2 *user* goals; it is achievement in the classroom that counts, not the changed minds of the students for life outside. Issues about native speakers and L2 users are relevant to task-based learning only to the extent that tasks refer to 'the world beyond the classroom' yet it is claimed that the relevance of tasks to external goals may be desirable 'but difficult to obtain in practice' (Skehan, 1998: 96). So what is the point of L2 learning confined to classroom tasks with neither internal nor external goals?

This lack of internal goals contradicts the stance in many national syllabuses, such as the UK National Curriculum (DES, 1990), which emphasises the benefits of language teaching in terms of cognitive processes and attitude change. In a sense this is inevitable; you can't learn another language without undergoing internal changes. All teaching has to live with this or profit from it, even if it does not openly acknowledge it. A major insight from the L2 user perspective is that teaching needs to take more account of the internal goals involving changes in the students' minds, thus paying more than lip-service to goals other than communication. Perhaps only the 'alternative' teaching methods that first emerged in the 1970s – such as Community Language Learning (CLL) (Curran, 1976), TPR (Seeley & Romijn, 1995) and Suggestopedia (Lozanov, 1978) – have taken this brief seriously. CLL for example has been used as part of the group therapy of mental illness in a London hospital.

The value of the L1 in the classroom should be emphasised

As we saw earlier, there was constant pressure in most twentieth-century language teaching to avoid the L1 in the classroom. At one level, national syllabuses insisted that it should be used as little at possible. In England 'Pupils are expected to use and respond to the target language, and to use English only when necessary (for example, when discussing a grammar point or when comparing English and the target language)' (DfEE, 1999). The avoidance of the L1 extends even to its use in tests: 'The form of a Target Language exam assumes also rubrics in the TL' (SCAA, 1994). At another level, methodology textbooks have moderated these claims with a grudging acknowledgement that the first language often creeps back into the classroom: the advice in task-based learning is 'Don't ban mother-tongue use but encourage attempts to use the target language' (Willis, 1996: 130).

In the classroom, then, students are never encouraged to see the first language as something that is part of themselves whatever they do and to appreciate that their first language is inextricably bound up with their knowledge and use of the second language. They are prevented from using the first language as a tool in learning the second language, in the ways to be described below.

In the light of these arguments, Cook (2001b) suggested that language teaching should re-examine its attempts to minimise the first language in the classroom. Rather than a blanket rejection of the first language, each of its possible classroom uses should be rationally examined. The overall motivation for the second language in the classroom must be that this is the only chance that many students will get to encounter it. Outside the class-room, students of Japanese in England are unlikely to encounter much Japanese; so the teacher has an obligation to provide as much Japanese as possible. A related justification comes from language functions; using the L2 for everyday classroom language shows the students how it is really used rather than the second-hand use shown in their textbooks.

While these two arguments speak to the need to maximise the L2, they do not preclude the use of the L1 for specific reasons; it may be an efficient shortcut, more related to the learning process the students are using, more natural or more relevant to their external goals. Based on studies of teach-ers' current behaviour by Macaro (1997) and Franklin (1990), there is a case for using the L1 in circumstances such as:

- Giving instructions about tasks. Useful as it may be to force students to understand instruction in the second language to carry out a class-room task, this sometimes takes considerably longer than the activity itself. Getting the students into the activity rapidly through the L1 may be more efficient than spending a long time setting it up in the L2. Macaro (1997) indeed found that teachers resort to the L1 after they have tried in vain to get the activity going in the L2.
- Translating and checking comprehension. Conveying the meaning of a word or a sentence of the L2 through the L1 can be a viable shortcut, partly for efficiency, partly to fit the learning processes in the students' minds, which invisibly make these links. The Bilingual Method (Dodson, 1967), for example, stresses this use.
- *Giving feedback to pupils.* Teachers sometimes prefer to give individual feedback to the students in their first language, presumably because this seems more natural, and relates to the students' real personalities rather than to their superficial L2 personalities in the pretend L2 situ-ation of the classroom.
- *Using the first language to maintain discipline.* Again teachers feel that saying 'Shut up or you will get a detention' in the first language shows that it is a serious threat rather than simply practising impera-

tive and conditional constructions. The L2 can rarely have the power of the L1 for classroom students.

- *Explaining grammar.* Though grammar-explanation has made an overt comeback as part of the FonF concept (Long, 1991), in which language should grammar be explained? Franklin (1990) found that over 80% of teachers used the first language for grammar explanation. In other words, where the emphasis is on understanding, teachers feel they cannot trust the second language. Perhaps the teacher's instincts should take precedence over the official advice to avoid the first language.

Conclusions

This chapter has argued that the L2 user perspective challenges several traditional teaching assumptions. It reminds us that the purpose of language teaching is to change the student positively. It suggests that these changes are not only the increasing ability to use language as an L2 user in a variety of contexts that a monolingual native speaker could not attempt but also cognitive abilities and attitudes that go beyond the thinking and perspective of monolingual native speakers. Language teaching transforms people into something they would not otherwise be. The L2 user concept reinstates language teaching as a profound influence on the students; it justifies language teaching educationally and restores it to the humanistic 'civilising' tradition, where it has barely figured for many years apart from the handful of people mentioned in Gomes-da-Matos's chapter.

Acknowledgements

I am grateful to Patsy Lightbown and Francisco Gomes de Matos for their helpful comments on earlier drafts of this chapter.

References

Bung, K. (1973) *The Foreign Language Needs of Hotel Waiters and Staff.* CCC/EES (73), 16.

Coleman, A. (1929) *The Teaching of Modern Languages in the United States.* New York: American and Canadian Committees on Foreign Languages.

Coleman, J.A. (1996) *Studying Languages: A Survey of British and European Students.* London: CILT.

Cook, V.J. (1970) Freedom and control in language teaching materials. In R.W. Rutherford (ed.) *BAAL Seminar Papers: Problems in the Preparation of Foreign Language Teaching Materials.* University of York: Child Language Survey.

Cook, V.J. (1983) Some assumptions in the design of courses. *University of Trier Papers* Series B, no. 94.

Cook, V.J. (1998) Relating SLA research to language teaching materials. *Canadian Journal of Applied Linguistics* 1 (1/2), 9–27.

Cook, V.J. (1999) Going beyond the native speaker in language teaching. *TESOL Quarterly* 33 (2), 185–209.

Cook, V.J. (2001a) *Second Language Learning and Language Teaching* (3rd edn). London: Arnold.

Cook, V.J. (2001b) Using the first language in the classroom. *Canadian Modern Language Review* 57 (3), 402–423.

Courtillon, J. and de Salins, G-D. (1995) *Libre Echange*. Hatier/Didier.

Cuban Ministry of Education (1999) *Principios que rigen la enseñanza del ingles en la escuala media*. Havana: Ministry of Education.

Curran, C.A. (1976) *Counselling-Learning in Second Languages*. Apple River, IL: Apple River Press.

DES (1990) *Modern Foreign Languages for Ages 11 to 16*. London: Department of Education and Science and the Welsh Office.

DfEE (1999) *The National Curriculum for England: Modern Foreign Languages*. Department for Education and Employment. On-line document: http://www.hmso.gov.uk/guides.htm.

Dodson, C.J. (1967) *Language Teaching and The Bilingual Method*. London: Pitman.

Ellis, R. (1996) SLA and language pedagogy. *Studies in Second Language Acquisition* 19, 69–92.

Franklin, C.E.M. (1990) Teaching in the target language. *Language Learning Journal* Sept, 20–24.

González-Nueno, M. (1997) VOT in the perception of foreign accent. *International Review of Applied Linguistics* XXXV/4, 251–267.

Guarnuccio, C. and Guarnuccio, E. (1997) *Ci Siamo*. CIS: Heinemann.

Halliday, M.A.K. (1968) The users and uses of language. In J. Fishman (ed.) *Readings in the Sociology of Language*. The Hague: Mouton.

HMSO (1995) *The National Curriculum*. London: Her Majesty's Stationery Office.

Holliday, A. (1994) *Appropriate Methodology and Social Context*. Cambridge: Cambridge University Press.

Howatt, A. (1984) *A History of English Language Teaching*. Oxford: Oxford University Press.

Institute of Linguists (1988) *Examinations in English for International Purposes*. London: Institute of Linguists.

Jacobson, R. and Faltis, C. (ed.) (1990) *Language Description Issues in Bilingual Schooling* (pp. 174–184). Clevedon: Multilingual Matters.

Jenkins, J. (2000) *The Phonology of English as an International Language*. Oxford: Oxford University Press.

Kemantarian Pendidikan Malaysia (1987) *Sukatan Pelajaran Sekolah Menengah: Bahasa Inggeris*. Malaysia: PPK.

Kramsch, C. (1998) The privilege of the intercultural speaker. In M. Byram and M. Fleming (eds) *Language Learning in Intercultural Perspective* (pp. 16–31). Cambridge: Cambridge University Press.

Krashen, S. (1993) *The Power of Reading*. Englewood, CO: Libraries Unlimited Inc.

Kurtz, S. and Silverman, J. (1996) The Calgary-Cambridge observation guides: An aid to defining the curriculum and organising the teaching in Communication Training Programmes. *Med Education* 30, 83–89.

Lado, R. (1964) *Language Teaching: A Scientific Approach*. New York: McGraw-Hill.

Littlewood, W. (1981) *Communicative Language Teaching*. Cambridge: Cambridge University Press.

Long, M. (1991) Focus on form: A design feature in language teaching methodology. In K. de Bot, R. Ginsberg and C. Kramsch (eds) *Foreign Language Research in Cross-Cultural Perspective* (pp. 39–52). Amsterdam: John Benjamins.

Lozanov, G. (1978) *Suggestology and Outlines of Suggestopedia*. New York: Gordon & Breach.

Macaro, E. (1997) *Target Language, Collaborative Learning and Autonomy*. Clevedon: Multilingual Matters.

Malakoff, M. and Hakuta, K. (1991) Translation skills and metalinguistic awareness in bilinguals. In E. Bialystok (ed.) *Language Processing in Bilingual Children* (pp.141–166). Cambridge: Cambridge University Press.

Ministère de l'Education (2000) *English Syllabus*. Quebec: Ministère de l'Education.

Nunan, D. (1995) *Atlas 1*. Boston: Heinle and Heinle.

Page, N. (1986) *A Conrad Companion*. Basingstoke: Macmillan.

Phillipson, R. (1992) *Linguistic Imperialism*. Oxford: Oxford University Press.

Prabhu, N.S. (1987) *Second Language Pedagogy*. Oxford: Oxford University Press.

SCAA (1994) *Modern Foreign Languages in the National Curriculum: Draft Proposals*. London: School Curriculum and Assessment Authority.

Seeley, C. and Romijn, E.K. (1995) *TPR is More Than Commands: At All Levels*. Berkeley, CA: Command Performance Language Institute.

Skehan, P. (1998) *A Cognitive Approach to Language Learning*. Oxford: Oxford University Press.

Thorley, W.C. (1918) *A Primer of English for Foreign Students*. London: Macmillan.

Tokyo, Shoseki (1990) *Course of Study for Senior High Schools: Foreign Languages*. Tokyo: Monbusho.

Wallerstein, N. (1983) The teaching approach of Paolo Freire. In J.W. Oller, Jr and P.A. Ricard-Amato (eds) *Methods that Work*. Rowley, MA: Newbury House.

Willis, J. (1996) *A Framework for Task-Based Learning*. Harlow: Longman.

Index